International Review of
RESEARCH IN
MENTAL RETARDATION

VOLUME 12

International Review of
RESEARCH IN
MENTAL RETARDATION

EDITED BY

NORMAN R. ELLIS

DEPARTMENT OF PSYCHOLOGY
UNIVERSITY OF ALABAMA
UNIVERSITY, ALABAMA

NORMAN W. BRAY

CENTER FOR DEVELOPMENTAL
AND LEARNING DISORDERS
UNIVERSITY OF ALABAMA
IN BIRMINGHAM
BIRMINGHAM, ALABAMA

VOLUME 12

1984

ACADEMIC PRESS INC.
(Harcourt Brace Jovanovich, Publishers)
Orlando   San Diego   New York   London
Toronto   Montreal   Sydney   Tokyo

ACADEMIC PRESS, INC.
Orlando, Florida 32887

United Kingdom Edition published by
ACADEMIC PRESS, INC. (LONDON) LTD.
24/28 Oval Road, London NW1 7DX

LIBRARY OF CONGRESS CATALOG CARD NUMBER: 65-28627
ISBN 0-12-366212-5

PRINTED IN THE UNITED STATES OF AMERICA

84 85 86 87   9 8 7 6 5 4 3 2 1

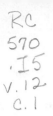

Contents

An Overview of the Social Policy of Deinstitutionalization

Barry Willer and James Intagliata

Community Attitudes toward Community Placement of Mentally Retarded Persons

Cynthia Okolo and Samuel Guskin

Family Attitudes toward Deinstitutionalization

Aysha Latib, James Conroy, and Carla M. Hess

Community Placement and Adjustment of Deinstitutionalized
Clients: Issues and Findings

Ellis M. Craig and Ronald B. McCarver

Issues in Adjustment of Mentally Retarded Individuals
to Residential Relocation

Tamar Heller

Salient Dimensions of Home Environment
Relevant to Child Development

Kazuo Nihira, Iris Tan Mink, and C. Edward Meyers

Current Trends and Changes in Institutions
for the Mentally Retarded

R. K. Eyman, S. A. Borthwick, and G. Tarjan

Methodological Considerations in Research on Residential Alternatives for Developmentally Disabled Persons

Laird W. Heal and Glenn T. Fujiura

A Systems Theory Approach to Deinstitutionalization Policies and Research

Angela A. Novak and Terry R. Berkeley

Autonomy and Adaptability in Work Behavior of Retarded Clients

John L. Gifford, Frank R. Rusch, James E. Martin, and David M. White

Contributors

Numbers in parentheses indicate the pages on which the authors' contributions begin.

Terry R. Berkeley (245), *Special Education Area, Louisiana State University, Baton Rouge, Louisiana 70803*

S. A. Borthwick (177), *Mental Retardation Research Center, Lanterman Research Group, University of California, Los Angeles, Los Angeles, California 91768*

James Conroy (67), *Developmental Disabilities Center, Temple University, Philadelphia, Pennsylvania 19122*

Ellis M. Craig (95), *Texas Department of Mental Health and Mental Retardation, Austin, Texas 78711*

R. K. Eyman (177), *School of Education, University of California, Riverside, Riverside, California 92521*

Glenn T. Fujiura (205), *Department of Special Education, College of Education, University of Illinois at Urbana-Champaign, Champaign, Illinois 61820*

John L. Gifford (285), *Department of Special Education, University of Illinois at Urbana-Champaign, Champaign, Illinois 61820*

Samuel Guskin (25), *Department of Special Education, Indiana University-Bloomington, Bloomington, Indiana 47405*

Laird W. Heal (205), *Department of Special Education, College of Education, University of Illinois at Urbana-Champaign, Champaign, Illinois 61820*

Tamar Heller (123), *Institute for the Study of Developmental Disabilities, University of Illinois at Chicago, Chicago, Illinois 60608*

Carla M. Hess (67), *Developmental Disabilities Center, Temple University, Philadelphia, Pennsylvania 19122*

James Intagliata (1), *University Affiliated Facility for Developmental Disabilities, University of Missouri at Kansas City, Kansas City, Missouri 64108*

Aysha Latib (67), *Developmental Disabilities Center, Temple University, Philadelphia, Pennsylvania 19122*

James E. Martin (285), *Department of Special Education, School of Education, University of Colorado at Colorado Springs, Colorado Springs, Colorado 80903*

Ronald B. McCarver (95), *Partlow State School and Hospital, Tuscaloosa, Alabama 35403*

C. Edward Meyers (149), *Mental Retardation Research Center, Neuropsychiatric Institute, University of California, Los Angeles, Los Angeles, California 90024*

Iris Tan Mink (149), *Mental Retardation Research Center, Neuropsychiatric Institute, University of California, Los Angeles, Los Angeles, California 90024*

Kazuo Nihira (149), *Mental Retardation Research Center, Neuropsychiatric Institute, University of California, Los Angeles, Los Angeles, California 90024*

Angela A. Novak (245), *Department of Health and Social Services, Madison, Wisconsin*

Cynthia Okolo (25), *Department of Special Education, Indiana University-Bloomington, Bloomington, Indiana 47405*

Frank R. Rusch (285), *Department of Special Education, University of Illinois at Urbana-Champaign, Champaign, Illinois 61820*

G. Tarjan (177), *Department of Psychiatry, School of Medicine, University of California, Los Angeles, Los Angeles, California 90024*

David M. White (285), *Department of Psychology, University of Illinois at Urbana-Champaign, Champaign, Illinois 61820*

Barry Willer (1), *Department of Psychiatry, School of Medicine, State University of New York at Buffalo, Buffalo, New York 14214*

Preface

There are few, if any, issues having a greater impact on the area of mental retardation than deinstitutionalization. The emotional fervor that has accompanied its debate and implementation is in many ways similar to that expressed regarding other important social problems, such as the assurance of human rights for racial minorities. Indeed, many have contended that the central issue is whether a society will assure the basic rights and freedoms of persons who have historically been denied these.

Amid the emotion of the debates on these issues, there has been frequent confusion of ideology and research facts, with ideology contributing more than the results of sound research. The purpose of the present volume is to examine the knowledge base generated by research on the multifaceted issue of deinstitutionalization. Each of the authors has conducted research on one or more of the many aspects of deinstitutionalization. Most have participated in the debates on this issue. For this book, however, they were asked to step aside from the debator's podium and present a dispassionate review of the research. They were asked to limit their discussion to what is clear from the research, to draw conclusions that are warranted by the data, and to suggest data-based issues that remain for further investigation. Thus, the aim of this book was to present the issues and data on deinstitutionalization in an objective manner. Because of the nature of this issue, there are limits on the extent to which authors can remove their ideologies from their work. Fingerprints follow each of us. Whether the objective has been fully realized is left for the reader to evaluate.

The ten articles may be divided into four major sections. These include (1) an overview of the policy of deinstitutionalization, (2) issues of community adjustment, (3) changes in the nature of large residential institutions, and (4) issues of research methods, theory, and application.

The first article, by Willer and Intagliata, provides an overview of deinstitutionalization as a social policy. They elaborate the idea that every social policy follows stages of development from initiation to termination or a major change in direction. In this context, it can be seen that research has contributed most to the implementation and evaluation stages and could, if done with foresight, contribute to the evolution of a new policy of service delivery.

Issues in community adjustment are reviewed in the next five articles. Okolo and Guskin discuss the research on attitudes of those living in neighborhoods where community residential facilities have been established. Their review indicates that many of the common assumptions made about community placement seem to be in error. Latib, Conroy, and Hess focus on attitudes of family members concerning deinstitutionalization. They review the literature and present new data on the follow-up of parental attitudes following placement of former residents of Pennhurst. Craig and McCarver, in an update of their article that appeared in this volume several years ago, review research on the reasons for institutionalization and the effect of institutionalization and personal characteristics on adjustment to community living. The article by Heller is concerned with variables that influence the degree of stress experienced by mentally retarded persons when they are relocated either within an institution or from an institution to a community facility. The research on this issue suggests ways that "transfer trauma" may be minimized. The final article on community adjustment is concerned with the assessment of home environments. Nihira, Mink, and Meyers review the research on the measurement of the characteristics of home environments as studied in the child development literature. Their review suggests that the use of these measures, in combination with a more theoretically guided approach to the effects of home environments, could add substantially to our understanding of the effects of community placement of the mentally retarded.

The article by Eyman, Borthwick, and Tarjan departs from the concern with community attitudes and adjustment and focuses on the effects deinstitutionalization has had on large residential institutions. The authors review changes in the composition of institutionalized populations, drawing heavily from their own data from California institutions. Although they were not directly concerned with community adjustment, their review suggests that community adjustment cannot be fully understood without carefully conducted longitudinal research of institutional discharges and readmissions.

The final three articles are concerned with research methodology, theory, and application. Heal and Fujiura examine methodological problems in research on deinstitutionalization from the perspective of both internal and external validity. Despite large gaps to be filled, they note some progress in refining research methodology and its application. Novak and Berkeley provide a general theoretical framework for research on deinstitutionalization. Adopting a systems approach, they delineate areas of strength and weakness of current research and issues for further investigation. They suggest that deinstitutionalization research has placed too much attention on client-centered processes and not enough on the contributions of the general social system. The final article by Gifford, Rusch, Martin, and White describes the application of research findings to the work behavior of mentally retarded adults. They describe the necessity of improving procedures for the development of autonomy and adaptability of the mentally retarded in the working community.

The next volume of this series will be devoted to cognitive processes in the mentally retarded. Although Volumes 12 and 13 are topical and were prepared by invited authors, for future volumes, we will continue to consider unsolicited manuscripts reviewing research and/or theory in any area of mental retardation and developmental disabilities. Potential authors are advised to contact one of the editors to describe the proposed chapter before submitting a completed manuscript.

NORMAN W. BRAY

University of Alabama in Birmingham

Announcement

We are pleased that Dr. Norman W. Bray is now serving as Coeditor of the series. Dr. Bray is the Director of the Division of Psychology at the Center for Developmental and Learning Disorders at The University of Alabama Medical School and Associate Professor of Psychology at The University of Alabama in Birmingham.

International Review of
RESEARCH IN
MENTAL RETARDATION

VOLUME 12

An Overview of the Social Policy
Of Deinstitutionalization

BARRY WILLER

DEPARTMENT OF PSYCHIATRY
SCHOOL OF MEDICINE
STATE UNIVERSITY OF NEW YORK AT BUFFALO
BUFFALO, NEW YORK

JAMES INTAGLIATA

UNIVERSITY AFFILIATED FACILITY FOR DEVELOPMENTAL DISABILITIES
UNIVERSITY OF MISSOURI AT KANSAS CITY
KANSAS CITY, MISSOURI

I. INTRODUCTION

There has been a great deal of interest and research on deinstitutionalization as a policy for services to mentally retarded persons since the late 1960s and during the 1970s and early 1980s. Craig and McCarver's article (this volume) discusses the circular nature of policies and how during this century most of the policy changes have related to different forms or purposes for institutionalization. With the advent of each new policy, there have been increasing numbers and proportions of mentally retarded persons placed in institutions. The most recent policy of deinstitutionalization was expected to represent a reversal of this trend and has been described by Bradley (1978) as revolutionary change.

The actual steps and stages of policy change and the factors that lead to the development of major policy shifts have not generally been studied by social scientists. Policy analysts have proposed various theories of the stages of policy development, including Brewer (1974), Cobb and Elder (1972), and Lynn (1978). There is not perfect agreement on the theoretical stages of policy development but there is a great deal of similarity. There is also not a great deal of research or discussion of research on specific policies such as deinstitutionalization, although the policy analysts present suppositions about the role of research and how research becomes important at various stages.

Craig and McCarver in their article (this volume) on research findings suggest policy change occurs regardless of research. Baumeister (1981) wrote specifically about the relationship of research to policy development and also suggests that research does not influence policy but that policy influences the type of research conducted. Since deinstitutionalization became widely accepted there has been a great deal more research on community placement, environmental effects, and the like. Baumeister adds that research has rarely influenced policy because most studies are not designed to provide the information necessary for policy makers. Lynn (1978) argues that policy change occurs under considerable pressure from events and interest groups and cannot wait for the research to be conducted. However, Lynn and others point out that research may not directly lead to policy change but can add significantly to some stages of policy development. Lynn suggests that the evaluation stage often relies on available research. Cobb and Elder (1972) suggest that research can help to keep a topic current and can be useful in maintaining the policy. Brewer (1974) suggests that research can also add to the likelihood of policy termination by demonstrating the negative or unintended consequences of the policy and its implementation.

The purpose of this article is to examine the most recent research on deinstitutionalization and relate this to the policy stages. For this, we elected to examine the policy of deinstitutionalization using Brewer's six stages of policy development: initiation, estimation, selection, implementation, evaluation, and termination. The first three stages are considered part of the early phase of policy development and are dealt with as one. In addition, research and discussion in the formal literature has tended to focus more on implementation and evaluation of deinstitutionalization. Brewer's inclusion of a termination stage to policy development is unusual and informative to consider. He suggests that termination or major policy redirection will eventually occur for every policy and naturally follows evaluation of that policy. Not only is the policy likely to fail in meeting all of its stated goals but it is likely to have numerous unintended consequences. In addition, the social and economic environmental context in which the policy was initiated is likely to change and such changes dictate changes in policy goals.

For the purposes of this article, deinstitutionalization is defined as the reduction in the number of admissions to public institutions, the development of alternative community methods of care, the return to the community of those individuals capable of functioning in a less restrictive environment, and the reform of public institutions to improve the quality of care provided (President's Committee on Mental Retardation, 1976). Deinstitutionalization policies have been initiated in a variety of service care sectors including the mental health, criminal corrections, and general health care systems. The discussion here, however, focuses on deinstitutionalization with the mental retardation service system.

II. STAGES OF POLICY DEVELOPMENT

A. The Early Stages

Issues of concern in every field are attended to in various ways. Not all issues impact on or lead to the formulation of specific policies. Cobb and Elder's (1972) model of agenda setting suggests that during the early stages an issue that leads to policy formulation must be highly consensual and affective; that is, it must be agreed that the issue is important and it must be an issue that affects our emotions. This is critical if the issue is to receive media attention, something which deinstitutionalization did receive with the help of "exposés" by Blatt (1966) and Rivera (1972).

Policy analysts point out that many issues of high import do not necessarily lead directly to policy formation. The social and economic climate must be conducive. The social climate of the late 1960s and early 1970s has been characterized as the "open society" with considerable attention paid to individual human rights (Baker & Schulberg, 1967). The economic climate was optimistic and there was relatively little concern for the level of public expenditure as long as the appropriated monies were intended to solve an important social issue.

Deinstitutionalization, in the beginning, reflected a concern for the rights of mentally retarded persons and as such was highly consistent with the social climate of the times. Further, while the government may have been willing to bear whatever additional costs that implementing deinstitutionalization efforts might have required in the relatively sound economic climate of the time, those advocating for deinstitutionalization promised that it would not only enhance the independence and quality of life for mentally retarded persons but also would save the government large sums of money. Clearly, deinstitutionalization appeared a very attractive policy.

Once a policy issue becomes recognized, it must be determined whether it should be adopted. In the Cobb and Elder model, the primary decisions are (1) is there an action that can be taken to resolve the issue, and (2) does resolution require government intervention? Policy analysts give the impression that such decisions are made by government agencies. While this may be true to some extent, the courts appear to have played a significant role in the adoption of deinstitutionalization as a policy by establishing that action could be taken to resolve the issue of inadequate care in institutions, and by mandating that government intervention was precisely what was required. The decision in *Wyatt v. Stickney* (1972) established that borderline and mildly retarded persons should not be admitted to an institution, and that no person should be admitted to an institution unless a prior determination has been made that residence in the institution is the least restrictive habilitative setting. A similar decision was reached in *Welsch v. Likins* (1974). The latter case also specified that the state is responsible to develop alternative residential care in the community. Other cases of litigation called for placement of mentally retarded persons out of large institutions such as Willowbrook (*New York Association of Retarded Children v. Rockefeller,* 1975) and Pennhurst (*Halderman et al. v. Pennhurst State School et al.,* 1978). Deinstitutionalization, as a policy issue, was clearly adopted and given high priority by most states in the United States as well as by most countries in the western world.

B. The Implementation Stage

For a policy issue to be adopted and then implemented, principles or guidelines that govern implementation are required. In the United States it had been established by President Kennedy that mental health and mental retardation were problems of national concern and should be attended to by the federal government (Bloom, 1977). This was an important guideline to implementation because other countries, such as Canada, left the responsibility for deinstitutionalization with the individual provinces. The national approach taken in the United States appears to have contributed to the much more rapid rate of deinstitutionalization that eventually took place in the United States.

Another guiding principle of deinstitutionalization was that of normalization, which began as a statement of rights for mentally retarded persons and eventually became a prescription for all services for mentally retarded persons. To begin with, the term normalization meant that all handicapped persons should have the same rights and benefits as all citizens (Nirje, 1969). Wolfensberger's (1970) variation on the theme suggested that handicapped persons should be exposed to experiences that encouraged normalized behavior. There were a number of other principles that with normalization, provided the ideology for deinstitutionalization. One of these is the developmental model, which suggests that mentally retarded persons progress through the same developmental stages as nonretarded persons, albeit, at a slower pace (MacMillan, 1977). The other important principle is least restrictiveness (Turnbull, 1981). The principle of least restrictiveness was spelled out in a number of court cases and suggests that treatment or habilitation services should take place in the least restrictive environment and/or the least restrictive fashion. Conversely, we should not incarcerate someone in an institution in the name of habilitation, when that person could be provided the same habilitation services in a less restrictive setting such as a group home.

Ideological concepts such as normalization, the developmental model, and least restrictiveness had implications for the ideal habilitative setting for mentally retarded persons. According to normalization, the ideal setting should be as close as possible to normal. The living environment should be separate and distinct from the school or work or treatment environment. The living environment should be located within easy access to generic services and homes for nonretarded persons. The developmental model encourages us to teach mentally retarded persons skills and behaviors that are age appropriate and which can direct the individual toward his/her maximum potential. The model implies that there is almost no limit to the developmental goals that may be attained. The principle of least restrictiveness suggests that there should not be any more restrictions placed on personal freedom than is absolutely necessary. It also suggests that when possible the individual should progress from more restrictive to less restrictive settings with the ultimate goal of independence.

These ideological concepts lay the groundwork for implementation and evaluation of deinstitutionalization efforts. The environment an individual is placed into should be normalized and can be evaluated using the PASS evaluation procedure (Wolfensberger & Glenn, 1975). PASS III, a more recent version of PASS, has been factor analyzed and four factors emerged: normalization of the habilitation programs, normalization of the physical setting, attention to individual rights, and access to generic services (Flynn, 1980). Evaluation of individual progress in community residential programs, as reviewed by Craig and McCarver (this volume), has tended to look at developmental growth of the individual particularly in areas of age appropriate behavior as measured by the Adaptive Behavior Scale. The principle of least restrictiveness has led some researchers to look at progress toward independence and/or failure to remain in the community setting and return to the institution. The procedures and outcome measures in this research have been consistent with the ideology of deinstitutionalization.

The ideology of deinstitutionalization provides the goal of the policy and determines to a large extent the implementation process at the clinical level. The most popular residential alternatives to institutions has been the group home, primarily because it meets most of the environmental goals spelled out by normalization and least restrictiveness. However, in order for the policy to be implemented, major issues related to funding, licensure, availability, and incentive for deinstitutionalization had to be resolved. In the United States most of the attempts to resolve these issues occurred at the federal level. There were various forms of legislation and legislative changes made that strongly encouraged states to endorse deinstitutionalization. Bradley (1978) provides an excellent overview of the federal legislation involved. The most significant of these is the change in Title XIX of the Social Security Act that made money available for partial funding of institutional care, and later made funds available for community-based intermediate care facilities. When the federal government became involved in funding institutions, new quality of care standards were imposed leading to significant institutional reform. In addition, the federal government was then in a position to develop agreements with states which included concrete plans for reduction in the use of and size of certain state institutions.

Deinstitutionalization could not have been considered without some provision for the development of residential alternatives. Funding for group home and intermediate care facility construction was made available through the Federal Department of Housing and Urban Development. Some states developed mechanisms for direct funding of group homes and/or supplements to social security incomes, which helped support the operation of community residential programs. The increase in the number of individuals residing in community residential programs required expanded use of available day training, sheltered work, or educational programs, and federal funds and some state funding became available for this.

There is a tendency to equate legislation with implementation of policy. The legislation changes and new legislation in the United States made deinstitutionalization possible, often by removing disincentives for community-based care. However, legislation alone does not make policy implementation likely. Deinstitutionalization occurred in Canada without federal involvement and without significant legislative changes. In both Canada and the United States there was a groundswell of support within certain interest groups who advocated on behalf of the mentally retarded. The most significant of these was the association of parents of mentally retarded persons. There was also considerable support among professionals in the field of mental retardation who had raised concern about the quality of care provided in institutions and provided some research support for this conclusion.

C. Evaluation of the Deinstitutionalization Policy

Evaluation of a policy such as deinstitutionalization can be provided in two forms. The first is an assessment of changes in the service delivery systems and ultimately how these changes affected the population served. The second is an assessment of the unintended effects of implementation of the policy. The evaluation of desired outcomes tends to focus on goals of the policy as represented by the ideology which supports the policy. Unintended effects are more often illusive and rarely come to light until the policy begins to be questioned, as when the policy begins to be modified or terminated (Brewer, 1974).

Evaluations of the intended effects of the policy of deinstitutionalization have tended to focus on the changes in institutional populations and the benefits for residents of placement in community residential alternatives. Research on the unintended effects of deinstitutionalization have focused on the problems of administering community residential programs, the increased costs of services, the reactions of parents to deinstitutionalization, and various other issues that only come to light once the policy implementation begins. Evaluations of intended benefits of policy implementation can be biased by methods of research which are also reflective of the ideology which supports the policy. Evaluations of unintended effects can be biased by some other usually unstated ideology. Craig and McCarver's article (this volume) provides an excellent summary of the research on deinstitutionalization and provides a graph describing the dramatic decline in the rate of institutionalization across the United States since 1967. Scheerenberger (1982) has provided numerous updates over the past few years on the progress of reducing institutional populations and cautions that we need to also be concerned about where these individuals are placed. An alarmingly high number of individuals have been placed in nursing homes and other settings not very different from institutions. Elderly mentally retarded persons, for example, are most likely to be placed in highly restrictive settings with fewer support services (Seltzer, Seltzer, & Sherwood, 1982). However, implementation of deinstitutionalization has clearly had a significant effect on institutions. There has been a steady decline in average institutional size, a steady increase in the staff-to-resident ratio (Lakin, Krautz, Bruininks, Clumpner, & Hill, 1982b), and significant changes in the type of residents in institutions. Eyman, Borthwick, and Tarjan's article (this volume) highlights the changes in two institutions. They point out that institutions are now housing an ever increasing proportion of older, more profoundly retarded persons with organic diagnoses and behavior problems. Best-Sigford, Bruininks, Lakin, and Hill (1982) describe the fact that the discharge of higher functioning residents from institutions has been a major factor in increasing the proportion of institutionalized residents in the severe or profound range of mental retardation.

Craig and McCarver also reviewed studies which demonstrated the improvement in adaptive behavior of individuals leaving institutions (e.g., Conroy, Efthimon, & Lemanowicz, 1982; Hemming, Lavender, & Pill, 1981; Schroeder & Henes, 1978). They point out that while most individuals do improve upon placement, these studies do not provide long-term (more than 1 year) evidence of change. As well, we know very little about the specific aspects of the residential environment which produced the desired changes. However, some still argue that there is sufficient information to demonstrate the efficacy of community placement and that no one should be left in or placed in an institution (Menolascino & Mcgee, 1981). Unfortunately for this argument, as noted by Heller in her article (this volume), several recent studies have found positive adaptive behavior gains for individuals placed from smaller to larger settings and for individuals placed in institutions (Ellis, Bostick, Moore, & Taylor, 1981; Schlottmann & Anderson, 1982). Further, Eyman and Arndt (1982) studied a large sample of individuals in both institutional and community residential settings and found no apparent differences in growth patterns of adaptive behavior.

Various studies of deinstitutionalization have produced results which can be used as arguments in favor of community residential programs. However, these same results can also be used to argue for institutional programs. Craig and McCarver's article (this volume) provides a review of the research on reinstitutionalization of deinstitutionalized individuals. The conclusion is that a significant proportion of individuals do not adjust well to community placement and must return to the institution. Those who support institutionalization might conclude that the rate of reinstitutionalization is reflective of the failure of community residential programs. Those in support of community placement could argue that the only way to prevent reinstitutionalization completely is to keep everyone in institutions. The more valuable research, from a policy evaluation perspective, is that which has identified the fact that reinstitutionalization is most likely for those individuals who have maladaptive behavior (Thiel, 1981; Intagliata & Willer, 1982). We also know that new referrals to institutions are much more likely to have behavior problems (Campbell, Smith, & Wool, 1982). This suggests that community residential programs are either less capable or less willing to provide programs for those with behavior problems. These conclusions have more practical significance than those which argue for either institutional placement or community placement on an ideological basis because they point to a weakness in the capability of community residential programs to serve all mentally retarded persons effectively.

Administrative problems with community residential programs have also been identified in the research literature. There is a very high turnover of staff in community programs and serious problems of morale relating to salary and career opportunities (Lakin, Bruininks, Hill, & Hauber, 1982a; O'Connor, 1976; Zaharia & Baumeister, 1979). These and other problems with the concept of community residences make one wonder why so much research has been devoted to community residential programs, especially group homes, while relatively few studies have compared these with other residential alternatives such as foster care and the natural home. The extreme popularity and unprecedented growth of community residential programs in the United States (Braddock, 1981; Bruininks, Hauber, & Kudla, 1980; Janicki, Mayeda, & Epple, 1983), and the apparent consistency between group homes and the principle of normalization are part of the explanation. Unfortunately, this has served to mask the potential value of familylike settings.

Scanlon, Arick, and Krug (1982) compared maladaptive behavior of residents in an institution, group homes, and natural homes. Individuals were matched on sex, chronological age, and language age. They found consistently fewer behavior problems among individuals living in the natural home. Willer and Intagliata (1982) compared foster care and group home placements and found similarly that individuals in foster care are more likely to overcome behavior problems. However, they also found that individuals in group homes were more likely to develop community living skills, pointing out a potential weakness in foster home settings. Research is hard pressed to demonstrate the appropriateness of institutions versus community placement, especially since this is essentially a political or legal decision. However, as Heller notes in her article (this volume), research has been useful in demonstrating the usefulness of a good fit between the individual needs and the characteristics of the placement setting. For example, Sutter, Mayeda, Yee, and Yanagi (1981) found placement success was enhanced when there was a good match between individual and care provider preferences.

A summary evaluation of deinstitutionalization would conclude that fewer individuals now reside in institutions and institutions are generally much smaller and better staffed than before deinstitutionalization was initiated. There has been a rapid expansion of the use of community residential alternatives (in particular, group homes), but there are unresolved issues regarding the relative efficacy of these settings when compared with other settings such as foster homes and natural family homes. Many of these unresolved issues will come to light as more attention is paid to the unintended results of deinstitutionalization.

D. Unintended Effects of the Policy

We pointed out earlier that evaluation of a social policy, particularly evaluation of unintended effects, generally occurs just prior to the stage of termination of that policy. It is appropriate at this juncture to define termination. Termination is not limited to the cessation of the policy. Termination also refers to a major redirection of the policy. Cameron (1978) describes termination of the community mental health program in California, which occurred more as a result of the unanticipated consequences of the policy implementation than through planned change. Planning for termination, Cameron argues, rarely occurs because individuals become so caught up in support of a particular ideology that they ignore the unintended consequences and refuse to consider alternative approaches.

The unintended consequences of deinstitutionalization of mentally retarded persons are only recently being attended to. However, a number of these unintended consequences have become apparent. The first and perhaps most significant of these is the alarming increase in out-of-home placements of mentally retarded persons. Institutions first served as an alternative to natural family care and families were encouraged to place their mentally retarded son or daughter in an institution. For most of this century there has been a steady increase in the number and proportion of mentally retarded persons placed in institutions. As graphically described by Craig and McCarver, the rate dropped noticeably in the years following 1967. However, studies of placements indicate that a large percentage of individuals placed out of institutions go to other publicly funded residential care programs. Meanwhile, a sizable percentage of individuals placed in group homes come from their natural family homes (Bruininks *et al.*, 1980). The result is an increase in overall number and proportion of out-of-home placements.

The increased use of out-of-home placements can be demonstrated graphically as well. Ontario, Canada began deinstitutionalization in 1973. The bar graph (Fig. 1) presents the number of persons per 100,000 in the general population who reside in publicly operated institutions and accordingly this number drops noticeably between 1973 and 1982. The proportion of persons in privately operated institutions, also presented in Fig. 1, remained relatively unchanged over the period and when added to the publicly operated facilities, the total proportion in institutional settings still declines. However, when we include the proportion of individuals in community residential facilities, the numbers and proportions show a dramatic increase.

This same result can probably be demonstrated for every province and

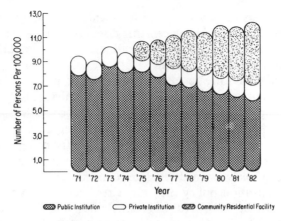

FIG. 1. Number of persons per 100,000 in the general population in residential programs for the mentally retarded in Ontario, 1971–1982.

state that has adopted the policy of deinstitutionalization and has endorsed community residential facilities (group homes) as the primary alternative. Until recently we have not had access to reliable data on the number of persons in community-based residential program. However, national surveys by Bruininks *et al.* (1980) and Janicki *et al.* (1983) have allowed us to make projections on the number of out-of-home placements across the United States. Figure 2 presents this projection for 1900 to the present. It would appear that the policy of deinstitutionalization and institutionalization share the com-

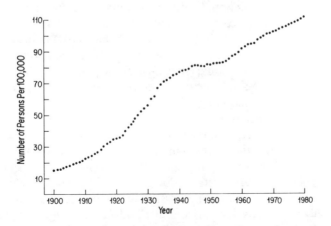

FIG. 2. Number of persons per 100,000 in the general population in out-of-home placements for the mentally retarded in the United States 1900–1980. Data on out-of-home placements from 1967–1980 include estimates of placements to community residential facilities.

mon theme of increasing out-of-home placements. It should be pointed out that the figure on out-of-home placements does not include those placed in nursing homes or foster homes and the addition of these would serve to increase the upward slope of the graph.

Wolfensberger (1969) predicted that out-of-home placements would increase with the expanded use of group homes for individuals for whom it is an age appropriate placement. Janicki *et al.* (1983) conclude that there will be increased use of group homes for individuals needing a homelike situation when movement out of the natural home is necessary or age appropriate. The implication is that group homes are serving as an alternative to natural homes rather than solely as an alternative to institutions. If this is a goal of the deinstitutionalization policy then more research should be directed at comparison of the relative benefits of group home living versus natural family care. If it was not part of the policy of deinstitutionalization then it is an unintended consequence that has serious policy implications that must be addressed.

There are several important spinoff effects which result from increased use of out-of-home placements. One is that the primary focus of residential services has shifted from the severely or profoundly mentally retarded to the mildly and moderately retarded. We know that the population of institutions has changed to include a much higher proportion of individuals who are older and more severely handicapped. However, the group home population, especially those who come directly from their natural home, are generally middle aged and are likely to be mildly impaired or borderline in intellectual functioning (Bruininks *et al.,* 1980; Jacobson & Schwartz, 1983). We also know that the depopulation of institutions has occurred largely because of restrictions placed on new admissions and younger, more severely handicapped individuals who would previously have been placed in an institution, are now remaining with their natural family. The end result is that the increased numbers of individuals in out-of-home placements includes an increased proportion of adult mentally retarded persons in the moderate to borderline range of functioning.

Another consequence of the dramatic increase in out-of-home placement is that public funded residential programs, institutional or otherwise, are much more expensive to operate than nonresidential services provided to individuals in their own home. Willer and Intagliata (1984) report that the total budget for operating mental retardation services in the State of New York increased by 275% between 1971 and 1981. This rate of increase was more than double that of the consumer price index and far exceeded the rates of increase to all other state departments. Some have argued that deinstitutionalization would eventually reduce costs for mental retardation services and provide cost comparisons between institutional placement and community placement for individuals (Baker, Seltzer, & Seltzer, 1974; Gardner, 1977; Heal & Laidlaw, 1980). However, from a policy perspective it is clear that the overall cost of services has increased dramatically and the current rate of increase probably cannot be sustained.

One further implication of increased use of out-of-home placement is the implied message for natural families of mentally retarded persons. As with the period of institutionalization, families are being encouraged to transfer the responsibility for care to the state (Suelzle & Keenan, 1981). The exception to this is families of severely or profoundly retarded persons, especially those who are young. Families of older, less handicapped individuals are encouraged to place them in group homes because "it is age appropriate." One of the problems with this is that individuals with the greatest needs for support services are in the natural home where they are less likely to receive the services.

This trend exists for individuals placed out of institutions as well. Willer and Intagliata (1983) found that individuals placed with the natural family were most likely to be female, severely or profoundly mentally retarded, younger, and more likely to have behavior problems. In addition, these families were less likely to be aware of or offered nonresidential services.

Natural family members apparently have a number of concerns about deinstitutionalization. The article by Latib, Conroy, and Hess (this volume) reviews the sources of concern for many parents who learn that their son or daughter is to be placed out of an institution. To begin with, they are concerned with the adequacy of community care and the availability of nonresidential services such as medical care. They wonder if funding for community residential programs is permanent or temporary. In general, they do not share the same beliefs about normalization, developmental theory, or least restrictiveness, the tenets of deinstitutionalization. Bartnik and Winkler (1981) studied attitudes toward community adjustment and found that parents wanted their sons or daughters to learn social skills and self-care skills while community service workers wanted them to learn decision making to become independent and "free from living with their parents' expectations."

It is not surprising that parents of institutionalized individuals do not agree with many of the goals of deinstitutionalization. It is natural that they feel threatened by the desires to reverse their decision to institutionalize. What is surprising is that the deinstitutionalization policy appears to have been implemented in such a fashion that parents' concerns have been essentially overlooked. Willer and Intagliata (1984) report that many parents in New York State were not asked for consent for placement even though it was stated as policy by the State Department of Mental Retardation. The Latib *et al.* article (this volume) on family responses describes a Nebraska court decision which proposed that parental consent not even be required and a guardian ad litem be appointed for all individuals proposed for placement out of the institution.

It is not stated that the policy of deinstitutionalization is opposed to parental participation in the process but the implementation of the policy appears to have created a certain level of this opposition. This is unfortunate given that parent involvement following placement has been found to be a significant factor in the long-term success of placement (Schalock, Harper, & Genung, 1981). It is also unfortunate because parents' concerns about the viability of community placement may be real rather than imagined. Willer and Intagliata (1984) found that parents who were most resistive to deinstitutionalization had sons or daughters who had the most behavioral adjustment problems following placement. One other unfortunate consequence of this is that a new lobby of parents of institutionalized persons opposed to deinstitutionalization may have been created as a reaction to the implementation process rather than the purpose of this policy.

There are a number of other unintended consequences of deinstitutionalization any one of which may become more significant as a backlash to deinstitutionalization occurs. There is concern over the possible deleterious effects of placement especially for elderly or severely handicapped individuals. This concern has been reviewed in the article by Heller (this volume) who suggests that placement shock may be an overstated concern but does not dismiss the possibility that relocation can produce sickness and possibly death if there is inadequate preparation of the individual concerned.

Another unintended consequence is the result of a significant transfer of responsibility of residential program management responsibility from the state to private, nonprofit agencies. Many of these agencies have endured rapid expansion and major administrative difficulties. In addition, because many of these agencies served originally as advocacy groups, they have essentially abandoned the advocacy function to become service providers. The growing threat of fiscal restraint is likely to leave many of these agencies wishing they had remained in the advocacy role.

E. Policy Termination

We have used Brewer's description of the life cycle of a policy because it includes a description of termination or redirection of the policy. Most authors of policy stages give little or no attention to the end point of a policy, perhaps because by the time a policy truly terminates it has already been replaced by a new policy which attracts much more attention. Albeit, there appears to be certain prerequisites for policy termination which are discussed in greater detail by Cameron (1978). At the risk of oversimplifying, these include the following:

1. Evaluation of the unintended consequences of the policy.
2. A growing disenchantment with the ideological basis for the policy.
3. Changes in the social and economic environment so that the policy and its ideology may no longer be supported.

We have already discussed some of the unintended consequences of deinstitutionalization. The concerns about ideological issues, in particular the appropriateness of normalization as the philosophical basis of mental retardation services, are less straightforward to assess. Cameron suggests that when the policy is initiated there is generally widespread acceptance of the ideology. However, with time, the ideology becomes criticized and restated, and its original intent is greatly altered. Butterfield (1977) has pointed out that normalization was originally adopted uncritically even though its intent changed from an initial concern for rights to a concern for the appropriateness of the environment for mentally retarded persons.

A debate over the appropriateness of normalization has begun to appear in the literature. Debates over ideologic issues, according to Cameron, do not allow for intelligent inquiry, that is, research. Indeed, the majority of the published articles do not make reference to research findings. For example, Schwartz (1977) contends that normalization by its nature places too much emphasis on the attainment of independence. Schwartz argues that the press toward independence will lead to increased behavior problems as defensive reactions on the part of mentally retarded persons. In addition, the goal of independence is not applicable to those who really need a secure living environment and long-term relationships, which includes the majority of mentally retarded persons. Rhoades and Browning (1977) and Hendrix (1981) also present the criticism that normalization does not attend to the interpersonal needs of mentally retarded persons and the press to live independently precludes the development of peer relationships. There is some evidence that individuals living in group homes have a greater likelihood of behavior problems than individuals living in other familylike settings, but it would be difficult to then conclude that this is the result of greater adherence to normalization principles. Increased behavior problems appear to be a common and natural outcome of living in any congregate living arrangement, for mentally retarded and nonretarded persons alike (Spivak & Spotts, 1966).

Aanes and Haagenson (1978) criticize normalization on the grounds that it has gradually become a conceptual nightmare, as the goal of normalization of the individual has become confused with normalization of the environment. Living in a group home with age appropriate surroundings has become the desired outcome rather than the process for attaining age appropriate behavior. The research on perceptions of the meaning of normalization by various interest groups such as parents, administrators, and direct care staff, has indicated widely divergent viewpoints. However, does this make the principle conceptually weak or does it simply mean that the various interest groups have different views on what is appropriate for mentally retarded persons?

Throne (1979) presents a different perspective on normalization and deinstitutionalization. He contends that the distinction between institutions and community-based congregate living arrangements is arbitrary. The widespread adoption of normalization and the association between normalization and group home living has made this form of living alternative automatically better than institutions. Throne warns that we may simply be creating a new form of institution that may be smaller and administered differently but that still retains the primary characteristics of institutions. The studies of staffing problems in group homes cited earlier in this article certainly suggest that there are some similarities betwen group homes and institutions. The staff-to-client interaction patterns, staff complaints about record keeping, and staff turnover are very similar across both settings.

Sproger (1980) wrote a response to Throne's provocative comments and argues that smaller settings such as group homes are inherently different from institutions and have been defined by various court decisions as less restrictive and therefore more appropriate. Sproger is correct about the judgments being handed down by the courts, but even some of the landmark court decisions are now being questioned. In a major review of *Wyatt v. Stickney,* Jones and Parlour (1981) suggest that the courts may have afforded rights to the mentally retarded that do not even exist for the general population. The authors even question whether the courts are an appropriate place to determine public policy.

Throne's comments on the institutional nature of group homes reflect less on normalization as a principle than on the translation of normalization into practice. If the concerns about the overuse of institutional alternatives are valid, then they become an even greater concern when we realize that group homes are being used as alternatives to natural families. The dramatic increase in out-of-home placements, particularly for mildly mentally retarded adults, implies that group homes must also be more appropriate than the natural family. This latter issue has been given relatively little attention in the research literature and discussions of deinstitutionalization, but may become a central issue in time as policy makers begin to realize that out-of-home placements are directly related to costs of services. In addition, as discussed earlier, the few studies which compare family living to group home living do not support the contention that mentally retarded persons are better off in group homes.

Advocates for the policy of dcinstitutionalization have responded to some of the criticisms of normalization. Most recently, the defense has been that normalization as a concept is a statement of the ideal which has not been fully adopted by most human service agencies (McCord, 1982). Therefore, we cannot criticize normalization but rather we must improve in its implementation. Dern (1983) argues that normalization simply cannot be adopted in most agencies and provides a long list of administrative and legal obstacles. Thus, the general acceptance of normalization appears to be coming into question and this may be an early sign of termination of deinstitutionalization as it has been implemented.

The other prerequisite for policy termination, outlined by Cameron, is change in the economic and social climate to support the policy. In the United States deinstitutionalization began during a period of high concern for individual rights and a relatively bouyant economy as evidenced by low unemployment and steady increase in the gross national product. The concern for rights is reflected in the principle of normalization, at least in its origin. Changes in social issues are likely to be reflected in growing concern for ideological principles such as normalization. We have already discussed many of these concerns. However, economic changes are likely to have an even greater effect on policy changes. There is little doubt that deinstitutionalization has been a costly policy. There have been major increases in expenditures for mental retardation services at both the federal and state levels in the United States and at the provincial level in Canada. The few available studies of costs of services cited earlier do not generally present the whole picture. Instead, they have concentrated on comparisons of one living situation to another. However, it will be the total cost of services that will become an issue for policy makers and may indeed end up as the major issue leading to policy termination.

In the United States we have already witnessed a changing attitude toward funding of human service programs, particularly at the federal level. Magaro, Gripp, and McDowell (1978) theorize that one of the covert functions of human service programs is to provide for employment of people who would otherwise be unemployed. They suggest that during periods of good economic times, human service programs expand and provide more opportunities for employment, particularly for young, idealistic persons with limited trade skills. During periods of poor economy the human service system contracts and provides less employment for nonprofessionals and generally fewer services to persons who are not truly in need. To extend their thesis to the mental retardation field, there will be cutbacks in programs generally and cutbacks in programs for mildly impaired individuals will be the most severe. Such cutbacks will most likely be accompanied by significant alterations in, if not the termination of, many current aspects of deinstitutionalization policy.

We may not accept the thesis that human services serve to employ the unemployable, but as Noble and Conley (1981) report, the current economic

climate will undoubtedly lead to major reductions in funding for social service programs. The shrinking budget for social programs will result in intense competition among various constituencies who, for the time being, will
also have to compete with other programs such as defense and education.
Noble and Conley suggest further, that recent policies in the human service
field have served to erode the responsibilities of natural families by encouraging them to place their disabled and elderly members in institutions,
nursing homes, and community residences. However, the high cost of these
programs will probably dictate an end to this trend if for no other reason
than the fact that we cannot afford for it to continue.

III. FUTURE POLICY DIRECTIONS

Brewer's description of the life cycle of a policy provides a useful context
for a review of research on deinstitutionalization of mentally retarded persons. It is particularly useful to include the stage of termination because it
places an entirely different perspective on the evaluation process. If we
assume that all policies must eventually terminate, then research findings
may be useful in both assessing and redirecting the policy. An analysis of the
intended and unintended outcomes of the current policy of deinstitutionalization provides useful clues to the future direction of services for mentally retarded persons. Individual research studies may not direct policy, but
research in the aggregate must be regarded as a source of valuable information.

It is unfortunate that as the deinstitutionalization policy comes into question, many of the intended outcomes that have been accomplished will be
overshadowed. Nevertheless, the success of the deinstitutionalization effort
is likely to play some role in dictating future policy. Community placement
will probably continue to be preferred over institutional placement, but economics will also play a major role in determining the type of community-
based care that will be used. Future policy will have to be more attentive to
costs and benefits of programs because economics has become an issue of
concern influencing all public policies.

There are a number of other issues, as yet unresolved, which may also play
a key role in future policy for mental retardation services. One is the development of goals and services to meet the special needs of the elderly and
severely/profoundly mentally retarded. These individuals have been somewhat overlooked by current policy. Their placement out of institutions
represents a risk, and the residential alternatives selected for them are often
no more appropriate than the institutions. Future policy will have to specify
what will be done to decrease the risk of placement shock while retaining the

benefits of community living. It is safe to assume that future policy will continue to emphasize community living. However, quality of life for residents who require long-term security and relationships will become more important than any efforts to increase independent living skills.

The concerns for the elderly and severely impaired mentally retarded raises the further issue of continued use of institutions. Proponents of deinstitutionalization originally advocated for the eventual elimination of all institutions. However, major reforms and the decreased size of public institutions have greatly improved the quality of life offered in institutions. Institutions are likely to continue to have a place within the continuum of residential services, particularly for the severely impaired, the elderly, and those with major behavior or psychiatric problems. Future policy will have to specify when institutional placement or continued institutional stay is appropriate.

Another unresolved issue which is likely to have a major influence in shaping future policy is the role of the natural family in the service delivery system. The White House Conference on Families led to a conclusion that public policies in the United States have tended to overlook the needs of natural families, and that such policies have served to undermine the role of families as a natural support system in American society (Dempsey, 1981). Deinstitutionalization, as it has been implemented, also appears to have overlooked the natural family in several respects. Few states and court cases which mandate deinstitutionalization have made provision for the valued responsibility of parents or guardians of individuals to be placed from institutions. Restrictions have been made on the new admissions to institutions but there has been little or no discussion of what services need to be developed for the body of families who have young, handicapped individuals still at home. What will be done to prevent the need for institutionalization now that we have eliminated institutionalization as an option for most families?

Individuals placed out of institutions into the natural home are generally more severely impaired than those placed in community residences. Future policy should address the needs of these individuals since they appear to have less access to support services. Meanwhile, the practice of community residences admitting mildly or borderline mentally retarded persons, directly from their own home simply because it is "age appropriate" must be reassessed. Future policy will probably treat all residential placements, community or institutional, as expensive interventions that must be used sparingly. To continue to allow community residencies to serve as an alternative to natural families can only lead to an unfair comparison between the two.

In this chapter we are suggesting that deinstitutionalization as a public policy will terminate or be greatly altered in its direction, probably within the current decade. Economic conditions have changed and the ideological basis for the policy is being reconsidered. The various unintended consequences of deinstitutionalization are now beginning to surface as are a number of unresolved issues. This is not meant to suggest that deinstitutionalization has been unsuccessful. To the contrary, the major reforms to institutions, the reduction in institutional populations, and the development of a more extensive community based system of services are major accomplishments that should not be overlooked. Future policy will probably continue to emphasize community-based services but must redirect service providers toward support rather than residential services. It must also reorient providers to the needs of the more severely impaired and elderly individuals. Finally, it must recognize that services and legislation must be directed at enhancing the role of natural families in the care and treatment of mentally retarded persons. Research on the policy of deinstitutionalization will provide invaluable information for the planners of future policies, and will eventually be directed at evaluation of the future policy itself.

REFERENCES

Aanes, D., & Haagenson, L. Normalization: Attention to a conceptual disaster. *Mental Retardation,* 1978, **16**, 55–56.

Baker, F., & Schulberg, H. C. The development of a community mental health ideology scale. *Community Mental Health Journal,* 1967, **3**, 216–225.

Baker, F., Seltzer, G. B., & Seltzer, M. M. *As close as possible: Community residences for retarded adults.* Boston, Massachusetts: Little, Brown, 1977.

Bartnik, E., & Winkler, R. C. Discrepant judgments of community adjustment of mentally retarded adults: The contribution of personal responsibility. *American Journal of Mental Deficiency,* 1981, **86**, 260–266.

Baumeister, A. A. Mental retardation policy and research: The unfulfilled promise. *American Journal of Mental Deficiency,* 1981, **85**, 449–456.

Best-Sigford, B., Bruininks, R. H., Lakin, C., Hill, B. K., & Heal, L. W. *American Journal of Mental Deficiency,* 1982, **87**, 130–140.

Blatt, B. *Christmas in purgatory.* Boston, Massachusetts: Allyn & Bacon, 1966.

Bloom, B. L. *Community mental health: A general introduction.* Monterey, California: Brooks/Cole, 1977.

Braddock, D. Deinstitutionalization of the retarded: Trends in public policy. *Hospital and Community Psychiatry,* 1981, **32**, 607–615.

Bradley, V. J. *Deinstitutionalization of developmentally disabled persons.* Baltimore, Maryland: Univ. Park Press, 1978.

Brewer, G. D. The policy sciences emerge: To nurture and structure a discipline. *Policy Sciences,* 1974, **15**, 239–244.

Bruininks, R. H., Hauber, F. A., & Kudla, M. J. National survey of community residential facilities: A profile of facilities and residents in 1977. *American Journal of Mental Deficiency,* 1980, **84**, 470–478.

Butterfield, E. C. Institutionalization and its alternatives for mentally retarded people in the United States. *International Journal of Mental Health,* 1977, **6**, 21–34.

Cameron, J. M. Ideology and policy termination: Restructuring California's mental health system. In J. V. May & A. B. Wildavsky (Eds.), *The policy cycle* (Vol. 5). Beverly Hills, California: Sage, 1978.

Campbell, V., Smith, R., & Wool, R. Adaptive behavior scale differences in scores of mentally retarded individuals referred for institutionalization and those never referred. *American Journal of Mental Deficiency,* 1982, **86**, 425-428.

Cobb, R. W., & Elder, C. D. *Participation in American politics: The dynamics of agenda-building.* Boston, Massachusetts: Allyn & Bacon, 1972.

Conroy, J., Efthimiou, J., & Lemanowicz, J. A matched comparison of the developmental growth of institutionalized and deinstitutionalized mentally retarded clients. *American Journal of Mental Deficiency,* 1982, **86**, 581-587.

Dempsey, J. J. *The family and public policy.* Baltimore, Maryland: Brookes, 1981.

Dern, T. A. Obstacles to the implementation of the normalization principle in human services: A response. *Mental Retardation,* 1983, **21**, 76.

Ellis, N. R., Bostick, G. E., Moore, S. A., & Taylor, J. J. A follow-up of severely and profoundly mentally retarded children after short-term institutionalization. *Mental Retardation,* 1981, **19**, 31-35.

Eyman, R. K., & Arndt, S. Life-span development of institutionalized and community-based mentally retarded residents. *American Journal of Mental Deficiency,* 1982, **86**, 342-350.

Flynn, R. Normalization, PASS, and service quality assessment: How normalizing are current human services? In R. J. Flynn & K. E. Nitsch (Eds.), *Normalization, social integration and community services.* Baltimore, Maryland: Univ. Park Press, 1980.

Gardner, J. M. Community residential alternatives for the developmentally disabled. *Mental Retardation,* 1977, **15**, 3-8.

Halderman et al. v. Pennhurst State School et al. Civil Action No. 74-1345. U.S. District Court, Eastern District of Pennsylvania, 1978.

Heal, L. W., & Laidlaw, T. J. Evaluation of residential alternatives. In A. R. Novak & L. W. Heal (Eds.), *Integration of developmentally disabled individuals into the community.* Baltimore, Maryland: Brookes, 1980.

Heller, T. Social disruption and residential relocation of mentally retarded children. *American Journal of Mental Deficiency,* 1982, **87**, 48-55.

Hemming, H., Lavender, T., & Pill, R. Quality of life of mentally retarded adults transferred from large institutions to new small units. *American Journal of Mental Deficiency,* 1981, **86**, 157-169.

Hendrix, E. The fallacies of the concept of normalization. *Mental Retardation,* 1981, **19**, 295-296.

Intagliata, J., & Willer, B. Reinstitutionalization of mentally retarded persons successfully placed into family care and group homes. *American Journal of Mental Deficiency,* 1982, **87**, 34-39.

Jacobson, J. W., & Schwartz, A. A. Personal and service characteristics affecting group home placement success: A prospective analysis. *Mental Retardation,* 1983, **21**, 1-7.

Janicki, M. P., Mayeda, T., and Epple, W. Availability of group homes for persons with mental retardation in the U.S. *Mental Retardation,* 1983, **21**, 45-51.

Jones, R., & Parlour, R. R. (Eds.). *Wyatt v. Stickney: Retrospect and prospect.* New York: Grune & Stratton, 1981.

Lakin, K. C., Bruininks, R. H., Hill, B. K., & Hauber, F. A. Turnover of direct-care staff in a national sample of residential facilities for mentally retarded people. *American Journal of Mental Deficiency,* 1982, **87**, 64-72. (a)

Lakin, K. C., Krantz, G. C., Bruininks, R. H., Clumpner, J. L., & Hill, B. K. One hundred years of data on populations of public residential facilities for mentally retarded people. *American Journal of Mental Deficiency,* 1982, **87**, 1-8. (b)

Lynn, L. E., Jr. *Knowledge and policy: The uncertain connection.* Washington, D.C.: National Academy of Science, 1978.

MacMillan, D. L. *Mental retardation in school and society.* Boston, Massachusetts: Little, Brown, 1977.

Magaro, P. A., Gripp, R., & McDowell, D. J. *The mental health industry: A cultural phenomenon.* New York: Wiley, 1978.

McCord, W. T. From theory to reality: Obstacles to the implementation of the normalization principle in human services. *Mental Retardation,* 1982, **20,** 247–253.

Menolascino, F. J., & McGee, J. J. The new institutions: Last ditch arguments. *Mental Retardation,* 1981, **19,** 215–220.

New York Association of Retarded Children v. Rockefeller. Civil Action Nos. 72–C–356, 72–357. E. D. N.Y., 1975.

Nirje, B. The normalization principle and its human management implications. In T. Kugel & W. Wolfensberger (Eds.), *Changing patterns in residential services for the retarded.* Washington, D.C.: U.S. Gov. Printing Office, 1969.

Noble, J. H., Jr., & Conley, R. W. Fact and conjecture in the policy of deinstitutionalization. *Health Policy Quarterly, 1981,* **1,** 99–124.

O'Connor, G. *Home is a good place: A national perspective of community residential facilities for developmentally disabled persons.* Washington, D.C.: American Association on Mental Deficiency, 1976.

President's Committee on Mental Retardation. *Mental retardation: Trends in state services.* Washington, D.C., 1976.

Rhoades, C., & Browning, P. Normalization at what price? *Mental Retardation,* 1977, **15,** 24.

Rivera, G. *Willowbrook: A report on how it is and why it doesn't have to be that way.* New York: Vintage Books, 1972.

Scanlon, C. A., Arick, J. R., & Krug, D. A. A matched sample investigation of nonadaptive behavior of severely handicapped adults across four living situations. *American Journal of Mental Deficiency,* 1982, **86,** 526–532.

Schalock, R. L., Harper, R. S., & Genung, T. Community integration of mentally retarded adults: Community placement and program success. *American Journal of Mental Deficiency,* 1981, **85,** 478–488.

Scheerenberger, R. C. Public residential services, 1981: Status and trends. *Mental Retardation,* 1982, **20,** 210–215.

Schlottman, R. A., & Anderson, V. H. Developmental changes of institutionalized mentally retarded children: A semilongitudinal study. *American Journal of Mental Deficiency,* 1982, **87,** 277–281.

Schroeder, S. R., & Henes, C. Assessment of progress of institutionalized and deinstitutionalized adults: A matched-control comparison. *Mental Retardation,* 1978, **16,** 147–148.

Schwartz, C. Normalization and idealism. *Mental Retardation,* 1977, **15,** 38–39.

Seltzer, M. M., Seltzer, G. B., & Sherwood, C. C. Comparison of community adjustment of older vs. younger mentally retarded adults. *American Journal of Mental Deficiency,* 1982, **87,** 9–13.

Spivack, G., & Spotts, J. *Devereux child behavior rating scale manual.* Devon, Pennsylvania Devereux Foundation, 1966.

Sproger, S. R. Misunderstanding deinstitutionalization: A response to a recent article. *Mental Retardation,* 1980, **18,** 199–201.

Suclzlc, M., & Keenan, V. Changes in family support networks over the life cycle of mentally retarded persons. *American Journal of Mental Deficiency,* 1981, **86,** 267–274.

Sutter, P., Mayeda, T., Yee, S., & Yanagi, G. Community placement success based on client behavior preferences of careproviders. *Mental Retardation,* 1981, **19,** 117–120.

Thiel, G. W. Relationship of I.Q. adaptive behavior, age, and environmental demand to community placement success of mentally retarded adults. *American Journal of Mental Deficiency,* 1981, **86,** 208–211.

Throne, J. M. Deinstitutionalization: Too wide a swath. *Mental Retardation,* 1979, **17,** 171–175.

Turnbull, R. H., (Ed.). *The least restrictive alternative: Principles and practices.* Washington, D.C.: American Association on Mental Deficiency, 1981.

Welsch v. Likins. Civil Action No. 451. U.S. District Court, District of Minnesota, Fourth Division, 1974.

Willer, B., & Intagliata, J. Comparison of family-care and group homes as alternatives to institutions. *American Journal of Mental Deficiency,* 1982, **86,** 588–595.

Willer, B., & Intagliata, J. *Promises and realities for mentally retarded persons: Life in the community.* Baltimore, Maryland: Univ. Park Press, 1984.

Wolfensberger, W. Twenty predictions about the future of residential services in mental retardation. *Mental Retardation,* 1969, **7,** 51–54.

Wolfensberger, W. The principle of normalization and its implications to psychiatric services. *American Journal of Psychiatry,* 1970, **127,** 291–297.

Wolfensberger, W., & Glenn, L. *PASS III: A method for qualitative evaluation of human services.* Toronto: National Institute on Mental Retardation, 1975.

Wyatt v. Stickney. Civil Action No. 3195 – N. U.S. District Court, Middle District of Alabama, North Division, 1972.

Zaharia, E. S., & Baumeister, A. A. Technician losses in public residential facilities. *American Journal of Mental Deficiency,* 1979, **84,** 36–39.

Community Attitudes toward Community Placement of Mentally Retarded Persons

CYNTHIA OKOLO AND SAMUEL GUSKIN

DEPARTMENT OF SPECIAL EDUCATION
INDIANA UNIVERSITY—BLOOMINGTON
BLOOMINGTON, INDIANA

INTERNATIONAL REVIEW OF RESEARCH IN
MENTAL RETARDATION, Vol. 12

I. PROLOGUE

The topic of this article may arouse in many readers an image of vociferous community members irrationally attacking proposals for humane, normal appearing residences for retarded persons in their neighborhood, driving these unhappy persons back to bedlamlike state hospitals. A vivid example of how one handicapped professional, a leader of community programs, viewed this situation is seen in Viscardi's (1972) description of the way fears and prejudices can be mobilized to oppose community programs for handicapped persons. The immediate stimulus to community action was a proposal to expand an education, training, and workshop facility which already existed within a suburban neighborhood. Members of the community hired lawyers, and brought a large number of neighborhood residents to the town hall where a requested change in zoning was being considered. What Viscardi referred to as a "mob scene" followed. Presenters for the handicapped facility were continually interrupted with shouts from the audience. They claimed they supported programs for the handicapped but they did not want to see a large building being constructed in their neighborhood. They put political pressure on the town board members and defeated the request for a change in zoning.

There is an alternative image, presented lucidly by Deutch (1976) who has opposed a community residence in his neighborhood. He suggests that those who support community residential facilities do not recognize the cost they are asking community members to bear, "a very real psychological cost of living in an atmosphere which is not normal, in the sense that their block or neighborhood will not reflect the ordinary composition of the community" (p. 347). He denies that the discomfort is due to unrealistic fears, prejudice, or ignorance. "The simple fact is that ordinary citizens seek a normal environment for their families that is in accord with the middle-class social mores and aspirations of the times." In short, his argument is that our attempts to normalize the lives of mentally retarded individuals are denormalizing the lives of nonretarded persons.

These two examples provide us with a picture of the range of alternative perspectives on community resistance to community placement of mentally retarded persons. What both have in common is their assumption that resistance is likely and an important phenomenon. Even these points are not universally agreed on by other writers nor are they supported by strong evidence. What this article attempts to do is to explicate the complexities of the phenomena involved, drawing on relevant theory and empirical findings where these are available. Finally, we try to indicate some of the implications of this analysis for further research and practical decision making.

II. INTRODUCTION

A. Common Assumptions

Most research and writing on community attitudes toward community placement of mentally retarded persons appears to be based on a core set of assumptions. First, it is assumed that the most appropriate residential placement is generally in the normal community, which to most professionals suggests a home and neighborhood much like the place in which they choose to live. This set of assumptions is formalized in the concepts and values discussed under the umbrella term "normalization" (Wolfensberger, 1972). It is presumed that the more normal the environment, the more normal the pattern of life, and the more satisfying the quality of life will be for the individual.

A second assumption appears to be that placement in large, isolated institutions was the result of hostile community attitudes toward the mentally retarded and that these same attitudes are a major source of the problems which have arisen in trying to establish small community residential facilities (CRFs) for mentally retarded persons.

Third, it seems to be assumed that community resistance is irrational and unrealistic and that if community members only knew the truth about the retarded and CRFs, they would be much more supportive. A related assumption is that the more exposure to, or contact with, retarded persons and CRFs, the more favorable the attitudes.

Finally, it is assumed that verbally expressed attitudes relate to overt behavior, e.g., resistance to CRFs. Thus, it is further assumed that if attitudes are changed, then overt actions opposing CRFs will also change.

As we review the empirical literature on this topic, the extent to which studies make these assumptions should become clear. Following the review, we shall come back to examine the extent to which these assumptions are justified. At that point, we shall also try to identify alternative conceptual frameworks and methodological approaches which might be more fruitful.

B. Defining the Constructs

All of the key terms in the title of this article, "community," "attitudes," "community placement," and "mental retardation" have had a wide range of meanings in writings on this topic. The purpose of this section is NOT to decide upon a single set of appropriate definitions nor a minimal set of criteria which operationally define these terms. We are not out to test an existing theoretical formulation by operationalizing these constructs. These terms are really just vague topical boundaries. The purpose of this section is to demonstrate the varied implications of the range of meanings alluded to.

"Community" is a term which is loosely used by professionals in the field of mental retardation but has been more systematically employed by urban sociologists (Davidson, 1983). It implies a cohesive interactive group holding common values, interests, and beliefs. Thus, an unorganized collection of individuals living within arbitrarily defined geographic boundaries would not be considered a community by some of these sociologists. While this distinction would not violate the meaning implied in the vivid example of collective action described in the prologue, it would raise serious questions about the way "community" is operationalized in most of the studies to be reported in this paper. Thus, we shall not limit our use of the term to the narrower definition but shall return to this conceptual issue following our review of the empirical literature.

"Attitudes" is a construct with a long definitional history. We shall use the term in its broadest sense here to incorporate all reactions by others to mentally retarded persons placed in the community, to residences for such persons in the community, and to related issues. Evidence for attitudes can come from formal instruments, primarily questionnaires, from less structured verbal measures, including interviews and content analysis of mass media, and from records of interactive behavior or decisions, e.g., to return a client to a large state hospital or not to open a group home.

"Community placement" is perhaps the most difficult but most central of these terms to deal with. Obviously, a small maximum security prisonlike structure constructed in the middle of an urban area should not qualify since we are primarily concerned with maximizing a normal environment and interaction with other community members. A foster home placement on an isolated farm might qualify but is not what we would typically think of. More specific definitions of types of community residential facilities (CRFs) are presented in Table I, which categorizes them as (1) family care facilities, serving less than five to seven residents or (2) group care facilities, serving five to seven residents or more. Many zoning ordinances and fire codes preserve this distinction between group and family care and become more restrictive when six or more residents are housed together (Lauber & Bangs, 1974). Although Table I provides a brief description of some typical group and family care facilities, the reader is cautioned that the names used in this table are rather arbitrary since a review of the literature indicates considerable variability and imprecision in terms used to refer to CRFs (Landesman-Dwyer, 1981). For example, "group home" is often used in conjunction with CRFs for the mentally retarded, while "halfway house" is often used to refer to comparable facilities for criminal offenders.

TABLE I
COMMUNITY RESIDENTIAL FACILITIES[a]

A. Group Care Facilities (5 to 7 or more residents)
   1. Group homes—24-hour care and supervision provided by live-in managers
   2. Miniinstitutions—24-hour care and supervision provided for 40 to 80 children and/or adults
   3. Workshops—dormitories—living units with associated work training programs
   4. Sheltered villages—segregated, self-contained communities for residents and live-in staff

B. Family Care Facilities (less than 5 to 7 residents)
   1. Natural/adoptive homes—parents have retained their natural child within the home or have adopted a mentally retarded person and retained him/her within the home.
   2. Foster or foster family care—care and supervision provided by family member(s) who receives payment for these services.
   3. Group homes—24-hour supervision provided by live-in managers.

C. Semiindependent or Independent Living
   Less than 24-hour supervision provided by a manager or agency staff (e.g., social worker)

[a]Adapted from Baker *et al.* (1977) and Lauber and Bangs (1974).

"Mentally retarded" persons can, of course, be defined by AAMD or governmental agency criteria, but the difficulty is the extent to which these definitions have changed over time. It is clear, however, that the degree of severity of the handicap must be considered in both conceptualizing and studying attitudes toward community placement. We shall also feel free to draw on literature with nonretarded populations when it adds to our understanding of the phenomena of interest.

C. Approaches to Research

Research on this topic has employed a variety of strategies, including opinion surveys of the general public, interviews with parents, neighbors, and group home managers, examining public laws and zoning regulations, determining geographic locations of CRFs and demographic characteristics of their neighborhood, checking housing prices near and away from CRFs, and field experiments on willingness to rent to mentally retarded persons. Most of the remainder of this article is devoted to a review of this body of literature.

III. REVIEW OF EMPIRICAL STUDIES

The first section of this review discusses research regarding community attitudes toward CRFs. The findings and limitations of empirical studies of attitudes toward CRFs are described and the results of studies that have examined the actual experiences of CRF developers, residents, and neighbors are presented. The second section examines the consequences of community opposition for CRFs and their residents, particularly as opposition affects the location and regulation of CRFs and the social and vocational integration of CRF residents. The third section discusses community concerns regarding CRFs and their residents, in an attempt to explicate the bases of negative attitudes and opposition. The final section provides a brief description of suggested strategies to facilitate the development of CRFs and more positive attitudes toward the community placement of persons with mental retardation.

A. Expressed Attitudes

Substantial research efforts have been devoted to the study of attitudes toward persons with mental retardation and other handicaps. Although this research has documented the existence of stereotypic expectations and negative attitudes, findings have often been inconsistent and contradictory. Methodological flaws in many studies, particularly unidimensional conceptualization of attitudes and researchers' failure to specify the attitude referent (Gottlieb, 1975; Gottlieb & Siperstein, 1976), render many findings uninterpretable. The reader is referred to the work of Gottlieb (1975) and Sandler and Robinson (1981) for comprehensive reviews of this body of attitudinal research.

Researchers have also studied public attitudes toward CRFs and CRF residents. In general, this body of research consists of two types of studies: (1) those that assess public attitudes toward the concept of community placement for persons with mental retardation and (2) those that examine attitudes toward a planned or actual CRF. The following sections summarize findings from both types of studies, and the reader is referred to Table II for methodological details of these studies.

1. ATTITUDES TOWARD THE CONCEPT
OF COMMUNITY PLACEMENT FOR PERSONS
WITH MENTAL RETARDATION

Illustrative of research exploring attitudes toward the concept of community placement is the widely cited Gallup Poll commissioned by the President's Committee on Mental Retardation (PCMR, 1975). This study indi-

TABLE II

EXPRESSED ATTITUDES TOWARD HYPOTHETICAL OR ACTUAL CRFs

Study	Methods	Relevant findings	Methodological strengths and weaknesses
Gottwald (1970), Public attitudes about mental retardation	Modified probability sample, 1515 respondents across United States. Likert scale questionnaire, administered through field interviews	48% agreed that "almost all" or "most" mentally retarded persons would make good neighbors	*Strengths:* large and representative sample *Weaknesses:* (1) no description of attitude referent, (2) items refer to broad and abstract social policies
Kastner *et al.* (1979), Assessing community attitudes toward mentally retarded persons	Control and threat groups, each consisting of 5–12 respondents, drawn from 10 residential areas and matched on demographic characteristics; 56 item questionnaire, items from Gallup (1974), Gottlieb & Corman (1975), Gottwald (1967). Threat group was told that a nearby house was being considered as a group home site	90% of control group and 81% of threat group would not object to a group home in the neighborhood; 95% of control group and 86% of threat group would not object to a mentally retarded co-worker	*Weaknesses:* (1) no description of attitude 'referent ("group home") provided to respondents, (2) sample limited to one community
Lewis (1973), The community and the retarded: A study in social ambivalence	Stratified random sample of 2661 adults in a Southern California city. Interview, administered after respondents were provided with a description of a moderately and severely retarded child	36% unconditionally recommended that a moderately retarded child be institutionalized; 74% unconditionally recommended that a severely retarded child be institutionalized	*Strengths:* provided a description of the attitude referent *Weaknesses:* sample limited to one city
Margolis and Charitonidis (1981), Public reactions to housing for the mentally retarded	80 landlords or rental agents on Eastern coast of New Jersey who had advertised apartments in local newspaper. Telephone contact to:	72.5% of landlords willing to rent to a mentally retarded adult	*Strengths:* (1) realistic situation, (2) attitude referent was described *Weaknesses:* sampled from a limited geographical area

(continued)

TABLE II (*continued*)

Study	Methods	Relevant findings	Methodological strengths and weaknesses
	(a) establish availability of apartment, (b) if apartment was available, repeat call in 20–30 minutes to request rental for a "mentally retarded adult who has just completed a rehabilitation program and has secured a job"		
President's Committee on Mental Retardation (1975), President's Committee on Mental Retardation Gallup Poll shows attitudes on mental retardation improving	Stratified random sample, Gallup poll survey (no other study details provided)	85% would not object to a home for mildly or moderately retarded adults on their block	*Weaknesses:* (1) no information available regarding sample, (2) items assess hypothetical and abstract situations
Smith (1981), Community acceptance of homes for mentally retarded people	2 rural communities in Michigan with similar demographic characteristics; one welcomed a group home for mentally retarded adults, other prevented its opening. Interviews conducted with neighbors and community leaders	Attitudes of community leaders were crucial for facilitating acceptance of a group home in the community	*Strengths:* studied community that had actually opposed a group home *Weaknesses:* sample limited to two communities

Trippi *et al.* (1978), Housing discrimination toward mentally retarded persons	100 landlords who advertised apartments in the local newspaper for $200 or less per month. Telephone contact to: (1) establish the availability of the apartment, (2) if apartment was available, return call 30 minutes later to request rental for a "mentally retarded adult who had just completed training and was ready for independent living"	1% of landlords were willing to rent to a mentally retarded adult	*Strengths:* (1) realistic situation, (2) attitude referent was described *Weaknesses:* sample limited to one city
Willms (1978), Retarded adults in the community: An investigation of neighborhood attitudes and concerns	75 adults at varying distances to a group home (same block, within 1000 feet and 1000–1400 feet); group home had been established 3 years prior to study and housed 36 residents. 56-item Likert scale to test concerns, 36-item test of knowledge about mental retardation; and 24-item test of attitudes toward integration	Primary concern of respondents was actual operation of group home, e.g., supervision of residents, competence of staff	*Strengths:* instrumentation carefully developed, described and validated *Weaknesses:* sample limited to neighbors of one group home

cated highly favorable attitudes, with 85% of the sample stating that they would not object to the following situation: "Suppose mildly or moderately retarded persons have been educated to live in the community. Would you object to six of them occupying a home on your block or not?"

Other studies have led to more pessimistic conclusions, however. Gottwald (1970), in one of the earlier studies of attitudes toward the mentally retarded as community members, reported that less than 50% of a nationwide sample agreed that "almost all" or "most" mentally retarded persons would make "good neighbors." Sigelman (1976) reported that only 44.7% of her respondents agreed that homes for retarded adults should be allowed in residential districts. In one of the few studies to provide a description of the attitude referent, Lewis (1973) assessed attitudes toward the community placement of retarded children. Respondents were first given descriptions of a mildly retarded child and a severely retarded child and then asked "if parents have such a child, what do you think they should do with him?" Twenty-three percent of the sample unconditionally recommended that the mildy retarded child be kept at home, 36% recommended institutionalization, and 41% provided an ambivalent response; that is, they indicated that the parents' decision could vary depending upon individual characteristics and circumstances. When queried about a severely retarded child, only 6% of the sample unconditionally recommended that the child remain at home, 74% recommended institutionalization, and 20% privided ambivalent responses. While Lewis concluded that ambivalent responses were indicative of confused and therefore unfavorable attitudes toward the retarded, it could be argued that ambivalent responses reflect respondents' cognizance of individual differences in tolerance and ability to care for a mentally retarded child. Moreover, it cannot be assumed that respondents who recommended institutionalization would take this action with their own child.

In summary, studies of attitudes toward the concept of community placement for mentally retarded persons have yielded inconsistent findings. Attitudinal studies often have employed a survey methodology (e.g., Gottwald, 1970; PCMR, 1975) to poll a representative sample of a state or national population and thus findings represent the aggregate score of a potentially diverse group of individuals (Lippman, 1976). A finding such as "95% of a sample of Americans believe mentally retarded persons should live in the community" does not predict that 95% of the people in a neighborhood where a CRF is scheduled to open will have a similar opinion. Moreover, one or two vocal opponents often are capable of preventing the opening of a CRF within the neighborhood (Baron, 1981; Sigelman, 1976).

The nature of the items used in these studies also introduces problems for the interpretation of results. Most studies have asked respondents about hypothetical situations, as illustrated by the following items from Gottwald's (1970) survey:

1. As far as you know, what proportion of the mentally retarded people would make good neighbors?
2. In your opinion, should most mentally retarded people drink liquor?
3. What proportion of mentally retarded people can be self-supporting?

Such items assess attitudes toward abstract social issues, and responses may be particularly vulnerable to social desirability bias. Moreover, respondents may not perceive abstract social policies to have a direct impact on their personal lives. Using a combination of items from other attitudinal studies (Gottlieb & Corman, 1975; Gottwald, 1970; PCMR, 1975), Kastner, Reppucci, and Pezzoli (1979) demonstrated that attitudes toward some issues became significantly more negative when respondents were led to believe that a hypothetical situation might become a reality. Thus, expressed attitudes toward hypothetical situations may be inaccurate predictors of attitudes toward actual situations.

The most serious criticism, however, must be levied against conclusions drawn from this body of research that fail to consider the tenuous relation between attitudes and behavior. In general, attitudinal research has failed to explicate this relationship, although research by Gottlieb and his colleagues (e.g., Gottlieb & Davis, 1973; Gottlieb & Gottlieb, 1977) is a notable exception. The literature offers little reason to conclude that persons who express highly favorable attitudes toward mentally retarded persons or deinstitutionalization will welcome mentally retarded neighbors or co-workers. In the absence of demonstrable relations between expressed attitudes and behavior, the majority of research exploring expressed attitudes toward the concept of community placement for persons with mental retardation is of dubious value.

2. ATTITUDES TOWARD PLANNED OR ACTUAL CRFs

Other studies have examined the attitudes of neighbors to a potential or actual CRF. The study by Kastner et al. (1979) is an example of this type of research. In this study, 5 to 12 households in proximity to a house for sale in each of 10 neighborhoods were defined as a "threat group," for a total of 99 threat-group respondents. Households in a control group were chosen to match those in the threat group on variables such as location, size, price of home, and neighborhood socioeconomic status. A 56-item questionnaire was administered to both control and threat groups in identical fashion, with the exception of the following introduction provided to the threat group: "for instance, that house (indicating the direction of target house with a gesture) is on the market. We would like to know what your views would be if that house was the location of a group home." Small but statistically significant differences between control and threat groups were found. For example, 90% of the control group indicated that they would not object to a group home in the neighborhood; however, this figure dropped to 81% for the threat group. Control and threat-group subjects also differed in their response to the question "would you object to having a trained worker who is mildly or moderately retarded employed where you work or not?" Ninety-five percent of the control group indicated they would not object, in contrast to 86% of the threat group. Kastner *et al.* felt that greater differences between groups on these and other items might have been obtained under a stronger threat condition; that is, if respondents were told that the house for sale would definitely become a group home. Further analyses indicated that the threat condition had no significant effect on questionnaire items designed to assess general attitudes toward and information about mental retardation, providing additional support that such items predict neither attitudes nor behavior in actual situations.

Willms (1978) developed a structured instrument to assess knowledge about mental retardation and concerns regarding CRFs. After administering this instrument to adults living at varying distances within 1400 ft of a residential facility, Willms reported that respondents were most concerned with factors related to the actual operation of the group home, including the supervision of residents, competence of the staff, reason for neighborhood selection, and sexual behavior of residents. A more comprehensive study was conducted by Smith (1981) in two rural Michigan communities; one that had opposed a group home for six persons with mental retardation and one that welcomed such a facility. Smith interviewed neighbors and community leaders in both towns and found that the attitudes and behaviors of community leaders were critical in facilitating positive community attitudes. In the accepting community, leaders had positive attitudes toward the group home and convinced community members that its opening would offer them additional employment opportunities.

At least two studies have assessed attitudes toward the mentally retarded as tenants in the community. Utilizing newspaper advertisements, Trippi, Michael, Colao, and Alvarez (1978) telephoned 100 landlords with apartments for rent. An initial call established the availability of the apartment. Thirty minutes later, a second call was made and the landlord was told that a "mentally retarded adult who had just completed training and was ready for independent living" was interested in renting the apartment. Only 1 of the 100 landlords was willing to rent the apartment under these conditions. A more recent replication of this study (Margolis & Charitonidis, 1981), in a different part of the country, produced drastically different findings. Eighty landlords were called and 72.5% indicated they would accept a mentally retarded tenant. By comparing the results of these two studies, it is tempting to conclude that attitudes toward the mentally retarded as community members have become more positive. Yet, these discrepant findings could also be explained by regional differences in attitudes, variation in the availability of rentals across the study locations, or the manner in which the questions were worded.

3. RESPONDENT CHARACTERISTICS
AND ATTITUDES

Although researchers have attempted to establish relations between attitudes toward CRFs and respondent characteristics, few conclusions can be reliably stated, as findings frequently contradict each other. Some studies have found females to be more positive (Gottwald, 1970), others have found no significant difference between sexes (Johnson & Beditz, 1981; Lewis, 1973). Sigelman (1976) found that blacks were more willing to recommend that group homes be allowed in single-family residential districts than Anglos or Mexican-Americans, while Lewis (1973) found that blacks were more likely to recommend institutionalization for mentally retarded children. Higher levels of income and education were found to be correlated with more positive and liberal attitudes in some studies (Gottwald, 1970; Lewis 1973), whereas other research has demonstrated that residents with low income but high educational attainment are more accepting of CRFs within the neighborhood (Segal, Baumohl, & Moyles, 1980).

The relation between neighbors' physical distance from a CRF and attitudes has also been explored, with some research indicating that persons at a further distance express more positive attitudes toward potential or actual CRFs (Baron & Piasecki, 1981; Nelson, 1978). Rothbart (1973) questioned neighbors of a halfway house for exconvicts and reported that people within 1 mile of the house were less favorable than people who lived 3 to 5 miles away, even though expressed attitudes of the two groups toward general prison reform were similar. Yet, contrary results are reported by Willms (1978) who found that distant neighbors had more concerns about a group home than did intermediate or immediate neighbors. Likewise, Knowles and Baba (cited in Lauber & Bangs, 1974) found that people familiar with a specific halfway house for exconvicts were highly favorable to it, in contrast to the community at large.

The relation between respondents' prior contact with mentally retarded persons and expressed attitudes has also been a popular research theme. Willms (1978) found that respondents with more reported contact had fewer concerns about a specific group home and Kastner et al. (1979) reported that both control and threat-group members with more contact responded more positively to attitudinal items. Yet, other researchers have not found similar correlations in their data (Sandler & Robinson, 1980). Some inconsistency may be attributed to variations in operational definitions of contact

(Altman, 1981). Some researchers have asked respondents to rate their degree of contact with the mentally retarded as "none," "some," or "considerable" (e.g., Sandler & Robinson, 1980; Willms, 1978). Others have used more elaborate definitions of contact, such as Kastner *et al.* (1979), who derived a contact score from responses to items that assessed (1) willingness to volunteer or visit neighborhood group homes, (2) previous interaction through personal friendship or contact with mentally retarded persons, and (3) reading relevant material or learning about the mentally retarded through formal instruction. Prior research on public attitudes toward mentally retarded persons also suggests that quality of contact is more critical than quantity (Gottlieb, 1975; Vurdelja-Maglajic & Jordan, 1974), but this hypothesis remains to be explored for attitudes toward CRF residents.

In conclusion, relations between respondent characteristics and attitudes must be interpreted with caution, given the limited number of studies and minimal consistency among findings. Moreover, the value of additional attempts to explicate these relations is questionable. Further refinement of the characteristics of the ideal neighborhood or neighbor will only produce statistical artifacts akin to the "average" person. Present research findings might suggest that the ideal neighbor is both young and a long-term resident of the neighborhood; certainly these two characteristics are contradictory. In any case, more pragmatic considerations, such as zoning restrictions or financial constraints, may not permit developers the luxury of choosing an "ideal" neighborhood for the location of a CRF.

B. Experiences of Community Residence Developers and Community Caretakers

Another series of studies has assessed developers', caretakers' and/or deinstitutionalized persons' perceptions of community attitudes and behaviors. A few of these studies have included interviews with nonhandicapped community members. This body of research provides reports of actual behavior toward CRFs and/or perceptions of that behavior, and thus supplies important insights into the relation between attitudes and behavior. Table III provides methodological details of the studies that are summarized below.

Three large-scale studies have assessed the experiences of deinstitutionalized persons in the community and community reactions to the mentally retarded person as a neighbor (Baker, Seltzer, & Seltzer, 1977; Gollay, Freedman, Wyngaarden, & Kurtz, 1978; O'Connor, 1976). All three studies were conducted by first collecting demographic data on a large sample of facilities and/or residents, and then selecting a smaller, representative sample for site visits and interviews. In the study conducted by Gollay *et al.* (1978), residents

TABLE III

TABLE III

EXPERIENCES OF COMMUNITY RESIDENCE DEVELOPERS AND COMMUNITY CARETAKERS

Study	Methods	Relevant findings	Methodological strengths and weaknesses
Baker et al. (1977), As close as possible: A study of community residences for retarded adults	Residences that (1) had been open for 6 or more months, (2) housed less than 80 adults, (3) considered themselves as alternatives to institutions. Two-part study: (1) 381 residences throughout U.S. that met above criteria were administered questionnaires, (2) 17 residences in 7 states were sampled for site visits; interviews conducted with mentally retarded residents, caretakers, and neighbors, observations conducted on site	35% of residences reported opposition to their opening	Strengths: interviews conducted with residents and neighbors
Berdiansky and Parker (1977). Establishing a group home for the adult mentally retarded in North Carolina	51 group home developers in North Carolina, group homes were usually located in central or transitional zones of cities or large towns. Fixed response and open-ended questions administered through interviews	Community opposition prevented group homes from opening in 12% of the cases	Weaknesses: (1) only assessed developers' perceptions of community attitudes, (2) sample limited to one state, (3) limited information provided about characteristics of sample
Colombatto et al. (1982), Perspectives on deinstitutionalization	192 superintendents of public residential facilities, members of the National Association of Superintendents of Public Residential Facilities for the Mentally Retarded. Questionnaires, administered through the mail	44% of superintendents described the community as indifferent, 35% described it as hostile to deinstitutionalization efforts	Weaknesses: (1) only assessed superintendents' perceptions of community reactions, (2) limited information about representativeness of sample

(continued)

TABLE III (continued)

Study	Methods	Relevant findings	Methodological strengths and weaknesses
Gollay et al. (1978), Coming back: The community experience of deinstitutionalized people	Two-part: (1) 250 institutions across U.S., (2) 440 deinstitutionalized residents, aged 6–40, released from 9 representative institutions at least 2 years prior to study. Majority of respondents were mild-moderately retarded. Institutions were mailed questionnaires regarding deinstitutionalization policies. Interviews were conducted with resident and a family member (i.e., parent, caretaker or social worker)	Caretakers of younger and more severely retarded perceived the community to be more friendly; 20% of caretakers stated that lack of community acceptance was a significant problem	Strengths: (1) large and representative sample, (2) residents' and caretakers' responses were compared and often found to agree
Justice et al. (1971), Foster family care for the retarded: Management concerns for the caretaker	59 foster mothers, each with 1 or more mentally retarded foster child under 18 (159 foster children). Half of children were severely or profoundly retarded, slightly more than half diagnosed as Down's syndrome. Structured interviews conducted with mothers	34% of foster mothers stated that "public misconceptions about the mentally retarded and lack of community acceptance", were problems	Weaknesses: study conducted in one geographically defined service area.
Mamula and Newman (1973), Community placement of the mentally retarded	20 foster care parents and 48 of their neighbors. Foster children were mentally retarded with no significant behavioral difficulties or physical anomalies. 80% had been	Neighbors were found to perceive the retarded individual "very favorably"	Weaknesses: (1) methodology and findings not described in detail

	Methods	Findings	Strengths/Weaknesses
	in home for 2 or more years. (1) 60 item true–false questionnaire to assess knowledge about mental retardation, (2) semantic differential instrument to assess attitudes		*Strengths*: large and representative sample *Weaknesses*: interviews conducted only with facility managers
O'Connor (1976), Home is a good place	(1) 611 community residences providing 24-hour care for 6 or more developmentally disabled persons, administered questionnaires. (2) 105 residences from above sample visited, structured interviews conducted with facility managers	33% of managers reported opposition to their facility	
Segal and Aviram (1978), The mentally ill and community-based sheltered care	Open-ended interviews conducted with "key people." 499 non-retarded persons with mental illness, aged 18–65, housed in sheltered care facilities (defined as "any residence, except licensed hospital, offering at least minimally supervised living arrangements"), 243 facility operators. Structured interviews conducted with facility operators and residents	19% of operators reported complaints from neighbors and 4% reported threats and harassment from neighbors; opposition did not seem to decrease over time	*Strengths*: use of open-ended interviews to develop structured instruments *Weaknesses*: sample limited to one state

were the unit of analysis. After surveying the deinstitutionalization patterns and procedures of 250 institutions across the United States, 440 deinstitutionalized residents from 9 representative institutions were identified and visited in their homes or in the institution (as 13% had been reinstitutionalized). Interviews were conducted with both the mentally retarded person and his or her caretaker. Overall, 20% of the caretakers felt that lack of community acceptance posed a significant problem. To facilitate the interpretation of issues explored by the study, Gollay *et al.* (1978) categorized study results by age of the deinstitutionalized person and by severity of retardation. Caretakers of the mildly retarded were least likely to see the community as friendly, in contrast to caretakers of persons with moderate and severe mental retardation. Differential results were also obtained for age; 94% of the caretakers of children rated the community as "friendly" or "very friendly," whereas only 42% of the caretakers of adults did the same. However, it is unlikely that age is related in a simple and consistent way to community acceptance, as suggested by Baron and Piasecki's (1981) finding that neighbors expressed more opposition to CRFs for young adults with mental illness than to CRFs for older adult clients.

In two other studies, the CRF was the unit of analysis. Baker *et al.* (1977) reported the results of site visits to 17 CRFs in seven states, during which a detailed history of the residence was obtained, staff and residents were interviewed, and community attitudes were assessed, where possible, through interviews with community members. Thirty-five percent of the residences in this study reported community opposition to their opening; 24% were opposed by "neighbors who complained," 12% experienced opposition through zoning disputes, 5% were opposed by political leaders, and 4% reported opposition from parents of retarded residents. All facilities indicated that opposition had decreased over time. Although other research has found correlations between the size of a CRF and the amount of community opposition (e.g., Segal & Aviram, 1978), Baker *et al.* did not find a relation between opposition and (1) size of residence or (2) severity of residents' retardation.

O'Connor (1976) reported the results of site visits and interviews with managers of 105 facilities for developmentally disabled persons. Similar to the results of Baker *et al.* (1977), one third of O'Connor's respondents reported opposition to their facility, with 83% of this opposition originating from neighbors and 11% from city/county officials and businessmen. O'Connor also was unable to establish relations between characteristics of the facility and amount of opposition.

Other studies have sampled a smaller and more restricted group of residents or facilities. Berdiansky and Parker (1977) interviewed group home developers in North Carolina. Community opposition was reported by approximately 25% of the respondents and was attributed to one or more of the following factors: (1) perceived danger of group home residents to the community, (2) fear of sexual deviance, (3) potential decreases in property values, (4) lack of supervision of group home residents, and (5) sexual racial composition of the home. In addition, respondents reported that each of these issues was resolved less than 50% of the time. In a more recent study, superintendents of public residential facilities were asked to describe the reactions of the surrounding community to deinstitutionalization efforts (Colombatto, Isett, Roszkowski, Spreat, D'Onofrio, & Alderfer, 1982). Forty-four percent described the community as "indifferent," while 35% described it as "somewhat hostile."

Few studies have attempted to determine the number of facilities that have not opened, or have closed soon after opening, due to community opposition. It should be noted that the amount of community opposition reported in most studies (e.g., Baker et al., 1977; Gollay, 1978; O'Connor, 1976) is probably underrepresentative, as facilities that were prevented from opening had no opportunity to be included in these samples. Piasecki (1975) reported that, for every existing residential facility in his sample, another had closed or never opened. Berdiansky and Parker (1977) reported a more encouraging figure, with 88% of planned group homes opening "but not always on time and not always without turmoil."

Other studies have examined community attitudes toward mentally retarded persons in foster care homes. After interviewing foster caretakers and neighbors of 20 foster care homes, Mamula and Newman (1973) reported that neighbors "perceived the retarded individual favorably." Very little information is provided about their methodology and findings, yet the authors do suggest that absence of behavioral difficulties and physical anomalies in their sample of foster children may have enhanced attitudes. A more informative study is described by Justice, Bradley, and O'Connor (1971) who interviewed 59 foster mothers, each with at least one mentally retarded child. Since about half these children were profoundly or severely retarded and slightly more than half were diagnosed as Down's syndrome, their handicap was likely to be visible to community members. "Public misconceptions about the mentally retarded and lack of community acceptance" was the most frequently named problem, cited by 34% of the sample. Examples of rejection included "open curiosity displayed toward the [child], antagonism of neighbors and friends, discrimination against caretakers and children, exclusion of [children] from community activities and imposition of restrictive zoning." Other studies of foster care have reported similarly negative responses from community members (Morrissey, 1966; Tinsley, O'Connor, & Halpern, 1973). Based on anecdotal reports, Cohen (1980) estimated that half of the caretakers affiliated with Bronx Developmental Services had experienced ridicule and abuse from neighbors. Caretakers in this sample often described the need to protect their foster child from community hostility and felt compelled to educate rejecting neighbors. Yet, caretakers apparently had positive interactions with neighbors as well, since half had received assistance from neighbors with baby-sitting, transportation and family activities.

One study found unfavorable attitudes to be a problem for natural parents and families of retarded children (Suelzle & Keenan, 1980). Fourteen percent of the respondents in this study felt their child had a negative effect on their ability to entertain at home while 21% felt their child affected their social activities outside the home. In addition, respondents indicated that community acceptance of their mentally retarded child decreased as the child grew into young adulthood, depriving him or her of opportunities for social integration at a time when such experiences may be critical.

In summary, this set of studies offers many useful findings about the prevalence and sources of negative attitudes toward CRFs and mentally retarded community members. By assessing the perceptions and attitudes of neighbors, caretakers, developers, and residents affiliated with an actual CRF or community placement, the difficulty of interpreting attitudes toward hypothetical situations is avoided. In particular, the research conducted by Baker *et al.* (1977), Gollay *et al.* (1978), and O'Connor (1976) is exemplary. By using careful sampling procedures and data from multiple sources, these authors have inspired confidence in their findings and have explicated a productive methodology for future research. Based on the studies reviewed in this section, community attitudes toward CRFs can be characterized as moderate, as opposition was typically reported by about one third of the respondents. Opposition that occurs with moderate frequency, however, has critical implications for the establishment of CRFs. Extra expenses may be incurred in public relations campaigns or promotional literature (Piasecki, 1975). In the face of persistent opposition, developers may have to locate another site and reapply for zoning and other permits, a process that is both costly and time consuming. Opposition appears to abate over time (Baker *et al.*, 1977; Nelson, 1978; Wehbring & Ogren, 1975), but the reasons for decreased opposition have not been adequately addressed. Longitudinal studies are needed to explicate the factors that facilitate community acceptance.

C. Parental Attitudes

The attitudes of parents with mentally retarded children and adults may also present an unexpected barrier to community placement, as parental requests to maintain their child in the institutional setting may be honored despite the availability of a community placement or its potential benefit to the resident. Furthermore, longitudinal studies have demonstrated that parental approval and family involvement in community placement are correlates of community adjustment (Schalock, Harper, & Genung, 1981; Willer & Intagliata 1981).

Parental opposition to the community placement of their mentally retarded son or daughter has been noted by many researchers and practitioners. Eighty-nine percent of the institutions in Sheerenberger's (1978) survey reported parental opposition to the community placement of their son or daughter. In addition, 67% of the institutional personnel who were surveyed indicated they would or might retain a minor resident in the face of persistent opposition, and 47% claimed they would retain an adult. Hill and Wehman (1980b) found that parental attitudes hindered the implementation of community training for severely retarded children, as parents were fearful, embarrassed, or had low expectations for their child. Birenbaum and Seiffer (1976) reported similarly negative attitudes among parents whose son or daughter was scheduled for placement in a sheltered-care community.

Parental opposition to community placement has also been expressed through class action suits targeted at deinstitutionalization efforts. For example, parents in *Halderman v. Pennhurst* (1977) argued that many residents were too old to adapt to the transition from institution to community placement and that residents' abilities had deteriorated due to the cumulative effects of institutional placement, leaving them ill prepared for community living. In *Connecticut Association for Retarded Citizens v. Mansfield Training School* (1979) parents expressed concern that their children would be placed in group homes without adequate monitoring or supervision.

Some research has specifically examined the reasons for parental opposition. Ferrara (1979) administered a questionnaire to 217 Philadelphians who were members of parents' organizations. The questionnaire consisted of a combination of demographic and attitudinal questions from other studies (Gottlieb & Corman, 1975; Gottwald, 1970), and two versions were developed. On the first version, parents responded to items about a general referent, for example "a mentally retarded child should go to a public school which has classes for non-retarded children." The second version required parents to respond to statements about their own child, for example, "my mentally retarded child should go to a public school which has classes for non-retarded children." For 42 of the 50 questionnaire items, responses were more positive to the general referent than to the specific referent. No interaction was found between parental age, parental sex, or the child's level of retardation, and responses toward the specific referent.

Meyer (1980) mailed a questionnaire to all parents or legal guardians of residents in an institution for mentally retarded persons. The questionnaire requested demographic and behavioral information about the resident and assessed parental satisfaction with institutional programming. A brief description was provided of a "small group home" and a "supervised apartment" and parents were asked to choose the most appropriate placement for their child both (1) now and (2) in the case that their child reached his or her potential in the institution. For both these items, over 75% of the respondents chose institutional placement. When asked to specify reasons for their choices, 37% of the parents mentioned the need for 24-hour care and supervision, 25% commented on the quality of care and availability of services in the institution, and 21% stated their child was happy and well adjusted at the institution. Younger parents were more likely to prefer community placement. Surprisingly, parents who indicated dissatisfaction with institutional programming were no more likely to prefer community placement than satisfied parents.

In summary, research has documented the existence of negative parental attitudes toward community placement for their institutionalized mentally retarded son or daughter. Parental opposition may be understandable, given the widespread and somewhat sensationalized accounts of "dumping" deinstitutionalized persons into the community without services (e.g., Santiestevan, 1975) and the unsupportive climate of the general community. One also must remember that professionals were once eager to convince parents of the advantages of institutional placement, and cited reasons such as "the need for 24-hour care and supervision." Thus, it should not be surprising that parents are uncertain about the desirability of community placement. Findings from this body of research suggest that CRF developers and practitioners should attend to parental attitudes and should attempt to actively involve parents in both the planning and the implementation of community placement for their son or daughter.

D. Consequences of Community Attitudes for Community Residential Facilities and Their Residents

Community opposition may have direct consequences for CRFs and their residents, including the location and regulation of CRFs within the community and the social and vocational integration of residents. Organized community groups or vocal community members may effectively prevent a CRF from opening in their neighborhood through the imposition and interpretation of zoning and/or other regulations. Such actions have been especially common in single-family residential districts (Chandler & Ross, 1976; Lauber & Bangs, 1974). Even after a CRF is established, continuing community opposition or negative attitudes may severely limit opportunities for residents' social and vocational integration.

1. LOCATION AND REGULATION OF CRFs

Community opposition has had a significant influence on the physical location of CRFs. Gollay *et al.* (1978) reported that 62% of 105 facilities they surveyed were located on residential streets. The facilities surveyed by Baker *et al.* (1977) were evenly distributed across different types of neighborhoods and Davidson (1982) reported that community-based treatment centers for mentally retarded persons were located in neighborhoods with relatively high income, educational attainment, and occupational prestige. In contrast, other research has indicated that CRFs for the mentally retarded (Berdiansky & Parker, 1977; O'Connor, 1976; Sigelman, 1973) and other disability groups (Keller & Alper, 1970; Segal & Aviram, 1978) are most often located in lower or lower-middle-class neighborhoods in the center of cities or large towns.

Although advocates of the normalization principle recommend that CRFs be located in single-family residential districts (Thomas, 1973; Wolfensberger, 1972), other researchers regard transient neighborhoods located in urban areas as advantageous sites, due to higher tolerance for individual differences, lowered potential for resistance, and the availability of community services (Davidson, 1982; Gerry, 1975; Segal & Aviram, 1978). In addition, facilities outside urban areas are less likely to be located near public transportation (Gollay *et al.,* 1978) and recreational and shopping facilities (Davidson, 1982).

Yet, transient neighborhoods may have disadvantages as well, including higher crime rates and less desirable living conditions. Although Segal and Aviram (1978) found that CRF residents in all white neighborhoods were socially isolated, so were residents in ghetto areas. Birenbaum (1980) reported that residents in an urban area were often afraid to travel about their community. Moreover, Davidson (1983) has presented evidence to suggest that transient neighborhoods are rapidly becoming adept at organizing to prevent the establishment of CRFs in their neighborhoods.

A community's zoning laws have often been effectively used to prevent the establishment of CRFs in single-family residential neighborhoods. Lauber and Bangs (1974) surveyed 200 municipal planning departments who subscribed to the Planning Advisory Service and found that 66% did not allow CRFs in single-family residential districts. "Family" is often narrowly defined as "relations by blood, adoption or marriage," a definition endorsed by the United States Supreme Court (*Boraas v. Village of Belle Terre,* 1974). Consequently, municipalities have won zoning battles on the claim that CRF residents do not constitute a family. In other instances, potential foster parents have been prevented from accepting a mentally retarded child into their home by neighbors' protests that foster care constitutes a "business use of property" impermissible in single-family residential districts (Chandler & Ross, 1976).

Rather than automatically prohibiting CRFs in certain districts, some communities require CRF developers to obtain special or conditional use permits (Chandler & Ross, 1976; Kressel, 1981; Lauber & Bangs, 1974). Special use permits typically initiate a process that includes notifying potential neighbors of intended property use and establishing procedures for appeals. Often, a hearing before a reviewing agency and local residents is required to demonstrate that certain conditions will be met, and the complete process may be both costly and time consuming (Kressel, 1981).

Recently, some states and/or municipalities have taken action to facilitate the establishment of CRFs in residential neighborhoods. One such measure is an extended definition of "family," such as the one created in Tuscon, Arizona: "family means any number of individuals customarily living as a single housekeeping unit and using common cooking facilities" (Kressel, 1981). In other cases, states have enacted legislation that preempts local zoning authority and requires zoning agencies to permit CRFs in residential neighborhoods. Even with facilitative zoning regulations, however, community members may generate sufficient pressure to prevent zoning approval.

At the present time, debate continues regarding the optimal nature and method of zoning reform (Hopperton, 1980) and a large amount of variability exists among and within states regarding zoning practices. Lauber and Bangs (1974) encourage planning departments to permit CRFs in residential districts after establishing controls to ensure adequate dispersal throughout the community. Deutch (1976) recommends that standards be set and enforced that allow neighbors to participate in the management of a CRF. Such standards may help to defuse potential opposition.

2. SOCIAL AND VOCATIONAL INTEGRATION OF CRF RESIDENTS

Community attitudes toward CRFs undoubtedly have important consequences for the successful community adjustment of CRF residents. Segal and Aviram (1978) studied the relation between community attitudes and CRF residents' integration in the neighborhood, as measured by a multidimensional scale that they developed. Of the nine variables entered into a regression equation, "positive response of neighbors," as defined by events such as neighbors initiating conversations with residents or inviting residents to their homes, was found to be the most significant predictor. Conversely, the number of complaints made to local authorities after a facility opened was found to have a deleterious effect on integration. For fiscal year 1976–1977, Sheerenberger (1978) reported that institutional personnel attributed 13% of their return rate to "community rejection of the retarded, the family or the retarded person." He speculated that attitudes may be improving, however, as this figure decreased from a reported 22% in 1973–1974. Compared to those successfully placed in the community, institutional returnees interviewed by Gollay et al. (1978) rated their community as significantly less friendly than did those residents who remained in the community.

Although empirical evidence suggests that CRFs and their residents are accepted over time (Baker et al., 1977; Mamula & Newman, 1973; O'Connor, 1976), the process by which communities come to accept their new neighbors and the factors that facilitate this acceptance are not clear. Moreover, decreased opposition may be more indicative of passive tolerance than of active acceptance. Most available data suggest that mentally retarded persons, as well as persons with other disabilities, remain isolated within the community.

One indication of isolation is the small percentage of residents who are employed in the community. Work may be viewed as a vehicle for establishing contact with persons outside the residence, as well as a means for enhancing self-esteem (Birenbaum & Seiffer, 1976; Moreau, Novak, & Sigelman, 1980). In studies of CRFs, the percentage of persons competitively employed has ranged from 14% (O'Connor, 1976) to 25% (Gollay et al., 1978). Residents are most often employed in sheltered workshops (Baker et al., 1977; Birenbaum & Seiffer, 1976; Gollay et al., 1978), and thus have social contacts with other handicapped persons, but not necessarily with the community at large.

It would be overly simplistic to propose that low rates of competitive employment are caused solely by negative attitudes. Many other factors undoubtedly influence employment rates, including the social and vocational competence of the worker, the availability of appropriate training programs, and prevailing economic conditions. However, recent research has demonstrated the vocational potential of mentally retarded persons (e.g., Bellamy, 1976; Gold, 1973; Karan, Wehman, Renzaglia, & Schutz, 1976) and employers' attitudes are critical to the development and implementation of training opportunities, as well as to the hiring and maintenance of mentally retarded persons in the work force. In addition, co-workers may play a significant role in job retention and success by providing assistance, encouragement, and support to the mentally retarded person. In contrast, negative attitudes may be manifested in harrassment, exclusion, and/or complaints to the supervisor, thus decreasing the mentally retarded person's chance for job success (Wehman, 1981).

It appears that few studies of attitudes toward mentally retarded workers have been conducted. Gottwald's (1970) survey included a relevant item, to which 42% of the sample responded that "some" mentally retarded persons would be "good employees." Cohen (1963) administered approximately 170 questionnaires to employers who had previous contact with mentally retarded workers through a training program and found that those with more contact tended to have more positive attitudes. However, Cohen also found that the failure of one retarded employee was sufficient to dissuade the employer from hiring other mentally retarded workers. Phelps (1965) reported that 65% of a sample of 132 personnel managers in six service occupations agreed that mentally retarded persons were capable of productive work and that most organizations should be able to hire them. Yet, employers from all six groups also felt that the physical appearance and emotional characteristics of mentally retarded persons would limit their potential to succeed in the workplace.

Hill and Wehman (1980a) surveyed 16 supervisors and 27 co-workers of 25 moderately and severely retarded persons in food service occupations. The workers were part of a training project that included a high degree of on-site training and supervision. All items of a 7-point questionnaire yielded average ratings of 5 or higher, indicating positive attitudes toward the mentally retarded worker on the part of co-workers and supervisors. However, as Hill and Wehman suggest, positive attitudes may have been engendered by the characteristics of the training program, as supervisors indicated that the mentally retarded workers would have difficulty in retaining their jobs without the on-site assistance of project staff.

Degree of participation in community activities is another indication of integration, and many studies have included an assessment of CRF residents' leisure time activities. O'Connor (1976) reported that 75% of her sample attended recreational activities in the community, but that over half of these were "special" activities attended only by disabled persons. Moreover, less than 60% of the residents in this study said they had friends outside the facility. Other studies have documented similar patterns of social isolation. Less than one third of Birenbaum and Seiffer's (1976) respondents attended community centers or parties outside the facility. Less than 20% of the respondents interviewed by Baker *et al.* (1977) attended club meetings and 33% of the caretakers and 21% of the mentally retarded respondents indicated that loneliness was a problem. In interviews with 18 parents of severely and profoundly retarded mentally retarded persons living at home, Hill and Wehman (1980b) found family life to be characterized by "nearly complete supervision of the child and a high degree of community isolation." Only eight parents stated that their son or daughter went on errands or community trips, often citing lack of community acceptance as a reason to leave their child at home.

Available data do not indicate that residents participate in more community activities over time. Schalock, Harper, and Carver (1981) interviewed 27 mentally retarded persons after they had successfully completed an adult training program and had lived independently in the community for 3 years. Respondents' most prevalent leisure time activities were television viewing and eating. One third stated they had no friends and interviewers described the respondents as lonely. A unique and commendable feature of this study was the verification of 40% of the data through interviews with a roommate or through direct observation. Respondents in Birenbaum and Seiffer's (1976) study were accompanied by staff during most community activities, and thus were dependent on staff for leisure activity. Two years later, interviews with the same residents indicated that staff-accompanied trips had decreased, yet there was no concomitant increase in independent community participation (Birenbaum & Re, 1979), leading the authors to conclude that residents had become more socially isolated over time.

Similar to employment rates, low rates of participation in community activities are undoutedly indicative of factors other than negative attitudes, including lack of transportation or financial resources, lack of knowledge of available activities, and lack of prerequisite skills. In addition, one could argue that the patterns of nonparticipation documented by various studies are not abnormal. Birenbaum (1980) points out that many urban residents who are marginally employed, lacking financial resources to afford leisure time activities and fearful of traveling in the city alone or at night, exhibit similar patterns of activity. Even unemployment is not uncommon or abnormal under current economic conditions, and thus lack of occupational success, at the present time, may not distinguish the mentally retarded community members from others. Moreover, Edgerton and Bercovici (1976) found considerable fluctuation in the community adjustment and quality of life of community-placed mentally retarded persons over a 12- to 14-year period. Thus, research that examines employment status or social integration at only one point in time may be vastly misleading. More longitudinal research is needed to determine patterns of integration over time. It is apparent, however, that the physical presence of a CRF in the neighborhood does not guarantee that residents will be able or welcome to participate in community activities. If integration of CRF residents within the neighborhood is to be achieved, community placement efforts must include provisions to provide CRF residents with appropriate leisure, social, and vocational skills, as well as strategies to facilitate more positive attitudes and active participation from community members.

E. Neighborhood Concerns Regarding the Establishment of Community Residential Facilities

A list of neighbors' concerns about the establishment of CRFs and the introduction of mentally retarded persons to the neighborhood may be culled from empirical studies and the experiences of CRF developers. An examination of these concerns provides a basis for explaining the prevalence of community opposition and negative attitudes discussed thus far. In the face of empirical evidence, many of these concerns cannot be supported. Yet, they have been presented by countless communities as sufficient justification for opposing a CRF.

One set of concerns arises from stereotypical fears and beliefs about persons with mental retardation and other disabilities, including fears of sexual deviance, crime and violence, and other norm-violating behaviors (Berdiansky & Parker, 1977; Lauber & Bangs, 1974; Segal & Avarim, 1978). Although misconceptions about handicapped persons may have decreased over the past two decades, they still may be sufficiently widespread to inspire negative reactions to potential CRF residents. Moreover, concerns about deviance and personal safety may be particulary salient for communities already preoccupied with escalating crime rates (Baron, 1981). Johnson and Beditz (1981) found that residents of a county that had opposed two community mental health centers expressed concerns about their own safety and that of their children among the ''rapists'' and ''criminals'' that would be introduced to the community. Opponents of a group home for six mentally retarded women in San Francisco felt that the women would be dangerous and have a bad influence on children (Wehbring & Ogren, 1975). The danger posed to the community by group home residents was a prevalent concern reported by group home developers in North Carolina (Berdiansky & Parker, 1977) and by superintendents of public residential facilities (Colombatto *et al.,* 1982). When asked about the possibility of renting an apartment to a mentally retarded adult, landlords often expressed fear for personal safety (Margolis & Charitonidis, 1981; Trippi *et al.,* 1978).

Yet, the bulk of available evidence does not support these concerns. Sitkei (1976) found that fewer than 1% of 1804 developmentally disabled residents living in the community had been in custody of the law over a 2-year period. Edgerton (1983) suggests that mentally retarded persons are more likely to be victims than perpetrators of crime. In a study of the adaptive behavior of community-placed mentally retarded persons, Nihira and Nihira (1975) found that only 9% of problem behavior incidents endangered community members (defined to include facility staff and family visitors as well) and Mamula and Newman (1973) reported that 96% of the mentally retarded persons in 20 family care homes had no recorded behavioral difficulties in the community.

Another set of concerns relates to the devaluation of community conditions and property subsequent to the introduction of a CRF. Believing that the CRF will decrease the quality of neighborhood life and thus depress the values of nearby property (Sigelman, Spanhel, & Lorenzen, 1979), this concern has been raised by current and/or potential neighbors to CRFs for the mentally retarded (Berdiansky & Parker, 1977; Colombatto et al., 1982; Wehbring & Ogren, 1975), the mentally ill (Johnson & Beditz, 1981; Segal & Aviram, 1978) and the criminal offender (Keller & Alper, 1970).

Empirical evidence suggests that concerns about the devaluation of property also are unfounded. Studies have shown no decreases in property values surrounding homes for retarded, mentally ill, and elderly (California Department of Planning, cited in Lauber & Bangs, 1974; Dear, 1977). A recent study by Wiener, Anderson, and Nietupski (1982) analyzed the property value of homes within one block of eight CRFs in Iowa. Their results indicated that, in six cases, property values were not depressed, and, in two cases, properties surrounding group homes had higher values than comparable properties in other communities. Other authors have reported similar increases in property values surrounding homes for both the mentally retarded (Thomas, 1973) and the mentally ill (Garr, 1973, cited in Segal & Aviram, 1978). In addition, there does not seem to be a differential turnover rate for homes in the proximity of CRFs (Hecht, Knowles, & Baba, cited by Lauber & Bangs, 1974). Furthermore, available evidence does not substantiate concerns regarding decreased quality of life when a CRF enters a neighborhood. Neither the California Department of Planning nor the San Francisco Planning Department found increases in traffic, noise, or parking problems in the vicinity of family and foster care homes (cited by Lauber & Bangs, 1974).

A third set of concerns revolves around the issue of community control. Citizens' groups or home owners' associations have typically sought to exert some control over the types of activities that occur within the neighborhood, particularly in single-family residential districts. Preemptive zoning legislation, designed to facilitate the development of CRFs by allowing states to overrule local zoning control, may only exacerbate these concerns. Neighbors may desire some control over the residential composition of their community as well, wishing not to be confronted with "aesthetically unappealing persons" (Lauber & Bangs, 1974) or with the reminder that "it might happen to someone in my family" (Viscardi, 1972).

The frequent occurrence of these three sets of concerns in research and anecdotal reports testifies to their widespread prevalence and suggests that CRF developers should anticipate that they will be raised by community members. Effective strategies for alleviating these concerns and for encouraging more positive attitudes toward CRFs and their residents have not been adequately researched, however. Some typical and recommended approaches are discussed in the next section of this article.

F. Strategies to Facilitate the Development of Community Residential Facilities and Attitudinal Change

Based on research and/or experience, professionals have offered two types of approaches in response to community opposition and negative reactions to CRFs. Some authors recommend a Machiavellian approach to community placement (Sigelman, 1976), suggesting that CRFs be established with a minimum of fanfare and advanced notice. Advocates of this approach suggest that attempts to notify and involve the community permit neighbors to mobilize opposition and increase the probability that the CRF will be prevented from opening.

In contrast to the Machiavellians, other authors recommend a collaborative approach to the establishment of CRFs (Baron, 1981). This approach is characterized by attempts to involve the community in the planning stages of a facility, to disseminate information and to change attitudes. Supporters of collaborative approaches claim that an open confrontation of issues helps to facilitate the development of a CRF and the subsequent acceptance of residents. It is difficult to evaluate the merits of either approach, however, as their relative effectiveness has not been adequately studied.

1. THE MACHIAVELLIAN APPROACH

The Machiavellian approach was first proposed by Sigelman (1976). Her finding that only 45% of a Texas community had favorable attitudes toward the idea of group homes in residential areas, along with other anecdotal evidence, led her to conclude that the "Machiavellian approach is no less effective than advance attitude sampling." She also found that 17 of 25 programs in five southern states did not attempt to inform neighbors in advance to the opening of a community facility. Willms (1978) also recommended a Machiavellian approach after discovering that distant neighbors, as well as people with less knowledge about mental retardation, expressed the most concerns about group homes. Sigelman *et al.* (1979) suggest that neighborhood concerns about increased crime rate, decreased property values, and impaired quality of life are not amenable to change through community education efforts and other authors have questioned whether the considerable time and expenses incurred through collaborative approaches can be justified (Baron, 1981).

Most available research and anecdotal material suggests that once a CRF is established in the neighborhood, community opposition decreases. In fact, some reports have stated that the strongest opponents to a proposed CRF later become its strongest supporters (Nelson, 1978; Wehbring & Ogren, 1975). Yet, this evidence does not necessarily support the Machiavellian position. Perhaps the factors that facilitate acceptance of CRFs and their residents over time could be more purposefully utilized to prepare the community prior to the opening of a CRF.

2. THE COLLABORATIVE APPROACH

Many authors feel that the Machiavellian approach is counterproductive to attitude change. Mamula and Newman (1973) suggest that community involvement is an integral component of any community placement program, stating that "few, if any, individuals can oppose a program which they have had a part in developing." These authors claim, as have others (Knox, 1979), that failure to involve communities in the planning stages of residential facilities has been the cause of subsequent opposition. Berdiansky and Parker (1977) found that group home developers in North Carolina often utilized a Machiavellian approach, but noted that "several . . . attribute much of their difficulty to their surreptitious approach." Wolfensberger and Menolascino (1970) testify to the importance of communication and publicity in the establishment of mental retardation services in Nebraska and call for long-range strategies to change attitudes. Mooring (1976) reports that community involvement during 2 years of preparations in Los Angeles produced a "community committed to a master plan it had developed." Research conducted by the California Department of Health (cited by Lauber & Bangs, 1974) suggests that negative community attitudes coincided with lack of knowledge regarding a program and its objectives. Other authors have recommended that systematic community education become a cornerstone of deinstitutionalization activities (Luckey & Newman, 1975; Thurlow, Bruininks, Williams, & Moreau, 1978).

A variety of collaborative strategies have been described in the literature. Nelson (1978) suggests various methods for presenting information to neighborhood groups before establishing a facility. Wehbring and Ogren (1975) describe developers' attempts to prepare a neighborhood by mailing a letter explaining the facility and then visiting door-to-door to answer questions. Willms (1978) suggests that developers may enhance attitudes toward group homes by sharing information about their actual operation. Tours of the residence or an open door policy has been recommended by some as an effective attitude change strategy (Nelson, 1978). Keller and Alper (1970) describe a unique approach that effectively squelched opposition to a halfway house for female criminal offenders. Community members were invited to visit their prospective neighbors in the reformatory. Those who did visit returned to the neighborhood and convinced opponents that their fears were unfounded and thus the home was established.

Advocates of a collaborative approach also recommend that media be used more effectively as a strategy for education and attitude change. Stereotypes may be perpetuated by fund raising appeals designed to elicit pity or guilt from the audience (Donaldson, 1980; Nelson, 1978). Utilizing volunteers in CRF activities may also be an effective strategy for the dissemination of accurate information about the mentally retarded and other disability groups. Such involvement should be structured, however, to ensure positive experiences for both volunteers and residents (Nelson, 1978).

3. COMBINING MACHIAVELLIAN AND COLLABORATIVE APPROACHES

Some professionals recommend that developers of community residences get to know the neighborhood first, then decide which strategy will work best (Baron, 1981; Soforenko & Sommer, 1973; Warren & Warren, 1975). In one of the few studies to examine this issue, Coates and Miller (1973) provide empirical evidence in support of such a tactic. These researchers evaluated attempts to neutralize community resistance to group homes for juvenile offenders. Three successful and three unsuccessful (i.e., never opened) homes were chosen for study and interviews were conducted with "key actors," including agency representatives, police, clergy, neighbors and city officials. Data were also collected through analyses of newspaper reports, letters of support and opposition, minutes of planning meetings and hearings, and other relevant documents. The authors found that knowledge of the community was a critical variable in facilitating the success of group home development and they conclude that developers must be aware of the type of people who reside in the larger community as well as the specific neighborhood where a CRF is to be established. Knowledge of the community's past responses to similar situations may provide important clues about community organization, power structure, interests, and concerns, and developers would be wise to "do their homework" before approaching a particular community regarding a potential CRF.

Based on their data, Coates and Miller (1973) suggest that the Machiavellian approach is adequate for communities characterized by mobility and diversity. However, a collaborative strategy aimed at communicating with both residents and community leaders seems necessary in middle-class neighborhoods. Finally, for communities with low organizational capability, they suggest that community leaders may play the critical role in shaping community policy and that collaboration and communication with these leaders may be sufficient.

In summary, based on an extremely limited amount of research, it appears that developers must consider the unique characteristics and organizational capabilities of a specific neighborhood and design individualized approaches to the establishment and acceptance of a CRF within that community. In addition, it seems safe to suggest that a surreptitious approach to the establishment of CRFs is undesirable in most cases. As community placement becomes more widespread, civic and neighborhood organizations are bound to become more sophisticated and vocal regarding their rights to information and participation (Baron, 1981).

IV. REEXAMINING COMMON ASSUMPTIONS

Now that we have reviewed the empirical literature, we shall return to what seemed to be the underlying assumptions behind research and practice in this field. In each case, we shall examine the extent to which the assumptions are supported by evidence and we shall make some alternative speculations.

A. Most Appropriate Environment

There seems little evidence to suggest that many of those living in CRFs are interacting with members of the community nor that those who do so generally have positive experiences. It seems best, then, to take the notion of individualized programming seriously, selecting specific environments for their appropriateness for specific mentally retarded persons.

B. Community Hostility toward Retarded Persons

The evidence reviewed suggests that attitudes toward mentally retarded persons living in the community are more positive than negative. A minority appears to actively oppose a minority of CRFs. This is obviously disturbing to those who have the responsibility for establishing such residences. But they are also disturbed by not being able to meet fire regulations, which are obviously designed to protect residents. Zoning regulations can aid those who oppose CRFs, but the regulations indicate a general hostility toward atypical uses in single-family residential areas, not necessarily a hostile reaction to mentally retarded persons.

C. Opposition Is Unrealistic

Certain specific fears held by community members are not supported by
evidence about crime rates, housing values, and the quality of life in neighborhoods housing CRFs. This is undoubtedly true regarding fears held
about other nontraditional housing uses, e.g., rentals to unrelated groups of
college students. However, the specified fears may only represent easily ver-
balized signs of a general uneasiness about changing the "feel" of the neighborhood, the discomfort people may feel when things are no longer the
same, including their discomfort in having to come in contact with people
who are not like themselves.

D. Contact Leads to More Favorable Attitudes

There is some evidence that opposition to CRFs reduces over time and that
immediate neighbors come to have more favorable attitudes than those a little farther away but still in the neighborhood. It appears likely that the prior
expectations about the characteristics of CRFs may be so negative that the
operation of the actual CRF may relieve anxieties. On the other hand, other
research does not suggest that those who know retarded persons better are
necessarily more favorable to them. The characteristics of most mentally
retarded persons with whom others have contact may be sufficiently deviant
as to make favorable social interaction difficult.

E. Expressed Attitudes Lead to Overt Actions

There is very little evidence regarding the relationship between expressed
attitudes toward community placement and actual support or opposition to
CRFs. It is probably safest not to assume either a predictive or causative relation but to treat both verbally expressed attitudes and overt actions as valid
but independent behaviors. A large body of literature has developed on the
more general topic of attitude–behavior relationships and this is addressed in
the next section.

V. THEORETICAL FORMULATIONS

An alternative to basing research and practice on these questionable assumptions is to utilize more systematic formulations. Although we have seen
that the literature on this topic tends to be atheoretical, formulations from
related areas can be drawn on. One source is the more general field of attitude study, particularly the relationship between attitudes and behavior.

Another promising source is the field of urban sociology, from which we can extract useful conceptualizations of the nature of communities.

A. Attitude-Behavior Relationship

The interest in community attitudes toward community placement lies in its presumed relationship to behavior. Writings suggest that negative community attitudes are demonstrated in public resistance to opening new group homes, that it is important to change attitudes so that such resistance will not occur, and so on. In other words, it is assumed that behavior is the result of attitudes or a sign of attitudes, i.e., of underlying beliefs and values held toward the retarded and toward their presence in the community. However, the history of research and theory on attitude-behavior relationships suggests that the matter is far more complex.

For some years, the lack of predictability of behavior from attitude measures led to skepticism of the utility of studying attitudes. More recently, scholars have suggested that the problem was that our thinking was oversimplified. Why should a verbal measure which asks about numerous beliefs and behaviors predict a single action, ignoring situational determinants and societal norms for behavior? Thus, it was shown that the best predictors of a single behavior were questions about that specific behavior. The best predictor of a whole range of behaviors, though, might be an attitude measure which taps a range of beliefs and actions (Ajzen & Fishbein, 1977). Other scholars have emphasized the inverse of our usual expectation that attitudes lead to behavior, suggesting that inducing changes in behavior can have important effects on attitude (Festinger, 1957). Most recently, Fazio and Zanna (1981) have suggested that attitudes which are based on behavioral experience are most likely to influence or at least predict future behavior.

What does this all mean for our understanding of community attitudes toward community placement of the mentally retarded? One implication is that we cannot expect that expressed feelings toward retarded persons in general will predict very well how people will react to having a group home next door to them. Second, we are unlikely to change such actions by an educational campaign which is limited to verbal propaganda. Third, if current attitudes are not based on experience with retarded persons in the community, they may be superficially held and open to change by concrete experiences. Fourth, behavior is likely to be strongly influenced by situational determinants and behavioral norms in the particular community, which may have little to do with retarded persons per se. Finally, if the reality of contact with retarded persons in the nearby community consists of unpleasant experiences, attitudes will ultimately become negative regardless of their current level.

This analysis suggests that although attitudes and behaviors may be related to one another, one cannot expect to predict or explain one from the other without a more careful specification of the attitudes and behaviors involved as well as the factors influencing each.

B. Community as a Social Network

A very different theoretical analysis can be drawn from the literature of urban sociology. Davidson (1982) suggests some of the implications of considering community as a social network to prepare clients for independent living. If "community" is viewed as "a tightly knit network of people occupying a common territory," and it is assumed that "participation in this network by community residents shapes the behavior of those residents," then a deinstitutionalized person introduced into that community will become resocialized to it and will become destigmatized. This is, of course, the hope of deinstitutionalization, expressed in the value of "normalization." However, as Davidson (1983) points out there are serious problems with this conceptualization. First, few communities are tightly knit social networks. Second, communities which are tightly knit might themselves be deviant and socialize clients to deviant behavior. Third, nondeviant tightly knit communities are unlikely to accept newcomers who have a deviant history.

These points bear an interesting relationship to the way in which normalization principles are implemented. Professionals are likely to identify nondeviant tightly knit communities as the most normalized and therefore the most desirable for location of community residences. Yet, these characteristics make them the least likely to accept deviant newcomers, whom they see as denormalizing their community. The most promising locations would seem to be in transitional neighborhoods in which there are weaker social bonds among residents. They have only a partial and voluntary investment in the community and thus they are more tolerant of deviant behavior (Davidson, 1983, p. 23).

Davidson (1983) suggests that we not assume the community is a preexisting entity. Instead, communities should be viewed as "emergent, unbounded, dynamic networks that must be created by each resident of the neighborhood . . . each person's community is defined by the people with whom he or she interacts regularly and is therefore different from everyone else's." Davidson goes on to suggest that "the task [of CRF program staff] becomes constructing their own community among sympathetic people and agencies in their environment instead of fitting into something that already exists and into which they have little right to venture" (p. 26).

This conception of neighborhood and community requires that we rethink what we mean by community attitudes toward community placement of the mentally retarded and how we study it. Methods which provide us with information on the beliefs held by the average member of a geographical area appear less appropriate, while data on the beliefs and relationships of those who interact with clients and staff become critical. Changes in interaction patterns over time are also important, including determining the extent to which networks grow and increase in supportiveness.

VI. DIRECTIONS FOR FURTHER RESEARCH

Although formulations derived from other areas may be useful in helping us recognize the extent to which our assumptions are oversimplified, the most promising approach may be to develop an understanding of these phenomena by grounding our concepts in intensive research in the natural setting. The approaches Glaser and Strauss (1967) term "grounded theory" and Guba and Lincoln (1981) term "naturalistic evaluation" require that we immerse ourselves in exploration of the phenomena or program, investing a great deal of time in interviewing and observation, in analysis of qualitative data, and in checking our interpretations by utilizing multiple data sources. Rather than attempting to obtain large and representative samples of the public or of CRFs, only one or a very small number of communities or residences or even retarded individuals may be studied in each investigation.

By focusing on a single case or a small number of such cases, it also becomes more feasible to extend the observations longitudinally. The importance of this approach is suggested in Edgerton and Bercovici's (1976) findings of considerable change over a several-year period in the adjustment pattern of mentally retarded adults discharged from a large residential institution and living in the community. Factors which were important in the first years after leaving the institution were of little predictive value in later years. Given the findings and speculations of prior research on CRFs, it would be of special value to trace community reactions from the time a CRF is proposed until it has been operating in the community for an extended period of time. "Thick descriptions" of the context for each case would be collected. Conceptions developed out of each such case could be checked against the findings of other case studies. The findings might also be cumulated utilizing qualitative metaanalytic methods (Pillemer & Light, 1980; Yin & Heald, 1975). Rather than reporting average values for acceptance or opposition, or correlations between demographic characteristics and attitudes, such summaries might present typical cases, characterizing the range of reactions and settings while maintaining the complexity of the natural phenomena. This method of synthesizing research should not only be of great value to other researchers, but should also assist those who must make practical decisions regarding community placement of mentally retarded persons, since they can compare their own situation in all its complexity with the detailed descriptions of the typical cases presented.

REFERENCES

Ajzen, I., & Fishbein, M. Attitude-behavior relations: A theoretical analysis and review of empirical research. *Psychological Bulletin,* 1977, **84**, 888–918.

Allport, G. W. *The nature of prejudice.* Reading, Massachusetts: Addison-Wesley, 1954.

Altman, B. M. Studies of attitudes toward the handicapped—the need for a new direction. *Social Problems,* 1981, **28**, 321–337.

Baker, B. L., Seltzer, G. B., & Seltzer, M. M. *As close as possible. A study of community residences for retarded adults.* Boston, Massachusetts: Little, Brown, 1977.

Baron, R. C. Deinstitutionalization at risk: Public response to community care. In D. D. Rutman (Ed.), *Planning for deinstitutionalization: A review of principles, methods and applications.* Human Services Monograph Series Number 28. Germantown, Maryland: Aspen Systems, 1981. (ERIC Document Reproduction Service No. ED 210 522).

Baron, R. C., & Piasecki, J. R. The community versus community care. In R. Budson (Ed.), *New directions for mental health services: Issues in community residential care* (Vol 11). San Francisco, California: Jossey-Bass, 1981.

Bellamy, G. T. *Habilitation of severely and profoundly retarded adults.* Eugene, Oregon: Research and Training Center in Mental Retardation, Univ. of Oregon, 1976.

Berdiansky, H. A., & Parker, R. Establishing a group home for the adult mentally retarded in North Carolina. *Mental Retardation,* 1977, **15**(4), 8–11.

Birenbaum, A. Social adaptation of the developmentally disabled adult in the community. In H. J. Cohen, D. Kliger, & J. Eisler (Eds.), *Urban community care for the developmentally disabled.* Springfield, Illinois: Thomas, 1980.

Birenbaum, A., & Re, M. A. Resettling retarded adults in the community—almost 4 years later. *American Journal of Mental Deficiency,* 1979, **83**, 323–329.

Birenbaum, A., & Seiffer, S. *Resetting retarded adults in a managed community.* New York: Praeger, 1976.

Boraas v. Village of Belle Terre, 476 F. 2d 806, 812 (2d Cir. 1973), rev'd 416 U.S.1, 1974.

Bruininks, R. H., Meyers, C. E., Sigford, B. B., & Lakin, K. C. *Deinstitutionalization and community adjustment of mentally retarded people.* Minneapolis, Minnesota: American Association on Mental Deficiency, 1981.

Chandler, J., & Ross, S. Zoning restrictions and the right to live in the community. In M. Kindred, J. Cohen, D. Penrod, & T. Shaffer (Eds), *The mentally retarded citizen and the law.* New York: Free Press, 1976.

Coates, R. B., & Miller, A. D. Neutralizing community resistance to group homes. In Y. Bakal (Ed.), *Closing correctional institutions.* Lexington, Massachusetts: Lexington Books, 1973.

Cohen, H. J. Finding and keeping family care providers. In H. J. Cohen, D. Kleiger, & J. Eisler (Eds.), *Urban community care for the developmentally disabled.* Springfield, Illinois: Thomas, 1980.

Cohen, J. S. Employer attitudes toward hiring mentally retarded individuals. *American Journal of Mental Deficiency,* 1963, **67**, 705–713.

Colombatto, J. J., Isett, R. D., Roszkowski, M., Spreat, S., D'Onofrio, A., & Alderfer, R. Perspectives on deinstitutionalization: A survey of the members of the National Association of Superintendents of Public Residential Facilities for the Mentally Retarded. *Education and Training of the Mentally Retarded,* 1982, **17**(1), 6–12.

Connecticut Association for Retarded Citizens v. Mansfield State Training School. Civil Action No. 14–78–653, D. Conn., 1979.

Davidson, J. L. Balancing required resources and neighborhood opposition in community-based treatment center neighborhoods. *Social Service Review,* 1982, **56,** 55–71.

Davidson, J. L. *The urban sociology of community-based treatment.* Unpublished paper, University of Delaware, 1983.

Dear, M. Impact of mental health facilities on property values. *Community Mental Health Journal,* 1977, **24,** 153–157.

Deutch, J. Reaction comment. In M. Kindred, J. Cohen, D. Penrod, & T. Shaffer (Eds.), *The mentally retarded citizen and the law.* New York: Free Press, 1976.

Donaldson, J. Changing attitudes toward handicapped persons: A review and analysis of research. *Exceptional Children,* 1980, **46,** 504–514.

Edgerton, R. B. Failure in community adaptation: The relativity of assessment. In K. Kernan, M. Begab, & R. Edgerton (Eds.), *Environment and behavior: The adaptation of mentally retarded persons.* Baltimore, Maryland: Univ. Park Press, 1983.

Edgerton, R. B., & Bercovici, S. M. The cloak of competence: Years later. *American Journal of Mental Deficiency,* 1976, **5,** 485–497.

Fazio, R. H., & Zanna, M. P. Direct experience and attitude-behavior consistency. In L. Berkowitz (Ed.), *Advances in experimental and social psychology* (Vol. 14). New York: Academic Press, 1981.

Ferrara, D. M. Attitudes of parents of mentally retarded children toward normalization activities. *American Journal of Mental Deficiency,* 1979, **84,** 145–151.

Festinger, L. *A theory of cognitive dissonance.* Stanford, California: Stanford Univ. Press, 1957.

Gerry, W. P. Selection of group homes. In J. S. Bergman (Ed.), *Community homes for the retarded.* Lexington, Massachusetts: Lexington Books, 1975.

Glaser, B. G., & Strauss, A. L. *The discovery of grounded theory.* Chicago, Illinois: Aldine, 1967.

Gold, M. W. Research on the vocational rehabilitation of the retarded: The present, the future. In N. Ellis (Ed.), *International review of research in mental retardation* (Vol. 6). New York: Academic Press, 1973.

Gollay, E. R., Freedman, R., Wyngaardern, M., & Kurtz, N. R. *Coming back: The community experience of deinstitutionalized people.* Cambridge, Massachusetts: Abt, 1978.

Gottlieb, J. Public, peer and professional attitudes toward mentally retarded persons. In M. J. Begab & S. A. Richardson (Eds.), *The mentally retarded and society: A social science perspective.* Baltimore, Maryland: Univ. Park Press, 1975.

Gottlieb, J., & Corman, L. Public attitudes toward mentally retarded children. *American Journal of Mental Deficiency,* 1975, **80,** 72–80.

Gottlieb, J., & Davis, J. E. Social acceptance of EMR children during overt behavioral interactions. *American Journal of Mental Deficiency,* 1973, **78,** 141–143.

Gottlieb, J., & Gottlieb, B. Stereotypic attitudes and behavioral intentions toward handicapped children. *American Journal of Mental Deficiency,* 1977, **82,** 65–71.

Gottlieb, J., & Siperstein, G. Attitudes toward mentally retarded persons: Effects of attitude referent specificity. *American Journal of Mental Deficiency,* 1976, **80,** 376–381.

Gottwald, H. *Public attitudes about mental retardation.* Reston, Virginia: Council for Exceptional Children, 1970.

Guba, E. G., & Lincoln, Y. S. *Effective evaluation.* San Francisco, California: Jossey-Bass, 1981.

Halderman et al. *v. Pennhurst State School,* 446 F. Supp. 1295, 1977.

Hill, J., & Wehman, P. Employer and nonhandicapped co-worker perceptions of moderately and severely retarded workers. In P. Wehman & M. Hill (Eds.), *Vocational training and placement of severely disabled persons. Project Employability* (Vol. 2). Richmond, Virginia: Virginia Commonwealth University, 1980. (a)

Hill, J., & Wehman, P. An initial assessment of the parental needs of severely and profoundly handicapped youth. In P. Wehman & M. Hill (Eds.), *Vocational training and placement of severely disabled persons. Project Employability* (Vol. 2). Richmond, Virginia: Virginia Commonwealth University, 1980. (b)

Hopperton, R. J. State legislative strategy for ending exclusionary zoning of community homes. *Urban Law Annual,* 1980, **19**, 47–85.

Johnson, P. J., & Beditz, J. Community support systems: Scaling community acceptance. *Community Mental Health Journal,* 1981, **17**, 153–160.

Justice, R. S., Bradley, J., & O'Connor, G. Foster family care for the retarded: Management concerns for the caretaker. *Mental Retardation,* 1971, **9**(4), 12–15.

Karan, O. C., Wehman, P. H., Renzaglia, A., & Schutz, R. P. *Habilitation practices with the severely developmentally disabled* (Vol. 1). Madison, Wisconsin: Rehabilitation Research and Training Center, University of Wisconsin, 1976.

Kastner, L. S., Reppucci, N. D., & Pezzoli, J. J. Assessing community attitudes toward mentally retarded persons. *American Journal of Mental Deficiency,* 1979, **84**, 137–144.

Keller, O. J., & Alper, B. S. *Halfway houses: Community-centered correction and treatment.* Lexington, Massachusetts: Heath, 1970.

Knox, T. Vermont's Project Awareness. In R. Wiegernink & J. W. Pelosi (Eds.), *Developmental disabilities: The DD movement.* Baltimore, Maryland: Brookes, 1979.

Kressel, L. Exclusionary zoning: The unseen threat. In R. Budson (Ed.), *New directions for mental health services: Issues in community residential care* (Vol. 11). San Francisco, California: Jossey-Bass, 1981.

Landesman-Dwyer, S. Living in the community. *American Journal of Mental Deficiency,* 1981, **86**, 223–234.

Lauber, D., & Bangs, F. S., Jr. *Zoning for family and group care facilities.* ASPO, Planning Advisory Service, Report No. 300, Chicago, Illinois: American Society of Planning Officials, 1974.

Lewis, J. F. The community and the retarded: A study in social ambivalence. In R. K. Eyman, C. E. Meyers, & G. Tarjan (Eds.), *Sociobehavioral studies in mental retardation* (Monogr. 1). Washington, D.C.: American Association on Mental Deficiency, 1973.

Lippman, L. D. The public. In R. B. Kugel & A. Shearer (Eds.), *Changing patterns in residential services for the mentally retarded.* Washington, D.C.: President's Committee on Mental Retardation, 1976.

Luckey, R. E., & Newman, R. S. President's panel recommendations today. Mental Retardation, 1975, **13**(4), 32–35.

Mamula, R. A., & Newman, N. *Community placement of the mentally retarded. A handbook for community agencies and social work practitioners.* Springfield, Illinois: Thomas, 1973.

Margolis, J., & Charitonidis, T. Public reactions to housing for the mentally retarded. *Exceptional Children,* 1981, **48**, 68–69.

Meyer, R. J. Attitudes of parents of institutionalized mentally retarded individuals toward deinstitutionalization. *American Journal of Mental Deficiency,* 1980, **85**, 184–187.

Mooring, I. Community planning for the mentally retarded. In R. Koch & J. C. Dobson (Eds.), *The mentally retarded child and his family: A multi-disciplinary approach.* New York: Brunner/Mazel, 1976.

Moreau, F. A., Novak, A. R., & Siegelman, C. K. Physical and social integration of developmentally disabled individuals into the community. In A. R. Novak & L. W. Heal (Eds.), *Integration of developmentally disabled individuals into the community*. Baltimore, Maryland: Brookes, 1980.

Morrissey, J. R. Status of family care programs. *Mental Retardation*, 1966, **4**(5), 8–11.

Nelson, R. *Creating community acceptance for handicapped people*. Springfield, Illinois: Thomas, 1978.

Nihira, L., & Nihira, K. Jeopardy in community placement. *American Journal of Mental Deficiency*, 1975, **79**, 538–544.

O'Connor, G. *Home is a good place: A national perspective of community residential facilities for developmentally disabled persons* (Monogr. No. 2). Washington, D.C.: American Association on Mental Deficiency, 1976.

Phelps, W. R. Attitudes related to the employment of the mentally retarded. *American Journal of Mental Deficiency*, 1965, **69**, 575–585.

Piasecki, J. *Community responses to residential services for the psycho-socially disabled: Preliminary results of a national survey*. Presented at the first annual conference of the International Association of Psycho-Social Rehabilitation Services. Philadelphia, Pennsylvania: Horizon House Institute, 1975.

Pillemer, D. B., & Light, R. J. Synthesizing outcomes: How to use research evidence from many studies. *Harvard Educational Review*, 1980, **50**, 176–195.

President's Committee on Mental Retardation. President's Committee on Mental Retardation Gallup Poll shows attitudes on mental retardation improving. *President's Committee on Mental Retardation Message*, 1975, **April.**

Rothbart, M. Perceiving social injustice: Observations on the relationship between liberal attitudes and proximity to social programs. *Journal of Applied Social Psychology*, 1973, **3**, 291–302.

Sandler, A., & Robinson, R. *Community acceptance of mentally retarded persons: Information, contact and attitude*. Unpublished manuscript, Temple University, 1980.

Sandler, A., & Robinson, R. Public attitudes and community acceptance of mentally retarded persons: A review. *Education and Training of the Mentally Retarded*, 1981, **16**(2), 97–103.

Santiestevan, H. *Out of their beds and into the streets*. Washington, D.C.: American Federation of State, County and Municipal Employees, 1975.

Schalock, R. L., Harper, R. S., & Carver, G. Independent living placement: Five years later. *American Journal of Mental Deficiency*, 1981, **86**, 170–177.

Schalock, R. L., Harper, R. S., & Genung, T. Community integration of mentally retarded adults: Community placement and program success. *American Journal of Mental Deficiency*, 1981, **5**, 478–488.

Segal, S. P., & Aviram, U. *The mentally ill and community-based sheltered care*. New York: Wiley, 1978.

Segal, S. P., Baumohl, J., & Moyles, E. W. Neighborhood types and community reaction to the mentally ill: A paradox of intensity. *Journal of Health and Social Behavior*, 1980, **21**, 345–359.

Sheerenberger, R. C. Public residential services for the mentally retarded. In N. Ellis (Ed.), *International review of research in mental retardation* (Vol. 9). New York: Academic Press, 1978.

Sigelman, C. K. (Ed.), *Group homes for the mentally retarded*. Lubbock, Texas: Research and Training Center in Mental Retardation, Texas Tech University, 1973.

Sigelman, C. K. A Machiavelli for planners: Community attitudes and selection of a group home site. *Mental Retardation*, 1976, **14**(1), 26–29.

Sigelman, C. K., Spanhel, C. L., & Lorenzen, C. D. Community reactions to deinstitutionalization: Crime, property values and other bugbears. *Journal of Rehabilitation*, 1979, **45**(1), 52–54, 60.

Sitkei, E. G. *Two year follow-up on mobility rates for a sample of group homes for developmentally disabled persons, or after group-home living—what alternatives?* Paper presented at the 100th annual meeting of the American Association on Mental Deficiency, Chicago, June 1976.

Smith, F. *Community acceptance of homes for mentally retarded people.* Unpublished doctoral dissertation, Ann Arbor, University of Michigan, 1981.

Soforenko, A. Z., & Sommer, D. K. Group homes in Connecticut: Genesis and program. In C. K. Sigelman (Ed.), *Group homes for the mentally retarded.* Lubbock, Texas: Research and Training Center in Mental Retardation, Texas Tech University, 1973.

Suelzle, M., & Keenan, V. *Outlook for families with developmentally disabled children in the 1980s.* Paper presented at the annual meeting of the Illinois Sociological Association. Chicago, October, 1980. (ERIC Document Reproduction Service No. ED 196 190).

Thomas, J. K. An overview of Washington state's group homes for developmentally disabled persons. In C. K. Sigelman (Ed.), *Group homes for the mentally retarded.* Lubbock, Texas: Research and Training Center in Mental Retardation, Texas Tech University, 1973.

Thurlow, M. L., Bruininks, R. H., Williams, S. M., & Morreau, L. E. *Deinstitutionalization and residential services: A literature survey. Project Report No. 1.* Minneapolis, Minnesota: Minnesota University, Department of Psychoeducational Studies, Jan. 1978 (ERIC Document Reproduction Service No. ED 204 976).

Tinsley, D. J., O'Connor, G., & Halpern, A. S. *The identification of problem areas in the establishment and maintenance of community residential facilities for the developmentally disabled. Working Paper No. 64.* Eugene, Oregon: Rehabilitation and Training Center in Mental Retardation, 1973.

Trippi, J., Michael, R., Colao, A., & Alvarez, A. Housing discrimination toward mentally retarded persons. *Exceptional Children,* 1978, **44**, 430–437.

Viscardi, H., Jr. *But not on our block.* New York: Ericksson, 1972.

Vurdelja-Maglajlic, D., & Jordan, J. E. Attitude-behaviors toward retardation of mothers of retarded and non-retarded in four nations. *Training School Bulletin,* 1974, **71**, 17–29.

Warren, D. I., & Warren, R. Six kinds of neighborhoods. *Psychology Today,* 1975, **9**(1), 74–80.

Wehbring, K., & Ogren, C. *Community residences for mentally retarded people: A study of seven community residences.* Arlington, Texas: National Association for Retarded Citizens, May, 1975 (ERIC Document Reproduction Service No. ED 181 809).

Wehman, P. *Competitive employment. New horizons for severely disabled individuals.* Baltimore, Maryland: Brookes, 1981.

Wiener, D., Anderson, R. J., & Nietupski, J. Impact of community-based residential facilities for mentally retarded adults on surrounding property values using a realtor analysis method. *Education and Training of the Mentally Retarded,* 1982, **17**, 278–282.

Willer, B., & Intagliata, J. Social-environmental factors as predictors of adjustment of deinstitutionalized mentally retarded adults. *American Journal of Mental Deficiency,* 1981, **86**, 252–259.

Willms, J. D. *Retarded adults in the community: An investigation of neighborhood attitudes and concerns.* Bethesda, Maryland: 1978. (ERIC Document Reproduction Service No. ED 162 474).

Wolfensberger, W. *The principle of normalization in human services.* Toronto: National Institute of Mental Retardation, 1972.

Wolfensberger, W., & Menolascino, F. J. Reflections on recent mental retardation developments in Nebraska. *Mental Retardation,* 1970, **8**(6), 28.

Yin, R. K., & Heald, K. A. Using the case survey method to analyze policy studies. *Administrative Science Quarterly,* 1975, **20**, 371–381.

Family Attitudes
toward Deinstitutionalization

AYSHA LATIB,
JAMES CONROY,
AND CARLA M. HESS

DEVELOPMENTAL DISABILITIES CENTER
TEMPLE UNIVERSITY
PHILADELPHIA, PENNSYLVANIA

I. INTRODUCTION

The aim of this article is to examine the impact on families when their mentally retarded relatives are moved from a large state institution to small community-based facilities. The setting we have studied is the southeastern region of Pennsylvania, the site of Pennhurst Center. In 1974, a suit seeking "institutional reform and damages" was brought against Pennhurst, a large state-supported institution for the mentally retarded. On December 23, 1977, Federal Judge Raymond Broderick rendered a 72-page decision, ruling that Pennhurst failed to provide minimally adequate habilitation for its residents, and on March 17, 1978, Judge Broderick ordered Pennhurst

INTERNATIONAL REVIEW OF RESEARCH IN
MENTAL RETARDATION, Vol. 12

closed and ordered the Commonwealth of Pennsylvania to "provide suitable community living arrangements for the retarded residents of Pennhurst." The Federal government, in turn, funded a longitudinal study of this process, beginning in 1979 and designed to continue for 5 years. The data in this article arise from that study.

Unlike his predecessors, who had primarily focused their attention on improvement of institutional settings, Broderick ruled that Pennhurst "by its very nature" was incapable of providing constitutionally appropriate care and habilitation. This finding led him to conclude that the residents of Pennhurst, those on the waiting list, and any other mentally retarded person in the community "at risk" of institutionalization at Pennhurst should be provided services in less restrictive settings in the community.

On the date of the Order, 1155 people lived at Pennhurst. In the ensuing months and years, over 400 of those residents have been moved to community residential facilities (CRFs). (In Pennsylvania, community residential facilities are known as "community living arrangements," or "CLAs.")

The Pennhurst decision was part of a national trend away from large, segregated public institutions for the total care of mentally retarded citizens. Although the trend has involved policy, statutes, family advocacy for reform, legal decisions, and philosophies, the practical aspect of the trend has been the reduction of populations of state institutions. From the turn of the century to the 1960s, the only option for an average income family faced with the need to place a retarded relative outside the home was a public institution. By the late 1960s, this situation was beginning to change. The peak of public institution population was 194,650 in 1967; the population then began declining. Currently, the population is at about 120,000. Similarly, first admissions declined from 7.8 per 100,000 population in 1965, to 5.4 in 1971, to about 2.7 in 1979 (Lakin, 1978). These numbers reflect the practical reality that the availability of institutions as an option for the family has declined.

The movement of persons who are mentally retarded from institutions to community living arrangements (CLAs) is known as "deinstitutionalization" and is related to the principle known as "normalization." Wolfensberger (1972) defined normalization as the "utilization of means which are as culturally normative as possible in order to establish or maintain personal behaviors or characteristics which are as culturally normative as possible" (p. 28). In addition to deinstitutionalization, implementation of normalization philosophy implies movement to the least restrictive alternative, and developmental programming, for mentally retarded citizens. The least restrictive alternative dictates that (1) mentally retarded persons shall not be placed in a residential setting which restricts their capacity to function at their highest level of independence, and (2) wherever mentally retarded persons may reside, the appropriate support services shall be provided to permit them to continue to function at that level of independence (Barnes, Krochalk, & Hutchinson, 1976). Similarly, developmental programming (the "developmental model") emphasizes growth and learning, rather than custodial care.

Despite the acceptance of deinstitutionalization philosophy by professionals and program planners, not everyone was (or is) caught up in the fervor of the movement. Ferrara (1979) documented that parents of mentally retarded children were more positive toward normalization activities for mentally retarded persons than they were for "*my mentally retarded child*." Payne (1976) identified a "deinstitutionalization backlash," a loosely knit countermovement of various local and statewide associations of parents organized in support of institutions as opposed to CLAs. While many parents see CLAs as a viable way to meet the needs for residential care for some persons, the parents of most persons now residing in large institutions have a distinct preference for that type of residential facility (Atthowe & Vitello, 1982; Frohboese & Sales, 1980; Payne, 1976).

Parents' resistance to deinstitutionalization can be said to center around five major, interrelated areas: (1) the ideology underlying community-based services; (2) the decision to deinstitutionalize as a reversal of the decision to institutionalize; (3) the adequacy of the community-based service system; (4) the process used to deinstitutionalize; and (5) funding.

A. Ideology

Beliefs held by families about mental retardation in general, and about their mentally retarded relatives in particular, play a significant role in families' opposition to deinstitutionalization. Some families believe that there are some mentally retarded individuals who will never be able to achieve the level of independence they think is necessary for community living; further, families think that it is damaging for professionals to create family expectations that their children will achieve such independence (NARC, 1977). Atthowe and Vitello (1982) found that 66% of families believed their relatives had reached their highest levels of educational and psychological development, and that their relatives would not progress much beyond their current levels of functioning. Parents' expectations about kinds of care for their relatives are similar: most families (54%) sent their children to the institution for custodial care, 30% expected that basic skills or self-care training would be provided, and only 5% believed vocational training to be a requisite element in services to be provided at an institution.

Parents believe mentally retarded persons are not normal and should not be treated as such; mental retardation is a permanent condition, and mentally retarded persons are "ever child-like" (Frohboese & Sales, 1980). It is not surprising, then, that families reject the concepts of deinstitutionalization and normalization. As Atthowe and Vitello (1982) found, "Whether or not families understand these concepts, they are suspicious of this ideology and want nothing to do with them" (p. 6).

Parents also fear the implications of the concept of least restrictive alternative: they fear that their children will not be properly protected in small community residential settings (NARC, 1977). As Willer, Intagliata, and Atkinson (1979) put it:

> In this instance, the individual is moved from a very secure situation where someone else, the state, is responsible for his safety and future. Alternative settings are, by definition, less restrictive, and the family is faced with the belief that increased risk of harm or abuse may occur. Thus, they may not have acquired an additional family member, but they believe that they have reacquired the legal, moral and psychological responsibility for a family member (p. 13).

Frohboese and Sales (1980) documented that families believed the stated institution to be the least restrictive alternative, due to a greater freedom of movement, independence, and a safe environment within the institution.

B. Deinstitutionalization as a Reversal

Parents of mentally retarded children have long had to decide whether to keep their children at home or to place them in an institution. Advice from professionals and friends has been contradictory, and what was a popular opinion several years ago may not be a popular opinion today (Frohboese & Sales, 1980, p. 55). One parent (Gorham, 1975) indicated that "In the past, we were made to feel guilty when we did not institutionalize our child, and now, under the new normalization principle, we are made to feel guilty if we do."

Stedman (1977) suggested that deinstitutionalization of a mentally retarded relative represents stress because it forces the family to question whether institutionalization is, or ever was, appropriate. The crisis of the deinstitutionalization decision parallels the crisis of the situations faced earlier by the family—diagnosis, burden of care, and institutionalization (Willer *et al.,* 1979). To those families who had chosen to institutionalize, deinstitutionalization represents a "painful revisitation" of the original decision (Willer *et al.,* 1979). Because the decision to institutionalize was most likely judged to be a final one, deinstitutionalization is also infused with an element of unexpectedness, thereby engendering crisis and opposition to the new policy. Atthowe and Vitello (1982) substantiated this: the majority of families (84%) believed that their child would stay institutionalized for the rest of his or her life.

Gorham (1975) pointed out other factors in the decision-making process which make families' decisions more difficult: parents were told repeatedly to institutionalize their children, often by professionals, only to have found out that the institutions were least well equipped to help their children. When parents then were told that the best place for their children was in the community, in a neighborhood with family or substitute family, the parents learned that there were not enough group homes to begin to meet the demand, and other alternative community placements were equally hard to come by.

C. Concerns about the Adequacy of Community-Based Service Systems

Parents are also concerned about the availability and quality of supervision, care, and other resources; many families believe that their relative needs 24-hour medical care, and feel this would not be provided in the community (Atthowe & Vitello, 1982; Frohboese & Sales, 1980; Meyer, 1980).

Payne (1976) found that parents were in favor of maintaining the institution and were skeptical of the advantages of small group homes. Parents agree fairly strongly that the large institution offered the advantages of a concentration of mental retardation expertise, the opportunity for people who are mentally retarded to be with persons like themselves, and the opportunity for people who are mentally retarded to be protected from the stress of community life. Additionally, parents believed that the large institution was the tried and true way of caring for the mentally retarded, and that the institution was a secure, permanent home, a place in which the person could stay after the parents died (Payne, 1976).

Meyer (1980) reported that most families who had a relative living in an institution were quite opposed to having that person placed in a CLA outside the institution. Even those families who were dissatisfied with the care and programming at the institution were just as likely to choose the institution as the best placement as those who were satisfied with the care and programming at the institution.

D. Process Used to Deinstitutionalize

Parental criticism also has been directed toward the deinstitutionalization process. Decisions regarding design and availability of services for mentally retarded persons were made by "experts"—doctors and lawyers—up to the 1930s. Parents as a group began to change their delegated, passive role, and major efforts by parents were directed toward ameliorating perceived lacks in existing services, expanding the range of service opportunities available to their mentally retarded sons and daughters, and changing societal attitudes toward mentally retarded persons. In 1951 parents' activism culminated in the formation of the National Association of Parents and Friends of Mentally Retarded Citizens, now called the National Association for Retarded Citizens (NARC).

Nonetheless, when the issue of parental involvement came before the court in 1973 (*Horacek v. Exon*), Judge Urbom questioned the legal propriety of parents bringing suits on behalf of their mentally retarded offspring, saying that "While parents in all good conscience may desire one remedy, or specific type or style of treatment for their children, it would not necessarily be in the best interests of the children." He decided that a guardian ad litem should be appointed, not to displace parents, but to ensure that someone would act in the best interests of the mentally retarded person in the event that a conflict between parental and client rights became apparent (Frohboese & Sales, 1980). So, while parents did have a forum for expressing their objections, they had no power to veto decisions made by "experts." Parents thus felt discriminated against, and felt they had been presumed wrong in advance, because the real decision-making power was in the hands of the experts. Parents believed they were being deprived of their "natural rights" to determine where their offspring should reside and what services they should receive (Atthowe & Vitello, 1982; Frohboese & Sales, 1980). As summarized by Frohboese and Sales (1980), the courts had broken the family sanctimony and infringed on an area formerly "untouchable by the court" (p. 74). This perceived infringement contributes to families' resistance to deinstitutionalization.

E. Funding

One of the greatest concerns of families about deinstitutionalization is the permanence of the community settings (Frohboese & Sales, 1980). The question of permanence, in turn, is linked to funding; the duration, amount, source, and policy intent of funding can all suggest how much one can trust the future of the program. The state institutions have existed for a long time, and were funded by states until recently. Under the Medicaid program, Federal funds became available in 1972 to assist in paying for state institutions (if the institutions met certain standards). By 1980, the Federal contribution exceeded $2 billion, and in 1982, it was over $3 billion. Nearly all institutional beds now qualify for this program of federal support (Braddock, 1974; Comptroller General of the United States, 1977). The institutions, then, have a long history of state support, as well as a more recent, but extremely large, and rapidly growing, Federal commitment to supply funds; and the Federal funds are an entitlement, not merely another program that may be defunded by the next Congress. Entitlements can be reduced, but they carry more weight and perceived permanence than simple funding statutes. From a funding perspective, then, it is reasonable to surmise that families perceive the institutions to be very secure in the long term.

The development of CLAs, on the other hand, is a more recent phenomenon, and the funding mechanisms provide less confidence for their permanence. Most states began their CLAs with their own funds in the 1970s, and the current economic situation suggests a fear of cutbacks in state legislatures. Many model programs began with short-term, Federally aided demonstration projects, which became a state burden when the demonstration money ended. The Federal assistance for CLAs has come in three forms. First, states could use creative mixtures of existing Federal funds to support CLAs: HUD for housing plus SSI for living expenses, Medicaid cards for medical care, perhaps adding food stamps. But states still need to pay for day programs, CLA staff, case management, monitoring, and administration. Moreover, HUD funds are now far more difficult to obtain than in the early 1970s. The funding mix approach, creative as it is, is a patchwork solution, and may not inspire confidence for many decades into the future. The second form of Federal assistance is the Medicaid program, which became available in the late 1970s for use in small (15 beds or less) community-based facilities. But the facilities must meet strict standards, and this means states must finance renovation. A few states (e.g., Minnesota, New York) have relied heavily on this program to assist them in their commitment to CLAs. However, the program is so recent, and so many states have not utilized it yet, that it may not provide the perception of permanence needed by many families. In 1980, 96% of clients supported under the Medicaid program were in large (over 15 beds) facilities. The third alternative is an option that became available in 1981: a more flexible use of the Medicaid program in community settings. By applying for a "waiver" of the Medicaid requirements, states can receive Federal reimbursement for case management, personal care attendants, day programs, habilitation, homemaker services, respite care, and other services, without meeting the strict physical standards of the "15 beds or less" program. This approach is entirely new and experimental.

In all, an analysis of funding history and current practices reveals that funding for institutions has continued for nearly 100 years, and Federal assistance has grown to become a vast commitment in the past decade. In contrast, funding for CLAs has been primarily in the form of state and/or short-term Federal demonstrations, while recent Federal initiatives have not been tested fully yet. For a family whose concern is that their relative be housed, fed, and clothed in the year 2020, institutional funding may appear to be a safer bet than the CLA approach.

It is clear that relatives of mentally retarded citizens overwhelmingly support institutions over community-based alternatives: when Judge Broderick ordered Pennhurst closed, and the clients moved to CLAs, it was obvious that the Pennhurst decision would have an impact on the families of clients, and possibly on families' attitudes toward deinstitutionalization, as well as on the clients themselves and on the communities into which they moved. Part of the Pennhurst Longitudinal Study is an assessment of the impact on families of clients.

The overall design of the Family Impacts portion of the Pennhurst Longitudinal Study is pre–post. Families were surveyed before clients were moved, and, as each client leaves Pennhurst, his/her family is interviewed at approximately 6 months postrelocation. The 6-month delay is intended to permit enough time for each family to develop familiarity with the CLA and for transitional relocation phenomena to fade.

We here report two sets of data: the Baseline Study of 472 families, which reveals their attitudes before their son or daughter was relocated, and interviews with 119 families 6 months after their relative was relocated. We will examine the results of both in some detail.

II. THE PENNHURST STUDY

The potential universe for the Baseline Study (Keating, Conroy, & Walker, 1980) consisted of the families of all residents at Pennhurst who originated from the five counties in the southeastern region of Pennsylvania as of May 29, 1980 ($N = 712$). Of the 630 residents of the institution who came originally from the southeastern region of Pennsylvania and who had any known family contact, information was collected for 472 residents (74.9%).

To ensure that the respondents were indeed representative of the population of family contacts for residents, a random sample of 25% of nonrespondents was telephoned and asked to respond to 16 critical items. Responses of the survey respondents and the telephone sample of non-respondents to those 16 items were then compared by the chi-square statistic. For no item was there a significant difference at the .05 level between the two groups. Therefore, the respondents were seen to be truly representative of the population.

In the Post-Relocation Study, we telephoned the families of the first 119 clients who moved to CLAs since the Baseline Study (June 1980). The telephone calls were made between July 1981 and May 1982. We telephoned only those families of clients who had already been in a CLA for at least 6 months; thus the Post-Relocation Survey concerns the families of clients who moved between June 1980 and September 1982.

The questionnaire for the Baseline Study was constructed to ascertain family attitudes toward deinstitutionalization (before their relative was moved to a CLA) and to obtain demographic variables such as education, sex, and race which might possibly relate to attitudes. A questionnaire developed by Barnes *et al.* (1976) served as a model for development of the first draft of our questionnaire, although no item from their questionnaire was used in ours. Based on recommendations of experts and pretest results, modifications were made. The final form of the instrument was ready in April 1980.

The Post-Relocation Survey questionnaire was designed to measure changes in families' attitudes 6 months after relocation of their retarded relatives. This post questionnaire was simply a subset of the items on the Baseline questionnaire. We also asked an open-ended question, intended to gather any perceptions, attitudes, or feelings not covered in the Survey.

The instruments contain many questions that address the attitudes of the respondent toward deinstitutionalization; a single scale reflecting a summary of such items has advantages. The validity of single items can be questioned, because errors and misinterpretation can bias any one particular response. This problem is reduced when many similar items are combined into a scale. We therefore composed a multiple-item scale from the questionnaires, tested the scale's reliability and internal consistency properties, and revised it. We derived the 25-item Attitudes Toward Deinstitutionalization Scale (ATDS), which is remarkably well structured and internally consistent. Statistical tests for internal consistency (Cronbach's alpha) indicated that 92% of the variation in scale score represented true variation in attitudes, the remaining 8% due to measurement error or "noise."

III. RESEARCH FINDINGS

A. Baseline Study

The most basic results to report are the percentage of respondents who answered each question on the Baseline Survey in a particular way. A total of 82.4% of the respondents were at least somewhat, if not very, satisfied with the services their relative received from the institution. It was not surprising, therefore, that 71.7% of the family members were at least somewhat unlikely to agree with their relative being selected for movement to the community. On the contrary, only 13.9% were very likely or somewhat likely to agree with such a decision. The picture that emerged was that a majority of family contacts preferred that their relative remain at the institution. Similarly, 76.5% of respondents agreed strongly or agreed somewhat that, when their relatives live away from the family, they should remain in the same place for their entire lifetimes.

The Survey also revealed that 60.1% of respondents strongly agreed with this statement: "I believe that my relative has reached his/her highest level of educational and psychological development and will *not* progress much beyond the level he/she is at now." Family response to this item was not related to the client's level of retardation, nor with the client's adaptive behavior level as measured by the Behavior Development Survey, although there was some difference in attitudes between parents of adults and parents of children: 76% of parents of adults agreed with the above statement, while 27% of parents of children agreed (mean responses were 1.8 and 3.3, $p = .001$). Thus, parents generally rejected the developmental model.

Three questions concerned philosophies. For normalization, only 36.3% strongly disagreed and 15.6% somewhat disagreed; for least restrictive environment, 37.3% strongly disagreed and 15.6% somewhat disagreed. When it came to deinstitutionalization, however, a relatively concrete philosophy having direct implications for relocation of clients, responses were considerably more negative: 56.5% strongly disagreed and 15.0% somewhat disagreed. Clearly, there are many families who do not express disagreement with normalization or least restrictive environment, but do disagree with deinstitutionalization. On the Attitudes Toward Deinstitutionalization Scale (ATDS), there was a preponderance of negative attitudes about deinstitutionalization among the families of current residents of the institution. The scale ranges from 1 (strongly agree) to 5 (strongly disagree); the overall mean score of respondents on the ATDS was 3.7.

Using the 25-item scale, we attempted to identify which client and/or family characteristics were related to the family's attitudes toward deinstitutionalization. During preliminary analysis, we used Pearson product-moment correlation coefficient or R for continuous variables.

Six variables were significantly correlated with attitudes. Although statistically significant, these correlations were all weak, suggesting that none would predict attitudes consistently and accurately by itself. An ANOVA was used to tap differences of ATDS score for categorical variables; two variables were significant. The remaining "candidate" variables were

Continuous
    Resident age
    Number of years institutionalized
    Family member's perceived urgency of resident's medical needs

Family member's educational level
Resident's maladaptive behavior level (Personal Adaptation score)
Family member's awareness of a court decision regarding Pennhurst

Categorical
Racial background of family (nonwhite)
Religion of family (Protestant–Catholic–Jewish–other).

Using these variables to tap partial relationships, we introduced multivariate statistics. Our first approach was to enter all the noncategorical variables (i.e., all but race and religion) to see which remained more important even after controlling for the impact of the others. Four variables remained: resident age, family member's perceived urgency of resident's medical needs, family member's educational level, and family member's familiarity with the Pennhurst decision. By analysis of covariance, the explanatory power of these five variables *and* the two categorical variables, race and religion, was assessed simultaneously (see Table I).

This analysis indicated that race was related to attitudes (nonwhites were more positive about deinstitutionalization), even controlling for age, familiarity, medical needs, and education ($p = .035$), but its contribution to explaining the variance in attitudes was relatively small compared to several other, stronger, variables. Religion appeared to have no significant impact on attitudes.

The resident's medical needs (as perceived by the family member) and age

TABLE I
PREDICTORS OF FAMILY ATTITUDES TOWARD DEINSTITUTIONALIZATION

	Sum of squares	Degrees of freedom	F	Significance
Main Effects				
Race	2.770	1	4.489	.035
Religion	.309	2	.250	.779
Covariates				
Resident's age	12.620	1	20.452	.001
Familiarity with court decision	5.174	1	8.385	.004
Perceived medical needs of resident	12.623	1	20.457	.001
Family education	2.700	1	4.375	.037
2-Way interactions				
Race × religion	.248	1	.402	.527
Explained	43.942	8	8.902	.001
Residual	222.757	361		

were the strongest variables here. Families who *believed* their relatives' medical needs were great were more likely to oppose deinstitutionalization, and older residents were more likely to have relatives who opposed deinstitutionalization. (Similarly, Payne, 1976, found that the greater the length of institutionalization, the greater the opposition to deinstitutionalization.)

The next best predictor was familiarity with the Pennhurst decision, with those most familiar being the most opposed to deinstitutionalization. This intriguing result, however, must be interpreted with caution. We *cannot* say that familiarity *causes* opposition, because it may be the other way around: Those who are most opposed may devote extra time to learning about the decision.

Relative to these three variables, the importance of race and education were quite small. Although they are statistically significant, they are probably of no practical significance. Perhaps the best summary statement about prediction is this: If we know *nothing* about a family's position on the subject of deinstitutionalization (that is, we are completely uncertain), but we *do* know the family's race, familiarity with the court decision, perceived urgency of their relative's medical needs, the education of the family respondent, and the age of the resident, we could reduce our uncertainty about the family's attitudes by only 16%. This is significant, but hardly awe inspiring.

B. Postrelocation Study

The 119 clients in the present study were generally very similar to the population of 472, except in age. The 119 were 4 years younger on the average, and, similarly, they were admitted to Pennhurst about 4 years later than the average for the 472. No differences were found with regard to the clients' gender, race, IQ, level of retardation, adaptive behavior, or maladaptive behavior. The 119 families did not differ from the population of families in age, race, or education.

Family visits hardly changed. Initially, 44% of the 119 reported visiting their relative at least once a month (the same as the 472, at 44%). After relocation, the figure was 53%. Though this change was statistically significant, the substantive change was hardly significant. Similarly, 13% of the 119 families reported that their relative came home for a visit at least once a month (much like the 472 at 11%), but this figure changed only to 16% after relocation of the relative to a CLA. Thus we found no confirmation of the notion that visits from or to the family would become more frequent upon deinstitutionalization.

The 119 families were initially very satisfied with Pennhurst. In the posttest, they expressed even higher satisfaction with the CLAs. The question was, "Overall, how satisfied are you with the services your relative is receiving from (Pennhurst/the CLA)?'' The responses were on a 5-point scale from 1 (very satisfied) to 5 (very dissatisfied). The average response of the 119 in 1980, while the clients were still at Pennhurst, was 1.7, which was identical to the average for all 472 families. After movement of the 119 relatives to CLAs, their families gave an average response of 1.5, which indicated a slight increase in satisfaction with the CLA compared to level of satisfaction at Pennhurst. The important point is that these families were satisfied with Pennhurst and now they are satisfied with CLAs. The same finding can be stated in another way. At the pretest, 85% of the 119 families were very or somewhat satisfied with Pennhurst, about the same proportion as in the population of 472 (82.4%). After relocation, 83% of the 119 were very or somewhat satisfied with the CLA. Thus these 119 families were just as satisfied with Pennhurst as the average family, but then reported satisfaction with the community service setting.

In analyzing the responses of the 119 families to the ATDS, we found that this group did not differ from the average Pennhurst family (472) before relocation, as Fig. 1 shows. The 119 were just as negative as the larger population at the Baseline.

The average initial (Baseline) ATDS scores for the 472 and the 119 families were 3.7 and 3.5, respectively. The posttest score for the 119, which represents attitudes at least 6 months after CLA placement of their relatives, was 2.4. These scores indicate that the attitudes of the 119 families were initially opposed, like the average for the 472 families: the 119 families changed sharply to more positive attitudes in the posttest [t (102) = 11.53, p = .000, 1-tailed].

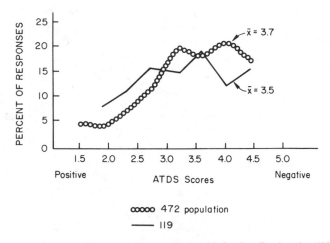

FIG. 1. Distribution of family attitudes toward deinstitutionalization for 472 and 119 at baseline.

We explored the components of the ATDS to determine which specific attitudes changed the most among the families of relocated clients. There were 25 items on the scale; 22 items showed a significant pre–post change among the 119 families; a discussion of these items follows.

A very direct question concerned agreement with the decision to move the retarded person from Pennhurst to the CLA. This item was also on a 5-point agreement scale.

Question 12 (Baseline):
    If your relative were to be selected for movement from Pennhurst to the community, how likely would you be to agree with this decision?
Question 12 (Posttest):
    Overall, since your relative was selected for movement from Pennhurst to the community, how do you feel about that move?

We present the distribution of responses in Table II. The 119 families initially tended to have strong negative feelings (52% strongly opposed), and were, on the average, like the population of 472 (63% strongly opposed). The change from pre to post for the 119, however, was dramatic. Only 4% of the families on the posttest strongly disagreed with the relocation, and 81% agreed strongly or somewhat.

Treating this item as a 1-to-5 scale (5 = strongly disagree), the 119 families were, on the average, slightly less negative (at 3.7) than the 472 (at 4.1) before relocation. The posttest response for the 119 was 1.7, a large change: It is apparent that many who were initially unsure or negative, after seeing their relatives in the CLAs, became convinced that the CLA was a good idea. The change was significant [paired $t(115) = 12$, $p = .001$].

TABLE II
FAMILY AGREEMENT WITH DECISION TO RELOCATE RELATIVE[a]

	472	119 Pre	119 Post
1. Strongly agree	9	20	64
2. Somewhat agree	5	7	17
3. Unsure	14	12	7
4. Somewhat disagree	8	9	8
5. Strongly disagree	63	52	4

[a]Agreements are given in percentages.

Question 13:

We are interested in how you think different aspects of your family's life (may change if/have changed since) your relative was placed in the community.

On the 14 items within Question 13, the 12 that showed significant pre–post changes are shown in Table III. Each item was on a 5-point scale ranging from 1 (large change for the better) to 5 (large change for the worse). For the 472 and the 119 Baseline, the means indicate *expectations*; for the 119 post, the means reflect *actual* changes. The initial responses of the 472 and the 119 are very similar. The expectations of the 119 families clustered about 3.5 at the Baseline, which meant they were basically pessimistic about expected changes. Their expectations were exceeded on the items shown in Table III. The *largest* change was in the retarded relative's general hap-

TABLE III
EXPECTED AND PERCEIVED CHANGES IN FAMILY LIFE

	472 (expected)	119 Pre (expected)	119 Post (actual)	Significance of pre–post change
a. Your own social life	3.7	3.6	2.9	.001
b. Your job	3.5	3.5	2.9	.001
d. Family recreation activities	3.5	3.4	2.8	.001
e. Your time alone	3.5	3.4	3.0	.001
f. Your time with your spouse	3.6	3.5	2.9	.001
h. Family vacation	3.5	3.5	2.9	.001
i. Your general happiness	3.8	3.6	2.1	.001
j. Your mentally retarded relative's relationships with other people	3.7	3.6	1.9	.001
k. Your mentally retarded relative's general happiness	3.9	3.5	1.7	.001
l. Your mentally retarded relative's relationship with you	3.3	3.1	2.5	.001
m. Your mentally retarded relative's relationship with your spouse	3.4	3.3	2.7	.003
n. Your mentally retarded relative's relationship with brothers and sisters	3.3	3.0	2.6	.008

piness, followed by his/her relationships with other people, and the family respondent's own general happiness. Table IV is but one illustration of the type of drastic changes that were prevalent; similar changes occurred in items "i" and "j." Examining the diagonal, from upper left to lower right, we see that there were 25 families (19 + 1 + 5) whose expectations matched their actual experience. For example, the 19 expected a large change for the better in their relative's general happiness, and then reported seeing exactly that. Above the diagonal are the families whose expectations were disappointed. There were only 2, who expected a large change for the better, but saw no change. All the other families, below the diagonal, perceived that the happiness of their relatives had improved beyond their expectations. In fact, at the extreme lower left of the table 17 families expected a large change for the worse, but actually saw a large change for the better.

In another part of the survey (Questions 14 to 22), we posed a series of 10 specific statements concerning deinstitutionalization, and asked for responses from 1 (strongly agree) to 5 (strongly disagree). All items changed in a positive direction, and 9 were statistically significant; these 9 are presented in Table V. These results follow one general pattern. First, the 119 were similar to the 472 in their negative Baseline responses (note that on Question 14, agreement implied a negative attitude); second, the 119 became more positive after their relatives were placed.

Two items in Table V were of particular interest. Item 14 was important because it concerned the developmental model, i.e., the belief that all people can grow and learn. This concept is one of the cornerstones of the new ideology in mental retardation services, yet the 472 families clearly disagreed with the notion in regard to their own relatives at Pennhurst. The 119 initially tended toward rejection of the developmental model, and at posttest

TABLE IV

CHANGE IN RETARDED RELATIVE'S GENERAL HAPPINESS

Pre (expected)		Post (actual)				
		Much better				Much worse
		1.	2.	3.	4.	5.
Much better	1.	19	0	2	0	0
	2.	3	1	0	0	0
	3.	6	3	5	0	0
	4.	8	3	2	0	0
Much worse	5.	17	8	9	4	0

TABLE V
Agreement with Specific Ideas

	472 (expected)	119 Pre (expected)	119 Post (actual)	Significance of pre–post change (paired t test) p
14. Relative will *not* progress beyond present level	1.8	2.1	2.9	.001
16. Prefer that relative should be moved from a more protected residential setting to an open setting as relative acquired greater self-help skills	3.6	3.5	3.1	.04
17. CLA personnel are knowledgeable and skillful	3.6	3.5	1.9	.001
18. CLA funding is secure	3.8	3.8	2.7	.001
19. All needed services are available in community	3.9	3.6	1.8	.001
20. Community placement does not add to family financial burden	3.0	2.7	1.6	.001
21. Normalization	3.4	3.1	1.9	.001
22. Least restrictive alternative	3.4	2.9 [a]	1.6	.001
23. Deinstitutionalization	4.0	3.5 [a]	1.9	.001

[a] The 119 were different from the 472 at $p = .01$.

changed only to neutrality. Both in the institution and the community, then, it appeared that families were not responsive to this relatively new philosophy.

The second item of special interest, item 18, concerned the security of CLA funding, a very important issue for families. The 472 and the 119 initially tended to disagree somewhat that funding for CLAs was secure and permanent. After relocation, the 119 families changed their opinion, but only to approximate neutrality. Their anxieties on this issue were reduced, but by no means eliminated.

At the conclusion of the structured interview, we asked an open-ended question: "Is there anything else you would like us to know about your relative's recent move from Pennhurst?" Interviewers were instructed to take comments verbatim, and not to ask additional questions. In this way, it was hoped that the spontaneous, subjective, personally meaningful perceptions of the respondents would be elicited.

Upon analysis of these responses, the predominant tone indicated that the majority of the respondents expressed very positive feelings about CLAs and the quality of service therein. A significant majority had not expected such services and were quite overwhelmed by the superior quality of the facilities. The general feeling was that the relatives had shown progress toward development of skills for independent living. This growth was, in their opinion, due to the personalized attention and interest of the staff, which was greatly facilitated by the small size of the facility and a high staff-to-client ratio. The respondents also reported that they enjoyed their visits to the CLAs. They had found visits to Pennhurst "scary" and were intimidated by converging crowds of retarded persons. Other respondents felt the CLA setting was conducive to bringing younger siblings for visits. Previously, parents had not wanted to expose their young children to the large, hospitallike, impersonal environment of Pennhurst.

In addition, most respondents indicated that the clients appeared happier at the CLAs. They enjoyed the small family and homelike environment and individual attention.

Though the general tone indicated a positive attitude toward mentally retarded persons living in the community, there were a few objections to the move from Pennhurst on the following grounds. Some respondents felt that it was "not safe" and rather "dangerous" for "these people" to "walk around alone." The implication was that mentally retarded persons need to be protected from the "normal" world; that they should not be free to walk around, since they are vulnerable. Given the level of functioning of these former Pennhurst residents, this belief was understandable. Another respondent opposed the move because CLAs do not have the advantage of having all the necessary facilities (medical, recreational, educational) on the premises. Another objection was made on the grounds that the respondent considered the court decision to move the relative to a CLA a violation of parental rights.

In addition, there were many expressions of concern about the security of funding for the CLAs from both those respondents who approved the move and those who did not. A number of respondents feared they might have to assume financial responsibilities for which they had no resources. Also, there was some apprehension about the effect of staff turnover. One respondent felt that the staff could not possibly be permanent since they would want to leave "to live their own lives," and feared that this would be emotionally damaging to his/her relative.

The retrospective evaluation of Pennhurst from these 119 families was that it was too large and crowded a place to offer adequate care and growth opportunities for the residents. It was felt to be a place where repetitive, institutional behaviors prevailed, due not only to the large numbers of persons housed, but also to the lack of educational programming and insufficient care and guidance from the staff.

Although the CLAs were seen as addressing the needs of the clients more favorably than Pennhurst, there was some fear that they would not have the permanence of a large institution like Pennhurst. This appeared to us to be the central counterpoint to the general extreme satisfaction expressed in the open-ended comments, and this paralleled the quantitative results of the survey.

IV. CONCLUSIONS

The most striking result of the Pennhurst family surveys was the overwhelmingly positive change among the families. In this discussion, we will treat a few of the most salient attitudes that changed (or did *not* change) and will then give a review of some theoretical frameworks available for attempting to understand these attitudes and attitude changes.

Before proceeding, we would like to stress the caveat that the Pennhurst results did not arise from families of individuals deinstitutionalized *at random*. We cannot be certain that the 119 families were representative of the population of 630 families in *every* way, although we found that they were so in nearly every way that we could measure. The usual cautions against perfectly confident generalization to the population, or to other facilities in other states, of course, must be applied to the Pennhurst results.

The negative attitudes toward deinstitutionalization expressed by families in the Baseline Study were consistent with the results obtained by Atthowe and Vitello (1982), Brockmeier (1975), Frohboese and Sales (1980), Klaber (1969), Meyer (1980), Payne (1976), and Willer, Intagliata, and Atkinson (1978). Further, although a substantial number of families in the Baseline Study strongly disagreed with the principles of normalization and least restrictive alternative, an even larger number disagreed with deinstitutionalization. A substantial number of respondents accorded value to these concepts, but family members of institutionalized relatives seemed to believe that the institution represented the most appropriate environment for their relatives.

Another apparent and, frankly, disturbing finding in the Baseline Study was that three quarters of the respondents felt that their relatives had reached the highest level of development possible. It appears that the message given by professionals in previous years—little, if anything, can be done for mentally retarded persons—was taken to heart by family members. The more recent message, that everyone, even severely and profoundly mentally retarded persons, can grow and develop (e.g., Gold, 1973), has not attained general acceptance among the families of institutional residents.

Even though families reported in open-ended comments in the Post-

Relocation study that their relatives had made surprising progress toward the development of skills for independent living, families still tended to believe that their relative had reached his or her maximum developmental potential. The quantitative item on developmental potential showed a statistically significant, but very small, change toward optimism. Though the families could report specific instances of development, their general belief structures about future development had apparently changed very little.

Even if families come to accept the developmental model, we cannot predict that family attitudes toward deinstitutionalization would change concomitantly. Meyer (1980) reported that families would prefer the institution to community placement even after recognizing the possibility of optimal development of their relatives in the community. There does appear to be more negative attitudes toward deinstitutionalization than simple rejection of the developmental model: for example, in the Baseline Study, family members were very concerned about their relatives' medical needs being met. Those respondents who perceived their relatives' medical needs as serious were more negative toward deinstitutionalization. This may be taken as one indication that families are concerned about the safety of their relatives; the institution apparently represents a secure environment to those respondents.

The concern is not limited to medical care: Atthowe and Vitello (1982), Frohboese and Sales (1980), Meyer (1980), Payne (1976), and our Baseline Study reported that a great fear of families with regard to community placement was that quality supervision, quality care, and other crucial resources might not be available in the community.

Families in the Baseline Study also were greatly concerned that the funding for community alternatives would not be secure and permanent. This may help to explain why people who have visited a CLA are no more positive toward deinstitutionalization than those who have never been to a CLA: if a family's perception is that the CLA system is insecure, it does not matter if they see, or even approve of, a community setting. Families will not support a system they cannot permanently depend upon one hundred percent.

The same fear was expressed in the responses of the 119 families in the Post-Relocation Study. Families are afraid that, although CLAs address the needs of their relatives more favorably than Pennhurst, the CLAs will not have the same permanence as Pennhurst. Regarding issues other than funding and permanence, some of the families in the Post-Relocation Study were so overwhelmed by the services and personnel in the CLAs that they expressed surprised disbelief at their own initial resistance to deinstitutionalization. They felt that their retarded relatives were happier and becoming more independent, and the families found both the concepts of normalization and least restrictive environment more agreeable. Most of the respondents, however, were doubtful that funding for CLAs was secure, and they expressed great anxiety in this regard. For a son or daughter who requires *lifetime* protection and training, such protection and training must be *at least* as secure as our century-old institutions. The prevailing attitude seems to be: "This new service model is good, and much better than expected, but will it be there 20 or 40 years after we pass on? We're *sure* the institution will be."

It is possible, as Meyer (1980) and Atthowe and Vitello (1982) have suggested, that those families who are prodeinstitutionalization were always a minority, although a very vocal minority. Given the fact that professionals, planners, and the law have come not only to support CLAs but are implementing the policy, and given that parents have no right to veto decisions made by the professionals, planners, and the law, it is urgent to survey families of previously institutionalized retarded individuals now living in CLAs, examining whether families' attitudes changed with the move. Wolfensberger and Menolascino (1970) said that cooperation, trust, and mutual dependence are essential ingredients in the parent and professional relationship for deinstitutionalization to succeed, and that "to gain credibility and acceptance from the public, and from parent and professional groups, some things must be said and done by parents and other things by professionals" (p. 27). Willer *et al.* (1978) found that most families "had come to accept and even approve" the original decision to have their relative discharged from the institution to CLAs and natural homes. While this study was post only—families relied on their memories of when their relative was institutionalized—the results are interesting.

Prior to relocation of their mentally retarded relatives, the 119 families in our longitudinal study were against deinstitutionalization, did not anticipate any positive changes in their social life, job, general happiness, or the happiness of the mentally retarded relative, and had doubts about the skill of personnel and security of funding of CLAs. All this, coupled with the fact that most of the respondents expressed satisfaction with Pennhurst, implied an attitude consistent with the belief that large-scale institutions are stable and workable. The very families who held a positive attitude toward the institution also experienced high stress when making the initial decision (an average of 24 years ago) to institutionalize their mentally retarded relative, implying that the proinstitutional attitude was arrived at with struggle. The struggle may have consisted of coming to terms with, and justifying, the idea of institutionalization, and eliminating guilt from "abandonment" of their relative that might have arisen from prevailing norms of family "togetherness."

Carver and Carver (1972) described a situation in which most parents experienced intense guilt and a sense of failure following the decision to place their son or daughter into an institution. Beddie and Osmond (1955), as reported by Wolfensberger (1971), likened the institutionalization of a retarded child to a child loss that engenders grief. "Institutionalization is a death without the proper rites. Parents have no socially constituted and approved way to express mourning, which may thus be delayed and prolonged" (p. 333). Furthermore, as in the death of a loved one, there is an ambivalence; emotions are extremely complex and may even be contradictory. There is a desire to maintain the tie with the loved one, yet at the same time a parallel tendency to break the bond.

The acceptance of institutionalization in years past meant the acceptance of a number of basic premises implicit in custodial care for mentally retarded persons: a rejection of the developmental model, deinstitutionalization, least restrictive alternative, and normalization, or, at least, the belief that the institution represented the most normalized, and least restrictive environment. Institutionalization as a treatment for mental retardation may have led to the assignment of a particular status to such persons. This means that ideas about mental retardation became consolidated in the social system through what is often referred to as the process of labeling. According to Rowitz (1974), labeling refers to the attachment of a deviant tag or status to an individual whose behavior does not appear normal to the identifier of the problem. Thus, the extent of deviation is determined not only by the behavior of the individual, but also by the norms used by the definer in making the judgment (Mercer & Brown, 1973). This perspective classifies mental retardation as "an acquired social status," a status that defines mental retardation as a debilitating problem with a stigma. Like any other social status, then, that of mentally retarded persons is defined by its location in the social system vis-à-vis other statuses and by the role prescriptions that define the type of performance expected of persons holding the status (Mercer & Brown, 1973).

The labeling theory can be used to understand the respondents' initial belief that their relative had reached his or her highest potential for growth. In addition, the negative attitudes of the 119 respondents reflected on the questions of normalization, least restrictive alternative, and deinstitutionalization in the Baseline Study can be viewed as an extension of this mindset. These relatives had struggled with the initial idea of institutionalization and had not only come to terms with the basic premises but had come to believe in what the institutional system stood for. Consequently, according to this theory, parents came to view their mentally retarded relatives as abnormal, with a disability that excluded living in the large community as an option, and for whom no conceivable intervention would change that situation. It does not come as a surprise, then, that, when these same parents were faced with the question of deinstitutionalization (which views institutionalization as unjust and detrimental to growth), 10 to 40 years after institutionalizing their relative, the parents became highly stressed and reacted by resisting the new movement.

Another theoretical explanation of the deinstitutionalization backlash is posed by Willer, Intagliata, and Atkinson (1981), who hypothesize that deinstitutionalization is a crisis event for families. "Crisis theory suggests that a crisis occurs when an individual or family encounter an abnormal or unexpected event (Jordan, 1962), which is a serious threat to life goals (Rapoport, 1962), appears to have no immediate solution, and leads to a short-term suspension of the usual coping mechanism" (Caplan, 1964, p. 39). There is no doubt that parents expected, when they institutionalized their relative, that their relative would remain at the institution for the rest of his or her life.

Mercer (1966) maintained that a crisis event occurs when there is a conflict between role expectations and role performance. Parents come to view the role of their mentally retarded relatives as that of institutionalized residents, segregated from the rest of society. To be told that there is a place in the community for their relatives, and there is potential for growth, is a contradiction to everything the parents have come to believe about their relative, thus creating stress, and a negative reaction to the new view.

Frohboese and Sales (1980) explain parental opposition on the basis of Brehm's Reactance Theory (Brehm, 1972), which posits that a person is motivationally aroused when a freedom which he or she believes to exist is threatened or eliminated. Arousal results in attempts to regain the freedom. Frohboese and Sales (1980) hypothesized that the courts' decisions to take away the parental power to veto the decision made by the experts to place a relative in a CLA was tantamount to taking away parents' freedom to make residency and service decisions about their mentally retarded relative. Thus, according to this theory, opposition to deinstitutionalization amounts to a psychological reactance to regain the freedom or right to make those residency and service decisions.

Keating (1981) explained the opposition in terms of cognitive dissonance theory, saying that parents are forced to choose between normal parenting roles and institutionalizing their child. After deciding to place their child into an institution, parents may experience what Festinger (1964) has referred to as cognitive dissonance. ["Two elements are in a dissonant relation if, considering those two alone, the obverse of one element would follow from the other" (Festinger, 1964, p. 13).] Placing a child into an institution implies the opposite of providing for that child, so the parents experience dissonance, an unpleasant state similar to anxiety or tension (Pallak & Pitman, 1972; Zanna & Cooper, 1974). Therefore, Keating (1981) said parents are motivated to reduce this tension by emphasizing the negative features of the "unchosen alternative" (p. 59).

The results of our Post-Relocation Study indicated that, initially, the 119 families, like the larger population of 472, displayed outright negative attitudes. After deinstitutionalization occurred, the 119 respondents expressed very positive attitudes. This change was succinctly captured in the words of one respondent: "I can't believe I filled out the first form. I was very much against the move and now I'm so happy about it all . . . We are exceptionally pleased with the arrangement." Given parental resistance, it *is* surprising that such drastic positive change in attitudes occurred in 6 months after relocation.

We conclude that no one theory explains families' attitudes: the theories do not take cognizance of families' legitimate concerns, like funding. So, while the theories may give partial explanations of parents' attitudes, they do not go *beyond* partial explanations. The cognitive dissonance theory, in particular, as Keating (1981) has acknowledged, is weak; in the predictability of dissonance-reducing outcomes it is imprecise. Cognitive dissonance theory is simplistic to the extent that the theory ignores the sociohistorical context of the current deinstitutionalization movement. Dissonance theory purports to explain parents' attitudes in a neat framework; what the theory actually does is reduce parents' attitudes to a psychological pathology.

The dramatic changes in family attitudes toward favoring deinstitutionalization is probably best explained by the fact that the actual observation of client progress and happiness in CLAs compelled the respondents to become believers in the new move. No labeling or ideas can combat the power of practical observation. Though they did not yet acknowledge the growth potential of mentally retarded persons, the respondents could not deny that CLAs were good for their mentally retarded relatives. Nevertheless, this positive impact on families clearly was tempered by a deep concern over security and permanence of the CLAs.

The major limitation of any attempt to explain parents' attitudes is that there has been no national study of "what parents of mentally retarded persons want," no matter where their offspring reside. Less than 19% of all mentally retarded people live in institutions; if it is true that those families most resistant to deinstitutionalization have relatives in institutions, it may turn out to be the case that those relatives will be left in institutions. A formal mechanism must be devised to involve all families in the deinstitutionalization process, and this cannot be done without knowing what families think.

In our case, the court-ordered deinstitutionalization of Pennhurst has abruptly interrupted the long-accepted way of life for these families and their mentally retarded relatives. The possibility of movement of the relatives is real. There was little opportunity in the years before the court decision for dissemination of information, or implementation of strategies to educate parents about developments which, in many cases, have come many years after their relatives were institutionalized. While the welfare of the mentally retarded person should remain the ultimate goal, and his or her rights must be protected, the opinions and feelings of the people whose lives have been so intimately intertwined with the lives of the clients are also important. A forum must be provided for a fair hearing of families' concerns prior to and during any community placement process.

This does not mean that families of an institutionalized retarded person, whether adult or child, should have the absolute power to veto any community placement. Our mutual opinion, developed over 4 years of the family impacts portion of the Pennhurst study, is that there should be fair hearings and full family participation—and that, for the vast majority of people residing in institutions, community placement would be beneficial. We must stress that, by community placement, we mean a residential arrangement in normal housing stock, with staff present at all times, a day program away from the residence for each person, and at least a minimal array of such supports as individual written plans, case management, and access to regular medical and therapeutic care.

ACKNOWLEDGMENT

This study was supported by the U.S. Department of Health and Human Services, Office of Human Development Services, Region III, Contract 130–81–0022.

REFERENCES

Atthowe, J. M., Jr., & Vitello, S. J. *Deinstitutionalization: Family reaction and involvement.* Unpublished manuscript, College of Medicine and Dentistry of New Jersey, Rutgers Medical School, 1982.

Barnes, D., Krochalk, P., & Hutchinson, J. *Comprehensive community residential care system study.* Los Angeles, California: Exceptional Children's Foundation, 1976.

Beddie, A., & Osmond, H. Mothers, mongols, and mores. *Canadian Medical Association Journal,* 1955, **73,** 167–170.

Braddock, D. L. U.S. federal funds: A policy study. In J. Wortis (Ed.), *Mental retardation and developmental disabilities: An annual review.* New York: Brunner/Mazel, 1974.

Brehm, J. W. *Responses to loss of freedom: A theory of psychological reactance.* Morristown, New Jersey: General Learning Press, 1972.

Brehm, J. W., & Cohen, A. R. *Explorations in cognitive dissonance.* New York: Wiley, 1962.

Brockmeier, W. E. Attitudes and opinions of relatives of institutionalized mentally retarded individuals toward institutional and noninstitutional care and training. *Dissertation Abstracts International,* 1975, **35,** 5163A.

Caplan, G. *Principles of preventive psychiatry.* New York: Basic Books, 1964.

Carver, J. N., & Carver, N. E. *The family of the retarded child.* Syracuse, New York: Syracuse Univ. Press, 1972.

Comptroller General of the United States. *Returning the mentally disabled to the community: Government needs to do more.* Report to the Congress, January 7, 1977 (HRD-76-152).

Ferrara, D. M. Attitudes of parents of mentally retarded children toward normalization activities. *American Journal of Mental Deficiency,* 1979, **84,** 145–151.

Festinger, L. *Public Opinion Quarterly,* 1964, **28,** 404–417.

Frohboese, R., & Sales, B. D. Parental opposition to deinstitutionalization. *Law and Human Behavior,* 1980, **4,** 1–87.

Gold, M. W. Research on the vocational habilitation of the retarded: The present, the future. In N. R. Ellis (Ed.), *International review of research in mental retardation* (Vol. VI). New York: Academic Press, 1973.

Gorham, K. A. A lost generation of parents. *Exceptional Children,* 1975, **3,** 521–525.

Horacek v. Exon, 357 F. Supp. 71, D. Neb., 1973.

Jordan, T. E. Research on the handicapped child and the family. *Merrill-Palmer Quarterly,* 1962, **8,** 243–260.

Keating, D. *Deinstitutionalization of the mentally retarded as seen by parents of institutionalized individuals.* Unpublished doctoral dissertation, Temple University, 1981.

Keating, D., Conroy, J., & Walker, S. *Family impacts baseline: A survey of families of residents of Pennhurst* (Pennhurst Longitudinal Study Technical Report PC-80-3). Philadelphia, Pennsylvania Temple University Developmental Disabilities Center, 1980.

Klaber, M. M. A study of institutions. In S. Sarason & J. Doris (Eds.), *Psychological problems in mental deficiency.* New York: Harper, 1969.

Lakin, C. *Demographic studies of residential facilities for the mentally retarded: An historical overview of methodologies and findings.* Minneapolis, Minnesota: Developmental Disabilities Project on Residential Services and Community Adjustment, University of Minnesota, Project Report #3, 1978.

Mercer, J. Patterns of family crisis related to reacceptance of the retarded. *American Journal of Mental Deficiency,* 1966, **71**(1), 19–32.

Mercer, J. R., & Brown, W. G. *Labeling the mentally retarded.* Berkeley, California: Univ. of California Press, 1973.

Meyer, R. J. Attitudes of parents of institutionalized mentally retarded individuals toward deinstitutionalization. *American Journal of Mental Deficiency,* 1980, **85**(2), 184–187.

National Association for Retarded Citizens. *The parent/professional partnership: The partnership—How to make it work.* New York: NARC, 1977.

Pallak, M. S., & Pittman, T. S. General motivational effects of dissonance arousal. *Journal of Personality and Social Psychology,* 1972, **21,** 349–358.

Payne, J. E. The deinstitutionalization backlash. *Mental Retardation,* 1976, **3,** 43–45.

Rapoport, L. The state of crisis: Some theoretical considerations. *Social Service Review,* 1962, **36,** 211–217.

Rowitz, L. Sociological perspective on labeling (A reaction to Macmillan, Jones, and Aloia), *American Journal of Mental Deficiency,* 1974, **79,** 265–267.

Stedman, D. J. Introduction. In J. L. Paul, D. J. Stedman, & G. Neufeld (Eds.), *Deinstitutionalization: Program policy development.* Syracuse, New York: Syracuse Univ. Press, 1977.

Willer, B. *Past institutional adjustment of the retarded returned to the natural family.* Paper presented at the 102nd annual meeting of the American Association on Mental Deficiency, Denver, May, 1978.

Willer, B. W., Intagliata, J. C., & Atkinson, A. C. *Deinstitutionalization as a crisis event for families of mentally retarded persons.* Unpublished manuscript, Division of Community Psychiatry, Department of Psychiatry, State University of New York at Buffalo, 1978.

Willer, B. W., Intagliata, J. C., & Atkinson, A. C., Crisis for families of mentally retarded persons including the crisis of deinstitutionalization. *British Journal of Mental Subnormality,* 1979.

Willer, B. W., Intagliata, J. C., & Atkinson, A. C. Deinstitutionalization as a crisis event for families of mentally retarded persons. *Mental Retardation,* 1981, **19,** 28-29.

Wolfensberger, W. Counseling parents of the retarded. In A. Bauneister (Ed.), *Mental retardation: Appraisal, education, and rehabilitation.* Chicago, Illinois: Aldine, 1971.

Wolfensberger, W. *The principle of normalization in human services.* Toronto: National Institute of Mental Retardation, 1972.

Wolfensberger, W., & Menolascino, F. Reflections on recent mental retardation developments in Nebraska. *Mental Retardation,* 1970, **8**(6), 20-28.

Zanna, M. P., & Cooper, J. Dissonance and the pill: An attribution approach to studying the arousal properties of dissonance. *Journal of Personality and Social Psychology,* 1974, **29,** 703-709.

Community Placement
and Adjustment of
Deinstitutionalized Clients:
Issues and Findings

ELLIS M. CRAIG

TEXAS DEPARTMENT OF MENTAL HEALTH AND MENTAL RETARDATION
AUSTIN, TEXAS

RONALD B. MCCARVER

PARTLOW STATE SCHOOL AND HOSPITAL
TUSCALOOSA, ALABAMA

I. INTRODUCTION

If a national survey regarding the best residential placement for mentally retarded people were conducted today, it is likely that the natural home

INTERNATIONAL REVIEW OF RESEARCH IN
MENTAL RETARDATION, Vol. 12

would be viewed the overwhelming favorite and public residential facilities the least desirable. This attitude is markedly different from the prevailing opinion only a few decades ago. In fact, thinking regarding the provision of services to mentally retarded citizens has traveled full circle in recent history. Prior to the twentieth century, families were expected to care for their own mentally retarded children. Help, if any, came from their community. Residential facilities were few in number and screened their admissions carefully. Today, most professionals and lawmakers expect the same. Families are encouraged to care for their own and get help, if any, from the community. Modern institutions are primarily reserved for clients with severely debilitating mental, and often physical and emotional, handicaps (Sloan & Stevens, 1976; McCarver & Cavalier, 1983; Scheerenberger, 1982). This shift in attitude has not occurred because of data generated by research comparing the efficacy of different types of placements. Research, as usual, has followed society's changing position. Some (e.g., Blatt, 1979) maintain that research has nothing to do with the issue. This is not a new state of affairs. Decisions about the fate of mentally retarded citizens are usually made on philosophical and political, as opposed to empirical, grounds.

As a consequence, most of the research available is retrospective and descriptive rather than predictive or explanatory. There is, however, a large body of literature available, beginning with Fernald's (1919) analysis of escapees from his institution (for reviews of the early literature see Windle, 1962; Eagle, 1967; McCarver & Craig, 1974). Subsequent reviews have been published (e.g., Heal, Sigelman, & Switzky, 1978) and at least four recent books are primarily devoted to research on this topic (Baker, Seltzer, & Seltzer, 1977; Bruininks, Meyers, Sigford, & Lakin, 1981a,b; Gollay, Freedman, Wyngaarden, & Kurtz, 1978; Rosen, Clark, & Kivitz, 1977). None of this work represents a complete review of the literature; no such document exists. The sheer number of relevant publications precludes such an effort. For example, McCarver and Craig (1974) cited 150 works but excluded most of the early literature unless it was deemed especially significant. Over 200 relevant articles published since that review were located in preparation for the current article, of which only a representative portion are referenced. This article will include research published since 1972 related to the community placement and adjustment of deinstitutionalized clients and will deemphasize the issues addressed in Heal *et al.*'s (1978) insightful work, which concentrated on the development of community residential alternatives. We will focus on the issues and research concerned with the current reasons for institutionalization and its effect on subsequent placement efforts.

II. DEINSTITUTIONALIZATION: HISTORICAL PERSPECTIVE

The deinstitutionalization movement of today should be considered within its historical context. In the 1840s, enthusiasm regarding the success of Seguin's "physiological method" was imported from Europe, and Samuel Howe, a Boston neuropsychiatrist, opened in 1848 the first residential training facility for the mentally retarded in this country (Sloan & Stevens, 1976). By 1868, there were 15 American institutions serving slightly over 4000 clients (Baumeister, 1970). Most of these early facilities were small and well staffed and admitted only those clients most likely to profit from training. In 1876, the "Association of Medical Officers of American Institutions of Idiotic and Feeble Minded Persons" was established. Included in its constitution was a statement dedicating the association to the establishment of institutions for the management and training of "idiots and feebleminded individuals" and research related thereto (Sloan & Stevens, 1976). Largely due to the lobbying efforts of this association, the number of residential training facilites slowly increased. However, attitudes began rapidly changing in the early 1900s. Due to a combination of the absence of any real cures in the experimental schools, the prevalent notion that moral and mental defectiveness were linked, and the eugenics movement, mentally retarded people began being regarded as a menace to society who should be isolated from the community in institutions, preferably in rural areas. A paper presented at the 1912 meeting of the American Association for the Study of the Feebleminded by Dr. Walter Fernald, a national leader in the field, aptly summarized current professional opinion. He stated that at least 80% of mental defects were inherited and described the mentally retarded as "a parasitic and predatory class never capable of supporting themselves or of managing their own affairs . . . a menace and danger to the community . . . a potential criminal." High-grade female imbeciles were seen as especially dangerous, being "twice as prolific as the normal woman," and "certain to become sexual offenders and to spread venereal disease or give birth to degenerate children" (Sloan & Stevens, 1976, p. 76). Fernald totally recanted this position in 1923, but the public was not so pliable. The demand for institutional care actually increased during the Great Depression, while the number of community special education programs were diminishing in many areas of the country (Baumeister, 1970; Sloan & Stevens, 1976). As shown in Fig. 1, the rate of building new institutions did not slow down until World War II. Although the number of institutions has only slightly decreased in recent years, the rate of institutionalization (see Fig. 2) and the absolute size of institutions (see Fig. 3) have dropped dramatically. The number of people

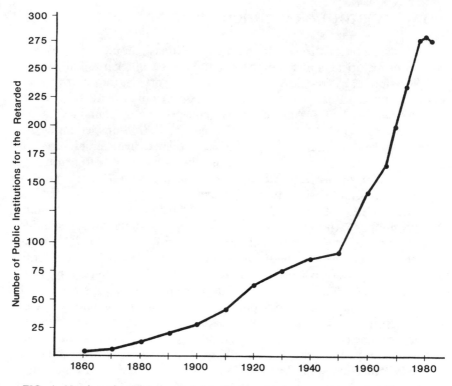

FIG. 1. Number of publicly supported institutions for the mentally retarded (Baumeister, 1970; Scheerenberger, 1976, 1979, 1982).

residing in residential facilities reached a peak in the middle 1960s. Since that time, the rate of institutionalization, the average size of institutions, and the total number of people in institutions have decreased steadily.

After more than 50 years, the consensus has drastically shifted, and now the rallying cry of concerned professionals has become "deinstitutionalization" rather than "institutionalization." The current movement began when the deplorable conditions of many public residential facilities for the mentally retarded were exposed in the early 1950s and 1960s (e.g., Blatt & Kaplan, 1966). After years of public indifference and legislative neglect, virtually every state had little to offer its mentally retarded citizens other than decaying, overcrowded, understaffed institutions with long waiting lists. Initial efforts were directed toward the upgrading of institutions and the building of new ones. However, by 1969, the deinstitutionalization movement had clearly been tied to the principle of normalization by Wolfensberger who later (1971) proclaimed that institutions should fade away and be replaced by

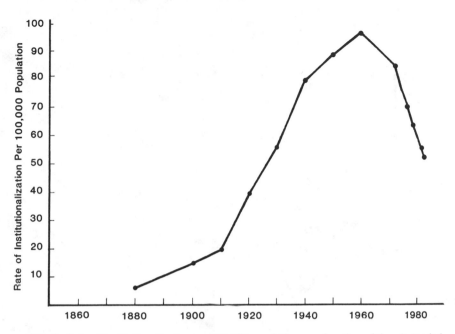

FIG. 2. Rate of institutionalization per 100,000 population as a function of time (extended from Baumeister, 1970, p. 19, with data from Scheerenberger, 1982, 1983).

small community residences because they were more normal. The movement has faced relatively little opposition and is now incorporated in laws, standards, and court orders. (See McCarver & Cavalier, 1983, for a more complete discussion of the philosophical and legal underpinnings of the deinstitutionalization movement.)

In many states deinstitutionalization is very nearly an accomplished fact. Several, including Maryland, Minnesota, Florida, Michigan, Illinois, and Pennsylvania have closed, or intend to close, public residential facilities to be replaced by community alternatives (NASMRP, 1982a). After peaking at just under 200,000 in 1967, the nationwide public institution population has steadily decreased every year. Scheerenberger has conducted demographic surveys of these facilities over the last 8 years. In the most recent analysis (Scheerenberger, 1983), the average daily population of these facilities had dropped to 119,335 for fiscal years 1981–1982. However, the number of new admissions had increased by 35% over the previous year (although it was down 10% from the first year of this series of surveys). An analysis of Scheerenberger's data indicates that the decrease in size of the institutional population has been due primarily to steady increases in releases from insti-

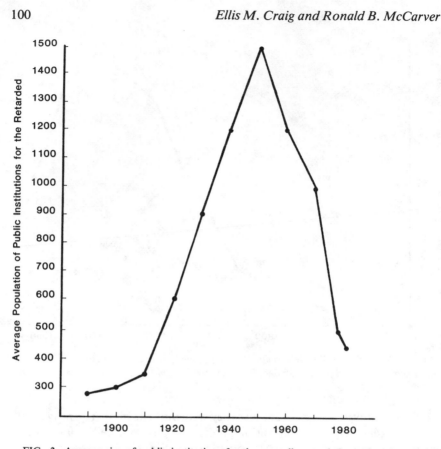

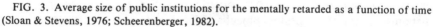

FIG. 3. Average size of public institutions for the mentally retarded as a function of time (Sloan & Stevens, 1976; Scheerenberger, 1982).

tutions, with the number of new admissions remaining stable or even increasing from year to year. It appears that some demand for institutional placement remains. In addition, legal and professional mandates for deinstitutionalization have weakened somewhat in recent times. The 1978 *Wyatt* hearings were marked with debate among the numerous experts who testified and prompted Roos (1979), among others, to be concerned about the apparent breakdown of professional consensus regarding deinstitutionalization and related issues. Judge Frank Johnson, in fact, stated in his 1979 ruling that an institution might be the least restrictive environment for some individuals, as did the Third Circuit Court of Appeals when it stayed the decision to close Pennhurst State School (see McCarver & Cavalier, 1983).

   In a related development, the Justice Department has begun to downgrade its involvement in right-to-treatment litigation following the Supreme Court's June 18, 1982 decision in the case of *Youngberg v. Romeo*

(NASMRP, 1982b). This ruling contains strong language indicating that decisions regarding the type of treatment and the setting in which it is provided should be left in the hands of professionals. Whether the pendulum will stop or reverse its direction remains to be seen, but it is apparent that we are at a crossroads. Some feel that ample research is available documenting the legal, ethical, and programmatic shortcomings of institutions (e.g., Roos, 1979; Wolfensberger, 1980), and others see insufficient evidence to draw firm conclusions (e.g., Ellis, 1979; Balla, 1976). The authors tend to agree with Blatt's pronouncement that research has little to do with the enactment of social policy. We, however, will attempt to summarize and analyze the available data in a step toward the ultimate goal of enlightened decision making.

III. LITERATURE REVIEW

The research conducted over the last decade differs in significant ways from earlier studies in postinstitutional adjustment. The absolute magnitude of the deinstitutionalization movement has probably been the major factor in this change. The drastically increased volume of community placements, sometimes under court order, has been an interesting sociological experiment. Some writers (e.g., Begab, 1975) have suggested that such a massive, rapid effort has been ill planned and a disservice to the individuals involved. If so, an increased failure rate or a higher incidence of community adjustment problems might be expected. As noted by Huey (1978), others have argued that the mentally retarded persons living in institutions are not essentially different from those who have been living in the community for some time. Thus, given an adequate network of services, successful community placement should be possible for the vast majority of institutionalized mentally retarded people. Much of the recent research (e.g., Gollay *et al.,* 1978) has, in fact, focused on the impact of community support services on successful community adjustment.

Other changes in the research over the last decade can be attributed to a growing methodological and conceptual maturity in the field. It has become clear that research focused on attempts to predict community adjustment on the basis of individual client characteristics is a futile effort. The interaction of client characteristics with a host of environmental variables has become the focus of attention. Such research has required a shift to more sophisticated analysis, primarily multivariate statistical techniques.

Despite such advances, some old problems remain unresolved. The lack of consistent criteria of successful adjustment is a prime example. This issue of client protection versus strong adherence to normalization principles is certainly not settled. Cost–benefit issues surrounding continued deinstitutionalization efforts have also recently emerged in the literature.

The following literature review will concentrate on the new research developments, although the relationship of the findings to past research will be considered. The review is organized into the following categories: (1) reasons for institutionalization, (2) effects of institutionalization, (3) client characteristics, (4) type of community placement, and (5) community training.

A.   Reasons for Institutionalization

A number of researchers remain concerned with the reasons for the continuing demand for institutional placement and the ultimate effect that the selection factors employed during the admission process have on deinstitutionalization efforts.

McCarver and Craig (1974) concluded that most mentally retarded people were institutionalized because the community would not tolerate their behavior, their families were unable to properly care for them, or community resources were not adequate. These still appear to be major reasons for current admissions.

The strong influence of behavior problems in institutional admissions has been noted by a number of recent authors. Spencer (1976) reported that 62% of the institutional admissions in England were because of behavior problems, as compared to 38% for physical infirmity and helplessness. Other recent studies including comparisons with control groups also support the importance of behavior problems. Wolf and Whitehead (1975) reported that parents of a group of institutionalized children were more likely to describe them as disruptive of family life than were the parents of a matched control group of noninstitutionalized children. Campbell, Smith, and Wool (1982) found significant differences on a number of maladaptive behavior domains of the Adaptive Behavior Scale between individuals referred for institutionalization and a matched sample who had not been referred. Eyman, Borthwick, and Miller (1981) also found a greater degree of maladaptive behavior among institutional admissions than among clients remaining in the community. They further reported that maladaptive behavior was more prevalent in mildly and moderately retarded individuals who were institutionalized than for the severely and profoundly retarded. Begab (1975) noted that mildly retarded people who are institutionalized often have been involved in delinquent activity and that community pressure for institutionalization is a common phenomenon, and Jacobson and Schwartz (1983) indicated that group home clients in their sample who were in danger of placement failure had more behavior problems. In the case of the more severely retarded, the inability of the family to care for the individual appears to be the most common precipitator of admission. Medical problems, lack of self-help skills, and a variety of maladaptive behaviors are frequently cited in such cases (e.g., Bjaanes, Butler, & Kelly, 1981).

There is considerable evidence, both direct and indirect, that lack of community resources is gradually becoming less of a factor. The dramatic growth of community-based residential facilities has played a major role (Bruininks, Hauber, & Kudla, 1980). On the basis of a nationwide survey, Janicki, Mayeda, and Epple (1983) reported that over 57,000 people lived in group home type community residences as of January 1982, a manyfold increase since the early 1970s. According to a survey reported by Bruininks, Kudla, Hauber, Hill, and Wieck (1981a), almost as many residents of such facilities came directly from their natural home as from institutions (32.4 vs 35%). Lakin, Hill, Hauber, and Bruininks (1982) noted that the average age of first admission (median = 16 years) to institutions has increased recently, after being relatively constant for years. One of their interpretations of this phenomenon is an increase in the availability of community programs, which is delaying the demand for institutional admission. Begab (1975) also commented on a developing trend to treat mentally retarded criminal offenders in the community rather than mixing them with more severely retarded people in institutions. However, Lakin, Hill, Hauber, Bruininks, and Heal (1983), recently completed a comprehensive analysis of new admissions and readmissions and reported that as many as 50% of new admissions have no secondary handicap and are not considered dangerous. They further indicated that the most common reason given for the admission of new clients is that the institution provides the best program for that particular client, which indicates that institutions still provide some programs that are not universally available in the community. In addition, Bock and Joiner (1983) reported that a significant percentage of the clients in institutions in Minnesota, traditionally a leader in the provision of community alternatives, possess the behaviors to function in group homes if they were available.

B. Effects of Institutionalization

The effect of institutional experience on subsequent community adjustment has often been assumed to have negative long-term effects. However, McCarver and Craig (1974) did not find strong support for this position. Studies in this area have typically analyzed the effects of institutional training and length of institutionalization on subsequent adjustment. Many researchers have shifted to comparisons between institutional and community populations, and comparisons between clients placed in the community and control groups remaining in the institution.

The notion of long-term ill effects of institutionalization is aptly captured by a quote from Edgerton (1975): "One lingering consequence of institutionalization seems to be the belief among retarded persons that one is never again a free agent, instead, one is always 'under the state.' " (p. 131) Apathy and dependency are frequently mentioned as consequences of institutionalization (e.g., Rosen *et al.,* 1977). De Vellis (1977) noted that the development of such behavior can be described as a case of learned helplessness, and offered a number of preventive and ameliorative suggestions. Bercovici (1981) commented that such dependency is probably a rational and adaptive response to not being in control of one's situation. The results of Edgerton's (1967) classic follow-up study might very well fit this description. He concluded that the successful adaptation of members of his sample was strongly influenced by their ability (or luck) in locating a helpful benefactor in the community. However, he changed this position on the basis of a second follow-up of the sample (Edgerton & Bercovici, 1976), which found that most members had become less dependent on others over time. It could be argued that the original interpretation was accurate, i.e., dependency in recently released clients is adaptive, but becomes less important over time and is not necessarily an irreversible consequence of institutionalization.

A number of recent studies have compared the behavior of clients placed in the community from an institution with a control group remaining in the institution. Close (1977) reported greater progress in social behavior and self-help skills for a group of eight severely and profoundly retarded adults 1 year after placement in a group home as compared to a matched control group that remained in the institution. Schroeder and Henes (1978) found that a community-placed group gained more adaptive behavior skills, especially communication, than a matched control group after 1 year. Conroy, Efthimiou, and Lemanowicz (1982) obtained similar results after a 2-year follow-up. Hemming, Lavender, and Pill (1981) found that a community-placed group initially exhibited an increase in maladaptive behavior, which subsided on subsequent assessments. Nevertheless, the group made significant adaptive behavior gains relative to the institutional control group after 9 months. Regardless of whether it can be argued that institutions have a deleterious effect on the residents, studies such as these suggest that adaptive behavior gains are likely to occur when residents are placed in appropriate community settings. In addition, as discussed in detail by Sandler and Thurman (1981), clinical studies, which have primarily focused on more subjective variables such as client satisfaction, also privide support for improvement following community placement, although the literature is less clear and contains contradictory findings.

If institutions did have a long-term negative effect on residents, it would be expected that length of institutionalization would be significantly related to measures of community adjustment. However, neither the earlier studies reviewed (McCarver & Craig, 1974) nor more recent ones indicate that it is an especially significant variable (e.g., Miller, Miller, Kim, Kutz, Lozier, & Misenheimer, 1975; Moen, Bogen, & Aanes, 1975; Schroeder & Henes, 1978). O'Neill (1977) reports mixed results by sex. One study (Gollay, 1976b) did find a positive correlation between length of institutionalization and community adjustment, but on the whole, it does not appear to be a particularly potent variable.

Prior to the widespread implementation of special education in the schools and an emphasis on community-based training programs, the need for training was a frequently cited reason for institutionalization (McCarver & Craig, 1974). Although there is some controversy regarding the benefits of formal training for some of the profoundly retarded (Ellis, 1979; Roos, 1979), the importance of training activities in institutional settings (regardless of their adequacy) is basically taken for granted (Rosen et al., 1977). It continues to be surprising that this area has received relatively little attention, a deficit pointed out in both the McCarver and Craig (1974) and Heal et al. (1978) reviews. One explanation for the frequent oversight of this area is the difficulty in quantifying it. For example, although the number of training hours might be calculated, this immediately leads to questions regarding training and staff ratios, comparability of different training activities, etc. Participation versus nonparticipation in a given training program is a rather gross and confounded categorization, although it has been reported to be a predictor of community outcome (e.g., Gollay, 1976a). Heal et al. (1978) discussed a rather unique approach to the measurement problem described in the Gollay study. Intensity of institutional programming, defined as per capita expenditures and average percentage of released residents who had participated in various programs, was treated as a general institutional variable and was associated with released residents remaining in the community. Schalock, Harper, and Genung (1981) reported that "formal" education received at the institution was a significant predictor of successful community placement in a multiple regression analysis, although the quantification of this variable was not specified. Perhaps a more meaningful variable is simply the client's level of development in various cognitive and adaptive behavior skills. Schalock et al. defined seven categories of these and identified them as training variables, making the point that ongoing training was occurring in areas with identified deficits. That is, it may be more appropriate to focus on the products of training rather than the process.

Although general institutional training has been insufficiently studied, a specific type—community preparation training—has received considerable attention. Rosen et al. (1977) make the point that any habilitation facility can simulate the "real" world to only a limited degree. Thus, when placement is anticipated, it is necessary to familiarize the client with that world through transitional experiences. Specific training on community survival skills has also been recommended (e.g., Weitz & Roll, 1977). There is evidence that such activities do not occur to an adequate extent in many placement programs. An illustrative example is provided by the results of a survey conducted by Bruininks, Williams, and Morreau (1978; described in Bruininks *et al.*, 1981a). Representatives of consumer groups, state planners, and state agency personnel in a six-state region rated the current level of development of 28 areas of deinstitutionalization and residential services. The area rated lowest in quality was preparing (training and counseling) institutional residents for community placement. A General Accounting Office (1977) report has also identified the lack of such preparation as a significant problem for deinstitutionalization efforts. That such efforts can facilitate the initial adjustment of clients and, perhaps, even prevent the "relocation syndrome" has some research support (e.g., Weinstock, Wulkan, Colon, Coleman, & Goncalves, 1979).

In summary, there is some support for gains in adaptive behavior when residents are placed in the community, but little evidence for the notion that institutionalization increases maladaptive behaviors (e.g., Eyman *et al.*, 1981), or that length of institutionalization is related to failure in the community. There is also limited evidence that participation in institutional training programs (especially those specifically designed to prepare residents for placement) increases the probability of a successful placement.

C. Client Characteristics

The area of client characteristics has traditionally received the most attention in studies of postinstitutional adjustment and yet is represented by a generally inconsistent pattern of findings (e.g, McCarver & Craig, 1974). However, the role of client characteristics in community adjustment has almost routinely been minimized in recent writings. Lakin, Bruinink, and Sigford (1981a,b), for example, argued that there is no need for further research on certain client characteristics, e.g., IQ. They point out that deinstitutionalization will continue regardless of research findings in that area. Gollay (1981) makes an even stronger statement in this regard. She argues that it is a failure of the service delivery system rather than the individual if a return to the institution is necessary. While it is difficult to justify continued research in an area where little significant new information is being discovered, the problem in this case may lie with the ingenuity of the researchers. It has been suggested that the lack of meaningful findings has resulted from considering client characteristics without attending to the nature of the community environment in which they are placed, a conceptually unsound approach (e.g., Heal *et al.*, 1978). As Landesman-Dwyer (1981) noted, however, the technology for assessing the interaction between individual and environmental characteristics is still relatively undeveloped. Quantification of environmental variables is especially in need of extensive development.

Studies investigating the interaction of client and environmental variables are beginning to appear. For example, Sutter, Mayeda, Yee, and Yanagi (1981) evaluated the match between community care providers' preferences for the type of clients they wanted to work with and the actual characteristics of the clients in the group homes. Clients who were mismatched with the care providers' preferences were significantly more likely to be unsuccessful, i.e., return to the institution.

In a particularly ambitious attempt, Latham, Campbell, Bailey, Sanders, and Teare (1982) investigated relationships between client and environmental variables and a multidimensional rating of clients' adjustments to their community residential placements. Results of stepwise multiple regression analyses indicated that client-related variables (practical living skills, maladaptive behavior, physical condition of the client, previous residence in a community setting), and residence-related variables (comfort and repair of the setting and habilitative orientation) accounted for approximately 46% of the variance in predicting a total adjustment score. This study represents one of the few to involve all levels of mental retardation, include environmental as well as client-related measures, evaluate a wide range of community placement options, view adjustment as multidimensional apart from institutional recidivism, and recognize that varying levels of adjustment are possible. However, the results should be viewed as tentative due to disparities in the numbers of settings within each placement category and limitations in the concept of adjustment.

Another study in this vein is that of Willer and Intagliata (1981). They used multiple regression analyses to predict five different outcome variables as a function of a variety of both client and environmental variables. A major finding was that environmental factors important in one type of setting (foster family care) were similarly influential in another (community residences), although the functioning levels of the clients varied across the two settings.

Although not all recent studies assessing the influence of client characteristics on community adjustment have considered such interactions, the use of multivariate analysis techniques is much more common. The client variables which have been most extensively researched include sex, age, IQ, adaptive behavior, maladaptive behavior, social skills, personal appearance, and personality.

1. SEX AND AGE DIFFERENCES

McCarver and Craig (1974) noted no consistent differences in community placement success rates of males and females. A similar pattern is present in the recent literature, i.e., in some studies males are more successful (O'Neill, 1977); females are in others (Schalock et al., 1981); and often there is no difference (Moen et al., 1975).

A similar situation exists with respect to age. In the older literature, there was a slight but inconsistent tendency for older individuals to be more successful (McCarver & Craig, 1974). In recent studies, there have typically been no significant age differences in success rates (e.g., Schalock & Harper, 1981; Thiel, 1981). Trends have tended to be in favor of younger age groups (e.g., Seltzer, Seltzer, & Sherwood, 1982).

2. INTELLIGENCE

In the older literature there was only a slight tendency for individuals with higher IQs to be more successfully adjusted (McCarver & Craig, 1974). It was pointed out that most of these studies involved clients in the mildly retarded range. With such a restricted range, it is not surprising that there is not a strong association between intellectual level and community success. This point was emphasized by Bell (1976), who included a broader range of IQ scores and found that higher IQ clients were more integrated into community life. Heal *et al.* (1978) added that IQ level is positively related to some measures of placement success and negatively to others (e.g., criminal behavior). The few recent studies that have included IQ comparisons of successful and unsuccessful groups have typically found little difference (e.g., Thiel, 1981). Jacobson and Schwartz (1983) did report that group home placements in danger of failure had higher IQ scores and were more independent than those deemed successfully adjusted by care providers. However, as in the older literature, most of these studies have involved groups with relatively homogeneous IQ scores.

3. ADAPTIVE BEHAVIOR

It has only been in recent years that adaptive behavior level has been granted equal status with IQ in the definition of mental retardation. Thus, the early literature rarely referenced this client characteristics as a predictor variable in studies of postinstitutional adjustment. Recently, changes in adaptive behavior have been frequently used as a measure of community adjustment (e.g., Hemming *et al.,* 1981), but relatively few studies have assessed the predictive value of preplacement adaptive behavior level. This is probably largely a result of the shift away from the study of client characteristics as a factor in deinstitutionalization efforts (e.g., Lakin *et al.,* 1981a,b). Also, clients of varying adaptive behavior levels are likely to be placed in different settings, making such comparisons less meaningful.

As with many other client characteristics, the available research on the influence of adaptive behavior skills on community adjustment yields mixed results. Schalock, Harper, and Carver (1981) identified several behavioral skill areas positively associated with success in independent living. Eyman, Demaine, and Lei (1979) and Intagliata, Crosby, and Neider (1981) found greater progress after community placement for clients with initially higher adaptive behavior levels. However, Gollay (1976a) found no difference in Adaptive Behavior Scale (Part I) scores between clients who remained in the community versus returnees. She later added (Gollay, 1981) that clients with lower adaptive behavior levels were perceived as adjusting slightly better, but were typically less integrated into the community and suggested that there are lower expectations for lower functioning clients. In a study by Cohen, Conroy, Frazer, Snelbecker, and Spreat (1977), clients were assessed with the Adaptive Behavior Scale prior to transfer from a large institution to a small facility, immediately following the relocation, and about 2 months later. Initially, higher functioning clients regressed in adaptive skills, which was interpreted as a manifestation of the relocation syndrome (i.e., withdrawal). Lower functioning clients, on the other hand, exhibited an initial increase in both adaptive and maladaptive behaviors.

Heal et al. (1978) concluded that the client characteristic which best predicts placement failure is the existence of maladaptive behavior. The general acceptance of this finding is a major reason for the higher prevalence of behavior problems in institutions than any other setting. Eyman and Call (1977) asserted that deinstitutionalization efforts will not proceed very far unless the behavior problems can be treated or special community facilities for such clients are established. In all the studies reviewed where preplacement maladaptive behavior patterns were assessed, behavior problems were predictive of community failure or poorer adjustment (Gollay, 1976a; Intagliata & Willer, 1982; Miller et al., 1975; Thiel, 1981).

4. SOCIAL SKILLS AND PERSONALITY

Although there has been considerable discussion of the importance of social skills for the community adjustment of mentally retarded people, few studies conducted within the last decade have directly examined this relationship. Schalock, Harper, and Genung (1981), found that measures of appropriate social–emotional behavior were significantly related to successful community placement, and several researchers have begun studying the social networks of retarded individuals. Cohen and Leland (1977), for example, argue that group placements may be more successful than individual ones because of the complementary skills of the members, and Landesman-Dwyer (1981) has advocated the need to closely consider the client's social network before implementing a transfer. Failure to do so has been related to the phenomenon of relocation syndrome (e.g., Cochran, Sran, & Varano, 1977).

Rosen et al. (1977) note that personality variables have considerable potential as a predictor of community adjustment, but that there has been little meaningful research in the area. They have been attempting to fill this gap, and one result of their research is a characterization of the "institutional personality." Five primary traits are identified: "lowered self-esteem and related motivational deficits, conditioned helplessness, acquiescence to authority, inappropriate behavior and sexual inadequacies." They concede that this complex of traits applies to noninstitutionalized retarded individuals as well. Nevertheless, it is a meaningful starting point in an area that has traditionally received very little attention (McCarver & Craig, 1974).

Two additional studies have added some significant information regarding the role of personality factors in postinstitutional adjustment. Bartnik and Winkler (1981) reported that employers, training staff, and parents of retarded individuals had discrepant perceptions of the key criteria of community adjustment. The degree of personal responsibility expected of retarded individuals appeared to be the main factor distinguishing these groups. Mullins and Hays (1980) identified a number of personality factors which were significantly related to work adjustment and yet independent of specific job skills.

5. PERSONAL APPEARANCE

One of the few client characteristics for which relatively consistent relationships with community adjustment has been found is personal appearance (McCarver & Craig, 1974). Fairly few studies have examined this variable; however, recent investigations continue to support its importance. Moen *et al.* (1975) identified poor grooming as a frequently cited factor in the reasons for community failure among their sample, and pointed out that it appeared to be more crucial to community than to institutional staff. Schalock, Harper, and Carver (1981) reported that personal maintenance and clothing care and use were significant predictors of placement success for individuals placed in independent housing. Finally, Gollay (1976a) found that interviewer ratings of physical attractiveness did not distinguish among outcome groups, but that ratings of personal appearance characteristics over which the individual had control did.

D. Type of Community Placement

Although much of the past research on types of community placements focused on comparative success rates of types of placements (McCarver & Craig), the more recent emphasis is on the need for a continuum of placement options (e.g., Baker *et al.,* 1977), a variety of which may be necessary during the life span of a given individual. Independent placement may be the goal for some, but not all (e.g., Schalock, Harper, & Carver, 1981). The most important criterion is the placement of the individual in the setting which most closely meets his needs and also provides the training necessary for continued development.

Eyman and Borthwick (1980) note that strong advocates of deinstitutionalization assume that all institutionalized retarded individuals can be adequately served in a community setting. However, this position has been challenged. It is argued that institutional settings may be the most appropriate for certain groups, such as the seriously medically involved (e.g., Begab, 1975). Further, suitable community placements are not yet available for all clients. Scheerenberger (1981) reported that only about half of the institutional clients identifed as needing community placement could be placed in available community living facilities. Baker *et al.* (1977) stress the need for a variety of placement options to meet the diverse needs of the mentally retarded population. Schalock and Harper (1981) add to this the need to ensure movement through a comprehensive system, involving increasing independence for the clients.

Best-Sigford, Bruininks, Lakin, Hill, and Heal (1982) provided a breakdown of the current variety of placement options on the basis of a survey of a random sample of releases from public institutions in 1978. The individuals released included 54.5% males and 45.5% females, essentially their same representation in the institutional population. By age, 30.9% of the releases were school aged and 68.5% adults (average age of 31.6). The releases tend to be younger than their general representation. There was a rather even distribution by adaptive behavior level of the releases, a marked shift from earlier years when the mildly retarded were the dominant group. The average length of institutionalization was 12.8 years, a shorter period than that for the institutional population. A significant number (21.9%) of the "releases" were to other public institutions, and thus were really just transfers. The most common placement (22.3%) was a small group home (15 or fewer residents). The natural or an adoptive home was the next most frequent (20.8%). Nursing homes were ranked third, accounting for 8.8% of the placements. Larger community residential facilities (16 or more residents) were used for 6.5% of the placements. Foster or family care included 5.5% and independent living 4.6%. Boarding homes and semiindependent living placements each accounted for 2.1% of the releases.

1. GROUP HOMES

Although community group homes of various types are mentioned throughout the postinstitutional adjustment literature, they have become a special focus of attention in recent years. Bruininks *et al.* (1980) reported that the number of such facilities doubled from 1973 to 1977 to a total of 4427 with a residential population of 83,688 and Janicki *et al.* (1983) located 6302 as of January 1982. Baker *et al.* (1977) provided a detailed account of different types of community residential facilities, pointing out the strong and weak features of each. Also, Heal *et al.* (1978) reviewed the research on this residential alternative.

Some of the key findings and issues in this research include the following:

Plans to establish such facilities often meet with considerable community opposition, especially from local neighborhood associations. However, this opposition usually decreases once the facility is established (e.g., Lubin, Schwartz, Zigman, & Janicki, 1982). Partly because of such opposition and for economic reasons, these facilities are often established in commercial rather than residential areas (e.g., Lakin *et al.*, 1981a). Although urban areas are usually advocated because of service availability, individuals placed in rural areas appear to be just as successful (e.g., Sanderson & Crawley, 1982). Although it is often assumed that small facilities are preferable, this is not necessarily the case. Landesman-Dwyer, Sackett, and Kleinman (1980), for example, found increased social interaction in larger facilities. Staff–client interaction patterns and integration into normalized activities in the community appear to be the most important factors. However, Campbell, Bailey, and Phronson (1984) evaluated 155 settings for degree of independence afforded residents, emphasis on clients' involvement in habilitation programs, and the extent of physical and social integration into the surrounding communities. Results indicated that settings rated as most extensively integrated, such as natural families, tended to provide less independence and habilitative emphasis than less normalized environments such as group homes and job training facilities. In a study comparing family care and group homes, Willer and Intagliata (1982) found that family care placements exhibited greater decreases in maladaptive behavior, but that group placements showed more improvement in community living skills.

2. FAMILY AND FOSTER CARE

Willer, Intagliata, and Wicks (1981) reviewed the research on returning clients to their natural homes. Although this was often discouraged in the past (McCarver & Craig, 1974), it is now being recognized as a viable and cost-efficient approach, especially if the family is assisted with the problems that originally led to institutionalization. Foster or family care homes have also received increased attention in recent years. In a recent review, Intagliata *et al.* (1981a) noted that the orientation of such homes has traditionally been more custodial than other types of placements. However, there are indications of increased training-oriented and normalizing activities in such settings. This has accompanied increased professionalization of foster family care providers, and, in fact, much of the research in this area focuses on care provider selection and training.

3. NURSING HOMES

A placement option that receives less than enthusiastic support is nursing homes. Bruininks *et al.* (1981a) discuss the results of a national nursing home survey conducted in 1977, which indicated that 6.1% or 79,800 residents were mentally retarded, a larger number than in community group homes. A General Accounting Office (1977) report indicated that such placements probably constituted another form of institutionalization. Relevant research (e.g., Brown & Guard, 1979) does suggest that these facilities tend to be custodial and nonnormalizing in orientation, and probably not appropriate for most mentally retarded people released from institutions.

E. Commmunity Training

A number of recent studies are concerned with training conducted in the community addressing behaviors which have traditionally resulted in reinstitutionalization. Such studies will become increasingly important if deinstitutionalization efforts begin to include even more problematic institutional clients. In the older literature, there was a fairly prevalent attitude that released clients experiencing difficulties in the community should be returned to the institution for additional training (McCarver & Craig, 1974). This may have been necessary at the time given the lack of development of community-based services. At present, however, there is an expectation that the client's problems will be dealt with in the community, and that if reinstitutionalization is necessary it may represent a failure of the service delivery system (Gollay et al., 1978).

A wide range of community-based training activities have been described in the literature. Basic self-help, grooming, and domestic skills are common areas (e.g., Doleys, Stacy, & Knowles, 1981; Johnson & Cuvo, 1981; Matson, 1981) as are the development of social skills and dealing with maladaptive behaviors (e.g., Rosen et al., 1977; Stacy, Doleys, & Malcolm, 1979). Although community vocational training has a long history, there is an increasing tendency to involve severely and profoundly retarded clients (e.g., Halpern, Browning, & Brummer, 1975).

Knowledge of the impact of such training on community adjustment is still in a relative state of infancy. However, it is anticipated that as deinstitutionalization efforts continue, research in this area will play an important role in evaluating this social policy.

IV. COMMUNITY ADJUSTMENT

There is such a wide diversity of community adjustment criteria and outcome measures that they are almost researcher specific. This is still current practice although the need for standardized measures has been stressed for years (e.g., Eagle, 1967; McCarver & Craig, 1974). The following are examples of this variety: Moen et al. (1975) classified subjects as unsuccessful if they had been returned to the institution at follow-up. Miller et al. (1975)

did not classify their subjects as successes unless they had remained in the community at least 2 years; for Schalock, Harper, and Carver (1981) the clients could not have moved to a more restrictive setting for 5-plus years. Intagliata, *et al.* (1981a) assessed changes in adaptive behavior. Edgerton and Bercovici (1976) used interviews and clinical judgment, stressing two factors: social competence and independence. Seltzer, Sherwood, Seltzer, and Sherwood (1981) argued that adjustment should be conceptualized as a positive change in multiple behavioral dimensions relative to the individual's own abilities. However, three key factors were identified: behavioral ability, maladaptive behavior, and client satisfaction. McDevitt, Smith, Schmidt, and Rosen (1978) identified four essential areas: vocational, economic, social, and personality. Willer and Intagliata (1981) assessed five key areas (self-care, behavioral control, community living skills, use of community resources, and social support).

Lakin *et al.* (1981b) discussed the problems caused by such a wide diversity of measures. However, they indicated that since the field is still so undeveloped that "all perspectives, with their varying operational definitions of adjustment, should be welcomed" (p. 29). There is merit in this view, although it does complicate the task of synthesizing and comparing the results of various studies. It is for this reason that some reviewers (e.g., Eagle, 1967; McCarver & Craig, 1974) have used an admittedly imperfect criterion—remaining in the community versus returning to the institution—as a baseline or standardized criterion. As Intagliata, Willer, and Wicks (1981b) have noted, this may be more a measure of community tenure than of adjustment. With such reservations in mind, the following analysis of success rates over the last decade is offered.

The majority of the studies have used measures other than institutional recidivism as success criteria. Although these criteria tend to be rather idiosyncratic, the results have suggested, in general, that the clients were adjusting relatively well and were better off than they had been in the institution, especially if the clients themselves were queried. Some examples of miniinstitutions in the community have been reported, and particular placement settings have been described as less normalizing than the institutions from which the clients were placed. Nevertheless, the consensus among researchers appears to be of an improved quality of life in the community for the clients they have been studying.

Perhaps because of the widespread criticism of the measure, relatively few studies conducted within the last decade have even mentioned institutional recidivism rates. Table I illustrates some of the few that have. The median return rate among these studies was 19%. This finding stands in marked contrast to the recidivism rate of almost 50% reported by McCarver and Craig (1974) for the 1960–1970 period of reported studies. This figure is also signif-

TABLE I

RECIDIVISM RATE OF RESIDENTS RELEASED
FROM INSTITUTIONS FOR THE MENTALLY RETARDED

	Number released and located	Number returned to institution	Recidivism rate (%)
Birenbaum and Re (1979)	63	21	33
Willer and Intagliata (1980)	477	168	26
Miller et al. (1975)	158	40	25
Baker et al. (1977)	—[a]	—	22
Sutter et al.	77	17	22
Schalock et al. (1981)	166	26	16
Moen et al. (1975)	85	13	15
Bell et al. (1981)	582	—	14
Gollay et al. (1981)	440	58	13
Aninger and Bolinsky (1977)	19	1	5

[a]—, Not reported.

icantly lower than the failure rate of 40% for the 1960–1970 decade reported by Gibson and Fields (1983). Several questions are raised by this pattern of findings. First, in the majority of studies was the recidivism rate not reported simply because it was not an issue? Or, has a recent commitment to deinstitutionalization with an accompanying increase in community support services truly slowed down the rate of recidivism? Conroy's (1977) results would suggest otherwise. He found that institutional readmissions were increasing at a higher rate than were releases over the 1970–1974 period. However, this may have been a temporary phenomenon associated with the initial push for deinstitutionalization. More recent data (Scheerenberger, 1983) suggest that readmission rates are decreasing. For example, Conroy noted that the number of readmissions represented 34% of the number of releases in 1974; Scheerenberger's (1982) data show 18%. Thus, on the basis of current data, it does appear that a true decrease in recidivism rate has occurred.

V. CONCLUDING REMARKS

Whether institutions will continue to fade away probably depends largely on the resources allocated to community support services. It has been commonly observed that institutions are gradually becoming populated almost entirely with behavior problems, the multiply handicapped, and the very severely retarded, all of which are difficult to serve in the community (e.g., McCarver & Craig, 1974; Scheerenberger, 1976, 1979). Thus, it might be assumed that institutions will always be necessary to serve such specialty groups efficiently and effectively (e.g., Ellis, 1975). A counterargument has been offered by Best-Sigford *et al.* (1982). They note that the "residual population" argument has been presented for decades, and yet the deinstitutionalization process continues, and also point out that 37% of the residents in licensed, nonpublic residential facilities are severely or profoundly retarded. However, Lakin *et al.* (1983) reported that fewer than one half of new admissions to institutions in their sample had serious behavior problems or secondary handicaps, and current data (Scheerenberger, 1983) suggest that the community placement trend is slowing, probably for economic and social (e.g., community and parental opposition) reasons rather than research demonstrating the failure of deinstitutionalization efforts. In fact, the available research indicates that, in the main, the deinstitutionalization movement has been successful in terms of the absolute number of clients released from institutions and the quality of life that released clients have in the community.

Lakin *et al.* (1983) see institutions as providing permanent placements for severely disabled clients for whom community alternatives are not yet generally available, stable alternatives for clients whose placement deteriorates, and transitional backup facilities for community programs. We tend to agree that institutions will remain with us for the forseeable future and predict that they will increasingly be viewed as a complement to the residential alternatives of the mentally retarded population. The concept of the least restrictive residential alternative has firmly taken root in the last decade. However, a significant number of mentally retarded people are still admitted to institutions. We only hope that researchers will continue to provide data that will someday allow decision makers to identify appropriate matches between mentally retarded people and their environments on an empirical basis.

REFERENCES

Aninger, M., & Bolinsky, K. Levels of independent functioning of retarded adults in apartments. *Mental Retardation,* 1977, **15**(4), 12–13.

Baker, B. L., Seltzer, G. B., & Seltzer, M. M. *As close as possible—Community residences for retarded adults.* Boston, Massachusetts: Little, Brown, 1977.

Balla, D. A. Relationship of institution size to quality of care: A review of the literature. *American Journal of Mental Deficiency,* 1976, **81**, 117–124.

Bartnik, E., & Winkler, R. C. Discrepant judgments of community adjustment of mentally retarded adults: The contribution of personal responsibility. *American Journal of Mental Deficiency,* 1981, **86**, 260–266.

Baumeister, A. A., The American residential institution: Its history and character. In A. A. Baumeister & E. C. Butterfield (Eds.), *Residential facilities for the mentally retarded.* Chicago, Illinois: Aldine, 1970.

Begab, M. J. The mentally retarded and society: Trends and issues. In M. J. Begab & S. A. Richardson (Eds.), *The mentally retarded and society: A social science perspective.* Baltimore, Maryland: Univ. Park Press, 1975.

Bell, N. J. IQ as a factor in community lifestyle of previously institutionalized retardates. *Mental Retardation,* 1976, **14**(3), 29–33.

Bell, N. J., Schoenrock, C., & Bensberg, G. Change over time in the community: Findings of a longitudinal study. In R. H. Bruininks, C. E. Meyers, B. B. Sigford, & H. C. Lakin (Eds.), *Deinstitutionalization and community adjustment of mentally retarded people.* Washington, D.C.: American Association on Mental Deficiency, 1981.

Bercovici, S. Qualitative methods and cultural perspectives in the study of deinstitutionalization. In R. H. Bruininks, C. E. Meyers, B. B. Sigford, K. C. Lakin (Eds.), *Deinstitutionalization and community adjustment of mentally retarded people.* Washington, D.C.: American Association on Mental Deficiency, 1981.

Best-Sigford, B., Bruininks, R. H., Lakin, K. C., Hill, B. H., & Heal, L. W. Resident release patterns in a national sample of public residential facilities. *American Journal of Mental Deficiency,* 1982, **87**, 130–142.

Birenbaum, A. The changing lives of mentally retarded adults. In M. J. Begab & S. A. Richardson (Eds.), *The mentally retarded and society: A social science perspective.* Baltimore, Maryland: Univ. Park Press, 1975.

Birenbaum, A., & Re, M. A. Resettling mentally retarded adults in the community—Almost 4 years later. *American Journal of Mental Deficiency,* 1979, **83**, 323–329.

Bjaanes, A. J., Butler, E. W., & Kelly, B. A. Placement type and client functioning level as factors in provision of services aimed at increasing adjustment. In R. H. Bruininks, C. E. Meyers, B. B. Sigford, & K. C. Lakin (Eds.) *Deinstitutionalization and community adjustment of mentally retarded people.* Washington, D.C.: American Association on Mental Deficiency, 1981.

Blatt, B. A drastically different analysis. *Mental Retardation,* 1979, **17**, 303–306.

Blatt, B., & Kaplan, F. *Christmas in purgatory: A photographic essay on mental retardation.* Boston, Massachusetts: Allyn & Bacon, 1966.

Bock, W. H., & Joiner, L. M. From institution to community residence: Behavioral competencies for admission and discharge. *Mental Retardation,* 1983, **20**, 153–158.

Brown, J. S., & Guard, K. A. The treatment environment for retarded persons in nursing homes. *Mental Retardation,* 1979, **17**(2), 77–82.

Bruininks, R. H., Hauber, F. A., & Kudla, M. J. National survey of community residential facilities: A profile of facilities and residents in 1977. *American Journal of Mental Deficiency,* 1980, **84**, 470–478.

Bruininks, R. H., Kudla, M. J., Hauber, F. A., Hill, B. K., & Wieck, C. A. Recent growth and status of community residential facilities. In R. H. Bruininks, C. E. Meyers, B. B. Sigford, & K. C. Lakin (Eds.), *Deinstitutionalization and community adjustment of mentally retarded people.* Washington, D.C.: American Association on Mental Deficiency, 1981.

Bruininks, R. H., Meyers, C. E., Sigford, B. B., & Lakin, K. C. (Eds.), *Deinstitutionalization and community adjustment of mentally retarded people.* Washington, D.C.: American Association on Mental Deficiency, 1981. (b)

Bruininks, R. H., Williams, S., & Morreau, L. *Issues and problems in deinstitutionalization in HEW Region V.* Minneapolis, Minnesota: University of Minnesota, Department of Psychoeducational Studies, 1978.

Campbell, V., Bailey, J., & Phronson, G. Differential characteristics of clients and environments as related to a typology for community residential services. Paper presented at the American Association on Mental Deficiency Annual Meeting, Minneapolis, Minnesota, 1984.

Campbell, V., Smith, A., & Wool, R. Adaptive Behavior Scale differences in scores of mentally retarded individuals referred for institutionalization and those never referred. *American Journal of Mental Deficiency*, 1982, **86**, 425–428.

Close, D. W. Community living for severely and profoundly retarded adults: A group home study. *Education and Training of the Mentally Retarded*, 1977, **12**, 256–262.

Cochran, W., Sran, P. K., & Varano, G. A. The relocation syndrome in mentally retarded individuals. *Mental Retardation*, 1977, **15**(2), 10–12.

Cohen, H., Conroy, J. W., Frazer, D. W., Snelbecker, G. E., & Spreat, S. Behavioral effects of interinstitutional relocation of mentally retarded residents. *American Journal of Mental Deficiency*, 1977, **82**, 12–18.

Cohen, H. G., & Leland, H. The workshop group: A case history of group processes among institutionalized mentally retarded men. *Mental Retardation*, 1977, **15**(6), 45–46.

Conroy, J. W. Trends in deinstitutionalization of the mentally retarded. *Mental Retardation*, 1977, **15**(4), 44–46.

Conroy, J., Efthimiou, J., & Lemanowicz, J. A matched comparison of the developmental growth of institutionalized and deinstitutionalized mentally retarded clients. *American Journal of Mental Deficiency*, 1982, **86**, 581–587.

De Vellis, A. F. Learned helplessness in institutions. *Mental Retardation*, 1977, **15**(5), 10–13.

Doleys, D. M., Stacy, D., & Knowles, S. Modification of grooming behavior in adult retarded. *Behavior Modification*, 1981, **5**, 119–128.

Eagle, E. Prognosis and outcome of community placement of institutionalized retardates. *American Journal of Mental Deficiency*, 1967, **72**, 232–243.

Edgerton, R. B. *The cloak of competence: Stigma in the lives of the mentally retarded*. Berkeley, California: Univ. of California Press, 1967.

Edgerton, R. B. Issues relating to the quality of life among mentally retarded persons. In M. J. Begab & S. A. Richardson (Eds.), *The mentally retarded and society: A social science perspective*. Baltimore, Maryland: Univ. Park Press, 1976.

Edgerton, R. B., & Bercovici, S. M. The cloak of competence: Years later. *American Journal of Mental Deficiency*, 1976, **80**, 485–497.

Ellis, N. R. Issues in mental retardation. *Law and Psychology Review*, 1975, **1**, 9–16.

Ellis, N. R. The Partlow case: A reply to Dr. Roos. *Law and Psychology Review*. 1979, **5**, 15–49.

Eyman, R. K., & Borthwick, S. A. Patterns of care for mentally retarded persons. *Mental Retardation*, 1980, **18**(2), 63–66.

Eyman, R. K., Borthwick, S. A., & Miller, C. Trends in maladaptive behavior of mentally retarded persons placed in community and residential settings. *American Journal of Mental Deficiency*, 1981, **85**, 473–477.

Eyman, R. K., & Call, T. Maladaptive behavior and community placement of mentally retarded persons. *American Journal of Mental Deficiency*, 1977, **82**, 137–144.

Eyman, R. K., Demaine, G. C., & Lei, T. Relationship between community environments and resident changes in adaptive behavior: A path model. *American Journal of Mental Deficiency*, 1979, **83**, 330–338.

Eyman, R. K., Silverstein, A. B., & McClain, R. Effects of treatment program on the acquisition of basic skills. *American Journal of Mental Deficiency*, 1975, **79**, 573–582.

Fernald, W. E. After-care study of the patients discharged from Waverly for a period of twenty-five years. *Ungraded*, 1919, **5**, 25–31.

General Accounting Office (GAO). Report to Congress by the Comptroller General of the United States. *Returning the mentally disabled to the community: Government needs to do more*. Washington, D.C.: Gov. Printing Office, 1977.

Gibson, D., & Fields, D. L. Fifty years of institutional habilitation outcomes: inventory and implications. *Education and Training of the Mentally Retarded*, 1983, **18**, 82–89.

Gollay, E. *A study of the community adjustment of deinstitutionalized mentally retarded persons. Vol. 5: An analysis of factors associated with community adjustment.* Contract No. OEC–074–9183, U.S. Office of Education). Cambridge, Massachusetts: Abt, 1976. (a)

Gollay, E. *A study of the community adjustment of deinstitutionalized mentally retarded persons. Vol. 4: Descriptive data on the community experiences of deinstitutionalized mentally retarded persons.* (Contract No. OEC–0–74–9183. U.S. Office of Education). Cambridge, Massachusetts: Abt, 1976. (b)

Gollay, E. An analysis of variables associated with the community adjustment of deinstitutionalized mentally retarded people. *Dissertation Abstracts International,* 1977, **38,** (1–A), 480. (a)

Gollay, E. Deinstitutionalized mentally retarded people: A closer look. *Education and Training of the Mentally Retarded,* 1977, **12,** 137–144. (b)

Gollay, E. Some conceptual and methodological issues in studying the community adjustment of deinstitutionalized mentally retarded people. In R. H. Bruininks, C. E. Meyers, B. B. Sigford, & K. C. Lakin (Eds.), *Deinstitutionalization and community adjustment of mentally retarded people.* Washington, D.C.: American Association on Mental Deficiency, 1981.

Gollay, E., Freedman, R., Wyngaarden, M., & Kurtz, N. R. *Coming back: The community experiences of deinstitutionalized mentally retarded people.* Cambridge, Massachusetts: Abt, 1978.

Halpern, A. S., Browning, P. L., & Brummer, E. R. Vocational adjustment of the mentally retarded. In M. J. Begab & S. A. Richardson (Eds.), *The mentally retarded and society: A social science perspective.* Baltimore, Maryland: Univ. Park Press, 1975.

Heal, L. W., Sigleman, C. K., & Switzky, H. N. Research on community residential alternatives for the mentally retarded. In N. R. Ellis (Ed.), *International review of research in mental retardation* (Vol. 9). New York: Academic Press, 1978.

Hemming, H., Lavender, T., & Pill, A. Quality of life of mentally retarded adults transferred from large institutions to new small units. *American Journal of Mental Deficiency,* 1981, **86,** 157–169.

Huey, K. Placing the mentally retarded: Where shall they live? *Hospital and Community Psychiatry,* 1978, **29,** 596–602.

Intagliata, J., Crosby, N., & Neider, L. Foster family care for mentally retarded people: A qualitative review. In R. H. Bruininks, C. E. Meyers, B. B. Sigford, & K. C. Lakin (Eds.), *Deinstitutionalization and community adjustment of mentally retarded people.* Washington, D.C.: American Association on Mental Deficiency, 1981. (a)

Intagliata, J., & Willer, B. Reinstitutionalization of mentally retarded persons successfully placed into family-care and group homes. *American Journal of Mental Deficiency,* 1982, **87,** 34–39.

Intagliata, B., Willer, B., & Wicks, N. Factors related to the quality of community adjustment in family care homes. In R. Bruininks, C. E. Meyers, B. Sigford, & K. C. Lakin (Eds.), *Deinstitutionalization and community adjustment of mentally retarded people.* Washington, D.C.: American Association in Mental Deficiency, 1981. (b)

Jacobson, J. W., & Schwartz, A. A. Personal and service characteristics affecting group home placement success: A prospective analysis. *Mental Retardation,* 1983, **21,** 1–7.

Janicki, M. P., Mayeda, T., & Epple, W. A. Availability of group homes for persons with mental retardation in the United States. *Mental Retardation,* 1983, **21,** 45–51.

Johnson, B. F., & Cuvo, A. J. Teaching mentally retarded adults to cook. *Behavior Modification,* 1981, **5,** 187–202.

Lakin, K. C., Bruininks, R. H., & Sigford, B. B. Deinstitutionalization and community adjustment: A summary of research and issues. In R. H. Bruininks, C. E. Meyers, B. B. Sigford,

& K. C. Lakin (Eds.), *Deinstitutionalization and community adjustment of mentally retarded people.* Washington, D.C.: American Association on Mental Deficiency, 1981. (a)

Lakin, K. C., Bruininks, R. H., & Sigford, B. B. Early perspectives on the community adjustment of mentally retarded people. In R. H. Bruininks, C. E. Meyers, B. B. Sigford, & K. C. Lakin (Eds.), *Deinstitutionalization and community adjustment of mentally retarded people.* Washington, D.C.: American Association on Mental Deficiency, 1981. (b)

Lakin, K. C., Hill, B. K., Hauber, F. A., & Bruininks, R. H. Changes in age at first admission to residential care for mentally retarded people. *Mental Retardation,* 1982, **20**(5), 216–219.

Lakin, K. C., Hill, B. K., Hauber, F. A., Bruininks, R. H., & Heal, L. W. New admissions and readmissions to a national sample of public residential facilities. *American Journal of Mental Deficiency,* 1983, **88**, 13–20.

Landesman-Dwyer, S. Living in the community. *American Journal of Mental Deficiency,* 1981, **86**, 223–234.

Landesman-Dwyer, S., Sackett, G. P., & Kleinman, J. S. Relationship of size to resident and staff behavior in small community residences. *American Journal of Mental Deficiency,* 1980, **85**, 6–17.

Latham, L., Campbell, V., Bailey, J., Sanders, N., & Teare, J. *Progress Report: Continuum of Services Project University of Alabama and Department of Mental Health.* Unpublished manuscript, February, 1982.

Lubin, R. A., Schwartz, A. A., Zigman, W. B., & Janicki, M. P. Community acceptance of residential programs for developmentally disabled persons. *Applied Research in Mental Retardation,* 1982, **3**, 191–200.

Matson, J. L. Use of independence training to teach shopping skills to mildly mentally retarded adults. *American Journal of Mental Deficiency,* 1981, **86**, 178–183.

McCarver, R. B., & Cavalier, A. R. Philosophical concepts and attitudes underlying programming for the mentally retarded. In J. L. Matson & F. Andrasik (Eds.), *Treatment issues and innovations in mental retardation.* New York: Plenum, 1983.

McCarver, R. B., & Craig, E. M. Placement of the retarded in the community: Prognosis and outcome. In N. R. Ellis (Ed.), *International review of research in mental retardation* (Vol. 7). New York: Academic Press, 1974.

McDevitt, S. C., Smith, P. M., Schmidt, D. W., & Rosen, M. The deinstitutionalized citizen: Adjustment and quality of life. *Mental Retardation,* 1978, **16**(1), 22–24.

Miller, S. I., Miller, P., Kim, M., Kutz, N., Lozier, J., & Misenheimer, B. Foster home adjustment of retardates. *The Indian Journal of Social Work,* 1975, **36**, 145–154.

Moen, M., Bogen, D., & Aanes, D. Follow-up of mentally retarded adults successfully placed in community group homes. *Hospital and Community Psychiatry,* 1975, **26**, 754–756.

Mullins, D., & Hays, J. R. Personality characteristics and employability of mentally retarded adults. *Psychological Reports,* 1980, **47**, 1063–1067.

National Association of State Mental Retardation Program Directors, Inc. *New Directions,* 1982, **12**. (a)

National Association of State Mental Retardation Program Directors, Inc. *Capital Capsule,* 1982, **July**. (b)

O'Neill, M. J. Factors associated with subsequent home adjustment of formerly institutionalized educable mentally retarded children and adolescents. *Dissertation Abstracts International,* 1977, **38**(3–A), 1331.

Roos, P. Custodial care for the "subtrainable"—Revisiting an old myth. *Law and Psychology Review,* 1979, **5**, 1–14.

Roos, S. The future of residential services for the mentally retarded in the United States: A delphi study. *Mental Retardation,* 1978, **16**(5), 355–356.

Rosen, M., Clark, G., & Kivitz, M. S. *Habilitation of the handicapped: New dimensions in programs for the developmentally disabled.* Baltimore, Maryland: Univ. Park Press, 1977.

Rosen, M., Floor, L., & Baxter, D. I.Q., academic achievement and community adjustment after discharge from the institution. *Mental Retardation,* 1974, **12**(2), 51–53.

Sanderson, H. W., & Crawley, M. Characteristics of successful family-care parents. *American Journal of Mental Deficiency,* 1982, **86**, 519–525.

Sandler, A., & Thurman, K. S. Status of community placement research. *Education and Training of the Mentally Retarded,* 1981, **16**, 245–251.

Scanlon, C. A., Arick, J. R., & Krug, D. A. A matched sample investigation of nonadaptive behavior of severely handicapped adults across four living situations. *American Journal of Mental Deficiency,* 1982, **86**, 526–532.

Schalock, R. L., & Harper, R. S. A systems approach to community living skills training. In R. H. Bruininks, C. E. Meyers, B. B. Sigford, & K. C. Lakin (Eds.), *Deinstitutionalization and community adjustment of mentally retarded people.* Washington, D.C.: American Association on Mental Deficiency, 1981.

Schalock, R. L., Harper, R. S., & Carver, G. Independent living placement: Five years later. *American Journal of Mental Deficiency,* 1981, **86**, 170–177.

Schalock, R. L., Harper, R. S., & Genung, T. Community placement and program success. *American Journal of Mental Deficiency,* 1981, **85**, 478–488.

Scheerenberger, R. C. A study of public residential facilities. *Mental Retardation,* 1976, **14**, 32–35.

Scheerenberger, R. C. *Public residential facilities for the mentally retarded.* National Association of Superintendents of Public Residential Facilities for the Mentally Retarded, 1979.

Scheerenberger, R. C. Deinstitutionalization: Trends and difficulties. In R. H. Bruininks, C. E. Meyers, B. B. Sigford, & K. C. Lakin (Eds.), *Deinstitutionalization and community adjustment of mentally retarded people.* Washington, D.C.: American Association on Mental Deficiency, 1981.

Scheerenberger, R. C. Public residential services, 1981: Status and trends. *Mental Retardation,* 1982, **20**(5), 210–215.

Scheerenberger, R. C. *Public residential services for the mentally retarded, 1982.* National Association of Superintendents of Public Residential Facilities for the Mentally Retarded, 1983.

Schroeder, S. R., & Henes, C. Assessment of progress of institutionalized and deinstitutionalized retarded adults: A matched-control comparison. *Mental Retardation,* 1978, **16**(2), 147–148.

Seltzer, M. M., Seltzer, G. B., & Sherwood, C. C. Comparison of community adjustment of older vs. younger mentally retarded adults. *American Journal of Mental Deficiency,* 1982, **87**, 9–13.

Seltzer, M. M., Sherwood, C. C., Seltzer, G. B., & Sherwood, S. Community adaptation and the impact of deinstitutionalization. In R. H. Bruininks, C. E. Meyers, B. B. Sigford, & K. C. Lakin (Eds.), *Deinstitutionalization and community adjustment of mentally retarded people.* Washington, D.C.: American Association on Mental Deficiency, 1981.

Sloan, W., & Stevens, H. A. *A history of the American Association on Mental Deficiency, 1975–1976.* Washington, D.C.: American Association on Mental Deficiency, 1976.

Spencer, D. A. New long-stay patients in a hospital for mental handicap. *British Journal of Psychiatry,* 1976, **128**, 467–470.

Stacy, D., Doleys, D. M., & Malcolm, R. Effects of social-skills training in a community-based program. *American Journal of Mental Deficiency,* 1979, **84**, 152–158.

Sutter, P. Environmental variables related to community placement failure in mentally retarded adults. *Mental Retardation,* 1980, **18**(4), 189–191.

Sutter, P., Mayeda, T., Call, T., Yanagi, G., & Yee, S. Comparison of successful and unsuccessful community-placed mentally retarded persons. *American Journal of Mental Deficiency,* 1980, **85,** 262–267.

Sutter, P., Mayeda, T., Yee, S., & Yanagi, G. Community placement success based on client behavior preferences of careproviders. *Mental Retardation,* 1981, **19**(3), 117–120.

Thiel, G. W. Relationship of I.Q., adaptive behavior, age, and environmental demand to community-placement success of mentally retarded adults. *American Journal of Mental Deficiency,* 1981, **86,** 208–211.

Weinstock, A., Wulkan, P., Colon, C. J., Coleman, J., & Goncalves, S. Stress inoculation and interinstitutional transfer of mentally retarded individuals. *American Journal of Mental Deficiency,* 1979, **83,** 385–390.

Weitz, S. E., & Roll, D. L. Survival skills for community-bound retarded youths. *Journal of Clinical Child Psychology,* 1977, **6,** 41–44.

Willer, B., & Intagliata, J. *Deinstitutionalization of mentally retarded persons in New York State (Final Report).* New York: Office of Human Development, U.S. Department of Health and Human Service, Region II, 1980.

Willer, B., & Intagliata, J. Social-environmental factors as predictors of adjustment of deinstitutionalized mentally retarded adults. *American Journal of Mental Deficiency,* 1981, **86,** 252–259.

Willer, B., & Intagliata, J. Comparison of family-care and group homes as alternatives to institutions. *American Journal of Mental Deficiency,* 1982, **86,** 588–595.

Willer, B., Intagliata, J., & Wicks, N. Return of retarded adults to natural families: Issues and results. In R. H. Bruininks, C. E. Meyers, B. B. Sigford, & K. C. Lakin (Eds.), *Deinstitutionalization and community adjustment of mentally retarded people.* Washington, D.C.: American Association on Mental Deficiency, 1981.

Windle, C. Prognosis of mental subnormals. *American Journal of Mental Deficiency,* 1962, **66,** (Monogr. Suppl.).

Wolf, L. C., & Whitehead, P. C. The decisions to institutionalize retarded children: Comparison of individually matched groups. *Mental Retardation,* 1975, **13**(5), 3–7.

Wolfensberger, W. Will there always be an institution? II: The impact of new service models: Residential alternatives to institutions. *Mental Retardation,* 1971, **9**(6), 31–38.

Wolfensberger, W. The definition of normalization: Update, problems, disagreements, and misunderstanding. In R. J. Flynn & K. E. Nitsch, (Eds.), *Normalization, social integration, and community services.* Baltimore, Maryland: Univ. Park Press, 1980.

Issues in Adjustment
of Mentally Retarded
Individuals to Residential Relocation

TAMAR HELLER

INSTITUTE FOR THE STUDY OF DEVELOPMENTAL DISABILITIES
UNIVERSITY OF ILLINOIS AT CHICAGO
CHICAGO, ILLINOIS

I. INTRODUCTION

Residential relocation has become a likely prospect for many mentally retarded people. Since the late 1960s, tens of thousands of mentally retarded people have been moved from large state institutions into smaller institutions or community-based facilities. The population in state institutions for the developmentally disabled has dropped from about 200,000 in 1967 to 125,000 in 1981 (Braddock, 1981). In a 1979 survey of 172 public residential facilities, 9% of the residents were transferred to similarly restrictive facilities and 62% to less restrictive facilities (Scheerenberger, 1981). In

INTERNATIONAL REVIEW OF RESEARCH IN
MENTAL RETARDATION, Vol. 12

many states, institutions for mentally retarded people have been closed or are in the process of closing.

This article reviews the literature and examines the major issues and concerns related to residential relocation of mentally retarded people. It includes relocations (1) from one institution into another, (2) from one unit of an institution to another within the same institution, (3) from an institution into a community-based facility, and (4) from one community facility into another. The following questions are addressed: Does relocation result in "transfer trauma" to the retarded individual? Which individuals are most likely to react adversely to relocation? What features of the old and new environments affect the subsequent adjustment to relocation? How can the relocation process be managed to mitigate stressful reactions?

II. EFFECTS OF RELOCATION

For mentally retarded residents, residential relocation is frequently involuntary and results in unexpected changes in physical surroundings, social relationships, vocational and educational programming, leisure activities, expectations, and basic daily functions. These disruptions in daily living and social patterns require major readjustments which may be stressful. Some theorists (Fried, 1963; Parkes, 1972) have made an explicit comparison between reactions to loss of loved ones or body parts and reactions to involuntary residential relocation. They note that such moves are often accompanied by symptoms of grief, "feeling of painful loss, continued longing, general depressive tone, frequent symptoms of psychological, social and somatic distress, sense of helplessness, occasional direct and displaced anger, and a tendency to idealize the lost place" (Fried, 1963, p. 151).

On the other hand, relocation to a new environment may have positive effects by facilitating changes in individual social and intellectual functioning and eventual integration into the community. Kelly (1968) has theorized that experience in a fluid environment provides more exposure to diversity and enhances adaptation to complex and changing future environments. Other potential benefits of residential relocation are that it may provide opportunity for better programming and staff, better housing, or more pleasant physical surroundings.

Many researchers have sought to determine the degree of stress ("transfer trauma") incurred as a result of institutional relocation, by studying individual adjustment following relocation. Indicators of the effects of stress have included mortality rates and changes in physical health, affect, and behavior.

A. Mortality

The most dramatic relocation effects reported have been increases in mortality rates for institutionalized elderly (Aldrich & Mendkoff, 1963; Aleksandrowicz, 1961; Bourestom & Tars, 1974; Jasnau, 1967; Killian, 1970; Markus, Blenkner, Bloom, & Downs, 1971; Marlowe, 1974; Shahinian, Goldfarb, & Turner, 1966). These findings have been frequently cited and used to resist many types of institutional transfers. However, even for the nonretarded elderly population several recent studies found either no increases or even decreases in mortality after transfers (Borup, Gallego, & Heffernan, 1979; Coffman, 1981; Kowalski, 1978; Miller & Lieberman, 1965; Novick, 1967; Watson & Buerkle, 1976; Zweig & Csank, 1975).

A major weakness of many of these mortality studies is the use of a baseline design, in which the death rates of groups in previous years or months are used as the baseline. The validity of this design depends on the comparability of the baseline groups with the relocated groups. For instance, changes in nursing homes' admission and release policies and services have changed the composition of nursing home populations from year to year. This casts some doubt on the similarities of resident characteristics and of incidence of mortality between the past and recent groups. Results of geriatric studies which did use the control group design are about equally divided between those finding increases in mortality (Bourestom & Tars, 1974; Killian, 1970; Marlowe, 1974) and those finding no significant changes in mortality (Borup *et al.*, 1979; Markson & Cumming, 1974).

Generally the studies of relocated mentally retarded people have not found any significant increases in death rate associated with relocation. The one exception is Miller's (1975) study of 342 profoundly retarded residents who were transferred from Pacific State Hospital to convalescent hospitals in California. In that study the mortality rate doubled after the transfer (4 versus 2%). Heller's (1982a) study of 50 multiply handicapped retarded children found no mortalities up to 6 months after a transfer but did note an increase in mortality rate for the more medically fragile residents. Three of these children died within a month of the move; throughout the previous year only two children had died in either of the two previous facilities from which they had transferred. Changes in mortality rate following relocation could be a serious problem; however, increased mortality rates following transfers have not been well documented.

B. Physical Health

The view that separation from familiar surroundings, objects, or people can precipitate the onset of disease has received some support in the medical literature (Engel, 1968; Schmale, 1958). Separation is often associated with feelings of helplessness and despair and concomitant medical symptoms. Increases in restriction of activity, hospitalization, health failure (Miller & Lieberman, 1965), and plasma cortisol (Kral, Grad, & Berenson, 1968) have been reported following relocation of elderly nursing home residents. Among mentally retarded residents, the one study that examined physical health (Heller, 1982a) found increases in medical symptoms (frequency of sick days) up to 3 months after a transfer from two community facilities into a new one.

C. Affect and Behavior

The most common symptoms of reported stress reactions to relocation are emotional, behavioral, and mental health changes. These effects have included pessimism, decreased social activity (Bourestom & Tars, 1974), deleterious changes in mental health, self-care and social capacities (Marlowe, 1973), and increases in confusion, memory deficits, and bizarre behavior (Miller & Lieberman, 1965) of geriatric residents. Other effects are short-term decrements in behavioral functioning of mentally ill residents (Lentz & Paul, 1971).

Several studies have reported no significant changes in psychiatric symptomology, adjustment, and life satisfaction subsequent to relocation of chronic mental patients (Barrington, Burke, & Lafave, 1962; Smith, Oswald, & Farucki, 1976). In fact, in some cases mental patients seem to actually benefit from relocation from one building of an institution (DeVries, 1968; Higgs, 1964) or ward (DiScipio & Wolf, 1974) to another.

Most studies of transferred mentally retarded residents have reported decrements in some positive behaviors, at least on a short-term basis. Cohen, Conroy, Fraser, Snelbecker, and Spreat (1977) found that 6 to 8 weeks after relocation from Pennhurst State School to Woodhaven Center, the intermediate care residents (mostly severely retarded) exhibited lower language development and greater withdrawal [as measured by the Adaptive Behavior Scale (ABS)] than that exhibited prior to the move. The skilled nursing (profoundly retarded) group, however, exhibited increases in maladaptive behavior as well as in adaptive behavior. Studies of facility closures (Heller, 1982a) and of intrainstitutional transfers (Carsrud, Carsrud, Henderson, Alisch, & Fowler, 1979) found short-term decreases in observed constructive activity and social interaction behaviors of multiply handicapped residents after the transfers. Similarly, in an intrainstitutional relocation (Schumacher, Wisland, & Qvammen, 1983), residents grouped for behavioral problems exhibited increased social isolation within 5 months after the transfer. Hemming, Lavender, and Pill (1981) investigated relocation effects on severely and profoundly retarded residents moved from large institutions in Wales to smaller new units. They found greater short-term (within 4 months) increases in maladaptive behavior (on the ABS Part II) and in prescriptions of antipsychotic drugs among the transferees than among a matched control group.

In a discussion of "transition shock," Coffman and Harris (1980), state that among nonretarded people, the key emotional reactions to transition difficulties are depression, anxiety, hostility, and nostalgia. They suggest that mentally retarded people are just as likely to experience these emotions, but that these symptoms are often inadequately recognized in them. Cochran, Sran, and Varano (1977) observed what they termed a "relocation syndrome" in which a few recently relocated mentally retarded adults became profoundly depressed, refused to eat, lost weight, and slept a great deal. One of these residents died shortly after the onset of depression. However, a large number of other individuals of the same age and overall mental functioning (largely moderately to profoundly retarded) were relocated during the same period without encountering extreme depression. One study of a voluntary relocation of mentally retarded residents from a large institution into a smaller facility found no adverse posttransfer effects (Weinstock, Wulkan, Colon, Coleman, & Goncalves, 1979).

Longer term positive effects of transfers, particularly from institutions into more community-based facilities, can outweigh the shorter term setbacks. Benefits in the areas of self-help, socialization, and communication have been widely documented in studies of community placements (e.g., Aanes & Moen, 1976; Close, 1977; Conroy, Efthimiou, & Lemanowicz, 1982).

One methodological problem common to relocation studies is the lack of appropriate control groups, since selection bias commonly occurs in determining placements of residents. Despite attempts to match on key characteristics, the control and experimental groups may differ on other important dimensions, such as physical attractiveness or behavioral repertoire. When large transfers occur out of an institution, the groups who remain, the controls, may actually undergo considerable changes as the population of the institution dwindles. Landesman-Dwyer's (1982) study, which used stratified, random assignment of residents to different programs, found that within 3 months both the transferred residents and those remaining in the old units exhibited increased stereotypic behaviors.

Another problem is the subjectivity of the behavioral ratings, which are usually done by staff members. When both the ratings before and after the move are done by the same staff, characteristics of the residents may be perceived as more stable than when they are done by different staff members. Also, whether the same or different staff members do the ratings or not, their expectations and evaluations of the relocated residents may differ in a new context. Although the behavioral functioning of a resident may be stable, it may be evaluated more negatively after the move if the residents of the new unit are higher functioning than those in the old unit. Also, in less restrictive settings, more negative ratings may reflect less tolerance for certain behaviors tolerated in the institution. Staff biases have been avoided in studies also using behavioral observations (Carsrud *et al.*, 1979; Heller, 1982a; Schumacher *et al.*, 1983) and medical records before and after the move (Heller, 1982a; Hemming *et al.*, 1981).

Among the studies utilizing behavioral observations, the most consistent findings were increases in social withdrawal (Carsrud *et al.*, 1979; Heller, 1982a; Schumacher *et al.*, 1983) and decreases in constructive behavior shortly after relocation (Carsrud *et al.*, 1979; Heller, 1982a). Although the two studies which investigated the medical records suggest that sick days (Heller, 1982a) and antipsychotic drug treatments (Hemming *et al.*, 1981) increase after residential transfer, the medical aspects need to be further tested in other studies.

This article indicates that residential transfer can result in physical and behavioral stress reactions, but that these effects are not consistent across different groups and settings. In order to understand the determinants of stressful or even positive reactions, it is necessary to examine the (1) individual characteristics of the residents, (2) the relocation process itself, and (3) the environmental characteristics of the sending and receiving facilities.

The sections that follow are divided into three parts. The first deals with the individual characteristics of transferred residents and attempts to identify groups which may be at risk for adverse reactions. The second section focuses on the relocation process itself. It discusses (1) the residents' reactions to relocation at different points in time, (2) the effect that preparations before the move have on the residents' cognitions, and (3) the effects of social disruption and social support from staff, peers, and family during relocation. The last section reviews the impact of the physical, social, and programmatic attributes of the receiving facilities on the transferred residents. It also discusses the joint influence of personal characteristics and setting characteristics on transferees' adaptation to new environments.

III. FACTORS INFLUENCING ADJUSTMENT TO RELOCATION

A. Individual Characteristics

Traditional stress theories attribute differential reactions to environmental change to individuals' personal characteristics. Psychoanalytic approaches tend to view reactions to these changes in terms of defense mechanisms that allow the individual to maintain psychological equilibrium. More recent approaches also consider individual competencies, resources, behavior patterns, motivation, attitudes, and values (Mechanic, 1974). Lazarus (1966) has hypothesized that environmental change is perceived as more stressful and has more drastic consequences for people with few available resources and supports (intelligence, education, finances, relatives, friends) and poorly differentiated or maladaptive coping mechanisms. From this perspective, one might expect relocation to have a particularly strong impact on more severely mentally and physically handicapped populations.

Several relocation studies of institutionalized populations have investigated the effects of the residents' initial physical health on subsequent adjustment. There is some evidence that among elderly residents relocation has the worst impact on those who are already in the poorest physical health (Goldfarb, Shahinian, & Burr, 1972; Killian, 1970; Marlowe, 1973) or suffer from severe brain syndrome (Aleksandrowicz, 1961).

One study of mentally retarded children (Heller, 1982a) found that following relocation the frequency of sick days increased more dramatically for the initially less healthy children than for the healthier ones. Also, the mortality rate only increased for the other more fragile relocated children who were not included in the study. One explanation is that the actual physical act of the movement (i.e., packing bags, traveling on buses, and climbing stairs) is more traumatic for the ailing person. Another is that the ailing person uses all his/her coping resources to deal with the disease and has little additional energy for moving.

The effect of intellectual functioning on relocation adjustment is not clear since there have been contradictory findings. The Cohen *et al.* (1977) study indicated that severely retarded residents became withdrawn and had decreased language functioning after the move, while the lower functioning profoundly retarded ones showed gains in domestic activity, self-direction, and responsibility as well as increases in maladaptive behaviors (antisocial, rebellious, and steroetyped). On the other hand, in the Carsrud *et al.* (1979) study profoundly mentally retarded residents decreased their activity levels after relocation. The Hemming *et al.* (1981) study found that higher functioning residents (IQ over 50) showed increases in language development and lower functioning ones (IQ less than 50) exhibited more withdrawal and maladaptive behavior.

In studies of nonretarded people, older people tend to be particularly vulnerable to the adverse effects of relocation. Neugarten (1968) has noted that with increased age there is less energy available for maintaining involvement with the outside world and a greater tendency to avoid rather than embrace change. The influence of age on adaptation to relocation has been rarely studied among mentally retarded people. In Landesman-Dwyer's

(1982) study older residents did not differ from younger residents in their reactions to transfers, with the exception of demonstrating a greater increase in sleeping behaviors.

Although some data support the contention that personal characteristics influence the impact of relocation on individuals, it is not clear which characteristics are the critical ones or how much influence they actually have. The most consistent finding has been that poor physical health is related to low relocation adjustment.

B.   Factors Inherent in the Relocation Process

1. TIME FACTORS

Several studies with mentally ill and mentally retarded residents have shown that the impact of relocation is strongest in the first few weeks after relocation. Higgs (1964) and DeVries (1968) both found that the significant gains in behavioral functioning made by mental patients 3 to 4 weeks after the move were not maintained 6 to 9 weeks after the move. Lentz and Paul (1971) found deleterious postmove effects among mental patients 4 weeks after, but not 22 weeks after relocation.

In the Cohen *et al.* (1977) study of mentally retarded residents, only 2 of the 10 ABS (Part I) domains, Language and Numbers and Time, continued to decrease from the 0 to 2 to the 6 to 8 weeks' period. Overall adaptive behavior scores only reached the premove levels 6 months after the transfer. In contrast with Cohen's results, both Hemming *et al.* (1981) and Heller (1982a) found increases in adaptive behavior after the transfer. Hemming *et al.*, who conducted 4-month, 9-month, and 2-year follow-ups, reported that the transferees had higher scores on the ABS than the controls in the first year (only significantly higher at 9 months), but that the improvement was not sustained the second year. On Part II of the ABS, an initial increase in maladaptive behavior at 4 months returned to baseline 9 months after the transfer. Heller found that scores on the Fairview Development scale (Giampiccolo & Boroskin, 1974) generally increased from the premove to the 6-week and 3-month follow-up times (an average increase of 3 months in developmental level over the 6 months).

Using observational methods, Heller (1982a) and Carsrud *et al.* (1979) found at least short-term decreases in constructive and social behaviors at 0 to 3 weeks and 0 to 6 weeks, respectively. However, in Heller's study the behavioral effects seemed to be short-lived; by 4 to 6 weeks most of the behaviors that deteriorated immediately after the move returned to the previous levels. By the 3-month follow-up, positive behavioral gains were generally maintained.

The physical effects seem to be maintained over longer periods of time. In

Heller's study, by 3 months after the transfer, the behavioral effects were no longer significant, while the number of sick days still remained higher than before the move. In a longer term study, Hemming *et al.* (1981) found that for the transferred residents increases in antipsychotic drug prescriptions were significant at the 9-month and 1-year follow-up, while increases in sedation prescriptions were significant at the 4-month follow-up. Two years after the transfer the drug prescriptions returned to the level before the move.

Relocation effects cannot be studied without examining the adaptation process longitudinally. The studies reviewed here suggest that most of the behavioral effects are very short-term; whereas the physical effects can last up to a year after the transfer. Changes in residents' functioning over time may also occur during the anticipatory phases before the move, particularly when there are also changes in staff behaviors. In the Carsrud *et al.* (1979) study, the decreases in positive behaviors after the transfer, in comparison with the 6-month premove baseline measures, were also evident immediately prior to the transfer. This finding emphasizes the importance of obtaining not only short- and longer term posttransfer measures, but also baseline measures obtained before the move prior to and after the transfer announcement. Also, the use of measures taken at two points in time prior to the move will help control for statistical regression effects. Unfortunately, opportunities for obtaining such baseline measures are rare, as researchers are usually not aware of large transfers until they are announced.

2. COGNITIONS ABOUT THE TRANSFER

Lazarus (1966) has emphasized the role of an individual's expectations and subjective evaluations of situations. The assumption is that an individual's ability to cope with a stressful experience such as relocation is more dependent on cognitive evaluations and expectations than on stable coping traits. Stressful events are those that are perceived as highly unfamiliar, ambiguous, and unanticipated. Other stressors are events that are viewed as a loss or that impede one's needs, goals, and aspirations (Marris, 1974). Anticipatory coping can mitigate unfavorable reactions to such events (Mechanic, 1974). For instance, ambiguity can be reduced by obtaining realistic information and participating in decisions about a new situation prior to its occurrence. Seligman's (1975) theory of learned helplessness has emphasized the role of perceived controllability in reducing stress.

There is some evidence that relocation adjustment depends on the degree to which residents are "psychologically prepared" for the change. Several geriatric institutional relocation programs which did not find adverse transfer effects provided supportive services, preparatory counseling, site visits, and realistic information about the new setting (Bourestom, Tars, &

Pastalan, 1973; Jasnau, 1967; Novick, 1967; Zweig & Csank, 1975). In the Novick (1967) study, staff members prepared residents by taking them on frequent bus trips to the new site and by constructing a full-sized model of the future bedroom and furniture. Lentz and Paul (1971) found that mental patients who received a preparatory program did not show relocation behavioral decrements while other patients did. Preparatory programs may serve to increase predictability and anticipatory coping.

Attitudes toward transfer might also depend on the degree that the desires of residents and their families are taken into account in the planning process. Occasionally residents can be involved in some aspect of the decision-making process. In one successful geriatric relocation project (Novick, 1967), residents decided what type of bedroom fixtures, windows, and doors they desired. However, another study (DeVries, 1968) did not find significant differences in relocation adjustment between mentally ill residents who gave their input in room and roommate assignments and those who did not.

In the one study of mentally retarded residents that used a transfer preparatory program, Weinstock *et al.* (1979) found no adverse adapative behavior or mortality effects. Unlike many of the other studies reported, the transfer was voluntary; residents' families were involved in the transfer decision and those residents who could discriminate the two environments were given voluntary choice with a visit to the new facility. Preparation for the move included notifying the residents of the date of transfer, giving them physical checkups, new clothes, explanations of the future transfer, information about their belongings, and opportunities to meet the new staff.

This study's findings may have limited applicability to the relocations occurring out of the large state institutions today, which involve many profoundly retarded residents with sensory handicaps. Involvement in the transfer process and decisions, visits to the new sites, and explanations may not benefit residents who are not able to understand these activities. Other aspects, such as family involvement and visits by the new staff, may have greater impact on these residents.

3. SOCIAL DISRUPTION AND SUPPORT

Social networks can potentially provide support when an individual experiences stress or other threats to normal adjustment (Gottlieb, 1981). Among nondisabled people this support has been associated with increased ability to recover from illness (DiMatteo & Hays, 1981), the loss of a spouse (Hinkle, 1974), and unemployment (Gore, 1978). Hence, one might expect that the major support systems of mentally retarded residents would also moderate the personal impact of relocation.

Residential transfers frequently involve not only a change in physical settings, but also social disruption entailing new resident groupings, new staff, and changes in family involvement. In a study of elderly people, Wells and McDonald (1981) report a substantial 31% reduction in number of close friendships among residents several months after transfers. Such disruption in social networks probably reduces the predictability and familiarity of new settings, and hence increases the adjustive demands on transferees. Coffman and Harris (1980) note that a person moving out of the institution to which he is accustomed encounters "missing cues": "The accustomed faces, voices, roles, and habits of staff members and other residents; all are lacking and unavailable either as guides to behavior or as implicit assurances that all is well and one is at home" (p. 4).

Relocations of elderly residents appear to be more successful when residents' relationships with staff, peers, family, and familiar belongings are retained (Bourestom & Tars, 1974; Novick, 1967). Bourestom and Tars (1974) found a higher mortality rate for residents who experienced radical environmental change, which included a move to a new physical environment with new staff, programs, and a new patient population, than for those who experienced minimal change involving only a move to a new building nearby, without any changes in staff, patient groups, or programs. Following the move the patients in the radical group were more likely to report pessimism about their physical health and to demonstrate a decrease in positive social activities and an increase in inappropriate behavior.

Although many mentally retarded people have extensive sensory and neuromuscular deficits and may not perceive the environment the same way as nonretarded individuals, there is evidence that their behavior is also affected by social environmental change (Hollis, 1965; Landesman-Dwyer, 1974). Goshgarian (1968) has shown that even profoundly retarded, nonambulatory children can recognize and prefer familiar people and places. Heller (1982a) investigated the effect of social disruption on mentally retarded children by randomly assigning children to a high or low social disruption group 3 weeks after relocation into a new facility. The low-disruption group retained most of the same daytime staff and programming, while the high-disruption group was cared for by totally different daytime staff and was integrated into daytime programs with new classmates. The high-disruption group demonstrated greater increases in abnormal behavior than did the other children during the first 3 weeks that the classroom changes were instituted. A limitation of Heller's study is that new programming, staff, and differential program quality were confounded, making it difficult to distinguish whether the behavioral change was caused by social disruption or by qualitative changes in programming.

Coffman's (1981) metanalysis of the elderly relocation studies of mortality provides further evidence for the important role of the social disruption variable in the adjustment of transferred residents. The metanalysis was conducted to determine what differentiated the elderly studies that found increases in posttransfer mortality rates from those that did not. The major difference was that the low-mortality relocations involved "intact" populations, in which a whole institution or ward population was moved, or in which individuals were moved from one stable population to another; whereas the high-mortality relocations involved a "disrupted" population, in which an institution was closed down or its members were redistributed.

The author attributed the increase in mortality for the "disrupted" group to a serious deterioration in the support system for these highly dependent persons. For these groups (Aldrich & Mendkoff, 1963; Bourestom & Tars, 1974; Killian, 1970) the transfer process involved long periods of high anxiety, tension, uncertainty, and confusion among patients and staff alike concerning their immediate and long-term futures. As in facilities for the elderly, in institutions for mentally retarded people the decision to close often becomes known by rumor, leading to apprehensiveness, considerable intrainstitutional transfers as buildings gradually close down, funding crises, litigations by families or employees, shifting deadlines for shutdown, and last-minute postponements that add to the confusion, anxiety, and poor morale of both the residents and the staff.

Coffman suggests that all relocations involve both disintegrative and integrative processes and that the ratio of these two processes is important. When the loss of support is faster and greater than replacement, the predominant process is disintegrative and potentially quite harmful. When replacement support is promptly and abundantly available, the overall process is integrative and potentially beneficial.

Since support systems seem to play an important role during transition periods, it is necessary to determine the characteristics of the residents' relationships with their staff, families, and friends. Undoubtedly, institutional closures and reductions in staff affect the morale and performance of staff, particularly those facing unemployment or transfer to other facilities. They are likely to withdraw from their previous attachments to the residents and the facility as they anticipate the transfer.

Experimental studies have repeatedly demonstrated that staff members' behaviors can be a powerful influence on residents (e.g., Schinke & Landesman-Dwyer, 1981). A survey conducted with former employees of a large state hospital for mentally ill patients (Cleveland State) after its closure, indicated that the vast majority (79%) felt that the staff exhibited loss of interest and initiative, and 29% felt that the patients received poorer care after the closure announcement (Schultz, Lyons, & Nothnagel, 1975). At the receiving facilities staff members may be inexperienced (e.g., Hemming *et al.*, 1981) and unaccustomed to working with the type of population coming from the institution, which most likely includes severely and profoundly retarded residents with behavioral or medical problems.

Families of residents facing transfers may be able to offer some support and continuity to the residents during relocation. Many family members have been quite vocal in expressing their resistance to transfers, particularly from the institution to the community (e.g., Conroy & Latib, 1982). This opposition largely centers around perceptions that the large institutions provide better care, more experienced staff, and greater stability for their relatives than would other smaller or community-based facilities (Payne, 1976; Vitello & Atthowe, 1982). Interestingly, several studies have noted that families' views dramatically change after the transfers, with very few reporting negative feelings about the placement outcome for their relatives (Conroy & Latib, 1982; Landesman-Dwyer, 1981; Vitello & Atthowe, 1982).

Few studies have investigated the effects of the pretransfer proceedings and the transfer itself on the actual behavior of the families. Do families visit more frequently or become more involved with their retarded relative after the transfer announcements or after the change in placement? What impact does continuity of family support have on the residents' adjustment to relocation? Although one might expect an increase in family visits after residents are moved into facilities closer to their families, Conroy and Latib (1982) found no such increase in family visits upon deinstitutionalization.

An important source of support for the relocated residents is their peers. There is considerable evidence that peer relationships play a critical role in the successful adjustment of mentally retarded adults in community settings (Romer & Heller, 1983). Heller and Berkson (1982) studied a residential relocation in which administrators were sensitive to the potential disruption of peer friendships following a facility closure. Residents were interviewed about their friendship choices and many were moved with their chosen friends or spouses. The findings were that stable friendships were associated with better posttransfer adjustment. Two and a half years after the transfer, residents moving with chosen friends tended to be rated as more sociable, more independent in self-care, and more likely to move into less restrictive settings than those who were separated from friends or those who did not express friendship choices before the move. Gollay, Freedman, Wyngaarden, and Kurtz (1978) reported that among residents released from institutions, 86% of those who remained in the community had friends, as opposed to only 46% of residents who were returned to the institutions. Of those who were successfully maintained in the community, two thirds still visited or kept in touch with some of their institutionalized friends. In both of these studies friendship stability may have resulted in less drastic social disruption and in a support network, which aided residents both emotionally and physically.

Disruption of familiar social relationships seems to adversely affect personal adjustment following relocations. Such disruptions could be minimized by maintaining intact resident groups and enhancing the social support systems of residents during the relocation process.

C. Facility Environments

Residental relocation research has generally paid insufficient attention to the objective physical design, programmatic, and social properties of sending and receiving facilities. Many studies have indicated that the behavior of the same people may differ substantially in different settings (e.g., Barker & Gump, 1964) and that consistent differences in settings can account for a significant degree of variance in behavior (Endler & Hunt, 1968). Although one would assume that relocations to environments offering a higher "quality" of life would facilitate successful adjustment, environmental attributes are seldom examined in a systematic manner in relocation studies. This could be attributed to the lack of theoretical approaches that fully conceptualize a broad range of environmental variables and to the difficulty of defining high "quality" facilities. Residential environments may not be better or worse according to a priori criteria, but may differ in suitability for different types of residents. The latter point has been emphasized by the ecological approach which assumes that successful adjustment to an environment depends on the joint influence of both individual and environmental characteristics.

In this review high "quality" environments are defined as those with optimal conditions for enhancing client development and growth. The following section first delineates key environmental factors which seem to impact significantly on residents' behaviors. It then examines the effect of (1) changes in the environmental characteristics of the old and new facilities and (2) the match between the person and the environmental setting.

In order to determine which conditions are most likely to facilitate development and growth for particular types of individuals, it is necessary to first conceptualize and measure environmental factors. Three major domains of environmental variables outlined by Moos and his associates (Moos & Lemke, 1983) include (1) architectural and design features, (2) policy, programmatic, and organizational factors, and (3) social climate and staff orientation. There is a growing body of literature that relates specific aspects of these facility dimensions to the well being of different population groups. For example, social climate characteristics of programs for mentally ill people have been related to the behavioral functioning of residents (Coleman, 1971; Cumming & Cummings, 1962; Fairweather, 1963) and to treatment outcomes, such as dropout rate, release, and community tenure (Moos & Schwartz, 1972; Moos & Petty, 1971). In elderly housing various physical design features and policies advocating autonomy, resident locus of control, and individualization have been associated with enhanced resident functioning (Lawton, 1975; Linn, Gurel, & Linn, 1977; Moos, Lemke, & David, 1983).

Most evaluations of facilities for mentally retarded people have measured their "quality" in terms of fixed "normalization" criteria that endorse culturally normative residences devoid of dehumanizing stigma. It is widely assumed that more "normalized" physical environments result in greater adaptive functioning of residents. Physical and architectural features of "normalized" settings would include smaller size, more homelike appearance, community accessibility, and, more individual space. Eyman, Demaine, and Lei (1979) used the PASS 3 (Wolfensberger & Glenn, 1975) to assess the physical attributes of residential facilities. They found that location and proximity of services, facility comfort and appearance, and facility openness and blending with neighborhood were positively associated with residents' progress.

The single feature most commonly assumed to affect residential functioning, facility size, has not consistently been shown to relate to residents' adaptive behavior (Balla, 1976). Similarly, modifications of physical design in institutions have only resulted in improved functioning for some groups of residents (Knight, Zimring, Weitzer, & Hollis, 1977; Landesman-Dwyer, 1982).

"Normalized" programmatic and organizational features would include higher staff–resident ratios, culturally appropriate staff behavior, habilitative programs, community integration, and recreational, vocational, and domestic activities. Landesman-Dwyer (1982) has indicated that increased staff–resident ratios do not necessarily result in increased interactions among staff members and residents or in changes in other resident behaviors. It appears that the key variable is not the mere number of staff present, but what type of interactions and program efforts are made by staff.

The social climate and staff orientation variables seem to most directly impact on the residents' progress. King, Raynes, and Tizard (1971) measured resident care practices with their Resident Management Practices Survey, which was based on Goffman's (1961) analysis of "total" institutions. Their survey focused on four categories: rigidity, block treatment, depersonalization, and social distance. Significant differences were found in management practices in three types of facilities: hospitals, voluntary homes, and group homes, with the latter being the most resident oriented and the hospitals the most institution oriented. Butler and Bjaanes (1977) found that a therapeutic orientation emphasizing habilitative programming, community involvement, and care-provider interaction with clients was related to client utilization of community services.

In Intagliata and Willer's (1980) study of family care homes, providers who encouraged resident autonomy and were tolerant rather than over-protective in their caring style [as rated by the Family Environment Scale (Moos, 1974)] facilitated significantly greater positive adaptive behavior changes. Additionally, residents in family homes characterized by cohesion, mutual support, and open expression of feelings exhibited less maladaptive behavior.

Bjaanes, Butler, and Kelley (1981) argue that "normalized" environmental settings are not sufficient for optimal client growth and development. In addition to "environmental normalization," it is also necessary to provide "client normalization" through habilitative programs aimed at enhancing skills. Four major services which address client deficiencies include (1) supportive counseling, (2) independent living skills training, (3) behavior therapy, and (4) social interaction training.

Several studies have noted long-term gains in adaptive behavior of residents upon deinstitutionalization (e.g., Aanes & Moen, 1976; Conroy *et al.,* 1982). However, Bjaanes *et al.* (1981) have questioned the common assumption that living in a community facility is necessarily qualitatively superior to living in an institution. Although clients placed in community facilities may have more "normalized" environments, they often lack the habilitative services which focus on the development of competence. Studies of resident relocations from one type of facility into another that carefully delineate environmental changes can shed light on the effects of these environmental factors on residents.

To assess changes in environmental "quality," it is necessary to assess both the sending and the receiving facilities. Schorr's (1970) review on the effects of housing quality on the individual indicated that residents' health and housing satisfaction after a move depended on how the quality of the present housing compared with that of the previous housing. The impact of institutionalization on mentally retarded children varies with the quality of their preinstitutionalization home background (Clarke, Clarke, & Reiman, 1958; Zigler & Williams, 1963) and the institution studied (Balla, Butterfield, & Zigler, 1974). Clarke *et al.* discovered that individuals coming from "deprived" homes showed gains in IQ upon institutionalization, while individuals coming from relatively "good" homes showed no such increases. In a similar vein, Conroy *et al.* (1982) found that mentally retarded clients from more "deprived" cottages (less normalized, individualized, and physically pleasant) showed greater gains in adaptive behavior (using the Behavior Development Survey, an adapted version of the ABS) upon deinstitutionalization. Degree of deprivation was measured by the PASS (Flynn & Heal, 1981), Resident Management Survey (King *et al.,* 1971), and ACMRDD accreditation data.

The new units in the Hemming *et al.* (1981) study differed from the old ones in that (1) management practices were more resident oriented [on the King & Raynes (1968) Scale of Management Practices], (2) staff–resident interactions were more frequent, (3) the staff had a substitute parent role instead of a nursing orientation, and (4) more habilitative programs were practiced. However, the majority of residents (80 versus 40% prior to the move) lacked regular daytime occupations when first transferred. This may have exacerbated behavior problems and increased sleeplessness at night. It is notable that most residents prescribed night sedation after the transfer no longer had regular daytime occupations. Although the staff had a substitute parent role, initially they were fairly inexperienced in applying behavioral analysis techniques used successfully in the previous institutions.

In two observational studies of social–environmental quality of pre- and postmove residential facilities for mentally retarded people (Carsrud *et al.*, 1979; Heller, 1982a), there was a relationship between social–environmental changes and resident behaviors. In Carsrud's study resident–staff interactions were related to decreases in constructive activity, social interaction, and yelling behaviors. Similarly, Heller found that children who received greater increases in structured programming and staff–child ratio demonstrated greater increases in both positive (object interaction) and negative (antisocial) behaviors.

The way individuals perceive and respond to their new environments depends not only on a comparison of the characteristics of the residents' previous living units with that of the new ones, but also on their personal characteristics (e.g., age, cognitive level, sensorimotor capacities, behavioral repertoire, and personal preferences). Although much has been written lately about the "person–environment" fit, few have considered it in evaluating the impact of relocations. Residential environments may differ in suitability for different types of residents.

Hemming *et al.* (1981) found that higher functioning residents (IQ over 50) from the more resident oriented pretransfer environments exhibited little or no improvement, whereas higher functioning residents from more restrictive pretransfer environments improved initially with some decrease 2 years after the transfer. Lower functioning residents from restrictive pretransfer environments not only improved initially, but also sustained these improvements over all assessments. In summary, the most able adults from the better units were the ones who benefited least from the transfer.

Landesman-Dwyer (1982), using a matched trio design in which two out of three subjects were assigned randomly to conditions, compared severely and profoundly retarded residents of institutions moved into remodeled units with those remaining in the old units. She found that certain clusters of subjects, based on their baseline patterns of behavior, were differentially affected by environmental changes. The most social and verbal residents seemed to be the least affected by the changes. Residents who were passive recipients of staff attention or highly oriented to objects, but were not extreme in any behavioral categories, seemed to benefit the most from living in the new units. Landesman-Dwyer suggested that individuals who are initially more dependent on the immediate environment are more likely to be affected by external changes than are those whose behaviors are less linked to their surroundings.

Much more research needs to be done on procedures which will enhance the reciprocal adjustment required of both residents and staff of facilities receiving new residents (Lakin, Bruininks, & Sigford, 1981). Schalock and Harper (1978) described a program which attempted to train candidates for residential placements in those skills demanded by the new settings. Their premise was that settings vary in the types of behavior both tolerated and expected. They demonstrated that the behavioral requirements of different settings can be specified and that success within the environment is predictable according to the degree the clients meet these requirements. Staff training programs may also increase staff tolerance and effectiveness in dealing with the residents. For example, in an institution receiving a large influx of transferees who function at a lower level than the current residents, staff may need training in working with such residents.

Although very few studies have systematically evaluated the features of both the old and new environments of relocated individuals, there is considerable evidence suggesting that environmental "quality" is an important consideration. Evaluations that isolate the physical, social, and programmatic variables and that evaluate the interaction between personal and environmental characteristics are needed in order to adequately assess the impact of relocation on individuals.

IV. CONCLUSION

The majority of studies indicate that relocation often has deleterious effects on people's physical health and behavioral functioning. However, relocation per se need not entail "transfer trauma"; in fact, in some cases it may be beneficial. These reactions are influenced by (1) individual differences in capabilities and resources, (2) individual perceptions and expectations, (3) social supports, and (4) the "quality" of the old and new environments. Of the individual difference variables studied, initial poor health is the major one associated with stressful reactions to relocation. The individuals' expectations about the move also seem to effect relocation adjustment. Preparatory programs can be instrumental in reducing anxieties and negative expectations prior to transfers. Social networks of residents, consisting of peers, staff, and/or families, can also provide support and moderate stressful reactions to relocation. Previous studies have largely ignored such key features as peer friendships, employee morale, family involvement, and adaptation of receiving facilities to new residents.

Environmental attributes of the receiving facilities that seem to be most critical to adaptive client functioning are the programmatic and social climate aspects. However, studies have only begun to systematically delineate the environmental features which optimize client adjustment and which are most suitable to various types of residents.

A major limitation in the literature reviewed here is the frequent absence of strong methodology. Many of the studies rely on subjective staff ratings, lack appropriate control groups, and ignore long-term effects. In particular, the problem of selection bias is pervasive in studies comparing the impact of various environmental features on residents. Hence, experimental research is needed to substantiate the findings on environmental "quality." Future research would benefit from prospective longitudinal studies using both subjective and objective measures of the "quality" of the environment and of the well being of the relocated residents. In addition, the use of randomized assignment (e.g., when there is a waiting list) or comparable control groups [as in Landesman-Dwyer's (1982) study] would greatly strengthen our ability to isolate the effects of relocation.

Since relocations may have adverse effects on individuals, we need to become more cognizant of the human costs involved in excessive transfers from one facility into another. Although relocation is seldom advocated, at times it is necessary because of institutional closings or because of a deinstitutionalization policy. In such cases this review suggests that adequate adjustment can be facilitated by proper planning of the relocation process.

The first suggestion is that caution be used in transferring those who are least capable of coping with stress and new situations, such as the medically fragile retarded residents. We need a more balanced viewpoint than has generally prevailed on the issue of "transfer trauma." The evidence does not indicate that trauma and increased mortality rates are inevitable in relocation and does not justify alarmist forecasts and extraordinary interventions. Rather, it does advocate recognizing the importance of everyday caretaking and support activities and proper management of the relocation process. Earlier studies conducted by Tarjan and his colleagues suggested that the increased mortality rates of retarded residents first entering institutions could be decreased by initial close medical monitoring of high-risk residents (young, low IQ, organically retarded) and by allowing residents to interact with their families shortly after admission (Tarjan, Brooke, Eyman,

Suyeyasu, & Miller, 1968; Tarjan, Eyman, & Miller, 1969). Similar policies could be effective in reducing medical risks of transferred residents.

Where applicable, the use of preparatory counseling, site visits, and family involvement is recommended. If the residents are capable, they may benefit from having some choice and participation in the movement process. Also, whenever possible, it would be advisable to move residents with chosen friends or to move units intact rather than moving people individually, so that friendships and a sense of continuity can be preserved. Heller's (1982b) review of involuntary residential relocations concluded that disruption of friendship networks is a key factor leading to poor relocation adjustment. The fact that broken friendships could adversely affect transferred residents is often ignored in placement decisions. The last point is that particular attention should be placed on moving people to new facilities which are environmentally more suitable and which enable a higher quality of life than did the previous one.

REFERENCES

Aanes, D., & Moen, M. Adaptive behavior changes of group home residents. *Mental Retardation*, 1976, **14**, 36–40.

Aldrich, C. I., & Mendkoff, E. Relocation of the aged and disabled: A mortality study. *Journal of the American Geriatrics Society*, 1963, **11**, 185–194.

Aleksandrowicz, D. Fire and its after-math on a geriatric ward. *Bulletin of the Meninger Clinic*, 1961, **25**, 23–32.

Balla, D. A. Relationship of institution size to quality of care: A review of the literature. *American Journal of Mental Deficiency*, 1976, **81**, 117–124.

Balla, D. A., Butterfield, E. C., & Zigler, E. Effects of institutionalization on retarded children: A longitudinal cross—institutional investigation. *American Journal of Mental Deficiency*, 1974, **78**, 530–549.

Barker, R., & Gump, P. *Big school, small school*. Stanford, California: Stanford Univ. Press, 1964.

Barrington, L., Burke, J. L., & LaFave, H. G. Mass transfer of two wards of chronic mental patients. *Psychiatric Quarterly*, 1962, **36**, 286–295.

Bjaanes, A. T., & Butler, E. W. Environmental variation in community care facilities for the mentally retarded. *American Journal of Mental Deficiency*, 1974, **78**, 429–439.

Bjaanes, A. T., Butler, E. W., & Kelly, B. R. Placement type and client functioning level as factors in provision of services aimed at increasing adjustment. In R. H. Bruininks, C. E. Meyers, B. B. Sigford, & K. C. Lakin (Eds.), *Deinstitutionalization and community adjustment of mentally retarded people*. Washington, D.C.: American Association on Mental Deficiency, 1981.

Borup, J. H., Gallego, D. T., & Heffernan, P. G. Relocation and its effect on mortality. *Gerontologist*, 1979, **19**, 135–140.

Bourestom, N. C., & Tars, S. Alterations in life patterns following nursing home relocation. *Gerontologist*, 1974, **14**, 506–510.

Bourestom, N. C., Tars, S., & Pastalan, L. *Alteration in life patterns following nursing home relocation.* Paper presented at the meeting of the Gerontological Society, Miami, 1973.

Braddock, D. Deinstitutionalization of the retarded: Trends in public policy. *Hospital and Community Psychiatry,* 1981, **32,** 607–615.

Butler, E. W., & Bjaanes, A. T. A typology of community care facilities and differential normalization outcomes. In P. Mittler (Ed.), *Research to practice in mental retardation: Care and intervention.* Baltimore, Maryland: Univ. Park Press, 1977.

Carsrud, A. L., Carsrud, K. B., Henderson, C. J., Alisch, C. J., & Fowler, A. V. Effects of social and environmental change on institutionalized mentally retarded persons: The relocation syndrome reconsidered. *American Journal of Mental Deficiency,* 1979, **84,** 266–272.

Clarke, A. D. B., Clarke, A. M., & Reiman, S. Cognitive and social changes in the feeble-minded: Three further studies. *British Journal of Psychology,* 1958, **49,** 144–157.

Close, D. Community living for severely and profoundly retarded adults: A group home study. *Education and Training of the Mentally Retarded,* 1977, **12,** 256–262.

Cochran, W., Sran, P., & Varano, G. The relocation syndrome in mentally retarded individuals. *Mental Retardation,* 1977, **15,** 10–12.

Coffman, T. L. Relocation and survival of institutionalized aged: A reexamination of the evidence. *The Gerontologist,* 1981, **21,** 483–500.

Coffman, T. L., & Harris, M. C. Transition shock and adjustments of mentally retarded persons. *Mental Retardation,* 1980, **18,** 3–7.

Cohen, H., Conroy, J. Q., Fraser, D. W., Snelbecker, G. E., & Spreat, S. Behavioral effects of interinstitutional relocation of mentally retarded residents. *American Journal of Mental Deficiency,* 1977, **82,** 12–18.

Coleman, A. *The planned environment in psychiatric treatment: A manual for ward design.* Springfield, Illinois: Thomas, 1971.

Conroy, J., Efthimiou, J., & Lemanowicz, J. A matched comparison of the developmental growth of institutionalized and deinstitutionalized mentally retarded clients. *American Journal of Mental Deficiency,* 1982, **86,** 581–587.

Conroy, J. W., & Latib, A. *Family impacts: Pre-post attitudes of 65 families of clients deinstitutionalized.* Philadelphia, Pennsylvania: Temple University Developmental Disabilities Center, 1982.

Cummings, J., & Cummings, E. *Ego and milieu.* New York: Atherton, 1962.

DeVries, D. L. Effects of environmental change and of participation on the behavior of mental patients. *Journal of Consulting and Clinical Psychology,* 1968, **32,** 532–536.

DiMatteo, M. R., & Hays, R. Social support and serious illness. In B. H. Gottlieb (Ed.), *Social networks and social support.* Beverly Hills, California: Sage, 1981.

DiScipio, W. J., & Wolf, S. Clinical and discharge status as a function of transfer from chronic to acute wards. *Journal of Community Psychology,* 1974, **2,** 144–147.

Endler, N., & Hunt, J. S-R inventories of hostility and comparisons of the proportion of variance from persons, responses, and situations for hostility and anxiousness. *Journal of Personality and Social Psychology,* 1968, **9,** 309–315.

Engel, G. L. A life setting conducive to illness: The giving up and given complex. *Annals of Internal Medicine,* 1968, **69,** 293.

Eyman, R., Demaine, G., & Lei, T. Relationship between community environments and resident changes in adaptive behavior: A path model. *American Journal of Mental Deficiency,* 1979, **83,** 330–337.

Fairweather, G. *Social psychology in the treatment of mental illness.* New York: McMillan, 1963.

Flynn, R., & Heal, L. A short form of PASS 3-A study of its structure, interrater reliability, and validity for assessing normalization. *Evaluation Review,* 1981, **56**, 357–376.

Fried, M. Grieving for a lost home. In L. J. Duhl (Ed.), *The urban condition.* New York: Basic Books, 1963.

Giampiccolo, J. S., & Boroskin, A. *Manual for the Fairview Development Scale.* Fairview State Hospital, California, 1974.

Goffman, E. *Asylums.* New York: Doubleday, 1961.

Goldfarb, A. I., Shahinian, S. P., & Burr, H. I. Death rate of relocated residents. In D. P. Kent, R. Kastenbaum, & S. Sherwood (Eds.), *Research planning and action for the elderly.* New York: Behavioral Publications, 1972.

Gollay, E., Freedman, R., Wyngaarden, M., & Kurtz, N. R. *Coming back: The community experiences of deinstitutionalized mentally retarded people.* Cambridge, Massachusetts: Abt, 1978.

Gore, S. The effect of social support in moderating the health consequences of unemployment. *Journal of Health and Social Behavior,* 1978, **19**, 157–165.

Goshgarian, N. K. *Visual preferences in retarded infants.* Unpublished masters thesis, University of Wisconsin, 1968.

Gottlieb, B. H. *Social networks and social support.* Beverly Hills, California: Sage, 1981.

Heller, T. Social disruption and residential relocation of mentally retarded children. *American Journal of Mental Deficiency,* 1982, **87**, 48–55. (a)

Heller, T. The effects of involuntary residential relocation: A review. *American Journal of Community Psychology,* 1982, **10**, 471–492. (b)

Heller, T., & Berkson, G. *Friendship and residential relocation.* Paper presented at the Gatlinburg Conference on Research in Mental Retardation. Gatlinburg, 1982.

Hemming, H., Lavender, T., & Pill, R. "Quality of Life" of mentally retarded adults transferred from large institutions to new small units. *American Journal of Mental Deficiency,* 1981, **86**, 157–169.

Higgs, W. J. *The effects of an environmental change upon behavior of schizophrenics.* Unpublished master's thesis, University of Illinois, 1964.

Hinkle, L. E. The effect of exposure to culture change, social change and changes in interpersonal relationships on health. In B. S. Dohrenwend & B. P. Dohrenwend (Eds.), *Stressful life events.* New York: Wiley, 1974.

Hollis, J. H. The effects of social and nonsocial stimuli on the behavior of profoundly retarded children: Part I. *American Journal of Mental Deficiency,* 1965, **69**, 755–771.

Intagliata, J., & Willer, B. *Factors associated with success in family care homes and community residential facilities.* Paper presented at the annual meeting of the American Academy on Mental Retardation, San Francisco, 1980.

Jasnau, K. F. Individualized vs. mass transfer of nonpsychotic geriatric patients from mental hospitals to nursing homes with special reference to the death rate. *Journal of the American Geriatrics Society,* 1967, **15**, 280–284.

Kelly, J. G. Towards an ecological conception of preventive interventions. In L. W. Carter (Ed.), *Research contribution from psychology to community mental health.* New York: Behavioral Publications, 1968.

Killian, E. C. Effect of geriatric transfers on mortality rates. *Social Work,* 1970, **15**, 19–26.

King, R. D., & Raynes, N. V. An operational measure of inmate management in residential institutions. *Social Sciences and Medicine,* 1968, **2**, 41–53.

King, R., Raynes, N., & Tizard, J. *Patterns of residential care: Sociological studies in institutions for handicapped children.* London: Routledge & Kegan Paul, 1971.

Knight, R. C., Zimring, C. M., Weitzer, W. H., & Hollis, C. W. *Social development and nor-*

malized institutional settings: A preliminary Research Report. Amherst, Massachusetts: Environment and Behavior Research Center, University of Massachusetts, 1977.

Kowalski, N. C. A home for the aged: A study of short-term mortality following dislocation of elderly residents. *Journal of Gerontology,* 1978, **33**, 601–602.

Kral, V. A., Grad, B., & Berenson, J. Stress reactions resulting from relocation of an aged population. *Canadian Psychiatrist,* 1968, **13**, 201–209.

Lakin, K. C., Bruininks, R. H., & Sigford, B. B. Deinstitutionalization and community adjustment: A summary of research and issues. In R. H. Bruininks, C. E. Meyers, B. B. Sigford, & K. C. Lakin (Eds.), *Deinstitutionalization and community adjustment of mentally retarded people.* Washington, D.C.: American Association on Mental Deficiency, 1981.

Landesman-Dwyer, S. *A description and modification of the behavior of nonambulatory, profoundly mentally retarded children.* Dissertation thesis, University of Washington, 1974.

Landesman-Dwyer, S. Living in the community. *American Journal of Mental Deficiency,* 1981, **86**, 223–234.

Landesman-Dwyer, S. *The changing structure and function of institutions: A search for optimal group care environments.* Paper presented at the Lake Wilderness Conference on the Impact of Residential Environments on Retarded Persons and their Care Providers, 1982.

Lawton, M. P. *Planning and managing housing for the elderly.* New York: Wiley, 1975.

Lazarus, R. S. *Psychological stress and the coping process.* New York: McGraw-Hill, 1966.

Lentz, R. J., & Paul, G. L. "Routine" vs. "therapeutic" transfer of chronic mental patients. *General Psychiatry,* 1971, **25**, 187–191.

Linn, M. W., Gurel, L., & Linn, B. S. Patient outcome as a measure of quality of nursing home care. *American Journal of Public Health,* 1977, **67**, 337–344.

Markson, E., & Cumming, J. A strategy of necessary mass transfer and its impact on patient mortality. *Journal of Gerontology,* 1974, **29**, 315–321.

Markus, E., Blenkner, M., Bloom, M., & Downs, T. The impact of relocation upon mortality rates of institutionalized aged persons. *Journal of Gerontology,* 1971, **26**, 537–541.

Marlowe, R. A. *Effects of environment on elderly state hospital relocatees.* Paper presented at the meeting of the Pacific Sociological Association, Scottsdale, Arizona, 1973.

Marlowe, R. A. *When they closed the doors at Modesto.* Paper presented at the National Institute of Mental Health Conference, Scottsdale, Arizona, 1974.

Marris, P. *Loss and change.* New York: Pantheon, 1974.

Mechanic, D. Social structure and personal adaptation: Some neglected dimensions. In G. V. Coelho, D. A. Hamburg, & J. E. Adams (Eds.), *Coping and adaptation.* New York: Basic Books, 1974.

Miller, C. *Deinstitutionalization and mortality trends in profoundly mentally retarded.* Paper presented at the Western Research Conference on Mental Retardation, Carmel, California, 1975.

Miller, D., & Lieberman, M. A. The relationship of affect state and adaptive capacity to reactions to stress. *Journal of Gerontology,* 1965, **20**, 492–497.

Moos, R. H. Systems for the assessment and classification of human environments: An overview. In R. H. Moos & P. M. Insel (Eds.), *Issues in social ecology: Human milieus.* Stanford, California: National Press, 1974.

Moos, R. H., & Lemke, S. Evaluating specialized environments for older people. In J. E. Birren & K. W. Schaie (Eds.), *Handbook of the psychology of aging.* Princeton, New Jersey: Van Nostrand-Reinhold, 1983, in press.

Moos, R. H., Lemke, S., & David, T. G. Environmental design and programming in residential settings for the elderly: Practices and preferences. In V. Regnier & J. Pynoos (Eds.), *Housing for the elderly: Satisfactions and preferences.* New York: Garland, 1983.

Moos, R. H., & Petty, C. *Treatment environment and treatment outcome: A replication.* Palo Alto, California: Stanford Univ. Press, 1971.

Moos, R. H., & Schwartz, J. Treatment environment and treatment outcome. *Journal of Nervous and Mental Disease,* 1972, **154,** 264–275.

National Association of State Mental Retardation Program Directors, *New Directions Newsletter,* July 1982.

Neugarten, B. L. *Middle Age and aging: A reader in social psychology.* Chicago, Illinois: Univ. of Chicago Press, 1968.

Novick, L. J. Easing the stress of moving day. *Hospitals,* 1967, **41,** 6–10.

Parkes, M. Components of the reaction to loss of limb, spouse, or home. *Journal of Psychosomatic Research,* 1972, **16,** 343–349.

Payne, J. E. The deinstitutionalization backlash. *Mental Retardation,* 1976, **3,** 43–45.

Romer, D., & Heller, T. Social adaptation of mentally retarded adults in community settings: A social - ecological approach. *Applied Research in Mental Retardation,* 1983, **4,** 303–314.

Schalock, R. L., & Harper R. S. Placement from community-based mental retardation programs: How well do clients do? *American Journal of Mental Deficiency,* 1978, **83,** 240–247.

Scheerenberger, R. C. Deinstitutionalization: Trends and difficulties. In R. H. Bruininks, C. E. Meyers, B. B. Sigford, & K. C. Lakin (Eds.), *Deinsitutionalization and community adjustment of mentally retarded people.* Washington, D.C.: American Association on Mental Deficiency Monograph, 1981.

Schinke, S. P., & Landesman-Dwyer, S. Training staff in group homes serving mentally retarded persons. In P. Mittler (Ed.), *Frontiers of knowledge in mental retardation. Vol. I -Social, educational, and behavioral aspects.* Baltimore, Maryland: Univ. Park Press, 1981.

Schmale, A. H. Relationship of separation and depression to disease. *Psychosomatic Medicine,* 1958, **20,** 259–267.

Schorr, A. L. Housing and its effects. In H. M. Proshansky, W. H. Ittelson, & L. G. Rivlin (Eds.), *Environmental psychology: Man and his physical setting.* New York: Holt, 1970.

Schultz, D. G., Lyons, T. F., & Nothnagel, G. E. *The effects of the closing of Cleveland State Hospital on its patients and staff.* Cleveland, Ohio: Case Western Reserve University, 1975.

Schumacher, K., Wisland, M., & Qvammen, B. *Relocation effects on adaptive and communication behaviors.* Paper presented at the annual meeting of the American Association for Mental Deficiency, Dallas, 1983.

Seligman, M. E. *Helplessness: On depression, development, and death.* San Francisco, California: Freeman, 1975.

Shahinian, S. B., Goldfarb, A. I., & Turner, H. *Death rate in relocated residents of nursing homes.* Paper presented at meeting of Gerontological Society, New York, 1966.

Smith, J. M., Oswald, W. Y., & Farucki, G. Y. The effects of relocation on the satisfaction of psychiatric inpatients. *Journal of Clinical Psychology,* 1976, **32,** 845–848.

Tarjan, G., Brooke, C. E., Eyman, R. K., Suyeyasu, A., & Miller, C. Mortality and cause of death in a hospital for the mentally retarded. *American Journal of Public Health,* 1968, **58,** 1891–1900.

Tarjan, G., Eyman, R. K., & Miller, C. R. Natural history of mental retardation in a state hospital revisited. *American Journal of the Disabled Child,* 1969, **117,** 609–620.

Vitello, S. J., & Atthowe, J. M. *Deinstitutionalization family reaction and involvement.* Paper presented at the Gatlinburg Conference on Research in Mental Retardation, Gatlinburg, 1982.

Watson, C. S., & Buerkle, H. R. Involuntary transfer as a cause of death and of medical hospitalization in geriatric neuropsychiatric patients. *Journal of the American Geriatrics Society,* 1976, **24,** 278–282.

Weinstock, A., Wulkan, P., Colon, C. J., Coleman, J., & Goncalves, S. Stress inoculation and interinstitutional transfer of mentally retarded individuals. *American Journal of Mental Deficiency,* 1979, **83,** 385–390.

Wells, L., & MacDonald, G. Interpersonal networks and postrelocation adjustment of the institutionalized elderly. *The Gerontologist,* 1981, **21,** 177–183.

Wolfensberger, W., & Glenn, L. *PASS: A method for the quantitative evaluation of human services* (Handbook). Toronto: National Institute on Mental Retardation, 1975.

Zigler, E., & Williams, J. Institutionalization and the effectiveness of social reinforcement: A three year follow-up study. *Journal of Abnormal and Social Psychology,* 1963, **66,** 197–205.

Zweig, J., & Csank, I. Effects of relocation on chronically ill geriatric patients of a medical unit: Mortality rates. *Journal of the American Geriatrics Society,* 1975, **23,** 132–136.

Salient Dimensions
of Home Environment
Relevant to Child Development

KAZUO NIHIRA, IRIS TAN MINK, AND C. EDWARD MEYERS

MENTAL RETARDATION RESEARCH CENTER
NEUROPSYCHIATRIC INSTITUTE
UNIVERSITY OF CALIFORNIA, LOS ANGELES
LOS ANGELES, CALIFORNIA

I. INTRODUCTION

> "I am what you have made me. Take all of the praise,
> take all of the blame; take all of the success,
> take all of the failure; in short, take me."
> (Charles Dickens, *Great Expectations*)

Literature, folklore, and scientific study of human development have long wrestled with the relationship of child behavior to family life and parental behavior. Early studies of this relationship focused on such structural and demographic characteristics as social status, family size, parental education,

INTERNATIONAL REVIEW OF RESEARCH IN
MENTAL RETARDATION, Vol. 12

occupation, age, and other descriptive variables. In time, the focus shifted from these distal variables to more proximal ones, such as the psychosocial climate or cultural atmosphere of the home. This shift began in the 1960s (Anastasi, 1967; Bloom, 1964; Hunt, 1961), and the last decade has witnessed an increasing number of studies directed to the quantification of the psychosocial environment of the home and its effect on the developing child.

The quantification of home environment appears to have followed three different theoretical approaches: (1) the study of general psychosocial climate of the home as perceived by the family members, a theme that can be traced from the need-press theory by Henry Murray (1938) and his followers (Stern, Stein, & Bloom, 1956; Moos, 1973; Insel & Moos, 1974); (2) work on environment process or the reinforcement analysis of learning environment which is an outgrowth of the social learning theory (Bandura, 1969; Mischel, 1968); and (3) research on child-rearing attitudes and practices (Baldwin, Kalhorn, & Breese, 1949; Baumrind, 1971; Becker, 1964; Kagan & Moss, 1962; Schaefer & Bell, 1958; Sears, Maccoby, & Levin, 1957; Sontag, Baker, & Nelson, 1958; Yarrow, Campbell, & Burton, 1968). These theoretical approaches have provided the framework for the development of various instruments to measure home environment which use observational as well as interview methods. The development of these instruments has undoubtedly stimulated much of the contemporary research on home environments. The use of standard instruments also permits generalization and comparability across different studies.

This article will describe several of the instruments developed to measure these three areas and the research which has employed these techniques. We will not attempt to review all instrumentation; we have only selected those which we found to be most helpful in our study of families with mentally retarded children.

II. PSYCHOSOCIAL CLIMATE OF THE HOME

In 1938, Murray defined press as environmental determinants of behavior. He further differentiated press into alpha press, those characteristics of an environment that exist objectively, and beta press, those characteristics of the environment as perceived by the participants within the environment.

A. Home Environment Questionnaire

Inquiries into the nature of alpha press have been made by Sines and his associates (Laing & Sines, 1982; Sines, 1982; Sines & Zimmerman, 1981). While acknowledging that beta presses are considered more important "proximal" causes of behavior, they favor the investigation of alpha press over beta press. They consider that the latter is a complex function of the objective environment plus characteristics of the perceiver, that is, "a product of some unknown combination of at least two unknowns" (Laing & Sines, 1982, p. 427). They also believe that concentration on alpha press will allow them to objectively validate the measures they derive.

Sines (1982) has developed the Home Environment Questionnaire (HEQ), a 134-item instrument which measures the alpha press dimensions of children's psychosocial environments. Items were initially selected to reflect Murray's 16 press dimensions of environments, life changes in the child's environment, and the academic–intellectual climate of the home. Subsequent data analysis yielded eight presses: Achievement, Aggression, Change, Play, Parent Absence, Affiliation, Sociability, and Academic–intellectual. Press Aggression has been subdivided into press External Aggression and press Home Aggression. Norms were established on a sample of nonretarded, nonneurologically impaired clinic children between the ages of 5 and 16.

To date there has been little research employing the HEQ. Using an earlier form of HEQ, Green (1970) found correlations between press Achievement ($r = .41$) and press Academic-Intellectual Behavior ($r = .71$) and socioeconomic status. Laing and Sines (1982) report that preliminary analyses performed during the development of the scale indicate the need for norms on unselected, nonclinic children and the removal of items which are inappropriate for single-parent families. Their correlation of the scales with variables measured by the Missouri Children's Behavior Checklist (Sines, Paulker, Sines, & Owen, 1969) revealed that press Aggression was the most salient scale. It correlated moderately with the behavior dimensions of activity level, somatization, sociability, and sleep disturbance, and significantly with aggressive behavior and inhibition. Sines and Zimmerman (1981) discuss a prospective study to be done on a group of adopted children in order to specify the various contributions of environment and heredity to a child's behavior.

B. Family Environment Scale

The investigation of beta press and social climate has been pursued by Moos and his colleagues (Moos, 1973, 1974, 1975; Insel & Moos, 1974; Moos, Insel, & Humphrey, 1974; Moos & Moos, 1981). Moos states that "environments have 'personalities' just as people do" and that they can be accurately measured (Moos, 1974, p. 1). His group has developed nine scales to measure four major categories of environments: treatment environments, total institutions, educational environments, and community settings. In the latter category is the Family Environment Scale (FES) which assesses the social climate of all types of families. "It focuses on the measurement and description of the interpersonal relationships among family members, on the directions of personal growth which are emphasized in the family, and on the basic organizational structure of the family" (Moos *et al.,* 1974, p. 3).

The FES contains 90 items which are divided into 10 subscales which measure the above-mentioned three dimensions. Within the Relationship dimension are the subscales of Cohesion, Expressiveness, and Conflict. The Personal Growth dimension contains Independence, Achievement Orientation, Intellectual–Cultural Orientation, Active–Recreational Orientation, and Moral–Religious Emphasis, while the System Maintenance dimension consists of Organization and Control.

Moos maintains that these 10 subscales are largely statistically independent. He uses classical scale construction methods, not factor analytic techniques (Moos & Moos, 1975, 1981). Several investigators who recognize the merits of Moos's instrument have tried to reduce the number of variables in the FES.

Using Moos's original sample of subjects (814 members of 240 families), Fowler (1981) presented a maximum likelihood factor structure of the FES. He considered a two-factor, varimax-rotated solution to be appropriate. The first factor was bipolar, Cohesion vs Conflict, and was felt to measure relationship-centered concerns. The second factor, Organization and Control, was concerned with system maintenance or the stability and integrity of the family unit.

We (Mink, Meyers, & Nihira, 1981; Nihira, Mink, & Meyers, 1981) have proposed and utilized a six-score version of the FES. FES scores from 411 families were factor analyzed and the resulting six factors were rotated by the direct oblimin method. We confirmed the independence of Expressiveness, Achievement Orientation, Moral–Religious Emphasis, and Control. However, the remaining six scales formed two factor-defined scales. Cohesion, Independence, Organization, and Conflict formed a bipolar factor which we named Cohesion vs Conflict. Intellectual–Cultural Orientation combined with Active–Recreational Orientation in a scale we call Intellectual–Recreational Orientation.

A search of the literature was made for studies of the psychosocial climate of families with children and adolescents. A good number of the studies were in the general literature but many were doctoral dissertations and master's theses, and several were presentations at conventions or privately circulated papers.

1. THE FES AND COGNITION DEVELOPMENT

In a group of trainable mentally retarded (TMR) families, Nihira *et al.* (1981) found that Moral–Religious Emphasis correlated significantly with IQ and that the bipolar factor Cohesion vs Conflict correlated significantly with Personal Self-Sufficiency, a dimension of adaptive behavior. In another study (Nihira, Meyers, & Mink, 1980), canonical correlation analysis revealed that for educable mentally retarded (EMR) families, more than for TMR families, an educationally stimulating home environment involved the psychosocial climate of the home (as measured by Organization, Cohesion, Active–Recreational Orientation, and Moral–Religious Emphasis). For the EMR families a culturally stimulating atmosphere and parental expectations for educational achievement were also important.

Fowler (1980), in a study of prekindergarten children, of whom 26% had behavioral problems, found that mothers' retrospective recollections of early developmental delay and speech–language deficits were reliably associated ($-.45$ and $-.30$) with mothers' perceptions of currently less cohesive family environments. Regression analysis revealed a moderate order of predictability ($r = .56$) between early behavioral problems and the relationship dimension of Cohesion vs Conflict.

Tabackman (1976) studied gifted adolescents and their families and found that, compared to the average family, families with gifted adolescents perceived themselves as more independent, permissive, intellectual, unstructured, and harmonious.

Gottfried and Gottfried (1984) employed the FES in their longitudinal study of children of middle-class families. In this study, the Cohesion, Expressiveness, and Intellectual–Cultural Orientation showed a pattern of significant correlations with the children's mental development assessed at each 6-month period between 12 and 42 months of age. These correlations were all positive and low magnitude ranging from .16 to .36. There were more significant correlations for the preschool than for the infant period.

2. THE FES AND SOCIAL DEVELOPMENT

The psychosocial climate of the home appears to be quite salient for prosocial and maladaptive behavior. Nihira et al. (1981) found that, in TMR families, Control was significantly correlated with social maladaptation and with misbehavior at school. Expressiveness was correlated with self-esteem, and Moral–Religious Emphasis was correlated with being outgoing and expressive at school. Even though factors from the FES were related to school adjustment, a stronger relationship was found for factors from the Home observation for Measurement of the Environment (see following section).

A study of the relationship between home environment and family adjustment (Nihira et al., 1980) revealed that in both TMR and EMR families, Cohesion and low Conflict are the most salient FES variables, although Expressiveness and Active–Recreational Orientation are also important. As in cognitive development, measures from the FES were more important in EMR families than in TMR families.

Longitudinal data on the same EMR families indicated significant relationships (*r*'s being in the high 20s and 30s) between Cohesion and low Conflict in the home during the first year and measures of social adjustment of the children secured at 2 subsequent years (Meyers, Nihira, & Mink, 1979, 1980). Longitudinal data on the TMR families also indicated the importance of Cohesion and low Conflict along with Control, Expressiveness, and Moral–Religious Emphasis (Nihira, Meyers, & Mink, 1983). In this study, the FES scores secured during the first year were used to predict the change in social adjustment of the children during the 3 subsequent years. The study also revealed some evidence of child effects on environmental factors as measured by Achievement Orientation and Moral–Religious Emphasis.

Ollendick, Berteaux, and Horne (1978) studied normal preschool children and their families. Mothers who scored high on Moral–Religious Emphasis reported fewer behavioral problems with their children. Also, mothers with internal locus of control had higher scores on Cohesion than did external locus of control mothers.

The Fowler (1980) study of prekindergarten children discovered that mothers' recollections of the child's early shyness and anxiety were associated ($r = -.31$) with less structural organization and control in the current family environment. There was also a discernible trend for early behavioral displays of aggression and hostility to be associated with less cohesive family structure.

In their study of family climate and female adolescents, Bell and Bell (1982) found that families with well-adjusted girls described themselves as more cohesive, more expressive of feelings, more independent, and less organized and controlling than did members of families with less well-adjusted girls. The Bells speculate that marital stress may be the cause of strained family climate.

A study of adolescents in a residential treatment facility (Malin, 1978) revealed that parents of these children scored lower on Cohesion, Independence, Intellectual–Cultural Orientation, Active–Recreational Orientation, and Moral–Religious Emphasis than did the normative sample. Family incongruence scores between parents and children revealed high disagreement.

Nowicki and Schneewind (1977), studying early and late adolescents in the United States and Germany, found that those with high internal locus of control described their families as cohesive, expressive, independent, high on participation in cultural and recreational activities, and low on conflict and controlling relationships. Similar patterning was found by Reinhart (1977) in a study of well-educated and economically stable one-parent families with adolescent children. The conclusion here is that some one-parent families are able to provide a milieu conducive to personal growth.

Steinbock (1978) compared three groups of adolescents and their parents: adolescents who ran away from home, adolescents in crisis but who did not run away, and a control group of adolescents not in crisis. With regard to parents' perceptions of their families, there were no significant differences between the three groups. However, runaway adolescents perceived much less Cohesion, Expressiveness, Independence, Intellectural-Cultural Orientation, and Active-Recreational Orientation, and more Conflict and Control in their families than did their parents or the control group of adolescents. The conclusion is that the incongruence of perception between runaway adolescents and their families is crucial.

Comparing children of schizophrenic parents with children of normal parents, Janes and Hesselbrock (1976) found that those having schizophrenic parents rated their families significantly lower on the subscales of Intellectual-Cultural Orientation and Active-Recreational Orientation. There were no differences between black and white children on any of the FES scales.

In a study of clinic and nonclinic families, Scoresby and Christensen (1976) found that those seeking help for family problems were lower on Cohesion, Expressiveness, and Organization, and higher on Conflict than the group of families not seeking help.

3. THE FES AND SCHOOL ACHIEVEMENT

Draper (1977) compared three groups of families: those whose children experienced no academic problems, those whose children experienced academic trouble, and those in which there was an academically successful and an academically troubled child. The families with academically troubled children were higher in Conflict than the other two groups and lower in Intellectual-Cultural Orientation than the academically successful families.

In the Tabackman (1976) study of gifted adolescents, families of high-achieving students (as measured by grade point average) were more likely than families of low achievers to perceive their family as cohesive, structured, and conflict free. Somewhat surprisingly, families of high achievers perceived themselves as less communicative and less active socially and recreationally than families of low achievers.

With the exception of Tabackman's findings on high-achieving gifted adolescents, an overview of the research which employs the FES scales indicates that good cognitive and social development and school achievement are associated with families who perceive themselves as cohesive, expressive (or communicative), and engaging in cultural and recreational activities. In contrast, children in families where the perception of conflict and control are high display adjustment and achievement problems at home and at school.

4. THE FES AND ENVIRONMENTAL TAXONOMIES

The study of psychosocial environments is a relatively new field, and, as is true in many emerging fields, there have been attempts to develop taxonomies or typologies of environments. Three typologies of families which utilize the FES have appeared in recent literature.

Moos and Moos (1976) developed an empirically based taxonomy of families. These families were recruited from church groups, from newspaper advertisements, through students at a local high school, and through minority research assistants. A clinic sample was obtained from a family psychiatric clinic and from a probation and parole department. The 10 FES subscale scores from these families were cluster analyzed and six distinctive family clusters emerged: Expression-Oriented, Structure-Oriented, Independence-Oriented, Achievement-Oriented, Moral-Religious-Oriented, and Conflict-Oriented. Some of these clusters were composed of subclusters so that altogether there were 10 different family types. Systematic differences between these family types were reported on such characteristics as family size, ethnic composition, drinking patterns, and family disturbance.

Several studies have employed the Moos and Moos family typology. Only two are relevant to this review. In his study of family care homes for moderately and severely retarded young people, Intagliata (1978) found that 85% of the family care homes for mentally retarded people were highly Structure Oriented. This contrasts sharply with Moos's findings that 8% of unselected families were Structure Oriented.

In a related study, Willer (1978) found that those families who accepted the return of their about-to-be-deinstitutionalized retarded offspring fell into somewhat different family types than those who requested alternative placement. About 50% of all natural families of retarded persons in this study were Structure Oriented. However, 44% of families who accepted their child's return were Structure Oriented as contrasted with 64% of those who requested alternative placement. More home placement families were Independence Oriented (28 vs 3% for alternative placement families). Also noteworthy was the absence of any Achievement-Oriented families in the home placement group as contrasted with 18% in the alternative placement group. Willer feels he is unable to predict future placement from the present data; however, he acknowledges the usefulness of family type in predicting whether a natural family who accepts a deinstitutionalized child will experience a crisis. Structure-Oriented families, which place a high emphasis on organization, expression, cohesion, and control, were much more unlikely to experience a crisis.

In a longitudinal study conducted by the authors of this chapter, samples of TMR, EMR, and educationally handicapped (EH) children between the ages of 8 and 12 were drawn from school programs designed to serve the educational needs of the children. A comparison of the Moos and Moos sample with our own revealed major differences between the samples. Even though Moos and Moos had included a group of clinic families, we felt that their sample's presenting problems were of a solvable, acute nature, whereas the problems faced by our families were of a chronic nature. Furthermore, the Moos taxonomy was based solely on the perceived environment. We decided to utilize a more extensive description of family environment in our taxonomy. It was our belief that parental childrearing practices and the provision of a supportive environment for learning were particularly important for the development of mentally retarded children.

We developed two separate taxonomies, one for families with TMR children (Mink, Nihira, & Meyers, 1983) and one for families with slow-learning (EMR or EH) children (Mink, Meyers, & Nihira, 1981, 1984). In the TMR taxonomy we used our six factors from the FES (see previous section), eight factors from the HOME (see following section), and five factors from the Home Quality Rating Scale (see following section). A cluster analysis yielded five distinctive clusters of families: Cohesive, harmonious; Control-oriented, somewhat unharmonious; Low-disclosure, unharmonious; Child-oriented, expressive; and Disadvantaged, low morale. Comparisons among the clusters revealed significant differences on such child characteristics as Down's syndrome, sex, ethnicity, IQ, Adaptive Behavior Scale scores, and self-esteem, and on such family characteristics as presence of a father figure, father assistance with child care, mother employment, child influence on the marriage, occurrence of stressful life events, and parental attitude to child impact.

In the EMR–EH taxonomy we employed the six factors from the FES, the five factors from the Home Quality Rating Scale, and three factors from the Henderson Environmental Learning Process Scale (see following section). Seven distinctive clusters of families were identified: Child-oriented, concordant; Learning-oriented, somewhat discordant; Low-disclosure, unharmonious; Disadvantaged with little concern for the child; Achievement-oriented, nonlearning supportive; Expression-oriented with few sociocultural interests; and Outer-directed with little achievement orientation. As in the TMR taxonomy, comparisons among the clusters on family and child characteristics and behavior yielded many significant differences.

We also compared the profiles of the five TMR and the seven EMR–EH family types. Three family types in each group closely resembled each other. These were the Cohesive, harmonious (TMR) and the Child-oriented, concordant (EMR–EH) families, the Low-disclosure, unharmonious families in both groups, and the Disadvantaged with low morale (TMR) and the Disadvantaged with little concern for the child (EMR–EH) families.

We are encouraged by the results of our taxonomies. We share Moos's view that empirically derived taxonomies of family environments may help us understand the relationship between environment and behavior. On the other hand, we are also cognizant of Mischel's warning of the futility of "searching for the final or ultimate taxonomy" (1977, p. 337). We agree with him that many different classifications are possible and useful, and that labeling environmental types can never substitute for "analyzing *how* conditions and environments interact with the people in them" (p. 338, emphasis original).

III. ENVIRONMENTAL PROCESS VARIABLES

The classical work of Benjamin Bloom, *Stability and Change in Human Characteristics* (1964), appears to have provided the major impetus toward the development of inventories to assess educationally relevant environmental process variables in the home. However, early attempts toward quantification of these variables suggest the influence of Murray's (1938) need-press theory. The Dave Index of Educational Environment (Dave, 1963) consists of six process dimensions: achievement press, language models, academic guidance, activeness of the family, intellectuality in the home, and work habits in the family. Majoribanks (1974) identified eight environmental presses in his instrument: press for achievement, press for activeness, press for intellectuality, press for independence, press for English, press for ethlanguage (second language spoken in the home), father dominance, and mother dominance. The authors of these inventories and other investigators (Kellaghan, 1977; Weiss, 1974) have found that environmental process variables show a generally stronger relation to the children's cognitive development, school achievement, and achievement motivation than more distal measures of social status or family structure.

The common thread among the environmental process variables appears to involve (1) educationally relevant stimuli and opportunities available for the child, (2) reinforcement practices parents use to modify the child's behavior, and (3) the expectation of parents regarding the child's educational achievement.

A. Home Observation for Measurement of the Environment

The two inventories called the HOME, for Home Observation for the Measurement of the Environment, are among the most frequently cited measures of the characteristics of the home as a psychological environment for the infant and young child. While there have probably been earlier versions of the scale, the form we have come to call the HOME appears to have been announced in 1966 (Caldwell, Heider, & Kaplan, 1966). The scale was developed to assess the subtle qualities and processes of child rearing as seen by an observer who visits the home and who asks direct questions about facilities and practices. The initial use was to appraise the home in infant and child stimulation programs. The scores obtained provide a measure of qualities considered to boost the child's cognitive development and emotional maturity. Score changes have been employed to measure improvement in mothers presumably in response to participation in home improvement or parenting programs. For example, Hamilton (1972) found that after 6 months, scores increased from 33 to 42 out of a possible 63. A similar employment and determination were reported by Metzl (1980).

The current infant version, designed for use from birth to 3 years, contains 45 items each marked *Yes* or *No,* the former indicating the presence of the assumed best practice or characteristic of the home; for example, expressing positive feelings when speaking to the child or *not* physically punishing the child. The HOME Infant distributes its items over six subscales that were based on a factor analysis of an earlier 72-item version. The six are listed in Table I. Items were placed in order of their loadings on the factor. Scores can be converted to stanines, based on the data of Caldwell and associates. An appropriately trained visitor requires about an hour to complete the HOME, employing observation and direct questions. We will not provide psychometric information, as to do so would take space from the principal purposes in this article, and also because the information is available elsewhere (e.g., Bradley & Caldwell, 1977; Caldwell, *et al.,* 1966; Elardo & Bradley, 1981). Validity of the HOME is, of course, addressed in our review of the investigations that have employed the scale.

A quick overview of the factors and the most representative items is given in order to permit a comparison later with the preschool versions. The comparative lists are given in Table I.

1. Emotional and Verbal Responsivity of Mother. "Mother spontaneously vocalizes to child at least twice during visit (excluding scolding)." The remaining 10 items also pertain to verbal communication with expressions of affection and attachment.

2. Avoidance of Restriction and Punishment. "Mother does not shout at child during visit." Other items refer to avoidance of expression of anger, irritation, etc. Two items loading here are "At least 10 books are present and visible," and "Family has a pet."

3. Organization of Physical and Temporal Environment. "When mother

TABLE I
FACTOR SUBSCALES OF THE VERSIONS OF THE HOME

Infant (45 items)
1. Emotional and Verbal Responsivity of Mother (11)
2. Avoidance of Restriction and Punishment (8)
3. Organization of the Physical and Temporal Environment (6)
4. Provision of Appropriate Play Materials (9)
5. Maternal Involvement with the Child (6)
6. Opportunity for Variety in Daily Routine (5)

Preschool, initial version (80 items)
1. Provision of Stimulation Through Equipment, Toys, and Experiences (21)
2. Stimulation of Mature Behavior (12)
3. Provision of a Comfortable Physical and Language Environment (12)
4. Avoidance of Restriction and Punishment (7)
5. Pride, Affection, and Thoughtfulness (16)
6. Masculine Stimulation (5)
7. Independence from Parental Control (7)

Preschool, revised version (54 items)
1. Stimulation through Toys, Games, and Reading Materials (11)
2. Language Stimulation (7)
3. Physical Environment: Safe, Clean, and Conducive to Development (7)
4. Pride, Affection, and Warmth (7)
5. Stimulation of Academic Behavior (5)
6. Modeling and Encouraging of Social Maturity (5)
7. Physical Punishment (4)[a]
8. Variety of Stimulation (8)[a]

[a]Not a factor.

is away, care is provided by one of three regular substitutes." Several items relate to being taken out, privacy of child's space, safety of environment.

4. Provision of Appropriate Play Materials. "Child has some muscle activity toys or equipment." Other items relate to materials for role playing and to literary and musical toys.

5. Maternal Involvement with Child. "Mother tends to keep child within visual range and to look at him often."

6. Opportunities for Variety in Daily Stimulation. "Father provides some caretaking every day." Items also included pertain to reading a story, eating with parents, visitors, having own books.

Through a moderately thorough search for research literature, we found over 20 research reports on or involving the infant level, 9 of these by Caldwell and one or more coauthors. Most of the reports relate to the appraisal of low-income or welfare families, both black and white.

1. THE HOME-INFANT AND COGNITIVE DEVELOPMENT

Factor and total scores failed to relate to 12-month Bayley mental scores, but factors correlated .24 and above, and the total HOME .50 with Binet at 3 years (Elardo, Bradley, & Caldwell, 1975). When extended to 54 months (Bradley & Caldwell, 1976a) these correlations were sustained; they were higher for HOME scores taken at 24 months than at 6 months. In both reports, the factors, Provision of Appropriate Play Materials and Maternal Involvement with Child, were most closely related to later IQ. Further data relating the 6-month HOME to later IQ were reported (Bradley & Caldwell, 1976b). A similar result obtained in the study of the consequences of early interaction of black mothers with preterm and full term babies (Bakeman & Brown, 1980). Absence of relationship with Bayley scores in the first 2 years was confirmed by Stevenson and Lamb (1979). Piper and Ramsay (1980) showed moderate relations between HOME and Griffith's Mental Developmental Scales in Down's syndrome children. Ramey, Farran, and Campbell (1979) demonstrated a prediction of HOME factors to 3-year IQ in a sample of children of high-risk families; early intervention modified this predictability. Taken all together, one finds prediction of IQ at 3 years and later from HOME scores taken even as early as 6 months of the infant's age.

Bradley and Caldwell (1976b) related HOME factor scores to changes in scores in children between 6 months on the Bayley Mental Development Index and 3-year Binet IQs. Increases were associated with Maternal Involvement with Child and Provision of Appropriate Play Materials. Decreases were related to inadequate Organization of Physical and Temporal Environment. Bradley and Caldwell employed discriminant function analysis with 91 mother–child dyads in an attempt to predict from 6-month HOME appraisals the IQ status at age 3, the latter divided into under 70, 70 to 89, and 90 or above. Seventy-one percent of the low group were correctly predicted and 62% of the others were properly placed. The most potent subscales were Organization of the Physical and Temporal environment, Provision of Appropriate Play Materials, and Maternal Involvement with Child.

The prediction of later IQ from observations of the home environment as early as 6 months suggest that later language could also be predicted. Elardo, Bradley, and Caldwell (1977) secured the 10 scores on the Illinois Test of Psycholinguistic Abilities (ITPA) at 3 years on the same subjects' studies for IQ at 3. The total ITPA correlated about .40 with 6-month HOME and about .60 with 24-month HOME. The corresponding multiple r's (using HOME factor scores) were higher. HOME scores at 24 months were more closely associated than 6-month scores, while the patterns of relationship varied somewhat between 6- and 24-month HOME factor scores. The relationships were higher for white than for black children. Wulbert, Inglis, Kriegsmann, and Mills (1975) compared 20 language-delayed preschool children with 20 nondelayed children who were otherwise matched in essential characteristics. The infant HOME was employed, demonstrating a clear distinction in scores between the homes of the two groups.

2. THE HOME-INFANT AND SOCIAL DEVELOPMENT

Piper and Ramsey (1980), comparing HOME with Griffith's scales, report the highest relation to be with the Griffith's Personal–Social scale. Bakeman and Brown's (1980) report on early interaction found that social competence and social participation at 3 years in a day camp correlated positively with earlier HOME scores, particularly Emotional and Verbal Responsivity of Mother. Stevenson and Lamb's (1979) study included assessment of sociability at 12 months. While unrelated to Bayley scores, the HOME scores were correlated with measures of social responsiveness.

3. THE HOME-INFANT AND SCHOOL ACHIEVEMENT

Van Doorninck, Caldwell, Wright, and Frankenburg (1981) report on the prediction of later school achievement of two groups that had 12-month HOME scores. The centiles of school achievement, letter grades, and curriculum levels of reading and math of 50 low-income children were examined 5 to 9 years after the HOME data had been secured. Among findings was a .37 correlation with achievement centiles. Twenty-four of the children were graded as having significant achievement problems; 68% were correctly classified by the HOME. This report also included a finding of interest regarding consistency of environment across siblings. In 21 middle-income families, HOME total scores secured 10 or more months apart for different siblings correlated .86.

4. OTHER RESEARCH USING THE HOME-INFANT

Bradley, Caldwell, and Elardo (1977) demonstrated that HOME total scores predicted IQ at 3 years better than socioeconomic status (SES), for both white and black families. The covariance of HOME with SES is evident in the trivial increase of r if SES is added to HOME—from .742 to .765. Hollenbeck (1978) presented data comparable to those as reported in the Caldwell Manual (1979) and comparable to those of Ramey, Mills, Campbell, and O'Brien (1975), indicating a close relation to HOME and SES. Hollenbeck "validated" HOME scores by relating them to family income and parent education, the r's being in the high .30s.

The issue of causal direction, whether, for example, highly reactive children elicit parental attention or vice versa, intrigues investigators. Rheingold and Eckerman (1975) had shown the child-to-parent direction in the first year of the child's life. Bradley, Caldwell, and Elardo (1979) presented a cross-lagged panel analysis employing HOME and Bayley scores at 6, 12, and 24 months. Child scores (Bayley) and environmental scores (HOME factor scores) were positive, suggesting mutual facilitation. Apart from that, using the assumption required for interpreting cross-lagged analyses that the variable of greater stability is more likely the source than the consequence, some interesting results obtained. It would appear that the more capable children invited more maternal responsivity, thus confirming Rheingold and Eckerman in part. After 12 months, higher maternal development seemed to boost Bayley scores. Altogether, however, clear causality escaped definition and the principal inference by the authors was one of mutuality between child and environment scores.

Gottfried and Gottfried (1984) conducted a longitudinal study of middle-class children in which both infant and preschool HOMEs were employed. The infant version was administered at 15 months and the preschool version at 39 months. The HOME scores were related to several measures of cognitive development including the Bayley Mental Development index and the McCarthy Scale of Children's Abilities. Among the HOME scores, the 15 month Variety of Stimulation subscale and the 39-month Stimulation of Academic Behavior subscale were the most pervasive and potent predictors of the children's cognitive development.

The infant-level HOME turns out to be an interesting and useful tool. In addition to its clear common sense appeal to those who seek the nature of home processes to be related to child development or to employ for other purposes, it appears to be able to predict later IQ in a manner no infant screening—Gesell, Bayley, etc.—has ever been able to do. Thus, it might well be employed to indicate families most in need of intervention. It also yields scores indicative of change in response to family participation in a stimulation and parenting program. Interviewer–visitors require only about an hour to secure information to complete the scale.

In order to continue the study of families under observation in the Little Rock study, Caldwell and associates provided a revised HOME suitable for children of ages 3 to 6 (Caldwell & Bradley, 1979). It has the same basic yes–no format for the visitor to complete, requires perhaps a little more time, and yields factor scores. The initial version contained 80 items arranged into clusters according to the six factors that had been obtained. The six factors are listed at the top of Table I. Bradley and Caldwell (1979a) announced a revision, reducing the scale to 54 items (they indicate 55, but only 54 are to be counted in their table), yielding a different pattern of subscale scores, of which not all are factors. These are listed in Table I. Except for minor wording improvements, the items retained in the revision are the same as found in the original. However, one notes in Table I a considerable alteration in the array of factors. Two of the subscales that are not factors contained items that had been found useful and predictive, according to the authors (Bradley & Caldwell, 1979a), and thus were retained. Other than those reported by the authors of this article, only a few studies that have employed the preschool version have appeared in the literature.

5. THE HOME-PRESCHOOL AND SCHOOL ACHIEVEMENT

One study (Bradley & Caldwell, 1981) utilized data gathered on the revised version in a validation with 60 black children, HOME scores having been secured when the children were 3 to 5 years old. Validation material was the Science Research Associates' (SRA) Achievement battery during primary grades, with correlations of .30, .40, and one of .50 reported (for reading vs Stimulation through Toys, Games, and Reading Materials). Reading and language arts scores were a bit better predicted than mathematics. The authors (Bradley & Caldwell, 1979b) also related HOME scores to locus of control in the children, studied by means of the Modified Intellectual Achievement Responsibility Questionnaire administered in the primary grades. For both sexes, some significant relations were found with the "positive" locus scores; in girls, the relationships were stronger and were found also for the "negative" scores. The findings proved difficult to interpret in theoretical terms.

6. THE HOME-PRESCHOOL AND SOCIAL DEVELOPMENT

In a series of reports on a sample of more than 100 TMR school children, the authors of this chapter have reported on the preschool HOME in several publications (Meyers, Nihira, & Mink, 1983; Nihira *et al.,* 1980, 1981, 1983). Briefly, the HOME figured in predicting school achievement and adjustment from scores determined from interviews in the home; relation to impact of the retarded child on the family and to the child's social and psychological adjustment in the home.

One study reported significant relationships between the HOME subscales and school adjustment of TMR children between 9 and 16 years of age with a mean age of 12.5 years (Nihira *et al.,* 1981). The first-order correlation and canonical correlation analysis indicated that the HOME measures are significantly related to the children's social status rating, self-esteem, and measures of social competency and inversely related to the children's maladaptive behavior in school (the r's being in the high .20s and .30s). Some of the significant HOME measures are (1) Provision of Stimulation through Equipment, Toys, and Experiences, (2) Stimulation of Mature Behavior, (3) Provision of Stimulating Physical and Language Environment, (4) Pride, Affection, and Thoughtfulness, and (5) Avoidance of Restriction and Punishment. The preschool version of the HOME inventory appears to assess aspects of home environment relevant to school adjustment of older TMR children.

In a longitudinal study of the growth and adjustment of TMR adolescents (Nihira *et al.*, 1983), some of the HOME measures obtained at the beginning of the project predicted the change in the adolescents' social adjustment observed during the 3 subsequent years. The result indicated that the HOME measures such as Stimulation of Academic Behavior, Language Stimulation, and Variety of Stimulation, have significant impact upon social and psychological adjustment and, in lesser degree, on the development of cognitive and self-sufficiency skills. The results also revealed that the adolescents' initial status on emotional adjustment predicted the subsequent change in some HOME measures, i.e., as Pride, Affection, and Warmth, and the Avoidance of Physical Punishment. The adolescents' initial status on cognitive development appears to influence the level of cognitive stimulation at home, such as Stimulation of Academic Behavior and Stimulation through Toys, Games, and Reading. Analyzing longitudinal data, this study demonstrated the reciprocal relationship between some measures of HOME and the cognitive and social development of TMR adolescents.

B. Henderson Environmental Learning Process Scale

Henderson, Bergan, and Hurt (1972) developed a self-administering or interview questionnaire entitled HELPS (the Henderson Environmental Learning Process Scale). The HELPS is designed to assess the home environment of school-aged children. The 51 Likert-type items are clustered into five factorially derived subscales: (1) Extended Interests and Community Involvement, (2) Valuing Language and School Related Behavior, (3) Intellectual Guidance, (4) Providing a Supportive Environment for School Learning, and (5) Attention. A recent factor analytic study involving families of EMR students yielded three factors. Two are similar to the first and fourth factors by Henderson *et al.* (1972), the third appears to measure educational expectations and aspirations (Silverstein, 1978).

1. THE HELPS AND SOCIAL DEVELOPMENT

In a longitudinal study of a group of EMR students and their families, HELPS was administered to the parents along with other measures of home environment (Nihira *et al.*, 1980). In this study, the canonical correlation analysis was used in order to define factorial dimensions of home environment relevant to the growth and adjustment of EMR students. Two subscales of HELPS (1) Providing Supportive Environment for School Learning and (2) Educational Expectations and Aspirations, have made major contributions (canonical loadings of .49 and .48) in the first canonical factor labeled Harmony and Educational Guidance. This factor was significantly related to the corresponding canonical factor labeled Adaptive Competence of the Child (canonical $R = .79$). The HELPS factor, Providing Supportive Environment for School Learning, also contributed (canonical loading of .40) to the second canonical factor labeled Family Harmony, which was, in turn, related to the students' social adjustment (canonical $R = .67$). The above study was based upon cross-sectional data, thus the results should be regarded to show the concurrent relationship between the HELPS measures and the child development and adjustment.

Meyers, Nihira, and Mink (1984) examined a longitudinal relationship between the home environment and the development of the same group of EMR students. The two factors of HELPS mentioned in the previous study were found to predict the students' social adjustment measured in the end of years 1 and 2.

2. THE HELPS AND SCHOOL ACHIEVEMENT

HELPS was administered to the mothers of 60 lower SES Mexican-American first graders and 66 middle SES Anglo-American first graders (Henderson *et al.*, 1972). Stepwise regression analysis revealed significant relationships between the children's performance on both the Stanford Early School Achievement Test and Boehm Test of Basic Concept and the HELPS scores ($r = .72$). Two factor scores, Valuing Language and School Related Behavior and Providing a Supportive Environment for School Learning, accounted for more than 90% of the predicted variance.

In a follow-up study of 35 Mexican-American children, Henderson (1972) reported significant predictive relationships (.39 to .61) between the HELPS scores taken when the children entered the first grade and their performance on a reading achievement test at the end of third grade.

Although only a few studies employing HELPS have appeared in the literature, the instrument seems to assess aspects of home environment relevant to school achievement of nonhandicapped children as well as social competency and adjustment of EMR adolescents.

IV. CHILD-REARING ATTITUDES AND VALUES

Decades of research have explored the association between child-rearing attitudes of parents and the developing personality and adjustment of children. The parent–child research may be traced through works by Baldwin *et al.* (1949), Schaefer and Bell (1958), Kagan and Moss (1962), Yarrow *et al.* (1968), Baumrind (1971), and others. Three salient dimensions that seem stable across studies are (1) loving acceptance vs rejection or disregard of the child; (2) restrictiveness vs permissiveness, ranging from authoritative control through laissez-faire; and (3) involvement with the child's development vs detachment. The position a parent takes in the three-dimensional space depicts his or her child-rearing attitudes and practices described by such terms as overprotection, domination, neglect, rejection, or responsibility.

Through longitudinal research of the families of TMR and EMR children, the authors of this chapter determined that certain existing inventories reviewed in the previous sections assessed aspects of home environment relevant to the development of handicapped children. None, however, yielded a sufficiently satisfying picture of the sense of love and attachment for the mentally retarded child, the family dynamics related to the child, or family cohesion in providing care, uncovered only by in-depth ethnographic observation (White & Watts, 1973). The Home Quality Rating Scale described below is an attempt to secure those characteristics of home environment that are not adequately covered by available standardized instruments.

The Home Quality Rating Scale

The HQRS (Home Quality Rating Scale) is designed to assess child-rearing attitudes and family adjustment to the mentally retarded child, and certain physical characteristics of the child's home environment (Meyers, Mink, & Nihira, 1977). The scale consists of 26 Likert-type rating scales to be completed by the person who visits the homes and interviews the parents. The scale provides the following five factor scores: (1) Harmony and Quality of Parenting, (2) Concordance in Support of Child Care, (3) Openness and Awareness of Respondent, (4) Quality of Residential Environment, and (5) Quality of Residential Area. The internal consistency reliabilities (Cronbach's alpha) of the factor scores are .83, .78, .76, .71, and .56 for each of the five factor scores.

1. THE HQRS AND SOCIAL DEVELOPMENT

The HQRS was employed in a longitudinal investigation of TMR and EMR students and their home environment. In this study the relationships between home environment, family adjustment, and the behavior of the mentally retarded children were examined by a series of canonical correlation analyses (Nihira *et al.,* 1980). In the TMR group, the HQRS factor, Harmony and Quality of Parenting, was the primary defining variable of the first canonical factor of the home environment. This canonical factor was related to the social adjustment of TMR students (canonical $R = .83$), the parents' level of coping with the child's problems (canonical $R = .84$), and negatively related to the impact of mental retardation on the family (canonical $R = .74$).

In the EMR group, the HQRS factor, Harmony and Quality of Parenting, contributed significantly to the first canonical factor of home environment labeled Harmony and Educational Guidance, and also to the second canonical factor labeled Family Harmony. The first canonical factor was related to the adaptive competence of EMR students (canonical $R = .79$). The second canonical factor was related to the social adjustment of the EMR students (canonical $R = .67$). In a separate canonical analysis of family adjustment problems, the same HQRS factor, Harmony and Quality of Parenting, was significantly related to the parents' level of coping with the child's problems (canonical $R = .82$).

The relationship between the HQRS factors and the students' developmental change in subsequent years was examined by stepwise multiple regression analysis (Meyers *et al.*, 1979, 1980, 1984). For both TMR and EMR groups, Harmony and Quality of Parenting contributed significantly to the prediction of the student's psychological adjustment 1 and 2 years later. Concordance in Support of Child Care and Openness and Awareness of Disability also contributed to the prediction of the students' psychosocial adjustment in the subsequent years.

These results were generally confirmed by a 4-year longitudinal study of the TMR students (Nihira *et al.*, 1983). In addition to the above-mentioned factors, Quality of Residential Environment and Quality of Residential Area were found to predict the change in Personal maladaptation of the TMR students during the 3 subsequent years. The study also indicated the reciprocal influence of the child on some of the HQRS factors during the study period.

2. THE HQRS AND SOCIAL ADJUSTMENT

Nihira *et al.* (1981) examined the relationship between home environment and school adjustment of TMR students. The HQRS was utilized in the study along with other measures of home environment. The HQRS factor, Harmony and Quality of Parenting, was significantly related to several measures of school adjustment including self-esteem measured by the Coopersmith Self-Esteem Behavior ($r = .39$), Outgoing-expressiveness measured by the Teacher Rating Scale ($r = .29$), Social status rating by teacher ($r = .26$), and inversely related to personal maladaptation ($r = -.37$), and social maladaptation ($r = -.30$) measured by the AAMD Adaptive Behavior Scale, and misbehavior score on the Teacher Rating Scale. In canonical correlation analysis, the HQRS factor, Harmony and Quality of Parenting, was the primary defining variable of the first canonical factor of home environment which was associated with the corresponding canonical factor of the students' adjustment in school (canonical $R = .82$).

V. SUMMARY AND CONCLUSIONS

In this article, we have reviewed child development research which utilized standard instruments to assess qualities of the home environment. The instruments were selected on the basis of their actual or potential application for research in mental retardation. We have identified at least three different theoretical trends in the assessment of psychosocial factors or proximal variables of home environment: (1) psychosocial climate and environmental press as perceived by the family members, (2) environmental process variables derived from the reinforcement analysis of the environment, and (3) parental attitudes and values.

The general psychosocial climate of the home as assessed by the FES apparently plays a significant role in the cognitive and social development of mentally retarded as well as normal children and adolescents. Among the FES factors, the significance of family cohesion and low conflict has been recognized repeatedly across different populations of children of all ages. Achievement Orientation, Moral–Religious Emphasis, Expressiveness, and the lack of Control are also found to be significant in some populations. In younger children, these factors appear to relate to both cognitive and social development, while for older children and adolescents, the factors appear to relate more to psychosocial adjustment than to cognitive development.

The HOME-Infant version, known as a measure of environmental process variables, has been extensively employed in the early childhood research. The accumulating evidence repeatedly indicates the effect of early stimulation upon the later cognitive development of young children. Evidence also suggests that some factors of HOME Inventory designed to stimulate cognitive development are related to the psychosocial adjustment of TMR adolescents. Conversely, the lack of cognitive stimulation at home appears to reinforce social maladaptation of these adolescents. The HELPS, another measure of environmental process variables, is found to predict school achievement in the lower primary grades, and social competency of EMR adolescents. The literature reviewed strongly supports the view that the environmental process variables measure significant aspects of learning environment that are not covered by socioeconomic status or family structure variables. The preschool version of HOME appears to be relevant to the studies of home environment of older TMR children.

The HQRS is the only instrument reviewed here that measures child-rearing attitudes and values. Two of its factors, Harmony and Quality of Parenting and Concordance in Support of Child Care, are related to several measures of psychosocial adjustment both at home and school. The reason for this finding may be the global nature of these factors, representing the clinical impression of the interviewers. It is our belief that the HQRS taps certain aspects of family dynamics not measured by other instruments reviewed in this chapter.

Some of the instruments reviewed have been used with white as well as black families (HOME), Mexican-American families (HELPS), and German families (FES). There is a need to further document the effectiveness of these instruments in other cultures and in various subcultures in America. Some instruments or certain items may be valid in selected cultures but others may be relevant across all cultures and subcultures.

Most studies cited examined the homes and children of specific age. Therefore, caution must be exercised in generalizing the findings to the children of other age ranges. A given environmental stimulus may not be equally potent to the children of different ages. Some authors even argued that environmental instruments should be modeled after IQ tests so that different items would be applied at each developmental level (Bradley & Caldwell, 1978; Elardo & Bradley, 1981). Theoretically, there will always be a set of critical environmental stimuli for every developmental level.

Another group of studies has attempted to answer the question of whether different types of home environment are related to different child behaviors. Three different taxonomies were cited (Moos & Moos, 1976; Mink *et al.*, 1984). They all have isolated different family types and have discovered significant differences between types on family and child characteristics and behavior.

The literature reviewed here reported significant relationships between child development and home environment. These results should not be interpreted as solely the effect of the environment on the child. Some of the studies are of a longitudinal nature, providing some justification for speculating on causal directions. Bradley *et al.* (1979) utilized the cross-lagged correlational analysis to examine the direction of causal effects and the reciprocal influence between children and their parents. Another study utilized a series of hierarchical multiple regression analysis to examine the predictive relationships in both directions, (Nihira *et al.*, 1983). The results provided a strong evidence of reciprocal interactions between the home environment and child development in TMR adolescents. Significant effects of the child's cognitive development and social adjustment were observed on several factors of HOME and HQRS, but only two of the FES factors were found to be influenced by the child's status.

It may be possible to speculate that those environmental factors that are proximal to the child, e.g., use of physical punishment, are more sensitive to the reciprocal effect than those less proximal, e.g., family cohesiveness. An emerging view in the literature is that there are changes that occur in both the child and home environment that influence their interactive pattern.

The last decade has witnessed a burgeoning interest in the relationship of home environment with child behavior. The existing measures of home environment have been largely based upon empirical studies without well-developed theories of environment–development relationship. However, just as the study of family structure gave way to the study of the psychosocial environment of the home, it is to be hoped that the next stage will be the development of theoretical models which will relate family environment to child behavior and further to adult behavior.

ACKNOWLEDGMENT

Preparation of this article was partially supported by grants from the National Institute of Child Health and Human Development.

REFERENCES

Anastasi, A. Psychology, psychologists and psychological testing. *American Psychologist,* 1967, **22,** 297–306.

Bakeman, R., & Brown, J. V. Early intervention: Consequences for social and mental development at three years. *Child Development,* 1980, **51,** 437–447.

Baldwin, A., Kalhorn, J., & Breese, F. The appraisal of parent behavior. *Psychological Monographs,* 1949, **63,** (4, Whole No., 299).

Bandura, A. *Principles of behavior modification.* New York: Holt, 1969.

Baumrind, D. Current patterns of parental authority. *Developmental Psychology Monographs,* 1971, **4,** (1).

Becker, C. Consequences of different kinds of parental discipline. In M. L. Hoffman & L. W. Hoffman (Eds.), *Review of child developmental research* (Vol. 1). New York: Russell Sage Foundation, 1964.

Bell, L. G., & Bell, D. C. Family climate and the role of the female adolescent: Determinants of adolescent functioning. *Family Relations,* 1982, **31,** 519–527.

Bloom, B. *Stability and change in human characteristics.* New York: Wiley, 1964.

Bradley, R. H., & Caldwell, B. M. The relation of infant's home environments to mental test performance at fifty-four months: A follow-up study. *Child Development,* 1976, **47,** 1172–1174. (a)

Bradley, R. H., & Caldwell, B. M. Early home environment and changes in mental test performance in children from six to thirty-six months. *Developmental Psychology.* 1976, **12,** 93–137. (b)

Bradley, R. H., & Caldwell, B. M. Home observation for Measurement of the Environment: A validation study of screening efficiency. *American Journal of Mental Deficiency,* 1977, **81** (5), 417–420.

Bradley, R. H., & Caldwell, B. M. Screening the environment, *American Journal of Orthopsychiatry,* 1978, **48** (1), 114–130.

Bradley, R. H., & Caldwell, B. M. Home observation for Measurement of the Environment: A revision of the preschool scale. *American Journal of Mental Deficiency,* 1979, **84,** 235–244 (a).

Bradley, R. H., & Caldwell, B. M. Home environment and locus of control. *Journal of Clinical Child Psychology,* 1979, **8,** 107–111. (b)

Bradley, R. H., & Caldwell, B. M. The home inventory: A validation of the pre-school scale for black children. *Child Development,* 1981, **52,** 708–710.

Bradley, R. H., Caldwell, B. M., & Elardo, R. Home environment, social status, and mental test performance, *Journal of Educational Psychology,* 1977, **69,** 697–701.

Bradley, R. H., Caldwell, B. M., & Elardo, R. Home environment and cognitive development in the first 2 years: Cross-lagged panel analysis. *Developmental Psychology,* 1979, **15,** 246–250.

Caldwell, B. and Bradley, R. *Home observation for measurement of the environment, manual.* The Center for Child Development and Education, Little Rock: Arkansas, University of Arkansas, 1979.

Caldwell, B. M., Bradley, R., & Elardo, R. Early stimulation. In J. Wortis (Ed.), *Mental retardation and developmental disabilities* (Vol. 7). New York: Brunner/Mazel, 1975.

Caldwell, B. M., Heider, J., & Kaplan, B. *The inventory of home stimulation.* Paper presented at the 64th annual convention of the American Psychological Association, New York, 1966.

Dave, R. H. *The identification and measurement of environmental process variables that are related to educational achievement.* Unpublished doctoral dissertation, University of Chicago, 1963.

Draper, J. *Specific aspects of family environment as they relate to a child's performance.* Unpublished masters thesis, George Peabody College for Teachers, 1977.

Elardo, R., & Bradley, R. H. The HOME observation for measurement of the environment (HOME) Scale: review of research. *Developmental Review,* 1981, **1,** 113–145.

Elardo, R., Bradley, R., & Caldwell, B. M. The relation of infant's home environments to mental test performance from six to thirty-six months: A longitudinal analysis. *Child Development,* 1975, **46,** 71–76.

Elardo, R., Bradley, R., & Caldwell, B. M. A longitudinal study of the relation of infant's home environments to language development at age three. *Child Development,* 1977, **48,** 596–603.

Fowler, P. C. Family environment and early behavioral development: A structural analysis of dependencies. *Psychological Reports,* 1980, **47,** 611–617.

Fowler, P. C. Maximum likelihood factor structure of the family environment scale. *Journal of Clinical Psychology,* 1981, **37,** 160–164.

Gottfried, A. W., & Gottfried, A. E. Home environment and mental development in young children of middle-class families. In A. W. Gottfried (Ed.), *Home environment and early mental development: Longitudinal research.* New York: Academic Press, 1984.

Green, L. W. Manual for scoring socioeconomic status for research on health behavior. *Public Health Reports,* 1970, **85,** 815–827.

Hamilton, M. Evaluation of a parent and child center program. *Child Welfare,* 1972, **51,** 248–258.

Henderson, R. Environmental predictors of academic performance of Mexican-American children. *Journal of Consulting and Clinical Psychology,* 1972, **38,** 297.

Henderson, R. W., Bergan, J. R., & Hurt, M. Development and validation of the Henderson Environmental Learning Process Scale. *Journal of Social Psychology,* 1972, **88,** 185–196.

Hollenbeck, A. R. Early infant home environments: Validation of the Home Observation for Measurement of the Environment inventory. *Developmental Psychology,* 1978, **14,** 416–418.

Hunt, J. McV. *Intelligence and experience.* New York: Ronald Press, 1961.

Insel, P. M., & Moos, R. G. Psychological environments: Expanding the scope of human ecology. *American Psychologist,* 1974, **29,** 179–188.

Intagliata, J. *The use of family care homes as a community placement for mentally retarded persons in New York state.* Paper presented at the annual convention of the American Association on Mental Deficiency, Denver, May, 1978.

Janes, C., & Hesselbrock, V. *Perceived family environment and school adjustment of children of schizophrenics.* Paper presented at the American Psychological Association convention, Washington, D.C., September, 1976.

Kagan, J., & Moss, H. A. *Birth to maturity: A study of psychological development.* New York: Wiley, 1962.

Kelleghan, T. Relationships between home environment and scholastic behavior in a disadvantaged population. *Journal of Educational Psychology,* 1977, **69,** 754–760.

Laing, J. A., & Sines, J. O. The home environment questionnaire: An instrument for assessing several behaviorally relevant dimensions of children's environments. *Journal of Pediatric Psychology,* 1982, **1,** 425–449.

Malin, N. *Pathways to child placement: Parental perceptions of adolescent children in residential treatment.* Unpublished doctoral dissertation, Department of Social Welfare, University of California, Los Angeles, 1978.

Marjoribanks, K. Environment, social class, and mental abilities. In K. Marjoribanks (Ed.), *Environment for learning.* Slough: NFER, 1974.

Metzl, M. N. Teaching parents a strategy for enhancing infant development. *Child Development,* 1980, **51,** 583–586.

Meyers, C. E., Mink, I. T., & Nihira, K. *Home quality rating scale.* Pomona, California: UCLA/Neuropsychiatric Institute-Lanterman State Hospital Research Group, 1977.

Meyers, C. E., Nihira, K., & Mink, I. *Home of retarded students: Characteristics and their relationship with development.* Paper presented at the 87th annual convention of the American Psychological Association, New York, September, 1979.

Meyers, C. E., Nihira, K., & Mink, I. T., *Problems of validating measures of community residential environments.* Paper presented at the 12th annual Gatlinburg Conference on Research in MR/DD, Gatlinburg, Tennessee, March, 1980.

Meyers, C. E., Nihira, K., & Mink, I. T. Predicting retarded students' short-term growth from home environment. *Applied Research in Mental Retardation,* 1984, **5,** 137–146.

Mink, I. T., Meyers, C. E., & Nihira, K. Lifestyles in families with slow learning children: A Taxonomy. *Working Paper of the Socio-Behavioral Group, No. 18,* Los Angeles, California: Mental Retardation Research Center, UCLA, 1981.

Mink, I. T., Meyers, C. E., & Nihira, K. Taxonomy of family life styles: II. Home with slow learning children. *American Journal of Mental Deficiency,* 1984, in press.

Mink, I. T., Nihira, K., & Meyers, C. E. Taxomony of family life styles: I. Homes with TMR children. *American Journal of Mental Deficiency,* 1983, **87,** 484–497.

Mischel, W. *Personality and assessment.* New York: Wiley, 1968.

Mischel, W. The interaction of person and situation. In D. Magnusson & N. S. Endler (Eds.), *Personality at the crossroads.* Hillsdale, New Jersey: Erlbaum, 1977.

Moos, R. H. Conceptualizations of human environments. *American Psychologist,* 1973, **28,** 652–665.

Moos, R. H. *The social climate scales: An overview.* Palo Alto, California: Consulting Psychologists Press, 1974.

Moos, R. H. *Evaluating correctional and community settings.* New York: Wiley, 1975.

Moos, R. H., Insel, P. M., & Humphrey, B. *Family, work and group environment scales manual.* Palo Alto, California: Consulting Psychologists Press, 1974.

Moos, R. H., & Moos, B. S. Families. In R. H. Moos (Ed.), *Evaluating correctional and community settings.* New York: Wiley, 1975.

Moos, R. H., & Moos, B. S. A typology of family social environments. *Family Process,* 1976, **15,** 357–371.

Moos, R. H., & Moos, B. S. *Family environment scale manual.* Palo Alto, California: Consulting Psychologists Press, 1981.

Murray, H. A. *Explorations in personality*. London and New York: Oxford Univ. Press, 1938.

Nihira, K., Meyers, C. E., & Mink, I. T. Home environment, family adjustment, and the development of mentally retarded children. *Applied Research in Mental Retardation*, 1980, **1**, 5–24.

Nihira, K., Meyers, C. E., & Mink, I. T. Reciprocal relationship between home environment and development of TMR adolescents. *American Journal of Mental Deficiency*, 1983, **88**, 139–149.

Nihira, K., Mink, I. T., & Meyers, C. E. Relationship between home environment and school adjustment of the TMR children. *American Journal of Mental Deficiency*, 1981, **86**, 8–15.

Nowicki, S., & Schneewind, K. *Relationship of family climate variables to locus of control orientation as a function of culture, sex and age*. Unpublished manuscript, Emory University, Atlanta, GA, 1977.

Ollendick, D. G., Berteaux, P. J., & Horne, A. M. Relationships among maternal attitudes, perceived family environments, and preschoolers behavior. *Perceptual and Motor Skills*, 1978, **46**, 1092–1094.

Piper, M. C., & Ramsay, M. K. Effects of early home environment on the mental development of Down syndrome infants. *American Journal of Mental Deficiency*, 1980, **85**, 39–44.

Ramey, C. T., Farran, D. C., & Campbell, F. A. Predicting IQ from mother-infant interactions. *Child Development*, 1979, **50**, 804–814.

Ramey, C. T., Mills, P., Campbell, F. A., & O'Brien, C. Infants' home environments: Comparison of high-risk families and families from the general population. *American Journal of Mental Deficiency*, 1975, **80**, 40–42.

Reinhart, G. *One-parent families: A study of divorced mothers and adolescents using social climate and relationship styles*. Unpublished doctoral dissertation, California School of Professional Psychology, San Francisco, 1977.

Rheingold, H., & Eckerman, C. Some proposals for unifying the study of social development. In M. Lewis & M. Rosenblum (Eds.), *Friendship and peer relations*. New York: Wiley, 1975.

Schaefer, E. S., & Bell, R. O. Development of a parental attitude research instrument. *Child Development*, 1958, **29**, 339–361.

Scoresby, A. L., & Christensen, B. Differences in interaction and environmental conditions of clinic and non-clinic families: Implications for counselors. *Journal of Marriage and Family Counseling*, 1976, **2**, 63–71.

Sears, R., Maccoby, E., & Levin, H. *Patterns of child-rearing*. Evanston, Illinois: Row & Peterson, 1957.

Silverstein, A. B. Personal communication, 1978.

Sines, J. O. *The home environment questionnaire*. Iowa City, Iowa: Psychological Assessment and Services, 1982. (P.O. Box 1031, Iowa City, Iowa, 52244).

Sines, J. O., Paulker, J. D., Sines, L. K., and Owen, D. R. Identification of clinically relevant dimensions of children's behavior. *Journal of Consulting and Clinical Psychology*, 1969, **33**, 728–734.

Sines, J. O., & Zimmerman, M. Assessing children's psychosocial environments. *Clinical Psychology Review*, 1981, **1**, 387–413.

Sontag, L., Baker, C., & Nelson, V. Mental growth and personality development: A longitudinal study. *Monographs of the Society for Research in Child Development*, 1958, **21** (2, Whole No. 68).

Steinbock, L. Nest-leaving: Family systems of runaway adolescents. (Doctoral dissertation, California School of Professional Psychology, San Francisco, 1977). *Dissertation Abstracts International*, 1978, **38**.

Stern, G. G., Stein, M. I., & Bloom, B. S. *Methods in personality assessment*. Glencoe, Illinois: Free Press, 1956.

Stevenson, M. B., & Lamb, M. E. Effects of infant sociability and the caretaking environment on infant cognitive performance. *Child Development,* 1979, **50**, 340–349.

Tabackman, M. A study of family psycho-social environment and its relationship to academic achievement in gifted adolescents. (Doctoral dissertation, University of Illinois at Urbana-Champaign, 1976). *Dissertation Abstracts International,* 1977, **37**.

Van Doorninck, W. J., Caldwell, B. M., Wright, C., & Frankenburg, W. K. The relationship between twelve-month home stimulation and school achievement. *Child Development,* 1981, **52**, 1080–1083.

Weiss, J. The identification and measurement of home environment factors related to achievement motivation and self-esteem. In K. Marjoribanks (Ed.), *Environment for learning.* Slough: NFER, 1974.

White, B. L., & Watts, J. C. *Experience and environment: Major influences on the development of the young child.* New York: Prentice-Hall, 1973.

Willer, B. *Post institutional adjustment of the retarded returned to the natural families.* Paper presented at the annual convention of the American Association on Mental Deficiency, Denver, May, 1978.

Wulbert, M., Inglis, S., Kriegsmann, E., & Mills, B. Language delay and associated mother-child interactions. *Developmental Psychology,* 1975, **11**, 61–70.

Yarrow, M., Campbell, J., & Burton, R. *Child-rearing.* San Francisco, California: Jossey-Bass, 1968.

Current Trends and Changes
in Institutions
for the Mentally Retarded

R. K. EYMAN

SCHOOL OF EDUCATION
UNIVERSITY OF CALIFORNIA, RIVERSIDE
RIVERSIDE, CALIFORNIA

S. A. BORTHWICK

MENTAL RETARDATION RESEARCH CENTER
LANTERMAN RESEARCH GROUP
UNIVERSITY OF CALIFORNIA, LOS ANGELES
LOS ANGELES, CALIFORNIA

G. TARJAN

DEPARTMENT OF PSYCHIATRY
SCHOOL OF MEDICINE
UNIVERSITY OF CALIFORNIA, LOS ANGELES
LOS ANGELES, CALIFORNIA

INTERNATIONAL REVIEW OF RESEARCH IN
MENTAL RETARDATION, Vol. 12

I. INTRODUCTION

The emphasis on deinstitutionalization of mentally retarded people in the past decade has resulted in major changes to the approach toward residential care and to the entire service delivery system. Bachrach (1981) defined deinstitutionalization as a process involving the avoidance of traditional institutional settings whenever possible for the mentally retarded, and the concurrent expansion of community-based facilities for the care of these individuals. Hence, deinstitutionalization is a complex phenomenon affecting not only those individuals who are moved from institutional settings to other placements, but also residual institution populations and the people who already live in community placements. Since 1970, considerable energy has been directed toward the development and use of alternate placements in the community, as vehicles for deinstitutionalization (Bruininks, Kudla, Hauber, Hill, & Wieck, 1981). An indication of the community influence, even in institutions, is the fact that placement decisions are often made by community-based agencies rather than by institutional staff.

It is widely known by this time that the number of clients who reside in large institutions in this country has drastically declined since the emphasis on deinstitutionalization (Scheerenberger, 1982). Moreover, because the more capable residents were most likely to be placed in community settings, residual institutional populations are considerably more impaired than earlier groups. New institutional admission criteria, characteristics of discharges and of readmissions all dynamically affect the nature of institutions and of community residences.

The purpose of this article is to examine trends in institutional population characteristics, admissions, discharges, readmissions, and mortality over the last three decades. We will attempt to provide a review of the existing literature on changes in the composition of institutions, and include the findings from a study we have recently completed on this topic. This effort will have implications for both institution and community placements within the total service system.

II. OUR RECENT WORK

The purpose of our investigation was to examine individual population movement, behavior, and demographic data for residents of an institution for the mentally retarded, from 1949 to 1982. A second institution was examined from 1971 to 1982. In contrast to the surveys conducted by Scheerenberger (1977, 1978a,b, 1979, 1982) and Rotegard, Bruininks, and Lakin (1982), the data reported from our study are based on continuous monitoring of the composition of the two sample institutions as well as all releases, retentions, and deaths over an extended period of time. This more in-depth movement and mortality data will be compared with the survey data of larger samples reported by Rotegard *et al.* (1982), Scheerenberger (1976, 1978b, 1979, 1981), and related studies.

Throughout this article we will refer to specific findings of our study. In order for our findings to be as meaningful as possible, a brief description of the study will be presented.

A. Sample

The populations of two institutions were examined. Lanterman State Hospital (formerly Pacific State Hospital) in Pomona, California, has been a public residential facility for the mentally retarded since 1927. Population movement data were available for this institution from 1949 until the present. A second western state hospital was also examined for comparison of trends and populations. In this report, Lanterman State Hospital is referred to as LSH, and the second western state hospital as WSH.

Cross-sectional distributions characterize the clients in residence at six cut-off points. Moreover, admission cohorts were followed for 3 years after intake, noting deaths, discharges, and readmissions. For the LSH sample we included the same cohorts (1949–1951, 1959–1961, 1966–1968) that had been examined in the Tarjan, Wright, Eyman, and Keeran (1973) study, adding adaptive behavior characteristics and two new cohorts to the Tarjan data. The new cohorts represent the final period prior to major deinstitutionalization efforts in 1972–1974, and it is the most recent data available for clients who could be followed for 3 years, from 1976 to 1978. A population movement data system was instituted in WSH in 1972; thus, the first cohort collection period is 1972–1974. In 1975–1976 another institution in the state was closed, as part of the deinstitutionalization process, and WSH was the recipient of a number of clients who were not placed in the community or transferred to other institutions. The final cohort for WSH was also 1976–1978. Cross-sectional data are also reported for both institutions for 1982 in order to present a current description of clients in these facilities. All clients who were in residence or on short home visits on June 30 of the years examined were included in the cross-sectional analysis.

B. Cohorts

Admission, discharge, and readmission practices differ between institutions and have also changed over the years. In order to provide a report with consistent interpretations, the following definitions were applied.

1. ADMISSION COHORTS

Five 3-year admission cohorts were comprised of clients admitted to LSH during the calendar years 1949–1951, 1959–1961, 1966–1968, 1969–1971, and 1976–1978. WSH cohorts included intake periods 1972–1974 and 1976–1978. The following people were excluded from the cohorts: (1) admitted for observation only, (2) diagnosed not mentally retarded, (3) directly discharged or placed in the community within 30 days of admission, and (4) transferred to another state hospital within 3 years. Each cohort member was followed for 3 years.

2. DISCHARGES

Discharges were defined as clients who were placed in the community within 3 years of admission, and who remained in the community for at least 6 months. Clients who were directly discharged to parental homes within 3 years were also included in this group.

3. READMISSIONS

Clients who met the criteria for discharges and who were readmitted to the hospital within 1 year of the discharge date were considered as readmissions.

4. DEATHS/MORTALITY RATES

Clients who died within 3 years of admission were included in the computation of death rates. Death rates per 1000 were computed for the first 6 months and the first 3 years, using the formula

$$\text{rate} = \frac{DT}{n - DT} \times 1000$$

where DT is the number of deaths in the time period (i.e., 6 months or 3 years), and n is the number of clients in the cohort with the characteristic being considered. The 3-year and 6-months death rates were computed by age, IQ, and diagnosis categories.

C. Client Characteristics

1. AGE GROUPS

The age groups were similar to those used in the Tarjan *et al.* (1973) study. Younger clients are grouped by preschool age (0–5 years), school age, preadolescence (6–11 years), and adolescence (12–17). Adult clients are 18 years and older.

2. IQ GROUPS

For historical reasons we used the same IQ groups that were selected for the Tarjan *et al.* (1973) study. The profoundly retarded are represented by IQ scores from 0 to 19, the moderately and severely retarded clients are in the IQ range from 20 to 49, and the mildly retarded are those with IQ scores from 50 to 70.

3. DIAGNOSIS

Four diagnostic groups were established: (1) retardation due to infections, intoxication, or trauma; (2) Down's syndrome; (3) functional retardation, including persons for whom medical examination did not indicate organic disease or pathological condition as accounting for retarded intellectual functioning (sometimes referred to as familial or undifferentiated conditions); and (4) other diagnoses, such as metabolic and gestational disorders, gross brain diseases, and unknown prenatal influences.

4. BEHAVIOR MEASUREMENT

Behavior characteristics were obtained by evaluating measures of adaptive behavior that have been collected annually at LSH since 1960, and at WSH since 1971. In all instances, we characterized clients as either having significant problems in an area and needing more assistance from others, or not having problems and requiring less assistance from others.

III. POPULATION CHARACTERISTICS

There are a number of studies that have examined the changing composition of public residential facilities for the mentally retarded (Eyman, 1976; Eyman & Borthwick, 1980; Janicki, Jacobson, Zigman, & Lubin, 1982; Lakin, Krantz, Bruininks, Clumpner, & Hill, 1982; Landesman-Dwyer & Schuckit, 1976; Rotegard *et al.*, 1982; Scheerenberger, 1978b, 1979; Tarjan *et al.*, 1973; Tarjan, Eyman, & Miller, 1969). All of these studies seem to be consistent in their general findings. The population of institutions is declining and the characteristics of individuals residing in institutions have changed. For example, it has been noted by both Scheerenberger (1978b) and Rotegard *et al.* (1982) that the mentally retarded population residing in institutions has declined from approximately 185,000 in 1969 to 135,000 in 1980. Rotegard *et al.* further report that 60% of mentally retarded people receiving residential services in 1969 were placed in an institution. This number declined to 42% of the retarded receiving such services who were placed in an institution in 1980.

A. Level of Functioning

Perhaps the most salient outcome of the deinstitutionalization process has been the movement of more capable residents into the community, and the subsequent lower functioning, residual populations in institutions. Tarjan *et al.* (1973) found the percentage of profoundly retarded in a California state institution to be 23% in 1950 and 50% by 1967. In our examination of the same institution, we found a continued increase in the percentage of profoundly retarded residents. There were 54% profoundly retarded in 1971, increasing to 78% in 1978, finally reaching 83% in 1982. The proportion of profoundly retarded residents in our second institution has also been increasing, although only 48% were in this category by 1982. Similarly, Rotegard *et al.* (1982) reported that the proportion of profoundly retarded residents in public institutions had doubled between 1965 and 1980. They estimated that by 1980, 55% of the residents in institutions nationally would be profoundly retarded, in comparison to 27% of such individuals institutionalized in 1965.

As would be expected, the findings of our study showed that the proportion of residents in the IQ category 50+ decreased in both institutions. The decline of these individuals was much more extreme in LSH than in WSH. The trends in level of functioning can be observed in Table I.

B. Sex

The incidence of mental retardation has been found to be higher among males than females (Farber, 1968; MacMillan, 1977; Mumpower, 1970). Moreover, males have historically made up the majority of residents in institutions (Rotegard *et al.*, 1982; Bruininks, Hauber, & Kudla, 1979; Scheerenberger, 1978b, 1982). According to Scheerenberger (1978b) the percentage of male residents in public residential facilities increased from 54% in 1976 to 65% in 1981. Hill and Bruininks' 1981 sample, however, consisted of only 55% males. In contrast to Scheerenberger's findings, the distribution of residents by sex remained reasonably stable for both institutions in our study. In 1950 and 1982 there were 58% males in LSH. In 1971 and 1982

TABLE I
PERCENTAGE OF RESIDENTS BY IQ GROUP

IQ	1971	1978	1982
LSH			
0–19	54	78	83
20–49	37	19	16
50 +	9	3	1
WSH			
0–19	11	47	48
20–49	51	24	24
50 +	38	29	28

there were 60 and 63% males in WSH, respectively. Rotegard *et al.* (1982) quite appropriately mentioned the fact that males made up only 49% of the population as a whole in 1981. Hence, all figures, including ours, suggest disproportionately greater numbers of males than females reside in institutions.

C. Age

Rotegard *et al.* (1982) reported that there had been an increase in the average age of mentally retarded persons in residential care facilities. Scheerenberger (1979) also found the percentage of adult residents had increased steadily from 1964 until it began to stabilize in 1978–1979 at 70%. Similar trends were found in our two samples (Table II).

Interestingly, the proportion of new admissions in the younger age groups has remained relatively stable. Rotegard *et al.* reported only 15% of all new admissions to public institutions were less than 11 years old (Bruininks *et al.,* 1979). In our 1976–1978 cohorts, 54% of new admissions to LSH were 11 years or younger, and 41% of those to WSH were 11 or younger. Rotegard *et al.* suggest a reason for this finding may be that many of the young residents are subsequently transferred to less restrictive settings. Our data suggest that while the discharge rate for residents from 0–5 years has increased only slightly, the discharge rate for clients 6–11 years has nearly doubled since 1971. The greatest increase in likelihood of release has been for clients 12–17 years. Conversely, adult residents are less likely to be discharged. Our mortality data also would indicate that some of the young admissions are likely to die within their first 3 years in the institution. Finally, the age distribution of the in-residence population over time is influenced by the process of natural aging which gradually moves residents from a younger category to an older one (Tarjan, Eyman, & Dingman, 1966).

TABLE II
PERCENTAGE OF RESIDENTS BY AGE

Age	1971	1978	1982
LSH			
0–11	21	4	4
12–17	32	12	11
18+	47	84	84
WSH			
0–11	15	5	4
12–17	26	16	13
18+	59	79	83

D. Diagnosis

The interpretation of admission trends by diagnosis must take into account the probable effects of increasing diligence in search of organic factors in addition to any "true" shift in the etiology of the residents. This change is of particular importance with regard to assignment to the "functional" group composed primarily of the "sociocultural" category, the proportion of which has declined over time. Although literature in this area is sparse, our study revealed dramatic changes in both in-residence clients and new admissions regarding the functional and other organic condition categories. Currently the majority of residents (as well as new admissions) receive a diagnosis implicating organic factors, i.e., "other." Residents with Down's syndrome, a relatively stable diagnostic condition, showed little change over time. Both sample institutions were reasonably consistent in these trends, supporting the contention that residents in institutions are individuals with more organic complications than were found in earlier years. Table III displays the trends in diagnosis.

E. Ethnicity

Bruininks et al. (1979) gathered data on the ethnic distribution of their national sample. The proportion of black clients in residential care (12%) was approximately equal to their numbers in the national population, although disproportionately more blacks were admitted to public facilities than to private, community-based facilities. Mentally retarded people of other minority groups, including Mexican-Americans, tended to be found in the service system in lower proportions than in the general population (Bruininks et al., 1979).

Our findings pertaining to ethnic status demonstrated differences between the institution serving an urban locality (LSH) versus the one serving a more

TABLE III
PERCENTAGES OF LSH CLIENTS BY DIAGNOSTIC CATEGORY

Category	1950	1961	1968	1971	1978	1982
Infection, intoxication, trauma	27	26	26	20	23	24
Down's syndrome	9	12	11	11	11	9
Functional	53	37	23	19	1	2
Other	11	25	40	50	65	65

rural area (WSH). LSH showed a general decrease of blacks and Mexican-Americans among residents (and admissions) through 1971, despite dramatic increases of these groups in the population catchment area of this facility. The establishment of classes for educable mentally retarded persons in the 1960s and the decreasing trend of institutionalization for minor delinquencies undoubtedly contributed to these shifts (Dingman, Tarjan, Eyman, & Mercer, 1967). Since 1971, there has been an increase in the proportion of Mexican-Americans in LSH, consistent with a larger number of admissions of this group in recent years. Moreover, the admissions reflect increases in the census figures for Mexican-Americans in the catchment area of the institution.

Although the numbers are small, there has also been a noticeable increase in the percentage of other minority groups, which is consistent with the migration of Asian and other groups to Southern California. The proportion of blacks (approximately 5%) has remained relatively stable since 1950. WSH has, over the years studied, continued to have a very small percentage of minority clients (range 4–5%), reflecting the makeup of its catchment area.

IV. POPULATION MOVEMENT

Changes in residential populations are dependent on the numbers and characteristics of the people who move in and out of institutions (Lakin, Bruininks, Doth, Hill, & Hauber, 1982). Lakin, Bruininks, Doth, and Hill (1982) and Best-Sigford, Bruininks, Lakin, and Hill (1982) have studied selected aspects of the population movement of institutionalized retarded individuals, based on records and interviews of sampled institutions and their staff. These studies suggested residents in all movement categories—discharges, admissions, etc—tended to be less severely impaired than the non-movers residing in institutions. In addition, 49% of the new admissions were reported to be transfers from other institutions, and 35% of these admissions were from the private sector. Although the authors cautioned the readers regarding the uncertainties involved in anecdotal data, these results are consistent with Tarjan *et al.* (1973) and Scheerenberger (1978b, 1979).

A. New Admissions

New admissions to institutions have decreased from about 8% of the total resident population in 1973 to 5% in 1976, and only 4% in 1979 (Scheerenberger, 1979). Our data indicated an overall decrease in the number of new admissions as well. The number of admissions to LSH steadily declined from 1140 between 1959 and 1961 to 216 between 1976 and 1978.

According to Eyman, O'Connor, Tarjan, and Justice (1972), by the 1970s admissions were largely determined by level of retardation, among other related factors. Scheerenberger's (1982, 1978b) surveys, however, have not supported the commonly held belief that new admissions are limited to the very young, severely or profoundly retarded person. In 1976 nearly half (47%) of the new admissions reported in his study were in the mild, moderate, and borderline categories of mental retardation. Only 53% were severely or profoundly retarded.

Our data support the findings of Eyma *et al.* (1972) and Rotegard *et al.* (1982), and appear contrary to Scheerenberger's results. Although the new admissions are higher functioning than some clients in residence, recent admission cohorts have become more debilitated, with fewer self-help or other independent living skills than earlier cohort groups. The percentage of new admissions to LSH who are profoundly retarded has nearly doubled, from 34% in the 1966–1969 cohort, to 64% in 1976–1978. Conversely, new admissions in the IQ range 20–49 have decreased sharply during the same period, from 48 to 23%. New clients in the mild level of retardation seem to have stablized at about 13%.

Table IV shows how the characteristics of new admissions have changed for the two latest cohorts, and how the most recent (1976–1978) cohort compares with the clients in residence in 1982. Specific abilities and skills of the new admissions for the final LSH cohort (1976–1978) closely approximate those of the in-residence population in 1982. Namely, 62% were nonverbal, and 80% needed help with both dressing and toileting. More than half of the admission cohort needed assistance when eating. More new admissions, however, tended to be nonambulatory (42%) than the in-residence population (32%). These figures suggest that new admissions will require as much or more assistance than existing residents.

The data from our second institution present a somewhat different picture with regard to new admissions. It reflects a trend that appears to be contra-

TABLE IV
CHARACTERISTICS OF ADMISSION COHORTS AND
IN-RESIDENCE POPULATION[a]

	1969–1971 Adm. cohort	1976–1978 Adm. cohort	Clients in-residence 1982[b]
LSH			
Profoundly retarded	48	64	83
0–5 years old	31	29	2
18+ years old	9	27	85
Nonambulatory	29	42	32
Needs help dressing	81	80	93
Not toilet trained	71	80	92
Needs help eating	38	54	69
Nonverbal	59	62	66
Aggressive	26	40	53
	1972–1974 Adm. Cohort		
WSH			
Profoundly retarded	57	47	48
0–5 years old	14	14	0
18+ years old	22	34	83
Nonambulatory	38	22	19
Needs help dressing	66	53	51
Not toilet trained	71	54	54
Needs help eating	57	45	48
Nonverbal	56	41	45
Aggressive	29	56	49

[a] Percentages.
[b] As of June 30th.

dictory to the LSH sample, yet it reveals an interesting reality that should not be overlooked. The new admissions in the 1976–1978 cohort for WSH were higher functioning, with more behavior problems than clients in the 1972–1974 cohort. The reason for this somewhat puzzling trend can be tied to the closure of a small institution serving moderately and mildly retarded clients with behavior problems in that state, who were subsequently transferred to WSH.

With regard to maladaptive behavior, recent studies by Eyman, Borthwick, and Miller (1981), Eyman and Call (1977), Eyman and Borthwick (1980), Hill and Bruininks (1981), and Landesman-Dwyer (1981) have all presented evidence that admissions to institutions are likely to evince aggressive or other maladaptive behavior. Whereas in the LSH 1966–1968 cohort only 13% of the new admissions were considered to have problems of aggression, as many as 40% of the final cohort (1976–1978) were identified as aggressive. Similarly, but less dramatic, 38 and 25% of the new admissions in the final cohort were considered to be hyperactive and self-injurious, respectively.

As noted regarding the in-residence population, the majority of recent admissions (1976–1978) to both LSH and WSH receive a diagnosis implicating organic factors, i.e., "other." The percentage of new admissions to LSH with Down's syndrome decreased from 8% for the 1969–1971 cohort to 4% in the 1976–1978 cohort, while admissions with infection, intoxication, and trauma increased from 19 to 29%. Similar trends were found for WSH.

The differences between our own samples, in addition to our differences with Scheerenberger's (1978b) conclusions, suggest that in some cases aggregate data for national samples can mask individual trends in institutions. Not only have states adopted varying rates of deinstitutionalization (Scheerenberger, 1980), but other factors, such as the opening and closing of institutions and the availability of community facilities, will influence residential placement patterns.

B. Discharges

Evaluation of discharges from institutions over time presents a special problem, because the definition of release and discharge has often (1) differed between institutions, (2) differed in studies reported, and (3) changed over time within an institution. Rotegard *et al.* (1982) and Lakin (1979) have noted the difficulties involved in obtaining accurate discharge and readmission data from state records. It is likely that such problems are due to changes in or interpretation of definitions of these terms. Moreover, because there are different ways to examine trends in release rates, comparisons across studies are difficult.

Previously, Tarjan *et al.* (1973) noted that the average time spent by clients who were on release to the community was on the rise between 1949 and 1968. In fact, time spent on release had generally quadrupled over the two-decade periods studied by Tarjan *et al.*, regardless of degree of handicap. Scheerenberger (1980) reported that the percentage of residents placed in 1979 (9.4% of the total resident population) was less than in previous years. In his recent report, however, Scheerenberger (1982) noted that the percentage had returned to the 1975 level of approximately 11%.

From another perspective, and one that seems most sensible to us, Lakin *et al.* (1982) compared ratios of releases to new admissions during 3-year periods of time. The number of discharges per 100 first admissions rose from an average of 61 in the 3-year period from 1963–1965, to an average of 283 in the period from 1978–1980. This ratio is, of course, influenced by the reduction in new admissions. It is difficult to compare these trends with Scheerenberger's, which are influenced instead by decreasing *total resident* populations. Nevertheless, both reports suggest mass moves out of institutions into community settings are no longer taking place, and placement rates have leveled off.

An interesting finding from Scheerenberger's (1982) survey was that respondents projected that only 60% of residents who were prepared for alternative placement would be placed during the forthcoming year. Community residential facilities have more latitude than institutions in selecting residents whom they choose to admit or release (Hill & Bruininks, 1981). Hence, it is possible that Scheerenberger's projections are partly tied to the availability of community residences for placement (Sutton, Sutter, Long, & Kelley, 1983). Scheerenberger (1977, 1979, 1981) and Lakin *et al.* (1982b) have examined the types of residence in which mentally retarded people who are released from institutions are placed.

Scheerenberger (1982) found that about two thirds (68%) of released residents were discharged to placements that were considered less restrictive than the institution. The other third consisted primarily of transfers to other state institutions. (It is important to note in comparisons with other studies that Scheerenberger's release rates include transfers to other institutions). Nursing home placements were down, from 15.5% of all placements in 1975–1976 to only 3.5% in 1980–1981. He also found a decreasing trend in the percentage of clients who were returned to their natural homes, from 22.2 to 18.6%, and who were placed in family care homes, from 14.7 to 6.4%. Conversely, Scheerenberger noted a significant increase in the use of group homes (from 15.9 to 23.5%), community intermediate care facilities (from 8.2 to 14.4%), and transfers to other institutions (from 11.6 to 22.6%).

Lakin *et al.* (1982b) reported release data by placement type for public and private institutions in 1977. Private residential facilities (average size = 15 mentally retarded residents), and natural/adoptive homes were the most popular placements, with 30.1 and 26.8% of releases, respectively. Transfers to other public institutions were also prevalent (22.1%). Other placements included family care (8.3%), nursing homes (11.4%), independent living, (14.7%), and other/unknown, (9.8%).

Because of different placement categories and different years examined, it is difficult to summarize the findings of Scheerenberger and Lakin *et al.;* however, some trends are evident. Transfers to other public institutions appear to make up nearly one fourth of all releases, and this proportion seems to be increasing over time. Group homes and community intermediate care facilities, of which there are many variations in size and other characteristics, are taking the largest percentage of clients released from institutions. Conversely, releases to family care appear to be declining. From the figures available, it is uncertain whether the proportion of clients being returned to their natural homes from the institution is declining, as Scheerenberger's data suggest.

In our study we examined yet another aspect of discharges—the relative likelihood of release for new admissions with particular characteristics. Evaluation of discharges over time in our two sample institutions presented special problems, in that the discharge procedures were different for the two institutions, and the definitions of release had changed over time. In the 1970s, many institutions, including the two sampled in our study, discharged residents rather than continuing a release program in which institution staff remained responsible for the welfare of the clients. In order to achieve some consistency over the study period, we considered a release that had lasted a minimum of 6 months as a discharge. A return to the institution within a year of discharge was treated as a readmission. "Discharge rates" refer to the percentages of release for clients who were admitted to the institution with certain characteristics. This rate seems more meaningful than actual percentages of release, because it takes into account the percentage of clients who were admitted with those characteristics. Clients who were transferred to other institutions were eliminated from the cohorts, hence, our discharges do not include this type of release. Table V displays pertinent data with regard to discharge rates.

The rate of discharges for mildly retarded (IQ 50+) residents in LSH increased from 33% in 1949–1951 to 86% in 1976–1978. This finding is opposite to what the percent of total discharged clients indicated, i.e., the actual percentage of releases who were mildly retarded *dropped,* but the likelihood of a new admission who was mildly retarded being released within 3 years increased substantially. The reason for the high percentage of mildly retarded who were discharged relative to the total number of clients discharged is simply that more individuals were mildly retarded in earlier cohorts compared to later admissions. Focusing on the rate discharged by level of retardation in LSH, it can also be observed that the discharge rate for the IQ group 20–49 rose from 1949–1951 to 1976–1978 (see Table II). Conversely, a consistent trend for discharge rates of the profoundly retarded (IQ 0–19) was not discernible. WSH exhibited higher discharge rates for all IQ levels, suggesting a general mandate to deinstitutionalize which had, in all probability, occurred earlier in LSH. Changes in the pattern of discharge rate of Mexican-Americans in the 1950s and 1960s reflected the disproportionate number of this group who had borderline IQs and were committed to an institution for minor offenses. The length of stay for such individuals was usually short. By the 1970s, admissions were largely determined by level of retardation among other related factors (Eyman *et al.,* 1972).

TABLE V

Characteristics of LSH Discharges:
Percentage of Cohort Discharged and Discharge Rate

	1949–1951	1959–1961	1966–1968	1969–1971	1976–1978
Number discharged	107	239	303	139	83
Percentage of cohort	20	21	33	25	38
IQ					
0–19	7[a](5)[b]	22(20)	28(30)	27(13)	31(20)
20–49	29(16)	48(25)	47(36)	49(30)	40(55)
50+	64(33)	30(38)	25(51)	24(45)	29(86)
Ethnic					
White	48(13)	77(26)	73(35)	76(25)	69(41)
Black	171(41)	8(26)	8(41)	6(17)	7(32)
Mexican-American	34(37)	13(28)	16(39)	17(26)	22(38)
Other	1 (9)	2(55)	3(53)	1 (6)	2(18)
Diagnosis					
Infection, intoxication, and trauma	12 (5)	18(20)	19(44)	21(26)	29(35)
Down's syndrome	7(14)	26(49)	14(72)	14(41)	14(43)
Functional	32(20)	7 (8)	2 (5)	0 (0)	0 (0)
Other	49(63)	49(35)	65(38)	65(21)	65(19)
Nonambulatory	—	12(14)	24(28)	22(19)	31(29)
Nonverbal	—	36(21)	41(28)	31(13)	45(28)
Not toilet trained	—	38(19)	51(30)	45(15)	64(31)
Aggressive	—	7 (6)	9(25)	24(22)	42(41)
Self-injurious	—	3 (9)	3(18)	17(20)	14(39)

[a] Percentage of discharged clients based on total discharged with this characteristic.
[b] Percentage of discharged clients based on total available for discharge with this characteristic.

Discharge rates by diagnosis of mental retardation exhibited some differential trends. For example, discharge rates for "other organic" categories showed a general *decrease* in LSH over the three decades while admissions and in-residence clients in this diagnostic category were *increasing*. In contrast, the discharge rates increased in the "other" category for WSH. Residents diagnosed as "functional" essentially disappeared among discharges in both LSH and WSH. It would appear that the old "socio-cultural" or "functional" group is no longer admitted and residual clients in this category are nearly nonexistent. The rise in admissions diagnosed as "other" concomitant with their decreasing discharge rate in LSH is probably a result of more accurate diagnoses over time as well as the increase of severe organic complications among clients admitted and retained in this institution.

In addition to level of retardation and diagnosis of mental retardation, individuals displaying aggression and self-injurious behavior showed interesting discharge rates. In this instance, both percent of discharges and discharge rates demonstrated an increase of residents released with these behavior problems. As stated earlier, the high percentage of these behavior problems relative to total discharges in the recent cohorts reflects the higher proportion of admissions with these problems compared to earlier admissions. However, the discharge rates verified that more residents with behavior problems are being released than was the case in earlier years. Both sample institutions demonstrated consistent trends regading these variables.

Although not as interesting as maladaptive behavior, there was a general inclination to release more clients with problems in self-help skills, e.g., non-ambulation or non-toilet trained. This is consistent with the discharge patterns found for the different IQ levels. Together with the trends found for maladaptive behavior, the general movement picture suggests increased emphasis on deinstitutionalization, for even previously more difficult to place clients.

C. Readmissions

There are a number of ways to examine trends in readmissions over time, and each method is likely to lead to a different conclusion with regard to changes in readmission "rates." Readmission rates have been defined as (1) the actual number of readmissions to institutions for a given period of time, (2) the ratio of readmissions to institution size, (3) the ratio of readmissions to the number of placements during a specified period, and (4) the percentage of discharges from an admission cohort who are readmitted within a given period of time. In general, the first three methods do not place a restriction on how long the person who is readmitted has remained in the community placement, while the fourth method (the one used in our study) counts only those clients who were discharged during a follow-up period and who returned within a specified time as readmissions. It is important to keep these differences in mind when interpreting trends and comparing studies.

Repeated readmissions have been associated with a "revolving door" label given to institutions for the mentally retarded (Keys, Boroskin, & Ross, 1973). Keys *et al.* (1973) found, however, that the revolving door label only applied to 1% of all placements from an institution in California during a 14-month period, while returns accounted for only 9.9% of all placements. Mayeda and Sutter (1981) discovered for the State of Hawaii that readmissions to the institution had increased to the point that by 1979 they outnumbered community placements. Taking another perspective, Lakin, Hill, Hauber, Bruininks, and Heal (1983) reported the ratio of total annual readmissions to the *average population of institutions* in the United States has increased over time, from 1:113.6 in 1964, to 1:65.4 in 1969, and 1:25.6 in 1980. However, this apparent increase in readmission rates seems to be more a function of declining institution populations than of placement "failures." Lakin *et al.* (1982b) reported the figures for readmissions had fluctuated between 1978 and 1980, and a trend in either direction was not evident. Estimating the actual number of readmissions, Scheerenberger (1982) reported the readmissions in 1981 had decreased by 28% since his 1975–1976 report. He further noted a decrease in the percentage of readmissions who were less than 22 years of age, and a corresponding increase in the percentage of readmissions who were 22 or older. The results by level of retardation indicated that rates were down for all levels of retardation, and the mildly retarded who were readmitted tended to be of school age, while the severe and profoundly retarded readmissions were older.

Despite the evidence suggesting that the residents in institutions are more severely retarded than in past years, maladaptive behavior appears to be the primary reason for community failure and continued institutionalization. Lakin *et al.* (1983) compared primary reasons for institutional placement of new admissions and readmissions. Sixty-nine percent of both new and readmission groups exhibited at least one kind of maladaptive behavior; however, unmanageable behavior was a far more frequent reason for readmission than for initial admission. Although new admissions and readmissions did not differ significantly on the presence of any particular category of maladaptive behavior, only 5.9% of new admissions exhibited five or more types of behavior problems, while 10.2% of readmissions had five or more problems. Scheerenberger (1980) found that behavior problems were ranked the primary problem by superintendents of institutions in placing residents in the community as well as the main reason for return to the institution. Pagel and Whitling (1978), Eagle (1967), and McCarver and Craig (1974) also concluded that community failure of most retarded individuals resulted from inappropriate behavior.

The results of our study revealed far fewer readmissions than reported by

Mayeda and Sutter (1981). We counted only those discharges who remained in the community for less than 1 year as a readmission. Like Scheerenberger (1982), both of our sample institutions showed decreasing rates of readmission from the early 1970s until the final cohort period. Although WSH had a somewhat higher percentage (14%) of readmissions than LSH (4%), the 1976–1978 rates were relatively low in each facility. An examination of the readmissions by client characteristics confirmed what Pagel and Whitling (1978) found with regard to the preponderance of individuals with behavior problems.

Lakin *et al.* (1983) suggested readmission rates reflect on the ability of institution personnel to prepare people for community living, of social service personnel to make appropriate placement decisions, and of community facilities and agencies to adapt their programs to the specialized needs of former residents of institutions. It is possible that the community regional center is at least partly responsible for the low readmission rate in California. Decisions to place clients back into the institution are made by agencies that have a community orientation, and are aware of all possible local alternatives at any given time. Conversely, an institution that still makes primary readmission decisions may return the client to his/her original placement in the institution, rather than seek out alternative community settings.

Our data suggest that more people can and will be released at least semi-permanently to the community. Other studies (Hill & Bruininks, 1981; Krantz, Bruininks, & Clumpner, 1979; Mayeda & Sutter, 1981) suggest that the readmissions will keep pace or even exceed admissions as discharges increase. A definitive resolution to this issue will require more studies based on prospective follow-up of community-placed individuals. As matters stand, successful community placement will probably depend on future support networks for the care providers as well as their tolerance for impaired retarded individuals, many of whom also exhibit maladaptive behavior.

D.　Mortality

Trends in the mortality rates of mentally retarded people will continue to be an important factor regarding the future composition of institutions as well as an indication of the general health status and effectiveness of medical interventions of the residents over time. Numerous studies have verified that mentally retarded individuals have a shorter life expectancy than the normal population (Balakrishnan & Wolf, 1976; Carter & Jancar, 1983; Forssman & Akesson, 1970; Heaton-Ward, 1968; Miller & Eyman, 1977; Patton & Weinstein, 1959; Roboz, 1972; Tarjan *et al.*, 1969, 1973; Thase, 1982).

Although medical advances have reduced some of the excess mortality in this population, recent studies have documented that such trends have not been as dramatic as hoped (Primrose, 1966; McCurley, MacKay, & Scally, 1972; Richards & Sylvester, 1969; Tarjan *et al.*, 1969, 1973). Forssman and Atkesson (1970) estimate that mildly deficient individuals suffer a mortality rate 1.7 times that of the general population, in contrast to 4.1 times the standard for severely deficient persons. Moreover, all of these studies are consistent regarding the association of the following factors with higher mortality among the mentally retarded:

1. The early admission or transfer period (up to 6 months) to a new placement is an extremely high-risk time interval, particularly among the younger, more profoundly retarded, and organically involved individuals. These children are considered generally more vulnerable and less adaptable to a change in environment.

2. The more superimposed handicaps, e.g., epilepsy, lack of toilet training, the greater the likelihood of death. This fact is particularly evident with respect to impaired mobility. As Roboz (1972) has stated "whatever the damaging agent or trauma might be, the post traumatic motor ability is of paramount importance in survival" (p. 221).

3. Although overall mortality rates have declined over the past decades, pulmonary diseases continue to be the most common cause of death, accounting for as much as 50% of all deaths. Some writers argue that such respiratory problems are more prevalent among the more severely retarded patients who are highly prone to infection and so succumb comparatively often to pneumonia (Chaney, Eyman, & Miller, 1979; Forssman & Akesson, 1970; McCurley *et al.*, 1972; Oster, Mikkelsen, & Nielson, 1964, 1975; Richards & Sylvester, 1969; Tarjan *et al.*, 1968; Thase, 1982). Other reasons include the fact that more profoundly retarded are immobile, a condition which restricts proper expansion of the lungs or ingestion of food without inhalation difficulty.

4. Common recommendations to improve survival include the use of smaller and more specialized placement facilities, intensive monitoring and specialized nursing care, restrictions on the admission or transfer of children less than 5 years of age to larger facilities, and limits on the number of admissions or transfers to the same facility over a comparatively short period of time.

Rotegard *et al.* (1982) reported stable mortality rates between 1978 and 1980, based on their cross-sectional surveys of institutions. Lakin *et al.* (1982) noted a general decrease in mortality rates per 1000 residents from 1925 to 1975. Scheerenberger (1981) found mortality rates reported by cooperating institutions to be about the same as those provided in the previous six surveys. Carter and Jancar (1983) investigated mortality from 1930 to 1980 at the Stoke Park hospital group which serves England and Wales. Mortality rates for all residents generally declined to 1950 and were relatively stable from that time until 1980. However, the decline in mortality rates for Down's syndrome was considerable and continued from 1930 to 1975.

Thase (1982), in an extensive review of the literature on Down's syndrome also revealed a great improvement in the life expectancy of Down's individuals. Most Down's persons did not survive to age 10 in the earlier studies, whereas the half-life of Down's persons in later studies reviewed by Thase was over 30 years of age.

Our mortality estimates were based on the follow-up of admissions to sample institutions rather than in-residence individuals who constituted the at risk group for most of the studies reviewed. Follow-up of admissions provides a more accurate and less biased estimate of mortality than the ratio of annual deaths to the in-residence population of a placement. Still, the two procedures should give approximately the same results.

Table VI provides mortality rates per 1000 for a 3-year and a 6-month follow-up of admission cohorts to LSH. Overall these rates were moderately high for the 1949–1951 admissions, decreasing sharply for the 1959–1961 admissions, and increasing again to almost three times the 1949–1951 rate regarding the 1976–1978 admissions. WSH demonstrated a slight decline in death rates from 1972–1974 admissions to 1976–1978 admissions.

It can be noted that very low mortality rates were realized in connection with the 1959–1961 LSH admission cohort. This occurrence may have been partly due to intensive programs associated with an experiment in the prediction of mortality among high-risk residents who were subsequently monitored closely by the medical staff at the institution (Dingman, Tarjan, Eyman, & Miller, 1964; Dingman & Eyman, 1970; Dingman, Tarjan, Eyman, & Mercer, 1967; Tarjan, Brooke, Eyman, Suyeyasu, & Miller, 1968). The dramatic increase in death rates for subsequent admission cohorts was probably related to the admission of more profoundly retarded nonambulatory individuals. Likewise the decrease in the death rates regarding WSH was probably associated with the transfer of the moderately and mildly retarded individuals from the closed institution in that state. All of these individuals would be expected to survive.

The death rates reported for LSH in Table VI reflect predictable trends in terms of the resident characteristics. Very young residents admitted to an institution are much more likely to die than older clients. Profoundly retarded residents have a higher death rate than less retarded individuals. Residents diagnosed with organic implications, i.e., infection or trauma as well as other conditions have a higher rate than Down's syndrome or functional diagnosis. Finally, young profoundly retarded residents were much more likely to die than other clients with the exception of older profoundly re-

TABLE VI
LSH Death Rates per 1000 for 3 Years and the First 6 Months by Admission Cohorts

| | Rates | | | | | | | | | |
| | 1949–1951 | | 1959–1961 | | 1966–1968 | | 1969–1971 | | 1976–1978 | |
	3 yr.	6 mo.	3 yr.	6 mo.	3 yr.	6 mo.	3 yr.	6 mo.	3 yr.	6 mo.
Age										
0–5	256	(155)	83	(21)	149	(53)	196	(114)	969	(658)
6–11	75	(65)	33	(14)	43	(23)	56	(22)	59	(0)
12–17	26	(5)	22	(0)	40	(17)	53	(26)	79	(25)
18+	61	(24)	35	(0)	86	(47)	14	(14)	94	(36)
IQ										
0–19	217	(129)	115	(28)	200	(85)	118	(68)	290	(200)
20–49	78	(54)	23	(7)	23	(10)	90	(48)	190	(87)
50+	26	(5)	17	(0)	35	(7)	14	(0)	120	(37)
Diagnosis										
Functional	30	(16)	7	(0)	0	(0)	0	(0)	0	(0)[a]
Down's	267	(135)	45	(12)	70	(34)	80	(38)	125	(125)
IIT	89	(60)	34	(15)	62	(23)	60	(25)	340	(189)
Other	217	(122)	85	(17)	100	(42)	107	(62)	212	(135)
Age by IQ										
Young–Low IQ	184	(119)	74	(23)	115	(46)	139	(75)	427	(289)
Young–High IQ	105	(82)	23	(4)	39	(15)	16	(8)	286	(125)[a]
Old–Low IQ	68	(26)	39	(0)	75	(40)	102	(59)	95	(45)
Old–High IQ	25	(5)	15	(0)	28	(9)	31	(15)	69	(0)
Actual number of deaths	46	28	52	13	64	28	49	28	42	28
Total rate	93	(54)	52	(12)	83	(35)	93	(51)	241	(149)

[a] Rates were based on total of nine admissions during 1976–1978 and likely to be spurious.

tarded residents of WSH admitted between 1972 and 1974. Otherwise the WSH death rates by resident characteristics were similar to those for LSH.

The overall trend in mortality rates for LSH and WSH approximated the death rates reported by Carter and Jancar (1983) from 1950 to 1975. However, the mortality trends by diagnosis given in Table VI are noteworthy. The death rates for both the functional and Down's individuals declined over time in contrast to the rates for infection and trauma or other organic conditions. The 125 per 1000 death rate noted for Down's in the 1976–1978 admission cohort was due to small sample size in that only nine Down's people were admitted during that period and one of them died over the 3-year follow-up, producing a spurious rate. With the exception of this artifact, the death trends given for LSH by diagnosis are consistent with declining rates reported by Thase (1982) and Carter and Jancar (1983), for Down's individuals in comparison to other institutionalized residents. It should also be apparent that residents diagnosed as functional mental retardation are nearly nonexistent in institutions since the late 1970s.

Miller and Eyman (1977) found that community and institution mortality rates were comparable if age, IQ, and ambulation were considered. This study suggested that mortality reflects the health condition of the retarded individuals rather than placement per se. The results pertaining to LSH and WSH support this contention. For example, as more debilitated clients were admitted to the urban institution, the mortality climbed considerably. In contrast, due to the closure of an institution for less debilitated clients with behavior problems in the rural state, admissions of these individuals to the nearby larger state institution lowered its mortality rate.

Although Carter and Jancar (1983) have documented increased longevity among retarded people over the last 50 years due to such factors as the introduction of new drug therapy, better diet, care, and environment, profoundly retarded young children still have a very limited life expectancy. Survival is even poorer if these children have organic conditions such as developmental cranial anomalies (Eyman, Grossman, Tarjan, & Miller, 1983). It appears that Down's individuals are among a select group of retarded people whose prognosis has been improved as the result of the newer medical interventions (Thase, 1982). Other groups of retarded individuals aided by improved medical techniques include those diagnosed as mental retardation associated with epilepsy and social cultural retardation (Carter & Jancar, 1983).

V. SUMMARY AND DISCUSSION

Findings of this investigation are generally consistent with the results reported elsewhere (Eyman & Borthwick, 1980; Lakin et al., 1982; Landesman-Dwyer & Shuckit, 1976; Rotegard et al., 1982; Scheerenberger, 1978b, 1979,

1980, 1982). There have been dramatic changes occurring in traditional institutions and it appears that these trends are still continuing. Basically, the composition of institutions seems to be evolving into an ever growing residual population of older, more profoundly retarded persons with organic diagnoses and concomitant behavior problems. The above literature as well as our investigation also shows that self-help skills such as ambulation, toilet training, dressing, eating, and the like are declining among residents in institutions.

Lakin *et al.* (1982) noted from their survey that all movement categories, i.e., admissions, discharges, transfers, involved less severely retarded clients who were less impaired than those remaining in institutions. Our data supported their findings, indicating that although admissions and discharges have followed the in-residence trends, the actual proportion of clients in the severely impaired categories is still smaller than for retarded individuals residing in the institution. Nevertheless, the discharge rates suggest more impaired individuals are being released to the community than in the past. Given that readmissions were not found to be very frequent in LSH or WSH compared to the numbers discharged, it appears that more individuals are being successfully placed in the community.

Systematic investigations and data collection of the follow-up of community-placed clients are essentially nonexistent. Hence, evidence tends to be based on institutional populations (Scheerenberger, 1978b, 1979, 1980) or anecdotal information from communities (Lakin *et al.*, 1982). Due to these limitations in prospective longitudinal data for community-placed clients as well as the continuing changes in the residents currently residing in institutions, it is difficult to speculate on how much further the deinstitutionalization of the residual population can proceed. Our data on discharges and readmissions suggest that more people can and will be released to the community. Yet other studies (Hill & Bruininks, 1981; Krantz *et al.*, 1980; Mayeda & Sutter, 1981) suggest that the readmissions will keep pace or even exceed admissions as discharges increase. A definitive resolution to this issue will require more studies based on prospective follow-up of community-placed individuals.

The mortality experience of the two sample institutions in our study was of particular significance. The sharp rise of mortality rates in LSH and the slight decrease in death rates in WSH, although seemingly contradictory, appear to be related to the severity of impairment of individuals admitted to those institutions. As noted before, apparent differences in death rates for an institution vs surrounding community placements disappeared when ambulation was controlled, along with the level of retardation and age (Miller & Eyman, 1977).

Two points need to be emphasized regarding the trends in death rates. First, as proportionately more admissions fell into the high-risk category for survival in LSH, it should not be surprising that mortality rates increased since fewer low-risk individuals entered into the denominator of the death rate. Second, with community agencies currently making the placement decisions, clients previously excluded from LSH because of their very young age and degree of illness can be now admitted to the institution regardless of the high mortality risk and burden of care. For example, very young residents made up only 2% of the total residents of LSH, but constituted about 30% of the new admissions to this facility. In the 1950s and 1960s institution staff at LSH resisted the admission of children under 2 years of age, particularly if such a move were considered a risk to the survival of the child. Many of these children would have died before admission to the institution was possible. Now, the burden of care for these very sick children is being shifted to the institution. No such trend was apparent in WSH, where institution staff have more control over admission.

Overall, the findings reported in this article support trends found elsewhere. Where there are inconsistencies, it seems more likely that the differences are due to operational definitions and methods of data collection rather than to descrepant results. The system of care is in a period of rapid transition in which the locus of administrative control and service delivery is being shifted from the institution to the community. Our results pertaining to California, where community regional centers make all placement decisions, suggest that many social service personnel still perceive a need for the institution. The national figures for new admissions and readmissions to institutions also support this notion. Hopefully, future guidelines regarding placement decisions will include strict follow-up and monitoring of the survival, development, and quality of life of the mentally retarded people who are affected by these decisions.

ACKNOWLEDGMENTS

This study was supported in part by the National Institute of Child Health and Human Development Research Grants HD–04612 and HD–14688.

REFERENCES

Bachrach, L. L. A conceptual approach to deinstitutionalization for the mentally retarded: A perspective from the experience of the mentally ill. In R. H. Bruininks, C. E. Meyers, B. B. Sigford, & K. C. Lakin (Eds.), *Deinstitutionalization and community adjustment of mentally retarded people.* AAMD Monograph No. 4, 1981.
Best-Sigford, B., Bruininks, R. H., Lakin, K. C., & Hill, B. K. Resident release patterns in a national sample of public residential facilities. *American Journal of Mental Deficiency,* 1982, **87,** 130–140.

Balakrishnan, T. R., & Wolf, L. C. Life expectancy of mentally retarded persons in Canadian institutions. *American Journal of Mental Deficiency,* 1976, **80,** 650–662.

Bruininks, R. H., Hauber, F. A., & Kudla, M. J. *National survey of community residential facilities: A profile of facilities and residents in 1977.* Minneapolis, Minnesota: University of Minnesota, Department of Psychoeducational Studies, 1979.

Bruininks, R. H., Kudla, M. J., Hauber, F. A., Hill, B. K., & Wieck, C. A. Recent growth and status of community based residential alternatives. In R. H. Bruininks, C. E. Meyers, B. B. Sigford, & K. C. Lakin (Eds.), *Deinstitutionalization and community adjustment of mentally retarded people.* AAMD Monograph No. 4, 1981.

Carter, G., & Jancar, J. Mortality in the mentally handicapped: A 50 year survey at the Stoke Park group of hospitals (1930–1980). *Journal of Mental Deficiency Research,* 1983, **27,** 143–156.

Chaney, R. H., Eyman, R. K., & Miller, C. R. Comparison of respiratory mortality in the profoundly mentally retarded and in the less retarded. *Journal of Mental Deficiency Research,* 1979, **23,** 1–7.

Dingman, H. F., Tarjan, G., Eyman, R. K., & Mercer, J. R. Epidemiology of institutionalized mental retardates. In J. Zubin & G. A. Jervis (Eds.), *Psychopathology of mental development.* New York: Grune & Stratten, 1967.

Dingman, H. F., Tarjan, G., Eyman, R. K., & Miller, C. R. Epidemiology in hospitals: Some uses of data processing in chronic disease institutions. *American Journal of Mental Deficiency,* 1964, **68,** 586–593.

Eagle, E. Prognosis and outcome of community placement of institutionalized retardates. *American Journal of Mental Deficiency,* 1967, **72,** 232–243.

Eyman, R. K. Trends in the development of the profoundly mentally retarded. In C. C. Cleland, J. D. Swartz, & L. W. Talkington (Eds.), *The profoundly mentally retarded,* Second Annual Conference Proceedings, 1976, 15–21.

Eyman, R. K., & Borthwick, S. A. Patterns of care of mentally retarded persons. *American Journal of Mental Deficiency,* 1980, **18,** 63–66.

Eyman, R. K., Borthwick, S. A., & Miller, C. Trends in maladaptive behavior of mentally retarded persons placed in community and institutional settings. *American Journal of Mental Deficiency,* 1981, **85,** 473–477.

Eyman, R. K., & Call, T. Maladaptive behavior and community placement of mentally retarded persons. *American Journal of Mental Deficiency,* 1977, **82,** 137–144.

Eyman, R. K., Grossman, H. J., Tarjan, G., & Miller, C. *Life Tables for Institutionalized Mentally Retarded,* Monograph of the American Association on Mental Deficiency, 1983, in press.

Eyman, R. K., O'Connor, G., Tarjan, G., & Justice, R. S. Factors determining residential placement of mentally retarded children. *American Journal of Mental Deficiency,* 1972, **76,** 692–698.

Farber, B. *Mental retardation: Its social context and social consequences.* Boston, Massachusetts: Houghton Mifflin, 1968.

Forssman, H., & Akesson, H. O. Mortality of the mentally deficient: A study of 12,903 institutionalized subjects. *Journal of Mental Deficiency Research,* 1970, **14,** 276–294.

Heaton-Ward, W. A. The life expectation of mentally subnormal patients in hospital. *British Journal of Psychiatry,* 1968, **114,** 1591–1592.

Hill, B. K., & Bruininks, R. H. *Physical and behavioral characteristics and maladaptive behavior of mentally retarded people in residential facilities.* Minneapolis, Minnesota: Department of Psychoeducational Studies, University of Minnesota, 1981.

Janicki, M. P., Jacobson, J. W., Zigman, W. B., & Lubin, R. A. *Group homes as alternative care settings: System issues and implications.* Washington, D.C.: NICHD Conference, 1982.

Keys, V., Boroskin, A., & Ross, R. The revolving door in an MR hospital: A study of returns from leave. *Mental Retardation,* 1973, **11**, 55–56.

Krantz, G. C., Bruininks, R. H., & Clumpner, J. L. *Mentally retarded people in state-operated residential facilities: Year ending June 30, 1979.* Minneapolis, Minnesota: University of Minnesota, Department of Psychoeducational Studies, 1980.

Lakin, K. C. *Demographic studies of residential facilities for the mentally retarded: An historical review of methodologies and findings.* Minneapolis, Minnesota: University of Minnesota, Department of Psychoeducational Studies, 1979.

Lakin, K. C., Bruininks, R. H., Doth, D. W., & Hill, B. K. *Selected data on long-term care for developmentally disabled people.* Minneapolis, Minnesota: University of Minnesota, Department of Psychoeducational Studies, 1982. (a)

Lakin, K. C., Bruininks, R. H., Doth, D., Hill, B., & Hauber, F. *Sourcebook on long-term care for developmentally disabled people.* Minneapolis, Minnesota: University of Minnesota, Department of Educational Psychology, 1982. (b)

Lakin, K. C., Hill, B. K., Hauber, F. A., Bruininks, R. H., & Heal, L. W. New admissions and readmissions to a national sample of public residential facilities. *American Journal of Mental Deficiency,* 1983, **88**, 13–20.

Lakin, K. C., Krantz, G. C., Bruininks, R. H., Clumpner, J. L., & Hill, B. K. One hundred years of data on populations of public residential facilities for mentally retarded people. *American Journal of Mental Deficiency,* 1982, **87**, 1–8.

Landesman-Dwyer, S. Living in the community. *American Journal of Mental Deficiency,* 1981, **86**, 223–234.

Landesman-Dwyer, S., & Schuckit, J. J. *Preliminary findings of the survey of state institutions for the mentally retarded.* Department of Social and Health Services, State of Washington, 1976, Library of Congress No. 76–620025.

MacMillan, D. L. *Mental retardation in school and society.* Boston, Massachusetts: Little, Brown, 1977.

Mayeda, T., & Sutter P. Deinstitutionalization: Phase II. In R. H. Bruininks, C. E. Meyers, B. B. Sigford, & K. C. Lakin (Eds.), *Deinstitutionalization and community adjustment of mentally retarded people.* Washington, D.C.: American Association on Mental Deficiency, 1981.

McCurley, R., MacKay, D. N., & Scally, B. G. The life expectation of the mentally subnormal under community and hospital care. *Journal of Mental Deficiency Research,* 1972, **16**, 57–66.

McCarver, R. B., & Craig, E. M. Placement of the retarded in the community: Prognosis and outcome. In N. R. Ellis (Ed.), *International review of research in mental retardation.* New York: Academic Press, 1974. Pp. 146–199.

Miller, C., & Eyman, R. Hospital and community mortality rates among the retarded. *Journal of Mental Deficiency Research,* 1977, **22**, 137–145.

Mumpower, D. L. Sex ratios found in various types of referred exceptional children. *Exceptional Children,* 1970, **36**, 621–622.

Oster, J., Mikkelsen, M., & Nielson, A. The mortality and causes of death in patients with Down's syndrome (mongolism). *Proceedings of the International Copenhagen Congress on the Scientific Study of Mental Retardation,* 1964, **1**, 231–235.

Oster, J., Mikkelsen, M., & Nielson, A. Mortality and life table in Down's syndrome. *Acta Pediatrica Scandinavica,* 1975, **64**, 322–326.

Pagel, S. E., & Whitling, C. A. Readmissions to a state hospital for mentally retarded persons: Reasons for community placement failure. *Mental Retardation,* 1978, **16**, 164–166.

Patton, R. E., & Weinstein, A. S. *Changing characteristics of the population in the New York State schools for mental defectives.* (Statistical Services Research Report No. 1). Department of Mental Hygiene, State of New York, February, 1959.

Primrose, D. A. A. Natural history of mental defiency in a hospital group and in the community it serves. *Journal of Mental Deficiency Research,* 1966, **10,** 159–189.

Richards, B. W., & Sylvester, P. E. Mortality trends in mental deficiency research. *Journal of Mental Deficiency Research,* 1969, **13,** 276.

Roboz, P. Mortality rate in institutionalized mentally retarded children. *The Medical Journal of Australia,* 1972, **1,** 218–221.

Rotegard, L. L. Bruininks, R. H., & Lakin, K. C. *Epidemiology of mental retardation and trends in residential services in the United States.* Washington, D.C.: NICHD Conference, 1982.

Scheerenberger, R. C. *Current trends and status of public residential facilities for the mentally retarded, 1976.* Madison, Wisconsin: National Association of Superintendents of Public Residential Facilities for the Mentally Retarded, 1977.

Scheerenberger, R. C. Public residential services for the retarded, In N. R. Ellis (Ed.), *International review of research in mental retardation.* New York: Academic Press, 1978. (a)

Scheerenberger, R. C. *Public residential services for the mentally retarded, 1977.* Minneapolis, Minnesota: University of Minnesota, Department of Psychoeducational Studies, 1978. (b)

Scheerenberger, R. C. *Public residential services for the mentally retarded.* Minneapolis, Minnesota: University of Minnesota, Department of Psychoeducational Studies, 1979.

Scheerenberger, R. C. *Community programs and services.* National Association of Superintendents of Public Residential Facilities for the Mentally Retarded, 1980.

Scheerenberger, R. C. Deinstitutionalization: Trends and difficulties. In R. H. Bruininks, C. E. Meyers, B. B. Sigford, & K. C. Lakin (Eds.), *Deinstitutionalization and community adjustment of mentally retarded people.* AAMD Monograph No. 4, 1981.

Scheerenberger, R. C. *Public residential services for the mentally retarded, 1981.* Minneapolis, Minnesota: University of Minnesota, Department of Psychoeducational Studies, 1982.

Sutton, M., Sutter, P., Long, K., & Kelley, D. *Barriers to community placement for the institutionalized mentally retarded.* Paper presented at the Western Psychological Association convention, San Francisco, 1983.

Tarjan, G., Brooke, C. E., Eyman, R. K., Suyeyasu, A., & Miller, C. R. Mortality and cause of death in a hospital for the mentally retarded. *American Journal of Public Health,* 1968, **58,** 1891–1990.

Tarjan, G., Eyman, R. K., & Dingman, H. F. Changes in the patient population of a hospital for the mentally retarded. *American Journal of Mental Deficiency,* 1966, **70,** 529–541.

Tarjan, G., Eyman, R. K., & Miller, C. R. Natural history of mental retardation in a state hospital, revisited. *American Journal of Diseases of Children,* 1969, **117,** 609–620.

Tarjan, G., Wright, S. W., Eyman, R. K., & Keeran, C. V. Natural history of mental retardation: Some aspects of epidemiology. *American Journal of Mental Deficiency,* 1973, **77,** 369–379.

Thase, M. E. Longevity and mortality in Down's syndrome. *Journal of Mental Deficiency Research,* 1982, **26,** 177–192.

Methodological Considerations in Research on Residential Alternatives for Developmentally Disabled Persons[1]

LAIRD W. HEAL AND GLENN T. FUJIURA

DEPARTMENT OF SPECIAL EDUCATION
COLLEGE OF EDUCATION
UNIVERSITY OF ILLINOIS AT URBANA-CHAMPAIGN
CHAMPAIGN ILLINOIS

[1]This article is a sequel to Heal (1984). Whereas the present article addresses issues of design validity in community integration research, that one discussed the issues that arise in each step of the research procedure: selecting subjects, selecting measures, making observations, analyzing data, and interpreting results.

INTERNATIONAL REVIEW OF RESEARCH IN
MENTAL RETARDATION, Vol. 12

I.   INTRODUCTION

Science begins with the observation and recording of empirical events. These records are then collected and organized in order to establish empirical regularities, called laws. Social scientists then deduce implications from these laws and invent experiments that are designed to demonstrate the generality of the empirical laws and the correctness of the scientists' logic. The purpose of the present article is to discuss the implications of this elegant ritual for the study of residential alternatives for developmentally disabled individuals.

Following the lead of Campbell and Stanley (1966), social scientists have come to evaluate research designs in terms of two broad perspectives: *internal validity,* the extent to which unbiased inferences can be drawn regarding the subjects, settings, measures, and conditions investigated (Campbell & Stanley, 1966; Cook & Campbell, 1979; Kratochwill, 1978; Sidman, 1960); and *external validity,* the extent to which experimental results generalize to subjects (population validity), settings (ecological validity), and measures (referent generality) beyond those that were actually investigated (Bracht & Glass, 1968; Campbell & Stanley, 1966; Cook & Campbell, 1979; Snow, 1974).

Validity of Measurement is a third major requirement for adequate research. Measures or observations are valid if they are accurate reflections of the constructs, concepts, or events that they are presumed to assess (Nunnally, 1978).

Another issue in research validity is what has been recently called social validity (Kazdin, 1982; Rusch, Schutz, & Heal, 1983). Social validity refers to the acceptability and importance of a study's goals, methods, and outcomes for the consumers of the research, especially for the subjects themselves. Valid research on socially important issues must necessarily provide evidence that the clients and practitioners who have a vested interest in the research see it as relevant to their needs.

The article that follows, then, is organized about these issues of the validity of research as they apply to residential alternatives for developmentally disabled children and adults.

II.   EXTERNAL VALIDITY

External validity means generality, the extent to which conclusions based on one set of observations from a particular set of subjects and a particular setting, apply reasonably to a broader set of measures, subjects, and settings.

A. Population Validity

One of the most perplexing challenges in the study of community integration is the identification of the study population. While epidemiological studies (see Conley, 1973, for an excellent review) set the prevalence of mental retardation at about 1% of the total population (i.e., 2 million individuals), the number in institutions has never reached 200,000 (Lakin, Krantz, Bruininks, Clumpner, & Hill, 1982), and the number in both public and community facilities is well under 250,000 (Bruininks, Hauber, & Kudla, 1980; Krantz, Bruininks, & Clumpner, 1978). Thus, the population of developmentally disabled citizens that is studied in the community integration literature is at most 10% of that which is assumed to exist nationally. While many others have been successfully integrated into the community, either as independent citizens or as adult dependents on relatives and friends, some fraction of this 90% has presumably escaped sampling because of inferior research procedures. The process of attaining population validity breaks down at three stages: defining the population, locating all its members, and sampling representatively from the members that have been located.

1. DEFINING THE STUDY POPULATION

The first threat to procedural adequacy is defining what is meant by public and/or community residential facilities. The taxonomies of community residential facilities utilized by the major national studies of community integration, are summarized in Table I. Brief definitions of these facilities were provided in Heal, Novak, Sigelman, and Switzky (1980) and will not be repeated here. These definitions are far from standardized. Every nation and state has uniquely defined models, undermining comparability in international and national studies.

2. STUDY POPULATION REGISTRY

After one defines facility type, the next task is to ensure that the facility registry is representative of those that have been defined. Two dimensions define this representativeness: *geographical scope* and *comprehensiveness*. Geographically, studies of residential alternatives have been international in scope (Howell & May, 1980; McCormick, Balla, & Zigler, 1975), national (e.g., Baker, Seltzer, & Seltzer, 1977; Bruininks *et al.,* 1980; Hauber, Bruininks, Wieck, Sigford, & Hill, 1981; Gollay, Freedman, Wyngaarden, & Kurtz, 1978; O'Connor, 1976), regional (e.g., Edgerton & Berkovici, 1976; Eyman, Silverstein, McLain, & Miller, 1977; Heal & Daniels, 1978; Intagliata & Willer, 1982; Schalock, Harper, & Carver, 1981a; Willer & Intagliata, 1981, 1982; Wolpert, 1978), or confined to a single facility (e.g.,

TABLE I
TAXONOMY OF RESIDENTIAL ALTERNATIVES FOR THE MENTALLY RETARDED[a]

Source:	Scheerenberger (1976, 1982) Research unit: Discharged resident:		Baker et al. (1977) Com. Res. Facil. N = 381		Hill et al. (1978) State & DC MR/DD coordinators N = 51		Gollay et al. (1978) Residents discharged to CRFs having 25 or fewer persons N = 440		Bruininks et al. (1980) N = 62,397 residents in 4427 facilities	
	%[b]	%		%[c]		%[d]		%[c]	Facil. %	Res. %
1. Independent living	1.4	5.4		5.0	a. Staffed apartments b. "Visiting professional"	56.9 9.8	a. Semiindependent b. Independent	10 10	a. 5.3 b. —	a. 2.4 b. —
2. Nat. or adopt. home	22.2	18.6		—[e]		—	See natural home	14	—	—
3. Other relative	2.3	1.6		—		—		0	—	—
4. Foster home	14.7	6.4		14.4		66.7		18	17.4	4.3
5. Group home	15.9	23.5		62.7	CRF	100.0		48	56.4	39.3
6. Commu. ICF	8.2	14.4	See group home	0	See CRF	0	See group home	0	3.0	13.8
7. Conval. home	1.1	1.3		10.0	See nursing home	0		—		
8. Nursing home	15.6	3.5	See conval. home	0		45.1		—		
9. County home	.2	.4	See conval. home	0	See CRF (!)	0		—		
10. Publ. Res. Fac.	11.6	22.6			a. Inst. or reg. cntr. b. Resid. schs. (children)	100.0 21.6		—		
11. Private Res. Fac.	.7	—	a. Mininstitutions b. Sheltered villages	1.3 2.4	a. See CRF b. Sheltered villages	0 2.0		—	a. 5.1 b. 0	a. 23.5 b. .1
12. Work placement	4.1	—			See CRF	0	See semiindependent	0		
13. Boarding home	1.3	2.4	cf. Group home	4.2		13.7	See group home	0	12.6	16.8
14. Mental hosp.	.2	3.7		0	See inst. or reg. entrs.	0		—	.1	.3
15. Prison and other	.2	.7		—		—		—		—
Total (rounded)	100.0	100.0		100.0		—		100	100.0	100.0

[a] Adapted from Heal et al. (1980).

[b] For the Scheerenberger study the first percentage column indicates the percentage discharged into each CRF category in FY 1975–1976; the second column indicates the corresponding percentage for FY 1980–1981.

[c] For the Baker et al., Gollay et al., and Bruininks et al. studies, the percentages are based on the proportion of the sampled Research Units that fell into the indicated categories.

[d] For the Hill et al. study the percentages are based on the proportion of the states that have facilities in the indicated categories.

Birenbaum & Re, 1979; Conroy, Efthimiou, & Lemanowicz, 1982; Soforenko & Macy, 1977, 1978).

In terms of comprehensiveness, some studies have included all facility types housing a target population (e.g., Scheerenberger, 1976, 1978, 1982); all facility types housing their volunteer subjects (e.g., Gollay *et al.*, 1978); all licensed facilities housing developmentally disabled (DD) residents who volunteer for study (e.g., Bruininks *et al.*, 1980; Bruininks, Hauber, Hill, Lakin, Sigford, & Wieck, 1981; O'Connor, 1976; Wyngaarden & Gollay, 1976); specific facility type(s) such as public residential facilities (PRFs) (e.g., Eyman, Demaine, & Lei, 1979; Nihira, Foster, Shellhaas, & Leland, 1974); specific locations in the subjects' life space (e.g., Berkson, 1981); or specific facilities (e.g., Birenbaum & Re, 1979; Conroy *et al.*, 1982; King, Soucar, & Isett, 1980). Oftentimes specific facilities have been described but not identified (e.g., MacEachron, 1983; Seltzer, 1981; Weber & Epstein, 1980), a questionable practice that has been exacerbated by society's current preoccupation with anonymity.

Either restricted geography or limited comprehensiveness can seriously limit research conclusions. The excluded facilities are likely to be smaller, less visible in the community, and have more residents per staff person than the included facilities. The narrower the registry, the more atypical its facilities are likely to be. For example, O'Connor (1976) reported that 53% of her national community residential facility (CRF) sample had come from PRFs, whereas Bruininks *et al.* (1980) reported that only 35% had come from this source. While it is possible that the year of sampling (1974 vs 1977) could account for this difference, it seems more likely that the comprehensiveness of their respective samples (611 vs 4427) or the different CRF definitions used in the two studies could account for the differences. For example, O'Connor excluded foster care and medical facilities, while Bruininks included them if they were specifically licensed for developmentally disabled residents. These biases in the development of a registry of residential facilities for the developmentally disabled have undermined all of the studies of community residential facilities to date, since the most careful sampling cannot correct for a biased registry. But, as we shall see, facility sampling can be even more challenging than facility definition and location.

3. SAMPLING

Sampling usually begins with the selection of a representative group of facilities from one's registry. Subsequently, residents, cottages, administrators, or caretakers may be sampled from each facility.

a. Sampling of Facilities. Once the facility roster has been developed, representative facilities are ordinarily sampled from all of those that have been defined as eligible. Because the truly random sample puts the experimenter at risk of missing certain critical types completely, most random samples have some constraints (Groves & Hess, 1975). For example, Hauber *et al.* (1981) stratified their sample so that four regions of the country were represented in proportion to their populations, and each size class was represented in proportion to its number of residents, larger facilities having larger sampling weights. Similarly, O'Connor (1976) used three stratifiers: facility size, facility administrative type (public, private nonprofit, entrepreneurial), and modal age of residents.

Once a facility has been sampled, the next task is to enlist participation. Universal participation is crucial to ensure the generalizability of results from the sample to the larger population. For example, in order to maximize participation, Bruininks *et al.* (1980) made three follow-up mailings and a follow-up phone call to nonrespondents on their original questionnaire. Similarly, Scheerenberger, (1976, 1978, 1982) routinely telephones his nonrespondents with a short form of his large questionnaire in order to achieve a 100% response rate.

Sampling biases resulting from nonresponses are probably more severe than those associated with incomplete facility rosters. A nonrespondent may fear comparison with other similar facilities, may have residents with serious behavior problems, may have a shortage of staff time for administrative tasks, and so forth. Replacement of nonparticipants can only partially compensate for these selection biases. For example, Hauber *et al.* (1981), the most comprehensive of the surveys on residential alternatives, had the cooperation of only one of the six CRFs with more than 400 residents, and found replacements for only 7 of their 21 other CRF nonparticipants and for only 3 of their 6 PRF nonparticipants. Presumably, replacement facilities, when they can be recruited, will be tainted by the correlates of voluntarism to a greater extent than facilities originally selected. Nevertheless, it seems desirable to replace nonrespondents to the extent possible. A corollary to the principle of replacement is the necessity to estimate the data of nonreplaced facilities by proportionately weighting the data from participants having characteristics similar to those of nonparticipants.

b. Sampling of Units within Facilities. Once the facility has been selected, a sample resident or caretaker within the facility is usually obtained. As in the case of sampling facilities, a truly random sample or a stratified random sample would be recommended (Groves & Hess, 1975), and the bias associated with nonrespondents may be severe. At the resident level, refusal to participate is, often paradoxically, an indication of normalized integration into the community. As Edgerton concluded in 1976, developmentally disabled individuals go through extreme efforts to "pass" as being unhandicapped. Presumably these efforts account for the fact that Soforenko and Macy (1977) could find only 48% of the residents released from Orient State

Hospital in Ohio over a 9-year period. On the other hand, the most promising residents may be selected for an "experimental" intervention, or some residents might be too sick or too uncontrollable to participate. Thus, missing information has an indeterminate but potentially biasing effect on the population validity of a study.

Sampling problems do not stop with the selection of a resident. Very often information about a resident is obtained from respondents who know the resident well. Explicit procedures for selecting respondents are essential. For example, Hauber *et al.* (1981) used respondents who had known the subject for at least 2 months and who worked with the subject regularly; but such specification is unusual in this research.

3. CONCLUSION

Population validity is fundamental to the discovery of general empirical laws. If the population under study cannot be defined, if defined members cannot be located, or if biases undermine sampling, then the results of the study apply logically only to its particular subjects, and any assertion that the results might apply to a more general population is made with indeterminate risk of error. While most studies make no pretense at universal relevance, readers and reviewers are often guilty of broadly interpreting very narrow findings. But even the studies that appear to be more general must be interpreted cautiously. For example, flaws are easily found in all five of the national CRF surveys of the 1970s (Baker *et al.*, 1977; Bruininks *et al.*, 1980, 1981; Gollay *et al.*, 1978; O'Connor, 1976). Defining the population is difficult in Gollay's national study of resident releases, since the rules by which she selected her releasing institutions were unclear. The definition of O'Connor's population is even more difficult. For example, it is impossible to tell whether licensed intermediate care facilities were included or excluded by her 24-hour, nonmedical, no-size-limit definition of CRF. The task of locating facilities after the population had been defined was extremely challenging and imperfectly accomplished in all of these studies. All describe a "grapevine" search, even for licensed facilities. Only recently (Bruininks, Hauber, Hill, Lakin, Rotegard, & White, 1983) have states and the Bruininks group established a reasonably comprehensive registry of all licensed CRF facilities. Finally, all these studies are plagued by sampling bias. Response rates were 51, 88, 82, 39, and 94% in the Baker *et al.* (1977), Bruininks *et al.* (1980, 1981), Gollay *et al.* (1978), and O'Connor (1976) studies, respectively. One must speculate that volunteer bias would be especially serious in mental retardation research; participants and nonparticipants might very well respond differently to sensitive questions. The fact is that nearly every study of community integration to date is undermined by its imperfect population validity.

B. Referent Generality

Once subjects have been selected, attention must be paid to the sampling of dependent measures, or what Snow (1974) calls referent generality. Just as subjects are sampled from a population of those possible, so are dependent variables (e.g., behavior change, success, service costs) sampled from a population of possible outcomes. The consequence of inadequate referent generality is the inaccurate representation of the effects of residential placement.

Early evaluations tended to employ only dichotomous outcome measures such as retention versus recidivism (Heal, Sigelman, & Switzky, 1978; McCarver & Craig, 1974). However, the notion of referent generality requires the experimenter to consider the population of all outcomes, of which recidivism may be only one, oversimplified facet. Based on their review of empirical evaluations of residential alternatives, Heal and Laidlaw (1980) identified six areas in which valid measures exist or could be readily constructed: normalization, residents' satisfaction, others' satisfaction, residential climate, cost, and skill improvement. Most studies fall far short of sampling the range of outcomes that may be expected from a community placement. For example, results of placement are often indexed in terms of a single dependent variable: e.g., Eyman, Borthwick, and Miller (1981; maladaptive behavior); Scanlon, Arick, and Krug (1982; the Autism Behavior Checklist); Seltzer (1981; the [multivariate] Community Adjustment Scale); and Schalock and Harper (1978), Schalock *et al.* (1981a), and Schalock, Harper, and Genung (1981b; the [multivariate] Independent Living Screening Test). Conroy *et al.* (1982), King *et al.* (1980), Sutter, Mayeda, Call, Yanagi, and Yee (1980), and Vitello, Atthowe, and Caldwell (1983), among others, relied almost entirely on the AAMD Adaptive Behavior Scale to index placement outcome. Another popular single-outcome measure is some index of resident management (e.g., Hemming, Lavender, & Pill, 1981; Howell & May, 1980; McCormick *et al.,* 1975; Pratt, Luszcz, & Brown, 1980). Even the broader studies have very circumscribed outcome measures. For example, of the large national surveys none estimated skill improvement, and only Wieck and Bruininks (1980) and Baker *et al.* (1977) published their cost data. In these studies, normalization, residents' satisfaction, and especially others' satisfaction were usually reflected only by remote proxies. Clearly, much more attention must be given to the many dimensions of outcome if we are to assess the complete effect of deinstitutionalization.

C. Ecological Validity

An investigation has ecological validity to the extent that its findings can be expected to generalize to different physical settings, to different temporal settings, and to different social settings; thus, the task of experimenters is to sample from the populations of places, times, and social demands without bias until they are satisfied that the target behavior of their study occurs in the targeted settings but not in nontargeted settings. A number of recent studies have made direct observations of their subjects performing in settings that occur naturally in the course of their daily living in order to achieve greater ecological validity (e.g., Berkson, 1981; Berkson & Romer, 1980; Bjaanes & Butler, 1974; Heller, Berkson, & Romer, 1981; Landesman-Dwyer, Berkson, & Romer, 1979; Landesman-Dwyer, Stein, & Sackett, 1978; Romer & Berkson, 1980a,b).

The very elaborate series by Berkson and his associates in 1980 and 1981 serves to highlight many of the features and difficulties of conducting ecologically valid research. The purpose of these studies was to observe and classify the free time activities of mentally retarded adults. In terms of place and time,

> Observations were done in situations in which informal social behavior was most probable. We specifically excluded situations (such as work situations or teaching situations) in which the staff members regulated the social behavior. Observations were carried out during coffee and lunch breaks at [four Chicago] workshops; during informal recreation periods at the [sheltered care] home; in streets, stores, and restaurants of the neighborhood; and on some recreational outings. (Berkson & Romer, 1980, pp. 222–223)

In terms of social demands, observations were made when formal staff constraints on social behavior were minimal. Furthermore, the observer obtrusiveness was reduced by occasional visits to the participating facilities during the month before formal observations were recorded.

While these are perhaps the most naturalistically focused studies of community social behavior of mentally retarded adults, they exemplify many shortcomings from the perspective of ecological validity. The constraint of place is explicit: Most of the 47,194 5-minute observations of the 315 clients were made in the four workshops, which were run by a single Chicago agency. No pretense can be made that these were typical of all Chicago workshops, to say nothing of workshops nationally. Furthermore, there was no effort to catalog any population of settings and times in order to permit the selection of a representative sample of those available for observation. Finally, the social demands were less than optimally controlled. There is no evidence that the observers were a neutral stimulus; subjects presumably inhibited an indeterminate amount of antisocial behavior, such as fighting, swearing, and arguing, in the presence of a university representative who had asked their permission to observe their social behavior.

Berkson's own data indicate the importance that setting plays in determining behavior. Berkson and Romer (1980) reported large differences in affiliation measures from one setting to the next. The workshops differed as much among themselves as they differed from the intermediate care facility, indicating that there are stable behavioral dispositions that are linked to settings more than to individuals. Furthermore, Berkson (1981) found that these differences could not be attributed to one's living arrangement. Clients from different living arrangements (independent living, natural home, and sheltered care) who were matched on a number of characteristics, had very similar social interaction profiles within each setting, although profiles differed markedly from one setting to another.

Thus, the act of making observations in a "natural setting" does not guarantee ecological validity. Only specification of the population of settings, times, and social demands, and subsequent random sampling from this population can guarantee ecological validity. While the studies done heretofore have contributed much to the methodology of studying deinstitutionalization, they must be seen as intermediate markers in the development of ecologically valid community integration research.

III. VALIDITY OF MEASUREMENT

A measure is valid if it is an accurate reflection of the attribute that it is intended to assess. Measurement is fundamental to all research. A major complication in the area of deinstitutionalization is the necessity of studying such abstractions as adaptive behavior, learning, motivation, and productivity. For example, an adaptive behavior test score is taken to be the operational definition of adaptation to the social, cultural, and economic environment (Coulter & Morrow, 1978; Hill & Bruininks, 1983; Nihira *et al.*, 1974; Scanlon *et al.*, 1982); respondent checklist responses index residential climate (Jackson, 1969; King, Raynes, & Tizard, 1971; Moos, 1975; Moos & Moos, 1976); the abstract attribute of normalization is defined operationally as a score on the Program Analysis of Services System (PASS-3) (Wolfensberger & Glenn, 1975a,b) or a more objective checklist (Hull & Thompson, 1980); self-report of satisfaction is taken as an index of happiness (Gollay *et al.*, 1978; Heal & Chadsey, 1983; Hull & Thompson, 1980; Seltzer & Seltzer, 1976); physical proximity is taken as an index of affiliation (Berkson & Romer, 1980; Heller *et al.*, 1981); and number of bicycle brakes assembled per unit time is taken as an index of production (Gold, 1973). While some of these measures are less abstract than others, they all share the property of operationalism (Bridgman, 1927): they are all intended to index an attribute of the subject which is an abstraction of the event actually observed. While Skinner (1953) and many others (see especially Johnston & Pennypacker, 1980, for a most compelling, scholarly analysis) have argued that these abstractions lie outside the realm of science, the tradition of defining them in terms of events that can be observed and recorded has become the foundation of contemporary social science. Every measured variable has a more or less tenuous correspondence to the construct that it purports to index. This analog approach to measurement of constructs in deinstitutionalization parallels that in social science generally.

Of all the topics in this chapter, measurement validity has the most extensive literature. General recent references include Cronbach (1970), Nunnally (1978), Salvia and Ysseldyke (1981), and Sackett (1978a,b).

A. Validity

While not neglected completely, investigators in the area of deinstitutionalization have usually given only token attention to the validity of the measures used. In their review of published tests used for exceptional children and adults, Salvia and Ysseldyke (1981) could point to only a handful whose standardization procedures, validities, and reliabilities were satisfactory to permit their use as referents for the performance that they were designed to assess. It is a rare paper (e.g., Conroy *et al.*, 1982; MacEachron, 1983) that publishes the reliability of the instruments using the data from the reported investigation. Because validity as a general topic can be studied elsewhere, the presentation here treats two validity topics with special relevance for research on residential alternatives: establishing construct validity and controlling response bias.

1. CONSTRUCT VALIDITY

All studies that compare residential alternatives are construct validity studies; all determine the extent to which their measures discriminate among residential alternatives that are presumed to be different on the examined variables. Thus, MacEachron's (1983) study is, in fact, a validation study of the Management Practices Scale (King *et al.*, 1971) and the AAMD Adaptive Behavior Scale (ABS), since she demonstrated predictable differences between her two institution building types on both variables. Similarly, Sutter *et al.* (1980) validated both Part I and Part II of the ABS since they replicated previously demonstrated differences among community facility types on both measures. To the extent that facilities differ as predicted on the measures employed, the measures are in fact partially validated as indices of the constructs that they purport to measure.

Other studies have been undertaken to demonstrate the discriminative power (i.e., validity) of a particular measurement instrument. For example, Flynn (1980) found two major factors of PASS-3 (Wolfensberger & Glenn, 1975a), Program Normalization and Setting Normalization. Comparisons of residential and day service facilities revealed that facilities had meaningfully different profiles on the two factors, evidence that supports the validity of PASS-3 as a measure of normalization. Similarly, Moos (1975) and Moos and Moos (1976) used discrimination of facility and home types as evidence for the validity of their environment typology scales. In a very elegant project, Eyman *et al.* (1979) related PASS-3 (normalization) factor scores to ABS scores and supported the validity of both instruments, evidenced by significant and meaningful correlations between ABS gains and normalization of environment.

The "Multi-trait Multi-Method" technique popularized by Campbell and Fiske (1959) is perhaps the most refined procedure available to evaluate construct validity. This technique features the assessment of two or more traits by two or more methods. For example, Futterman and Arndt (1983) assessed both adaptive behavior and mental age by (1) program assignments, (2) psychometric tests, and (3) a psychologist's ratings. High intercorrelations among the three measures of mental age and among the three measures of adaptive behavior were taken as evidence that all measures "converged" on the same construct or referent. Unfortunately, the measures' intertrait correlations (i.e., between adaptive behavior and mental age) were in the same range as intratrait correlations (i.e., between methods for either mental age or adaptive behavior), indicating low discriminant validity between measures of different traits.

Flynn and Heal (1981) did a similar analysis on dimensions of Flynn's "short form" of Wolfensberger and Glenn's (1975a,b) PASS-3. Their "multi-methods" were actually "multi-raters" (Kavanagh, MacKinney, & Wolins, 1971). The correlation coefficients for 16 institutional cottages were .57 for program normalization and .78 for setting normalization, indicating substantial convergence among raters. Intertrait monorater and intertrait cross-rater correlations were near zero, indicating high discriminant validity as well. Thus two lines of evidence supported referent validity: (1) Different raters agreed on their setting normalization and program normalization ratings of each cottage, and (2) facilities' ratings for program normalization and setting normalization were independent: a cottage's rating on one characteristic did not apparently influence its rating on the other.

2. RESPONSE BIASES

A special issue in validity is the degree to which respondent biases influence observation records. Although they did not deal with mental retardation, Sudman and Bradburn's (1974) massive metanalysis of interview effects is very relevant to this issue. Their review covered no less than 935 references to methodological studies from 95 different social science journals as well as numerous dissertations, monographs, and books. They classified dependent variables according to (1) behavior (e.g., Did you buy any milk last week?) or (2) attitude (e.g., Should the United States supply

England with warships to fight Nazi Germany?). Their 46 independent variables were classified as (1) task variables (e.g., home vs out-of-home, face-to-face vs self-administered, importance of the interview question for the respondent, deliberate deception); (2) interviewer roles and characteristics; and (3) respondent roles and characteristics. Attitude responses were influenced by virtually every independent variable that they investigated, whereas behavior responses were influenced only by method of questionnaire administration—respondents tended to underreport behaviors that they were asked to recall in self-administered questionnaires as opposed to other forms of inquiry.

These findings have special relevance for mental retardation research, which depends so often on the responses to questionnaires by informants. A nonexhaustive list would include Adaptive Behavior Scale (Nihira et al., 1974), the PASS-3 measure of normalization (Wolfensberger & Glenn, 1975a), the questionnaires used by Willer and Intagliata (1981) and Intagliata and Willer (1982), the adaptive behavior and normalization instruments employed by Hull and Thompson (1980), and the omnibus survey questionnaires used by Baker et al. (1977), Bruininks et al. (1980, 1981, 1983), Gollay et al. (1978), and O'Connor (1976). The inference from Sudman and Bradburn's conclusions is that the validity of interview and questionnaire results is maximized by the use of behavioral (Does X have daily visitors to his/her room?) rather than nonbehavioral items (Is X happy living here?).

In addition to the ordinary problems associated with interviewing any respondent, there is substantial evidence that mentally retarded respondents are especially prone to certain response biases. Sigelman, Budd, Spanhel, and Schoenrock (1981a) and Sigelman, Schoenrock, Winer, Spanhel, Hromas, Martin, Budd, and Bensberg (1981b) have confirmed that mentally retarded respondents, especially those who are more severely impaired, are somewhat unreliable, and are prone to "acquiescence" bias, i.e., the disposition to say "yes" whatever the question asked of them (Sigelman, Budd, Winer, Schoenrock, & Martin, 1982). In order to neutralize the acquiescence bias, Sigelman et al. (1982) recommended the use of either–or questions instead of yes–no questions. Another approach is to assess acquiescence directly and make regression adjustments for it on other subscales (Heal & Chadsey, 1983).

An effective yet infrequently used procedure for controlling response biases is the triple-blind procedure. The highest quality research employs triple-blinding procedures. In addition to the subject, the investigator and the intervenor are instructed in a way that blinds them from any anticipated results of the investigator. For example, Ellis, Bostick, Moore, and Taylor (1981) had respondents assess the adaptive behavior of their subjects from information that was gleaned from unidentified facility file folders. Interrater correlations ranged from .82 for maladaptive behavior to .95 for independent skills and for language development. Unfortunately, these procedures have been overlooked by the vast majority of the investigators in community integration research.

B. Reliability

The literature on reliability is extensive. Fortunately, two recent papers (Berk, 1979; Hollenbeck, 1978) discuss reliability in the context of mental retardation research and elaborate on many of the foibles of researchers in this area. The three major types of reliability: *test–retest reliability, interrater agreement,* and *internal consistency,* are sensitive to different sources of measurement error. Table II summarizes the reliability and agreement indices recommended by Hollenbeck (1978). For each type of unsystematic error the preferred statistic is shown for nominal and for interval scales. An important nuance distinguishes test–retest reliability from interrater agreement: A Pearson's correlation (r) is a suitable index of test–retest reliability but not interrater agreement. If one rater has a consistent leniency bias (rates all subjects higher), that "error" in judgment should reasonably be called unreliability since, by definition, raters disagree to the extent that one is more lenient. But r is insensitive to overall interrater differences. For example, Ellis *et al.* (1981) reported correlations of .95, .95, .93, and .82 between two raters' estimates of partial ABS scores for Independent Functioning,

TABLE II

OPTIMAL RELIABILITY STATISTICS

Case	Test–retest	Interrater agreement	Internal consistency
Type of error	Time-related changes in examinees	Individual differences in raters' perceptions	Variations in sampling of items from the content domain
Preferred statistic(s)			
Nominal scale	Phi (binary r)	Cohen's Kappa[a]	—
Interval scale (items may be *yes–no*)	Pearson's r	Robinson's[b] a	Cronbach's alpha[c]

[a] Cohen (1968).
[b] Robinson (1957).
[c] Cronbach (1951).

Socialization, Language Development, and Maladaptive Behavior, respectively. While it is commendable that reliability data were gathered, it is impossible to determine the degree of leniency error of one rater or another. The intraclass correlation or Robinson's *a* is a more appropriate agreement index of interrater agreement, but to our knowledge neither has been used in the mental retardation literature. While Robinson's *a* is applied to variables measured on an interval scale, an analogous procedure, Cohen's Kappa (Cohen, 1968), should be used to index percentage agreement for categorical data. Kappa has the virtue of correcting for chance agreement if one or both raters guess at their subjects' scores.

Internal consistency indexes the degree to which items on a scale agree with one another. Cronbach's alpha (e.g., Cronbach, 1951), which equals the average of all possible split-half correlations among the items on an instrument, is the recommended index. The index of internal consistency is no substitute for either interrater agreement or test–retest reliability. Indeed, all three are necessary but not sufficient conditions for the validity of a measure.

The foregoing discussion and Table II must be seen as a transitional summary of reliability procedures, one whose recommendations will correct past errors, but one that falls short of the more elegant, but mathematically difficult, approach, *generalizability theory* (Berk, 1979; Cronbach, Gleser, Nanda, & Rajaratnam, 1972). This sophisticated analysis of the variance associated with all tractable sources of unreliability is the strategy of choice for social science research.

IV. INTERNAL VALIDITY

Internal validity refers to the validity of an empirically based inference in support of a tentative empirical law (a hypothesis). In the prototypical case, called the *"true" experiment,* subjects are *randomly* assigned to either of two groups, an experimental group (which gets a critical intervention), and a control group (which is treated exactly the same as the experimental group except for the absence of the critical intervention or, better, the substitution of a placebo intervention). Random assignment is critical to internal validity, for only random assignment assures that the backgrounds of the two groups are equated. However, studies employing random assignment of individuals to living facilities is rare in residential research. Thus, nearly all designs for testing hypotheses about community integration are called *quasi* experimental: the independent variables are manipulated by sampling groups of subjects from different populations, and experimental and "control" groups may differ in many ways besides their difference on the independent variable. Notwithstanding their inherent weaknesses, these designs can address many of the threats to internal validity.

A. Quasi-Experimental Designs

The five designs in this section have been labeled "pre-experimental" by Campbell and Stanley (1966) since they rule out very few internal validity threats.

1. ONE-GROUP POSTTEST-ONLY DESIGN

In this design, measurements are made after treatment on a single group of individuals. There are no pretests or comparisons to no-treatment groups. For example, McDevitt, Smith, Schmidt, and Rosen (1978) described a case study of the adjustment and quality of life of 18 deinstitutionalized mildly handicapped individuals. All of the subjects were living independently in the community. The investigators assessed vocational, economic, social, and personal adjustment through intensive interviewing. As a group, the subjects were described as confident, adjusted, and satisfied with community living. The analysis by McDevitt *et al.* is necessarily descriptive. Although suggesting that their subjects had greater personal satisfaction in their community settings, the authors made no attempt to attribute causal relationships to the residential changes. The absence of comparison to nontreatment groups is the fundamental limiting deficiency of this design. Without these comparisons the effects of experimentally irrelevant variables cannot be evaluated. Indeed, even the attribution of satisfaction to deinstitutionalization is fallible: lacking pretreatment measures, change in the dependent measure cannot be assumed. This simple design is appropriate only for very primitive descriptive objectives. There are no satisfactory controls for threats to internal validity.

2. ONE-GROUP PRETEST–POSTTEST DESIGN

The addition of pretest assessment prior to treatment provides a modest improvement over the posttest-only design. Comparison of assessments allows some evaluation of changes in the dependent variable. However, causal statements regarding treatment effect (or lack of effect) cannot be supported. Although pretest measurement provides a baseline of performance, making it possible to detect subjects' change, no threat to internal validity is adequately controlled.

Aninger and Bolinsky (1977) described changes in adaptive behavior in 18 retarded adults transferred from an institutional setting to supervised apartment living facilities. Pretest measures were taken before placement and 6 months after placement. Modest increases in adaptive behavior were indicated in the AAMD scale and interview posttest scores, and modest decreases in the Burks' Rating Scale. Taken as a whole, pretest–posttest differences were not statistically significant, and the authors concluded that the independent living environment failed to increase independent functioning in these individuals. Birenbaum and Re (1979) and King *et al.* (1980) are other recent studies of this type. Birenbaum and Re found that from 1974 to 1977 the residents of Gatewood, a large ($N = 63$) CRF, engaged in fewer integrative activities and were managed with more rules. King *et al.* found that 142 residents at Woodhaven, a transitional facility, increased significantly in their adaptive behavior but remained unchanged in their maladaptive behavior. These studies of resident improvement exemplify five internal weaknesses: history, attrition, maturation, regression, and instrumentation effects.

A major threat to design validity is the *"history"* of concomitant events that covary with the intervention. Moving into a new residence involves making new friends; attracting the attention of old friends, advocates, and family; placing oneself in situations where new learning can occur that has nothing to do with placement per se; etc. Collateral vocational, medical, and spiritual interventions often accompany placement. All of these might be expected to improve adaptive behavior, either directly or indirectly.

A special type of historical concomitant is *attrition*. Logically, lost cases are atypical. Thus, when cases are lost in the interval between a pretest and a posttest, these measures are taken on logically different populations. For example, attrition could easily have pressured the Birenbaum and Re posttest scores downward, since the 21 subjects lost during the course of their study were presumably the most capable.

Another class of artifacts is *maturation*—including growth or degeneration, or in the shorter term, warm-up and fatigue. Even in adults, it is reasonable to assume that many adaptive and social skills are developing quite independent of residential placement. Thus, the growing dissatisfaction expressed by the subjects of Birenbaum and Re may have reflected social maturation, not domiciliary variation.

A fourth class of threats to internal validity is *regression*. Regression is the statistical drift of scores on an unreliable variable: Individuals who have extreme scores on an unreliable measure at first testing, statistically tend to have scores that are less extreme on subsequent testings. This effect is very likely in community placement research, since individuals are selected for placement because of their momentarily high adaptive and social skill assessments. These can be unreliable variables, especially when they are measured by the judgment of institutional caretakers and case workers

(Landesman-Dwyer & Sulzbacher, 1981). Thus, one would expect some regression of residents' measured social and adaptive skills after they have been placed, even if their real skills had been stable.

Finally, typical of research in community placement, these studies made no effort to control for *measurement instrumentation* effects. Interviews, for example, are a particularly reactive measurement process (Sigelman *et al.,* 1982). Having had the pretest, Aninger and Bolinsky's subjects might have consciously practiced the adaptive behavior items and rehearsed answers to the interviews. Another jeopardy comes from the failure to blind observers or to assess interobserver agreement. Behavior and interview ratings were undoubtedly influenced by observers' preconceptions about housing mentally retarded adults in community apartments.

Longitudinal research (e.g., Balla, Butterfield, & Zigler, 1974; Zigler, Butterfield, & Capobianco, 1970) has the structure of the one-group pretest–posttest design. These studies by Zigler *et al.* were undertaken to demonstrate that IQ degeneration often observed after institutionalization could be attributed to the examinee's increased desire to interact with the tester, which in turn resulted from the social deprivation of the institutional environment relative to the preinstitutional environment. Their moderate support for this hypothesis was undermined by all of the threats described above: history, attrition, maturation, regression, or measurement reactiveness.

Quite aside from the logical threats to the pretest–posttest design, are the undesirable measurement properties of the gain score as a dependent variable. Cronbach and Furby (1970) and Linn and Slinde (1977) discuss these properties in detail. Briefly, the gain score has two problems. First, it is usually less reliable than the pretest and posttest scores individually. Second, because of the regression effect described above and because subjects crowd the "ceiling score" as they progress, gain scores tend to be negatively correlated with pretest scores. Thus, gain scores should be used only with very reliable measures that have an unconstrained ceiling, and only then with covariance adjustments for pretest scores. Even so, Cronbach and Furby (1970) and Linn and Slinde (1977) argue that gain scores are so fallible that they should be avoided in empirical research.

3. INTACT GROUPS, POSTTEST ONLY

The third preexperimental design is that of comparative research. This design is also called static group comparison (Campbell & Stanley, 1966) or ex post facto research (Cook & Campbell, 1979). The five major national surveys of deinstitutionalization (Baker *et al.,* 1977; Bruininks *et al.,* 1980, 1981; Gollay *et al.,* 1978; O'Connor, 1976) are examples of the posttest-only design. All feature "one-shot" descriptions and comparisons of different residence types.

Also included in this group are studies of placement success. Examples include Intagliata and Willer (1982), Sutter *et al.* (1980), and Thiel (1981), all of whom reported that extrapunitive maladaptive behavior was a consistent impediment to successful placement. Using the same design, Schalock and Harper (1978) and Schalock *et al.* (1981b) concluded that basic skills, especially language skills, were the important attributes of successful clients. Other studies using this design include Eyman *et al.* (1981), Pratt *et al.* (1980), Scanlon *et al.* (1982), Vitello *et al.* (1983), and Willer and Intagliata (1981).

The posttest-only comparative design, like the other preexperimental variants, cannot confirm causal relationships. Its fundamental weakness is the absence of control for *selection biases.* Group differences are as likely to be a function of administrative and clinical variables that determine placement as they are a consequence of the placement itself (Butterfield, 1982). As an example, Baker *et al.* reported that semiindependent facilities had greater resident autonomy, responsibility, and work activities than other facility types; but this finding cannot be validly attributed to facility placement per se. Residents of this group were also the most capable of the total CRF sample. In these studies, individual characteristics and group treatment are inextricably confounded.

The foregoing critique is not intended to demean the importance of these seminal investigations. Indeed, in placement success studies it is almost nonsensical to consider assigning subjects at random to recidivism and nonrecidivism groups. The question of interest is to determine the variables that correlate with placement success in the real world, so that individuals and conditions can be selected to optimize the match of residents and facilities. But in this determination there should be no pretense that comparing intact groups is equivalent to conducting a true experiment.

4. INTACT GROUPS, PRETEST, AND POSTTEST DESIGN

The addition of pretest measures strengthens internal validity by partially controlling some extraneous variables. Inclusion of both a pretest and a comparison nontreatment group in a design can increase interpretability of treatment effects when historical factors are comparable for the two groups.

Eyman *et al.* (1981) and Willer and Intagliata (1982), among others, employed pre- and posttest assessments in comparisons of behavior change across residential alternatives. These studies did not attempt to preestablish matched comparison groups, although in both, pretest data on subject characteristics were presented in order to argue that groups were comparable before placement. From what we have said previously, it is clear that these group posttest differences are most reasonably attributed to selection factors and subject characteristics rather than to placement site. Thus, we find that the comparison of intact groups is an imperfect strategy for evaluating tentative empirical laws, even when pretest measures permit a modicum of confidence in the comparability of groups prior to their differential treatment. One might suspect that this design would be improved by the intentional matching of groups prior to assignment. However, as we shall see in the next section, matching intact experimental and control groups is an imperfect substitute for the random assignment of subjects to these groups.

5. PREMATCHED CONTROL GROUP DESIGN

In this design, treatment and control groups are matched on pretest evaluations; treatment effect is assessed in the comparison of posttest or gain scores. As in all quasi-experimental designs, the groups are *intact* collectives of subjects, not randomly assigned to the experimental and control groups.

The classic example of a matched control group design is Skeels' study of environmental enrichment and intellectual development (e.g., Skeels, 1966). Skeels and his students placed a group of 13 orphaned infants on wards for adult female residents in an institution for the retarded. These adults functioned as "surrogate mothers." A "matched," control group of 12 children was *subsequently* selected at the orphanage, where stimulation from adults was at a minimum. Over the years striking differences emerged between the groups, with the experimental subjects manifesting dramatic increases in IQ and successful adaptation to adult life (Skeels, 1966). This study has been highly criticized because control subjects and experimental subjects had not been randomly assigned to their respective groups. Indeed, the control group was selected after the experimental subjects had been placed (e.g., Longstreth, 1981). Thus, most threats to internal validity, especially differential selection and regression of experimental and control groups, offered alternative explanations for group differences. Nevertheless, the prematched intact control group design continues to appear frequently in the literature in this area (e.g., Berkson, 1981; Conroy *et al.*, 1982; Hemming *et al.*, 1981; Kastner, Reppucci, & Pezzoli, 1979; Scanlon *et al.*, 1982; Wolpert, 1978).

The study reported by Conroy *et al.* (1982), exemplifies the problems with this design. Seventy individuals were released from a single institution into community facilities. Using preplacement data, placed subjects were matched individually with residents remaining at the releasing institution. Matching variables included sex, years of institutionalization, scores on a self-sufficiency scale, and IQ. Simple *t* tests yielded no significant differences between groups on these variables. Subsequent to matching, additional analyses were conducted on characteristics reflecting secondary disabilities (e.g., seizure problems, ambulation, and other physical disabilities). On these variables, individuals placed in the community were at least as impaired as the control sample. Although there were no differences in adaptive or maladaptive pretest scores, significant posttest differences in adaptive and maladaptive behavior favored the community group. During the 2 years following their release, the community group exhibited large gains in adaptive behavior; maladaptive scores were stable. Among control subjects, there was minimal change in adaptive behavior; the significant difference in maladaptive scores between the two groups was due to increases in these behaviors by the control group. Conroy et al. concluded that subjects in the community group were less dependent than they would have been had they remained at the institution.

Two possible flaws are especially threatening to prematched control group designs: selection interactions and statistical regression. Although groups had been assessed and matched for equivalence, one cannot assume the entire array of relevant variables had been held constant. For example, these matched groups could have differed in physical appearance, parental support for placement, or advocates in the institution and the community. Posttest differences could be explained by invoking interactions of maturation, history, etc., with bias due to capabilities selectively present in the treatment group not considered in the original matching. Threats such as these can never be ruled out with certainty, but the experimenter can limit their plausibility. For example, Conroy et al. took special care to select matching variables that had been deemed relevant in the literature of community placement success and then demonstrated that groups did not differ statistically on these measures.

But the greatest threat to the validity of the matched group design is statistical regression, the tendency for extreme scores to be less extreme upon remeasurement. Some residents are selected for placement because of their promise; others are passed over for their lack of it. Thus, at the moment of selection, those who are placed are irrefutably seen to be more promising than those who are not, regardless of any matching on psychometric and personal characteristics. This state of affairs has two implications for regression effects. On the one hand, it could be argued that the scores of the community group should regress toward the institution mean. On the other hand, the control subjects, whose momentary formal assessment has qualified them for placement although their informal assessment has not, are handpicked for their "regression potential," and can probably be expected to regress even more than the placed subjects. This interpretation is consistent with the Conroy et al. finding that maladaptive behavior worsened for the institution group, but not the community group.

A final problem with matched groups designs is the constraint on the differences between groups at the beginning of an experiment. While this constraint has logical appeal, it tends to bias statistical tests on posttest scores against the detection of group differences. This bias is corrected by controlling for the matching variable statistically using a covariance or regression analysis.

B. The True Experiment

The foregoing discussion of quasi-experimental designs is sobering in its implications. All such designs are compromises. Research comparing residential alternatives can only be conclusive if conducted using true experimental designs, with random assignment to groups. In view of the logical weaknesses of quasi-experimental designs, it is surprising that so few hypothesis confirmation studies in this literature are true experiments. But there are a few (Close, 1977; Heal, Colson, & Gross, 1984; Landesman-Dwyer, 1983; MacEachron, 1983; Matson, 1981; Matson, Marchetti, & Atkins, 1980; Tizard, 1964). Butterfield (1982), citing Kiesler (1982), reports 10 others for mentally ill populations.

1. TRADITIONAL TRUE EXPERIMENTS

Tizard (1964), Close (1977), MacEachron (1983), and most recently, Landesman-Dwyer (1983) randomly assigned institutionalized residents to placement and nonplacement groups. Tizard compared residents of a large English institution with matched peers who were placed into an experimental group home. Seven months after initial placement, two subjects from the experimental group were returned to the institution because of their aggressive behavior and severe seizure activity. Two residents from the institution replaced them in the group home. While experimental and control groups both increased mean verbal and nonverbal mental age (MA) scores over the 2-year study period, the difference between groups on verbal MA was large (8 months) and statistically significant.

Close (1977) randomly selected 8 institutionalized severely and profoundly retarded adults from a sample of 15 for placement into a community group home program; the 7 remaining subjects formed the control group. Placement into the group home was accompanied by an intensive self-care and social skills training program. One-year posttest score comparisons yielded significant differences on all dependent measures in favor of the experimental group. As in Tizard's study, attrition reduced the sample over the course of the investigation. An "aggressive resident" from the experimental group was returned to the institution after 10 weeks; data were retained in both pretest and posttest group means. The two other lost cases, an experimental subject who died after 10 months in the group home and a control subject placed into the community, were excluded from the data analysis.

In MacEachron's (1983) study 160 subjects in a Massachusetts institution were randomly selected from the eligible pool of 289 for placement from old, conventional, institution buildings into new, "homelike" cottages. Extensive environmental and program differences between the new and old buildings were documented, although the staffing patterns were similar. After a year's residence, the adaptive behavior of the group moved to the new building was significantly higher than those who remained in the old structures. The temptation to conclude that homelike structures facilitate growth in adaptive behavior is undermined by the fact that, despite random assignment, there was some evidence that the experimental group was the more intelligent (point biserial $r = .17, p < .05$).

The last of the true experiment studies of placement was reported by Landesman-Dwyer. She evaluated behavioral changes in residents placed from a large state institution to an "innovative community," comprised of duplexes in an institution. For a variety of administrative reasons Landesman-Dwyer and her host institution negotiated a "match-trios" design: One of three matched subjects was selected for placement by the institution that hosted her project; of the remaining two, one was randomly chosen for placement, the other being a control remaining in the institution. Assessments showed that the experimental duplexes were significantly less "institutional" in appearance, environment, management practices, and social context. Behavioral changes, on the other hand, were small.

Tables III and IV summarize the threats to internal validity in the present analysis. Five major classes of threat to internal validity are identified, two of which are subdivided into subclasses. Each threat is defined with an example, and one or more control strategies are recommended (Table III). Table IV presents this information more cryptically, with threats listed as rows and controls as columns. Table IV indicates that random assignment of subjects to conditions reduces or eliminates many, but not all, of these threats. Selection, maturation, and regression are all logically neutralized. As these tables indicate, historical threats to internal validity are of three conceptually different types: extrinsic, intrinsic, and attrition. Random assignment controls only for the first of these.

Perhaps the greatest challenge in establishing causal relationships is the control of historical events that are *intrinsic* to the intervention. This threat is called multiple treatment interference by Campbell and Stanley (1966) and Cook and Campbell (1979). The notion of intrinsic historical threat depends upon the definition of the treatment variable, i.e., on the specificity of the causal attributions of the investigation. For example, when the intervention is defined in the narrow sense as simple change in domiciliary arrangement,

TABLE III

APPROACHES TO THE CONTROL OF THREATS TO INTERNAL VALIDITY IN COMMUNITY INTEGRATION RESEARCH

Threat	Description	Example	Control strategy
Selection bias	More promising cases selected for placement than for control group	Comparison of intact groups in a posttest-only study (Baker et al., 1977; Bruininks et al., 1981)	Randomly assign subjects to placement and control conditions; compare intact groups to assess their similarity
History	Events occur coincidentally with placement		
Events extrinsic to research design	Collateral events are independent of placement	Cut in funding, change in day program	Include near by control group in design; the control group must experience the same history as the placed group
Events intrinsic to research design	"Multiple treatment interference"; collateral events are correlated with placement	Placement and programming are confounded (Close, 1977; Tizard, 1963)	Define treatment carefully. Partition treatment into setting and intervention components; employ blinded intervenors who have no vested interest in the success of placement
Attrition	Loss of subjects due to mortality, upward mobility, or downward mobility	Changes in subject status and apparently arbitrary replacement rules (Birenbaum & Re, 1979; Tizard, 1963)	Include various attrition results as scale points on dependent variable; replace lost subjects by preselected, matched substitutes; compare attrited and retained groups on pretest(s) to assess their similarity

Maturation	Growth, degeneration, warm-up, and fatigue that impact on the dependent variable(s) regardless of any intervention	Spontaneous growth in a one-group pretest–posttest design (Aninger & Bolinsky, 1977; King et al., 1980)	Include a randomly constituted control group whose extra-placement developmental activities are comparable to those of the placed group
Measurement	Measurement of the dependent variable(s) create the illusion of a treatment effect where none exists in reality		
Reaction to assessment	Responsiveness to placement is catalyzed by testing or observation	Improvement noted from repeated testing in the absence of intervention (Heal et al., 1984)	Omit pretests for all or a random half of all study groups; use unobtrusive measures, especially before and during intervention
Biased testers or observers	Examiners whose scores are based on information other than that provided by the subject	Examiners who have a vested interest in obtaining a particular outcome (Virtually all placement studies)	Employ blinded subjects and observers, who know only what they are measuring, not why
Floor or ceiling effects	The range of a measure is constrained so that the performance of a high-scoring subject is underestimated or that of a low-scoring subject is overestimated	Part II of the Adaptive Behavior Scale (Nihira et al., 1974) whose modal value is zero for most populations assessed	Employ measures whose ranges extend well above and below the levels that occur in the subjects of study
Regression to true scores	The statistical tendency for individuals with extreme scores on one occasion to achieve more nearly average scores on subsequent occasions	After a placement group has been selected, a control group is matched with it on the basis of above-average adaptive behavior scores (Conroy et al., 1982; Skeels, 1966)	Assign subjects randomly to placed and unplaced groups; never select subjects on the basis of scores that are higher (or lower) than those expected in a random sample from the same population

TABLE IV

SUMMARY OF CONTROLS FOR THREATS TO INTERNAL VALIDITY

Threats	Controls										
	Assess extent of equivalence	Nearby control group	Careful Treatment specif.	Scale value for lost cases	Omit pretests	Blinded observers & SBS	Blinded intervenors	Full range measures	Matched groups	Random assignment	Reversal and multiple baseline
Selection bias	?								?	X	X
History											
Extrinsic		X							X	X	X
Intrinsic			X				X				
Attrition	?			X							X
Maturation									?	X	X
Measurement											
Reactivity					X	?					
Bias						X	X				
Floor or ceiling								X			
Regression to true scores										X	X

intrinsic concomitants may include (1) extraordinary parental interest after placement, (2) neighborhood support or animosity, and (3) the presence of a neighborhood. Behavioral changes in residents can be attributed to them rather than to domiciliary change itself. On the other hand, a broader definition of treatment might include all these events—parental interest, community interactions, and neighborhood appearance—as parts of the "collage" of movement to a new environment and, thus, as valid elements of the intervention itself. For example, experimental subjects in the Landesman-Dwyer study were placed into new and apparently superior settings but they were apparently not the recipients of dramatic increases in training. Behavioral change for these individuals was minor. In contrast, there were large positive changes for experimental subjects in the Tizard (1964), Close (1977), and MacEachron (1983) investigations, where facility change was accompanied by increased programming. These results strongly suggest that noninstitutional management or programming, not placement itself, occasions resident behavior changes. Unfortunately, management system, programming, and environmental change were confounded in these earlier investigations, so there is no way to determine whether their outcomes would have resulted from programming alone.

While random assignment eliminates selection bias it does not guarantee comparability of groups at posttest. *Attrition* that is systematically related to treatment is perhaps the single greatest threat to the internal validity of both Tizard's and Close's true experiments. In Tizard's investigation, subjects with behavioral and health problems were replaced by presumably more adaptive residents. The pattern of consistent verbal mental age gain for both experimental and control groups, albeit at a slower rate for control subjects, could be interpreted in terms of a selection–maturation bias in favor of the experimental group. Similar threats weaken Close's investigation. The two excluded cases favor positive outcomes in the experimental group. Poor health may have been a precursor to the death of the experimental subject. Omitting such data selectively biases the sample in favor of healthier, more physically competent individuals. In the instance of the excluded control subject placed into the community by the institution, possible bias in favor of treatment outcome is introduced by the removal of a skilled individual from the control group. Subject loss was not reported in Landesman-Dwyer's study. However, her plan to replace lost subjects with their matched cohort represents a compromise with respect to maintaining randomly attained group equivalence. These examples highlight a serious problem: To the extent that attrition has been selective, the internal validity of the true experiment degenerates toward that of a quasi-experimental, nonequivalent groups design.

Close (1977) chose to retain the data of the aggressive experimental subject who was returned to the institution after 10 weeks in the group home. In this instance, retention of the data for a subject not receiving full treatment could reduce its apparent effects. Cook and Campbell (1979) suggest other alternatives. First, pretest measures of the original sample can be compared to those of the subjects remaining in the groups at the study's conclusion. Equivalence of the original and final groups can be assessed. Additionally, pretest differences in the remaining experimental and control subjects can be compared; if significant, attrition-induced sample bias is suggested. Zigler *et al.* (1970) used this strategy to argue that attrition did not jeopardize their conclusion that social deprivation fosters social responsiveness in institutionalized residents. When a variety of pretest measures is employed, attrition may result in different patterns among the measures. Cook and Campbell recommend analysis of each measure individually.

The matching of subjects merits special attention here. Random assignment guarantees only probablistic equivalence. Sampling variability can lead to initial group nonequivalence on critical variables. Close (1977) chose to evaluate equivalence by testing group difference on the dependent measures after assignment. Ideally, subjects should be matched in blocks (e.g., pairs) prior to random assignment, as was done in MacEachron's (1983) and Tizard's (1964) studies. In a randomized block design, error variance (blocks by treatments) is disassociated from individual (block) differences, thereby increasing the design's precision and power to detect subtle intervention effects. However, the effect of matching on the power of the significance test is directly related to the correlation of the matching variable(s) and outcome measure. If this relationship is not strong (the matching variable is not related to group differences) then matching may cause a net loss on a design's statistical power.

2. CROSS-GROUP AND CROSS-GROUP CROSSOVER DESIGNS

One important true experiment alternative that has been overlooked by applied social scientists is a *"cross-group"* assignment of experimental task components. In this design, subjects are randomly divided into two groups, and the training tasks are divided into two sets. Each group then serves as a *randomly constituted control group* for the other on half the tasks. Subsequent manipulation, called a cross-group crossover design, involves interchanging the two groups and intervention tasks so that all subjects receive the total intervention. The applications of cross-group and crossover variations have special significance for residential research in applied settings where the withholding of treatment is both administratively difficult and unethical. For example, Heal *et al.* (1983) evaluated a secondary school program to train severely mentally handicapped students in community and living skills. During the fall of 1978, one group of students was trained on one set of tasks, and the other group on the second set. Both groups were pre- and posttested on both sets of tasks, so that each group served as a randomly constituted control group for the other on half the tasks. This cross-group design is unquestionably a true experiment in that all extraneous variables have been randomized. Furthermore, it appears to be a marked improvement upon the classical true experiment, where superior performance achieved by the experimental group over the control group might be due solely to differential attention to the trained subjects, not to the particular intervention under study. In the cross-group design, both groups are given comparable training, provided that the skills taught are equivalent. Furthermore, a vast number of factors associated with classroom and school variations are held constant. In the spring of 1979, Heal, Colson, and Gross interchanged the experimental and control tasks for their two groups; so during one semester or the other all students were trained on all tasks, half in the fall and half in the spring. This was the *cross-groups crossover* manipulation. Assuming that growth on the measures is not restrained by a ceiling effect, the crossover feature adds the precision of using subjects as their own controls to the logic of true experimental control. Using these designs for 2 years with six tasks each semester, Heal *et al.* found that trained students had higher posttest scores than untrained students on all 24 comparisons, after covariance adjustments for each semester's pretest performance.

These are not, of course, new designs. For example, Winer's (1971, p. 712, plan 5) is precisely a cross-group crossover design with three sets of materials and three training periods. In view of the lament over the use of quasi-experimental designs in applied social research, it is surprising that cross-group and cross-group crossover variations have not been more generally applied.

C. Some Time Series Alternatives

Time series, a refreshing approach to the science of behavior, solves many of the problems of Internal Validity. According to Birnbrauer, Peterson, and Solnick (1974), research in this tradition is defined by four characteristics: (1) repeated measures on the same subject(s) under controlled conditions; (2) the use of reliable measures of directly observable behaviors; (3) the use of interventions that are defined in sufficient detail to allow their replication; and (4) the demonstration of repeatable behavioral effects of those interventions. Thus, time series designs assess the effects of intervention(s) relative to *intra*individual performance variations, whereas conventional designs assess these effects relative to *inter*individual variations in performance (Kazdin, 1982).

There are two popular strategies for demonstrating a "functional" (i.e., presumed causal) relationship between an independent variable and a dependent variable in this tradition, *reversal* and *multiple baseline*. A study by Martin, Rusch, James, Decker, and Trtol (1982b) provides both a reversal and a multiple baseline example. Upon being placed into apartments from a large intermediate care facility, several mentally retarded adults were in immediate need of learning to cook. The established routine was to provide direct instruction, "preinstruction and instructional feedback." Disappointed in the learner's dependence on the trainer under this routine, Martin *et al.* constructed a step-by-step flip chart of photographs and printed instructions for each of five balanced meals. The step-by-step performance of three subjects was assessed for at least 2 weeks under a baseline routine of preinstruction and instructional feedback conditions. The percentage of steps completed independently was about 50%, but it seemed to be increasing over days for all three subjects. After baseline, picture cards were added to the instructional routine, starting on different days for different subjects (multiple baseline) to minimize the interpretation that some extraexperimental historical event, rather than the picture intervention, might be responsible for any improvement. For all three subjects this second phase was associated with modest, gradual increases in the percentage of steps completed independently. Because there was some question that the rise in performance during the picture condition was simply an extension of the gradual rise in performance during baseline, pictures were withdrawn for the subject whose improvement seemed least dramatic, i.e., seemed most continuous with the gradual baseline rise. This reversal resulted in a sudden and unambiguous decrement in performance. After one cycle of the menus (five meals), pictures were reinstated for this subject, and her performance returned abruptly to its prereversal level. Thus, Martin *et al.* concluded that their picture series facilitated the cooking performance of their subjects.

Other time-series, community-integration papers have been recently reviewed by Martin, Rusch, and Heal (1982a). Examples include Bauman and Iwata (1977) whose apparently successful intervention to improve the housecleaning by a pair of roommates was undermined by their failure to use either a reversal or a multiple-baseline procedure to control for history, maturation, or measurement artifacts; Lowe and Cuvo (1976), whose intervention to teach money valuation was presented in a multiple-baseline design over different coins, thereby controlling for many of these threats to internal validity; and Vogelsberg and Rusch (1979), who eliminated many of these threats by demonstrating the degeneration of their subject's street-crossing performance toward her baseline level when the intervention (direct instruction) was withdrawn (i.e., "reversed").

By their nature, time-series designs control most threats to internal validity. *Selection* bias is perfectly controlled in that the experimental and control conditions are vested in the self-same subject(s). *History* is controlled by repeating intervention and baseline alternations (reversal strategy) or by varying the time at which intervention begins in different behaviors (multiple-baseline strategy). *Maturation* is assessed by ongoing measurements; intervention effects can be seen against the baseline of ambient growth or degeneration, if any. *Regression* effects are controlled by extending baseline measurements until they become stabilized about their "true score" values. Only *measurement bias* and *reactiveness* form a serious threat to these designs. Especially problematic is the repeated measurement by an experimenter who comes to know his subject extremely well, and who often develops a personal and emotional as well as a theoretical commitment to a successful intervention. The typical procedure in this research is to record the data daily and decide each day whether the intervention should be maintained or modified. This decision is presumably based on unrecorded cues given by the subject during experimental sessions. Thus, while procedures can be accurately reported, their replicability is usually open to question. Blinding of observers seems crucial in such research, but it is seldom done, and may be impossible in repeated measures, small-*n* investigations.

D. Synopsis of the Threats to Internal Validity

The logic of internal validity is extremely complex. The true experiment, with random assignment of subjects to groups, controls logically for *selection bias,* for *maturation effects,* and for *regression* to true scores. However, many additional controls must be applied in order to logically reduce threats from *historical factors* of the intrinsic, extrinsic, and attrition varieties; *maturation* and degeneration, both short- and long-term; and *measurement artifacts,* including reactivity, bias, and constrained scales of measurement; and regression.

V. SOCIAL VALIDITY

Kazdin (1982), Wolf (1978), and others have proposed that experimental results be considered socially valid only if targeted performance of the experimental condition is (1) worthy of pursuit, (2) uses "acceptable" procedures, and (3) falls within the range of socially acceptable levels, as evidenced either by *empirical comparison* to the performance of a group of the subjects' peers or by the *subjective evaluation* of those (e.g., subjects, peers, parents, supervisors) whose own well being is affected by the performance.

These social validation considerations were woven into the procedures used by Rusch, Weithers, Menchetti, and Schutz (1980) to evaluate the social validity of an intervention to reduce "repetition of topics" by a moderately retarded food services employee during lunches and dinners. Supervisors and co-workers regarded this repetition to be excessive and annoying (*socially valid research problem*). Following baseline measurement, co-workers were provided preinstruction in how to give feedback when a topic was repeated (*socially valid procedure*). Results indicated that co-workers were effective in reducing topic repetition only when they were prompted to provide feedback themselves by an experimenter. Data collected on the number of co-worker topical repetitions (*comparative validation measure*) revealed that the mentally retarded employee and his nonhandicapped peers repeated themselves equally often. However, contrary to the direct comparison data, ratings by the co-workers (*subjective validation measure*) did not show a reduction in repetitions.

Another example is provided by Matson (1981) who established grocery shopping performance standards for his mentally retarded group by observing and scoring a blinded group of nonretarded subjects who were matched with the target group on age and sex. After training, his subjects achieved 12.4 of 14 "correct steps"; the normal comparative social validation group had completed 12.1 steps "correctly." Trained subjects significantly surpassed untrained, randomly assigned controls, who completed only 2.5 correct steps.

These studies reveal the intertwining of social validity and experimental validity in applied research: If applied research is to have social relevance, then the social scientist must demonstrate the acceptability of its goals, procedures, and results in the judgment of those to whom the research would apply. Yet, as Brooks and Baumeister (1977) have charged, few investigators have taken this responsibility seriously.

VI. THE ETHICS OF APPLIED SCIENCE

From the above it is clear that an elaborate system of methodological conventions has been developed, and that the validity of research in residential alternatives for developmentally disabled individuals depends upon its adherence to these conventions. But research on residential alternatives has fallen short in all regards. Ecological validity has usually been ignored and must be assumed from the unsystematic (as opposed to random) selection of settings and times from the population available (e.g., Bjaanes & Butler, 1974; Landesman-Dwyer *et al.,* 1979). Population validity has been approached in only a few studies (e.g., Hauber *et al.,* 1981; Krantz *et al.,* 1978,

1979, 1980; O'Connor, 1976; Scheerenberger, 1978, 1982). Referent generality has been compromised in all community integration research; studies often report only one outcome measure.

Measurement validity is nearly always assumed by the author, and the few promising measures, such as the Adaptive Behavior Scale (Nihira *et al.*, 1974) and the Resident Management Practices Scale (King *et al.*, 1971), are often passed over in favor of untried, author-developed substitutes.

Internal validity has been flawed by the unfortunate custom of using intact, rather than randomized, groups. The applied researcher must challenge the assertion of practitioners that "best practice" is incompatible with this essential prerequisite of internal validity. The number of studies (e.g., Close, 1977; Heal *et al.*, 1984; Landesman-Dwyer, 1983; MacEachron, 1983; Matson, 1981; Matson *et al.*, 1980; Tizard, 1964) that have accomplished random assignment has been embarrasingly few. But random assignment of subjects to conditions does not guarantee internal validity. Measurement artifacts, for example, have been controlled by blinding data gatherers in very few studies (e.g., Ellis *et al.*, 1978; Landesman-Dwyer & Sulzbacher, 1981; Sigelman *et al.*, 1982). In addition, specification of the intervention in order to avoid the threat of "multiple treatment interference" is necessarily imperfectly accomplished in all applied research.

Finally, social validity is seldom assessed. It is not surprising that social scientists' activities are seen to be irrelevant by the very consumers whose social problems they putatively address. Quite aside from the public relations value of asking consumers to participate in the formulation of research, it seems axiomatic that only the consumers can identify or exemplify the goals, the procedures, and the ideal performance standards that will render the research valid for the population studied.

We are remiss as scientists to tolerate the present state of affairs. We charge ourselves with the responsibility of providing society with information that it needs to make decisions about the provision of residential services for its developmentally disabled citizens. With this responsibility comes the obligation to advocate for the best methodology we know. We have clearly failed to meet this obligation.

REFERENCES

Aninger, M., & Bolinsky, K. Levels of independent functioning of retarded adults in apartments. *Mental Retardation,* 1977, **15**(4), 12–13.

Baker, B. L., Seltzer, G. B., & Seltzer, M. M. *As close as possible.* Boston, Massachusetts: Little, Brown, 1977.

Balla, D., Butterfield, E. C., & Zigler, E. Effects of institutionalization on retarded children: A longitudinal cross-institutional investigation. *American Journal of Mental Deficiency,* 1974, **78**, 530–549.

Bauman, K. E., & Iwata, B. A. Maintenancy of independent housekeeping skills using scheduling plus self-recording procedures. *Behavior Therapy,* 1977, **8,** 554–560.

Berk, R. A. Generalizability of behavioral observations: A clarification of inter-observer agreement and inter-observer reliability. *American Journal of Mental Deficiency,* 1979, **83,** 460–472.

Berkson, G. Social ecology of supervised communal facilities for mentally disabled adults: V. Residence as a predictor of social and work adjustment. *American Journal of Mental Deficiency,* 1981, **86,** 39–42.

Berkson, G., & Romer, D. Social ecology of supervised communal facilities for mentally disabled adults: I. Introduction. *American Journal of Mental Deficiency,* 1980, **85,** 219–228.

Birenbaum, A., & Re, M. A. Resettling mentally retarded adults in the community—almost four years later. *American Journal of Mental Deficiency,* 1979, **83,** 323–329.

Birnbrauer, J. S., Peterson, C. R., & Solnick, J. V. Design and interpretation of studies of single subjects. *American Journal of Mental Deficiency,* 1974, **79,** 191–203.

Bjaanes, A. T., & Butler, E. W. Environmental variation in community care facilities for mentally retarded persons. *American Journal of Mental Deficiency,* 1974, **78,** 429–439.

Bracht, G. H., & Glass, G. V. The external validity of experiments. *American Educational Research Journal,* 1968, **5,** 437–474.

Bridgman, P. W. *The logic of modern physics,* New York: Macmillan, 1927.

Brooks, P. H., & Baumeister, A. A. A plea for consideration of ecological validity in the experimental psychology of mental retardation: A guest editorial. *American Journal of Mental Deficiency,* 1977, **81,** 1–416.

Bruininks, R. H., Hauber, F. A., Hill, B. K., Lakin, K. C., Sigford, B. B., & Wieck, C. A. *Brief #5. 1978–1979 in-depth national interview survey of public and community residential facilities for mentally retarded persons.* Minneapolis, Minnesota: University of Minnesota, Department of Psychoeducational Studies, September, 1981.

Bruininks, R. H., Hauber, F. A., & Kudla, M. J. National survey of community residential facilities: A profile of facilities and residents in 1977. Minneapolis, Minnesota: University of Minnesota, Department of Psychoeducational Studies, 1979. Also available in *American Journal of Mental Deficiency,* 1980, **84**(5), 470–478.

Bruininks, R. H., Hauber, F. A., Hill, B. K., Lakin, C. K., Rotegard, L., & White, C. Personal communication relating to the 1982 national survey of residential facilities. Minneapolis, Minnesota: University of Minnesota, Center for Residential and Community Services. October 3, 1983.

Butler, E. W., & Bjaanes, A. T. Activities and the use of time by retarded persons in community care facilities. In G. P. Sackett (Ed.), *Observing behavior Vol. 1; Theory and applications in mental retardation.* Baltimore, Maryland: Univ. Park Press, 1978.

Butterfield, E. C. *Why and how to study the influence of living arrangements upon the mentally retarded.* Paper presented at the Lake Wilderness on the Impact of Residential Environments on Retarded Persons and Their Care Providers, August, 1982.

Campbell, D. T., & Fiske, D. W. Convergent and discriminant validation by the multitrait-multimethod matrix. *Psychological Bulletin,* 1959, **56,** 81–103.

Campbell, D. T., & Stanley, J. C. *Experimental and quasi-experimental designs for research.* Chicago, Illinois: Rand McNally, 1966.

Close, D. W. Community living for severely and profoundly retarded adults: a group home study. *Education and Training of the Mentally Retarded,* 1977, **12,** 256–262.

Cohen, J. Weighted kappa: Nominal scale agreement with provision for scaled disagreement or partial credit. *Psychological Bulletin,* 1968, **70,** 213–220.

Conley, R. W. *The economics of mental retardation.* Baltimore, Maryland: Johns Hopkins Press, 1973.

Conroy, J., Efthimiou, J., & Lemanowicz, J. A matched comparison of the developmental growth of institutionalized and deinstitutionalized mentally retarded clients. *American Journal of Mental Deficiency,* 1982, **86,** 581-587.

Cook, T. D., & Campbell, D. T. *Quasi-experimental design and analysis issues for field settings.* Boston, Massachusetts: Houghton-Mifflin, 1979.

Coulter, W. A., & Morrow, H. W. *Adaptive behavior: Concepts and measurements.* New York: Grune & Stratton, 1978.

Cronbach, L. J. Coefficient alpha and the internal structure of tests. *Psychometrika,* 1951, **16,** 297-334.

Cronbach, L. J. *Essentials of psychological testing* (3rd ed.). New York: Harper, 1970.

Cronbach, L. J., & Furby, L. How we should measure "change"—or should we? *Psychological Bulletin,* 1970, **74,** 68-80.

Cronbach, L. J., Gleser, G. C., Nanda, H., & Rajaratnam, N. *The dependability of behavioral measurements: Theory of generalizability of scores and profiles.* New York: Wiley, 1972.

Edgerton, R. B. *The cloak of competence: Stigma in the lives of the mentally retarded.* Berkeley, California: Univ. of California Press, 1967.

Edgerton, R. B., & Bercovici, S. M. The cloak of competence: Years later. *American Journal of Mental Deficiency,* 1976, **80,** 485-497.

Ellis, N. R., Bostick, G. E., Moore, S. A., & Taylor, J. J. A follow-up of severely and profoundly retarded mentally retarded children after short-term institutionalization. *Mental Retardation,* 1981, **19,** 31-35.

Eyman, R. K., Borthwick, S. A., & Miller, C. Trends in maladaptive behavior of mentally retarded persons placed in community and deinstitution settings. *American Journal of Mental Deficiency,* 1981, **85,** 473-477.

Eyman, R. K., Demaine, G. C., & Lei, T. Relationship between community environments and resident changes in adaptive behavior: A path model. *American Journal of Mental Deficiency,* 1979, **83,** 330-338.

Eyman, R. K., Silverstein, A. B., McLain, R., & Miller, C. Effects of residential settings on development. In P. Mittler (Ed.), *Research to practice in mental retardation.* Baltimore, Maryland: Univ. Park Press, 1977.

Flynn, R. J. Normalization, PASS, and service quality assessment: How normalizing are current human services. In R. J. Flynn & K. E. Nitsch (Eds.), *Normalization, social integration, and community services.* Baltimore, Maryland: Univ. Park Press, 1980.

Flynn, R. J., & Heal, L. W. Short form of PASS #3. *Evaluation Review,* 1981, **5,** 357-376.

Futterman, A. D., & Arndt, S. The construct and predictive validity of adaptive behavior. *American Journal of Mental Deficiency,* 1983, **87,** 546-659.

Gold, M. W. Research on the vocational habilitation of the retarded: The present, the future. In N. R. Ellis (Ed.), *International review of research in mental retardation* (Vol. 6). New York: Academic Press, 1973.

Gollay, E., Freedman, R., Wyngaarden, M., & Kurtz, N. R. *Coming back; community experiences of deinstitutionalized mentally retarded people.* Cambridge, Massachusetts: Abt, 1978.

Groves, R. M., & Hess, I. An algorithm for controlled selection. In I. Hess, D. C. Riedel, & T. B. Fitzpatrick (Eds.), *Probability sampling of hospitals and patients* (2nd ed.). Ann Arbor, Michigan: Health Administration Press, 1975.

Hauber, F., Bruininks, R., Wieck, C., Sigford, B., & Hill, B. 1978-1979 in-depth national survey of public and community residential facilities for mentally retarded persons: Methods and procedures. Minneapolis, Minnesota: University of Minnesota, Department of Psychoeducational Studies, 1981.

Heal, L. W. Methodology for community integration research. In R.H. Bruininks and K. C. Lakin (Eds.), *Living and learning in the least restrictive environment.* Baltimore, Maryland: Brooks, 1984.

Heal, L. W., & Chadsey, J. *The lifestyle satisfaction scale*. Unpublished, University of Illinois at Urbana-Champaign, 1983.

Heal, L. W., Colson, L. S., & Gross, J. C. Progress made on adult living skills by severely handicapped students in a behavioral secondary program evaluated using a true experimental design. *American Journal of Mental Deficiency*, 1984, in press.

Heal, L. W., & Daniels, B. S. *A cost-effectiveness analysis of residential alternatives for selected developmentally disabled citizens of three northern Wisconsin counties*. Paper presented at the 1978 meeting of the American Association on Mental Deficiency, Denver, May, 1978.

Heal, L. W., & Laidlaw, T. J. Evaluation of residential alternatives. In A. R. Novak & L. W. Heal (Eds.), *Integration of developmentally disabled individuals into the community*. Baltimore, Maryland: Brookes, 1980.

Heal, L. W., Novak, A. R., Sigelman, C. K., & Switzky, H. N. Characteristics of community residential facilities. In A. R. Novak & L. W. Heal (Eds.), *Integration of developmentally disabled individuals into the community*. Baltimore, Maryland: Brookes, 1980.

Heal, L. W., Sigelman, C. K., & Switzky, H. N. Research on community residential alternatives for the mentally retarded. In N. R. Ellis (Ed.), *International review of research in mental retardation* (Vol. 9). New York: Academic Press, 1978.

Heller, T., Berkson, G., & Romer, D. Social ecology of supervised communal facilities for mentally disabled adults: VI. Initial social adaptation. *American Journal of Mental Deficiency*, 1981, **86**, 43–49.

Hemming, H., Lavender, T., & Pill, R. Quality of life of mentally retarded adults transferred from large institutions to new small units. *American Journal of Mental Deficiency*, 1981, **86**, 157–169.

Hill, B. K., & Bruininks, R. H. Maladaptive behavior of mentally retarded people in residential facilities. *American Journal of Mental Deficiency*, 1984, in press.

Hill, B. K., Sathen, L. B., Kudla, M. J., & Bruininks, R. H. A survey of types of residential programs for mentally retarded people in the United States in 1978. Department of Psychoeducational Studies, University of Minnesota, 1978.

Hollenbeck, A. R. Problems of reliability in observational research. In G. P. Sackett (Ed.), *Observing behavior, Vol. II: Data collection and analysis methods*. Baltimore, Maryland: Univ. Park Press, 1978.

Howell, H. H., & May, A. E. Resident-care practices in the county of Somerset, England. *American Journal of Mental Deficiency*, 1980, **84**, 393–396.

Hull, J. T., & Thompson, J. C. Predicting adaptive functioning of mentally retarded persons in community settings. *American Journal of Mental Deficiency*, 1980, **85**, 253–261.

Intagliata, J., & Willer, B. Reinstitutionalization of mentally retarded persons successfully placed into family-care and group homes. *American Journal of Mental Deficiency*, 1982, **87**, 34–39.

Jackson, J. Factors of the treatment environment. *Archives of General Psychiatry*, 1969, **21**, 39–45.

Johnston, J. M., & Pennypacker, H. S. *Strategies and tactics of human behavioral research*. Hillsdale, New Jersey: Erlbaum, 1980.

Kastner, L. S., Reppucci, N. D., & Pezzoli, J. J. Assessing community attitudes toward mentally retarded persons. *American Journal of Mental Deficiency*, 1979, **84**, 137–144.

Kavanagh, M. J., MacKinney, A. C., & Wolins, L. Issues in managerial performance: Multitrait-multimethod analysis of ratings. *Psychological Bulletin*, 1971, **75**, 34–49.

Kazdin, A. E. *Single-case research designs: Methods for clinical and applied settings*. London and New York: Oxford Univ. Press, 1982.

Kiesler, C. A. Mental hospitals and alternative care. Noninstitutionalization as potential public policy for mental patients. *American Psychologist*, 1982, **37**, 349–360.

King, R. D., Raynes, N. V., & Tizard, J. *Patterns of residential care: Sociological studies in institutions for handicapped citizens.* London: Routledge & Kegan Paul, 1971.

King, T., Soucar, E., & Isett, R. Brief reports: An attempt to assess and predict adaptive behavior of institutionalized mentally retarded clients. *American Journal of Mental Deficiency,* 1980, **84**, 406–410.

Krantz, G. C., Bruininks, R. H., & Clumpner, J. L. *Mentally retarded people in state-operated residential facilities: Year ending June 30, 1978.* (2nd Ed.). Minneapolis, Minnesota: University of Minnesota, Department of Psychoeducational Studies, 1978.

Krantz, G. C., Bruininks, R. H., & Clumpner, J. L. *Mentally retarded people in state-operated residential facilities: Year ending June 30, 1979.* Minneapolis, Minnesota: University of Minnesota, Department of Psychoeducational Studies, 1979.

Krantz, G., Bruininks, R., & Clumpner, J. *Mentally retarded people in state-operated residential facilities: Year ending June 30, 1980.* Minneapolis, Minnesota: University of Minnesota, Department of Psychoeducational Studies, 1980.

Kratochwill, T. R. *Single subject research: Strategies for evaluating change.* New York: Academic Press, 1978.

Lakin, K. C., Krantz, G. C., Bruininks, R. H., Clumpner, J. L., & Hill, B. K. One hundred years of data on populations of public residential facilities for mentally retarded people. *American Journal of Mental Deficiency,* 1982, **87**, 1–8.

Landesman-Dwyer, S. The changing structure and function of institutions; a search for optimal group care environments. In S. Landesman-Dwyer & P. Vietze (Eds.), *The social ecology of residential environments: Person X setting transactions in mental retardation.* Baltimore, Maryland: Univ. Park Press, 1983.

Landesman-Dwyer, S., Berkson, G., & Romer, D. Affiliation and friendship of mentally retarded residents in group homes. *American Journal of Mental Deficiency,* 1979, **83**, 571–580.

Landesman-Dwyer, S., Stein, J. G., & Sackett, G. P. A behavioral and ecological study of group homes. In G. P. Sackett, (Ed.), *Observing behavior, Vol. I: Theory and applications in mental retardation.* Baltimore, Maryland: Univ. Park Press, 1978.

Landesman-Dwyer, S., & Sulzbacher, F. M. Residential placement and adaptation of severely and profoundly retarded individuals. In R. H. Bruininks, C. E. Meyers, B. B. Sigford, & K. C. Lakin (Eds.), *Deinstitutionalization and community adjustment of mentally retarded people.* Washington, DC: American Association on Mental Deficiency, 1981.

Linn, R. L., & Slinde, J. A. The determination of the significance of change between pre- and posttesting periods. *Review of Educational Research,* 1977, **47**, 121–150.

Longstreth, L. E. Revisiting Skeels' final study. *Developmental Psychology,* 1981, **14**, 620–625.

Lowe, M. L., & Cuvo, A. J. Teaching coin summation to the mentally retarded. *Journal of Applied Behavior Analysis,* 1976, **9**, 483–489.

MacEachron, A. E. Institutional reform and the adaptive functioning of mentally retarded persons: A field experiment. *American Journal of Mental Deficiency,* 1983, **88**, 2–12.

Martin, J. E., Rusch, F. R., & Heal, L. W. Teaching community survival skills to mentally retarded adults: A review and analysis. *Journal of Special Education,* 1982, **16**, 243–268. (a)

Martin, J. E., Rusch, F. R., James, V. L., Decker, P. J., & Trtol, K. A. The use of picture cues to establish self-control in the preparation of complex meals by mentally retarded adults. *Applied Research in Mental Retardation,* 1982, **3**, 105–119. (b)

Matson, J. L. Use of independence training to teach shopping skills to mildly mentally retarded adults. *American Journal of Mental Deficiency,* 1981, **86**, 178–183.

Matson, J., Marchetti, A., & Atkins, J. A. Comparison of operant- and independence-training procedures for mentally retarded adults. *American Journal of Mental Deficiency,* 1980, **84**, 486–494.

McCarver, R. B., & Craig, E. M. Placement of the retarded in the community: Prognosis and outcome. In N. R. Ellis (Ed.), *International review of research in mental retardation* (Vol. 7). New York: Academic Press, 1974.

McCormick, M., Balla, D., & Zigler, E. Resident care practices in institutions for retarded persons: A cross-institutional, cross-cultural study. *American Journal of Mental Deficiency,* 1975, **80**, 1–17.

McDevitt, S. C., Smith, P. M., Schmidt, D. W., & Rosen, M. The deinstitutionalized citizen: Adjustment and quality of life. *Mental Retardation,* 1978, **16**, 22–24.

McGuigan, F. J. The experimenter: A neglected stimulus object. *Psychological Bulletin,* 1963, **60**, 421–428.

Moos, R. M. *Evaluating correctional and community settings.* New York: Wiley, 1975.

Moos, R. H., & Moos, B. S. A typology of family social environments. *Family Process,* 1976, **15**, 357–371.

Nihira, K. Factorial dimensions of adaptive behavior in mentally retarded children and adolescents. *American Journal of Mental Deficiency,* 1969, **74**, 130–141.

Nihira, K., Foster, R., Shellhaas, M., & Leland, H. *AAMD adaptive behavioral scale, 1975 revision.* Washington, DC: American Association on Mental Deficiency, 1974.

Nunnally, J. *Psychometric theory.* New York: McGraw-Hill, 1978.

O'Connor, G. *Home is a good place.* Washington, D.C.: American Association on Mental Deficiency, 1976.

Pratt, M. W., Luszcz, M. A., & Brown, M. E. Measuring dimensions of the quality of care in small community residences. *American Journal of Mental Deficiency,* 1980, **85**, 188–194.

Robinson, W. S. The statistical measurement of agreement. *American Sociological Review,* 1957, **22**, 17–25.

Romer, D., & Berkson, G. Social ecology of supervised communal facilities for mentally disabled adults: II. Predictors of affiliation. *American Journal of Mental Deficiency,* 1980, **85**, 229–242. (a)

Romer, D., & Berkson, G. Social ecology of supervised communal facilities for mentally disabled adults: III. Predictors of social choice. *American Journal of Mental Deficiency,* 1980, **85**, 243–252. (b)

Romer, D., & Berkson, G. Social ecology of supervised communal facilities for mentally disabled adults: IV. Characteristics of social behavior. *American Journal of Mental Deficiency,* 1981, **86**, 28–38.

Rusch, F. R., Schutz, R. P., & Heal, L. W. The validity of sheltered and nonsheltered work behavior research: A review and discussion. In J. L. Matson & J. A. Mulick (Eds.), *Comprehensive handbook on mental retardation.* Oxford: Pergamon, 1983.

Rusch, F. R., Weithers, J. A., Menchetti, B. M., & Schutz, R. P. Social validation of a program to reduce topic repetition in a nonsheltered setting. *Education and Training of the Mentally Retarded,* 1980, **15**, 208–215.

Sackett, G. P. (Ed.), *Observing behavior, Vol I: Theory and applications in mental retardation.* Baltimore, Maryland: Univ. Park Press, 1978. (a)

Sackett, G. P. (Ed.) *Observing behavior, Vol II: Data collection and analysis methods.* Baltimore, Maryland: Univ. Park Press, 1978. (b)

Salvia, J., & Ysseldyke, J. E. *Assessment in special and remedial education* (2nd ed.). Boston, Massachusetts: Houghton-Mifflin, 1981.

Scanlon, C. A., Arick, J. R., & Krug, D. A. A matched sample investigation of nonadaptive behavior of severely handicapped adults across four living situations. *American Journal of Mental Deficiency,* 1982, **86**, 526–532.

Schalock, R. L. *Independent living screening test standardization manual.* Hastings, Nebraska: Mid-Nebraska Mental Retardation Services, 1979.

Schalock, R. L., & Harper, R. S. Placement from community-based MR programs: How well do clients do? *American Journal of Mental Deficiency,* 1978, **83** (3), 240–247.

Schalock, R. L., Harper, R. S., & Carver, G. Independent living placement: Five years later. *American Journal of Mental Deficiency,* 1981, **86**, 170–177. (a)

Schalock, R. L., Harper, R. S., & Genung, T. Community integration of mentally retarded adults: Community placement and program success. *American Journal of Mental Deficiency,* 1981, **85**, 478–488. (b)

Scheerenberger, R. C. Public residential services for the mentally retarded. Madison, Wisconsin: National Association of Superintendents of Public Residential Facilities for the Mentally Retarded, 1976.

Scheerenberger, R. C. *Public residential services for the mentally retarded.* Madison, Wisconsin: National Association of Superintendents of Public Residential Facilities for the Mentally Retarded, Central Wisconsin Center for the Developmentally Disabled, 1976. (b) Also available in N. R. Ellis (Ed.), *International review of research in mental retardation* (Vol. 9). New York: Academic Press, 1978.

Scheerenberger, R. C. Public residential services, 1981: Status and trends. *American Association on Mental Retardation,* 1982, **20**(5), 210–215.

Seltzer, G. B. Community residential adjustment: The relationship among environment, performance, and satisfaction. *American Journal of Mental Deficiency,* 1981, **85**, 624–630.

Seltzer, G. B., & Seltzer, M. M. *The community adjustment scale.* Cambridge, Massachusetts: Educational Projects, 1976.

Sidman, M. *Tactics in scientific research.* New York: Basic Books, 1960.

Sigelman, C. K., Budd, E. C., Spanhel, C. L., & Schoenrock, C. J. When in doubt, say yes: Acquiescence in interviews with mentally retarded persons. *Mental Retardation,* 1981, **19**, 53–58. (a)

Sigelman, C. K., Budd, E. C., Winer, J. W., Schoenrock, C. J., & Martin, P. W. Evaluating alternative techniques of questioning mentally retarded persons. *American Journal of Mental Deficiency,* 1982, **86**, 511–518.

Sigelman, C. K., Schoenrock, C. J., Winer, J. L., Spanhel, C. L., Hromas, S. G., Martin, P. W., Budd, E. C., & Bensberg, G. J. Issues in interviewing mentally retarded persons: An empirical study. In R. H. Bruininks, C. E. Meyers, B. B. Sigford, & K. C. Lakin (Eds.), *Deinstitutionalization and community adjustment of mentally retarded people.* Washington, D.C.: American Association on Mental Deficiency, 1981. (b)

Skeels, H. M. Adult status of children with contrasting early life experiences. *Monographs of the Society for Research in Child Development,* 1966, **31**(3), 1–65.

Skinner, B. J. *Science and human behavior.* New York: Free Press, 1953.

Snow, R. E. Representative and Quasi-representative designs for research on teaching. *American Educational Research Journal,* 1974, **44**, 265–291.

Soforenko, A. Z., & Macy, T. W. *A study of the characteristics and life status of persons discharged from a large state institution for the mentally retarded during the years 1969–1977.* Orient, Ohio: Orient State Institute, 1977.

Soforenko, A. Z., & Macy, T. W. Living arrangements of MR/DD persons discharged from an institutional setting, *Mental Retardation,* 1978, **16**(3), 269–270.

Sudman, S., & Bradburn, N. M. *Response effects in surveys: A review and synthesis.* Chicago, Illinois: Aldine, 1974.

Sutter, P., Mayeda, T., Call, T., Yanagi, G., & Yee, S. Comparison of successful and unsuccessful community-placed mentally retarded persons. *American Journal of Mental Deficiency,* 1980, **85**, 262–267.

Thiel, G. W. Relationship of IQ, adaptive behavior, age, and environmental demand to community-placement success of mentally retarded adults. *American Journal of Mental Deficiency,* 1981, **86,** 208–211.

Tizard, J. *Community services for the mentally handicapped.* London and New York: Oxford Univ. Press, 1964.

Vitello, S. J., Atthowe, J. M., Jr., & Cadwell, J. Determinants of community placement of institutionalized mentally retarded persons. *American Journal of Mental Deficiency,* 1983, **87,** 539–545.

Vogelsberg, R. T., & Rusch, F. R. Training severely handicapped students to cross partially controlled intersection. *AAESPH Review,* 1979, **4,** 264–273.

Weber, D. B., & Epstein, H. R. Contrasting adaptive behavior ratings of male and female institutionalized residents across two settings. *American Journal of Mental Deficiency,* 1980, **84,** 397–400.

Wieck, C. A., & Bruininks, R. H. *The cost of public and community residential care for mentally retarded people in the United States.* Minneapolis, Minnesota: University of Minnesota, Department of Psychoeducational Studies, 1980.

Willer, B., & Intagliata, J. Social-environmental factors as predictors of adjustment of deinstitutionalized mentally retarded adults. *American Journal of Mental Deficiency,* 1981, **86,** 252–259.

Willer, B., & Intagliata, J. Comparison of family-care and group homes as alternatives to institutions. *American Journal of Mental Deficiency,* 1982, **86,** 588–595.

Winer, B. J. *Statistical principles of experimental design* (2nd ed.). New York: McGraw-Hill, 1971.

Wolf, M. M. Social validity: The case for subjective measurement or how applied behavior analysis is finding its heart. *Journal of Applied Behavior Analysis,* 1978, **11,** 203–214.

Wolfensberger, W., & Glenn, L. *PASS 3, program analysis of service systems field manual.* Toronto: National Institute on Mental Retardation, 1975. (a)

Wolfensberger, W., & Glenn, L. PASS 3. *program analysis of service systems handbook.* Toronto: National Institute on Mental Retardation, 1975. (b)

Wolpert, J. *Group homes for the mentally retarded: An investigation of neighborhood property impacts.* Study prepared for the New York State Office of Mental Retardation and Developmental Disabilities, August, 1978.

Wyngaarden, M., & Gollay, E. *Profile of national deinstitutionalization patterns 1972–1974* (Vol. II), of a study of the community adjustment of deinstitutionalized mentally retarded persons. Cambridge, Massachusetts: Abt, 1976, Contract No. OEC-0-74-9183, U.S. Office of Education.

Zigler, E., Butterfield, E. C., & Capobianco, F. Institutionalization and the effectiveness of social reinforcement: A five- and eight-year follow-up study. *Developmental Psychology,* 1970, **3,** 255–263.

A Systems Theory Approach to Deinstitutionalization Policies and Research

ANGELA R. NOVAK

DEPARTMENT OF HEALTH AND SOCIAL SERVICES
MADISON, WISCONSIN

TERRY R. BERKELEY

SPECIAL EDUCATION AREA
LOUISIANA STATE UNIVERSITY
BATON ROUGE, LOUISIANA

!. INTRODUCTION

Systems analysis represents a theoretical approach to organizing "certain aspects or perspectives of reality" (von Bertalanffy, 1968, p. 94) into a structured model, intended to facilitate the understanding of the consequences of human interactions. Its application to the interpretation of and solutions for

INTERNATIONAL REVIEW OF RESEARCH IN
MENTAL RETARDATION, Vol. 12

social problems is based on the assumption that singular, unidimensional approaches fail to solve social problems because they only address one part of a complex system.

The systems theory approach was originated by a biologist who, just prior to World War II, was dissatisfied with molecular, cellular, and reductionist approaches (von Bertalanffy, 1968). Von Bertalanffy's approach, an organismic viewpoint, shifted the view of living organisms from a focus on parts to the definition of organisms as organized beings. The purpose of biology was refocused to the discovery of organization, its effects, and the reason for its existence.

The most general definition of a system is "a complex of elements in interaction, these interactions being of an ordered, non-random nature" (von Bertalanffy, 1968). Components or elements can exist in isolation or together but if they remain unchanged by their association with each other, they simply form a collection, not a system. In contrast, the components of a true system are necessarily changed by their association with each other; the whole is more complex and more than just a collection of parts.

II. COMPONENTS OF SYSTEMS ANALYSIS

Systems analysis offers the field of mental retardation a framework for interpreting and guiding research and policy decisions on the issues of deinstitutionalization and community integration. This framework consists of several elements including (1) identification of the *structure* of the system, including an analysis of the subsystems within the larger system of which it is a part, (2) clarification of the *function* and *response* of the system, and (3) understanding the *outputs* of the system.

A. Structure

The first basic concept of systems language defined by Cortés, Przeworski, and Sprague (1974) is *structure*, which is defined as the relations between social elements that are invariant for some period of historical time. For example, monogamous marriage and the exchange of labor for money wages are structural features of social systems. The structure of any system is as important as its individual components. Structure influences the behavior of both the components and the system.

The structure of the system is also inextricably tied to the boundaries, either concrete or abstract, between the components of a system. The boundaries between elements of the system (for instance, between a person with retardation and his neighborhood, or a retarded child and her schoolmates) may be determined by the beliefs, values, expectations, resources, and history of both parties. A fundamental organizational principle is that higher level components exercise control over the lower level elements, and each level maintains control over its own boundary conditions (Kernberg, 1974). An example (Stein, 1974) is both the social worker's social control function of boundary maintenance (the retarded person as helpee and worker as helper) and the client's active participation in maintenance of the helping system itself (the dependent role of helpee).

Communication of information between component elements is the basis of transactions between elements of the system, contributing to the constant tension, and thus the possibility for transformation and systems change, inherent in the composition of the system. That tension derives from the primary function of the system, which can be either self-regulation and system self-maintenance, or movement toward accomplishment of specific goals. When a system's variables are forced beyond their range of stability, stress occurs. Tension is a constant, and can often lead to "systems disablement" (Wolfensberger, 1982) in addition to the possibility for the accomplishment of specific goals and systems change.

In considering the case of a single individual who finds it difficult to learn and to live as independently as others do and thus needs assistance to do so, several different analyses of the social structures designed to provide that assistance have been proposed. These analyses have seen the social structure for a person with mental retardation as a series of increasingly complex levels of organization, such as (1) client, (2) family or group, (3) community, (4) organizational level such as agencies, (5) institutional level (local, state, and federal governments), and (6) societal level (Cantor, 1979; Goffman, 1961; Reiff, 1971; Thompson & Wray, 1985).

A very useful and well-articulated analysis of the structure of systems in which persons with mental retardation find themselves is Bronfenbrenner's (1977, 1979) adaptation of Brim's (1975) terminology regarding ecological environments. In this approach, the ecology of a human being and his development depends upon progressive, mutual accommodation throughout the life span between the human organism and the changing environments in which it lives. That process is affected by the relations within and between the individual and the environment, within and between environments, and within and between those settings and larger social contexts, both formal and informal.

Within Bronfenbrenner's ecological environment, there are four successive levels in a nested arrangement of structures, each contained within the next:

1. A *microsystem* is the complex of relations between the person and envi-

ronment in an immediate setting containing that person, such as home, school, workplace. Such factors as place, time, physical features, activities, participants, and roles constitute the element of a setting.

2. A *mesosystem* is comprised of the interrelations among major settings which contain the person at a particular point in life. For a mentally retarded person, the mesosystem might typically encompass the interactions among family, group home, sheltered workshop, church, and peer group, or the interactions among different departments within an institution, such as ward, school program, and work program. A mesosystem is a system of microsystems.

3. An *exosystem* embraces other special formal and informal social structures that do not directly contain the individual but rather influence or encompass the immediate settings in which that person is found. Those structures thereby influence, limit, and determine what goes on in the immediate settings. Such structures include the major societal institutions as they operate at a concrete local level, such as the world of work, the neighborhood, the mass media, government agencies, and informal social networks.

4. *Macrosystems* differ from the preceding three forms in that they do not refer to specific contexts but rather to general prototypes existing in the culture or its subcultures that set the pattern for the activities and structures occurring at the concrete level. For instance, one school classroom, one sheltered workshop, or one doctor's office look and function like all others, as if they were all constructed from the same blueprint; these "blueprints" are the macrosystems of Bronfenbrenner's analysis. Although there are specific laws, regulations, and rules that are explicit examples, most macrosystems are implicit and informal. They are carried as ideology in the minds of the members of society and manifest through custom and practice in everyday life (Bronfenbrenner, 1977, pp. 514–515).

By definition, macrosystem refers to the institutional patterns of the culture or subculture, such as the economic, social, educational, legal, and political systems, of which micro-, meso-, and exosystems are the concrete manifestations. Macrosystems are carriers of information and ideology that endow meaning and motivation to particular agencies, social networks, roles, activities, and their interrelations.

The sociological mapping for a child with mental retardation which begins at the moment of birth, or at times even prior to birth, operates in specific micro-, meso-, exo-, and macrosystems defined for that child by his/her retardation. These sometimes operate in conjunction with systems defined by the sex, race, or social class of the child, but are quite distinct because of the retardation. The mentally retarded person's relationship and interactions in the immediate environment of family are influenced and formed by the entire host of influences on each family member, on the family as a unit, on members of the family's neighborhood and extended family, and on the economic, social, legal, and political influences which affect the larger social contexts within which the family operates.

B. Function and Response

The second basic concept of systems languages, *function,* denotes "a relation between a part of a system and some selected state of the whole" (Cortés *et al.* 1974, p. 9). Analysis of a system attempts to answer the question, Given the structure of this system, what is its function? Functionalists assert that certain "functions" must be performed in order for the system to "survive." The function is the rule by which the elements of the set that is being transformed are associated with the elements of the set that results from the process of transformation, the end state of the whole. The function is the manner or mode of transformation by which some social condition, the input, becomes another social condition, the output.

If this transformation process is known, then the *response* of the system, the third element of analysis, can also be examined. Variations in the external environment enter the system as inputs, and the system responds by transforming those inputs. The result of the response, or output, depends both on the structure of the system and the history of its environment. By definition, "The response of a system is the output that the system yields given a particular history of inputs" (Cortés *et al.,* 1974, p. 10).

1. FUNCTION OF EARLY RESIDENTIAL SERVICES

A particularly revealing example of the function and response of the mental retardation system can be gleaned from an examination of the early history of residential services for persons with mental retardation. Wolfensberger (1976), for instance, has summarized the shift in the function of the residential services system characterized by the development of the large public institution.

In Wolfensberger's historical analysis, a large number of institutions were founded in the nineteenth century in the United States primarily for purposes of education. By congregating a large number of retarded individuals in one place, isolated from other distractions of society, expert tutorial attention could be focused on them. Wilbur (1852) and Howe (1852) were quite adamant that the function of these early schools was intensive training aimed at returning persons to their communities "as more wholly functioning members of society . . . nearer the common standard of humanity . . . more capable of understanding and obeying human laws . . . more capable of self-assistance, self-support, self-respect" (Wilbur, 1852, pp. 31–32). The first institutions were temporary boarding schools, located in the very heart of their commnities, with standards for admission based on the modifiability of retardation. "The institution is not intended for epileptic or insane children, nor for those who are incurable hydrocephalic or paralytic, and any such will not be retained, to the exclusion of more improvable subjects" (Howe, 1852).

A shift in function took place, however, as the superintendents began to discover that only a proportion of the institution population could be successfully returned to independence in the community. Although a large proportion of those who had seemed to benefit from school training could return to the protection of their families, the only alternative for those who had no families had been public almshouses (Fernald, 1893). As it began to become evident that a number of institutionalized individuals needed life-long care and supervision, the superintendents and institution staff began to be unwilling to remove these individuals from their care, and "begged that they might be allowed to remain where they could be happy and kept from harm" (Fernald, 1893, p. 210). Within 20 years, the function of the institution altered from educating the deviant individual to become a less deviant member of his community to that of protection of the retarded person. Between 1870 and 1880, the shift in the function of the residential model was from education and development to pity, charity, and loving protection.

The villages and communities for these simple-minded "children of God" began to be built as "cities of refuge" (Kerlin, 1885) and "Gardens of Eden," isolated from the rest of society. They gradually expanded, and began to elicit public concern about public expense. "Schools" became "asylums."

In the mid 1880s, according to Wolfenberger's (1976) analysis, the third stage of evolution began to emerge. An ever present current of negative attitudes toward retarded persons became more vocal, and new conceptualizations of retarded persons contributed to the trends of isolation, enlargement, and economization. Contemporary writers were tying mental retardation to concepts of crime (Dunphy, 1908), uncontrollable passions (Wilmarth, 1902), and the need for control (Johnson, 1903). Goddard, Davenport, and Tredgold (cited by Fernald, 1915) provided "scientific evidence" that feeble-mindedness was transmitted from generation to generation, while more research "definitely proved that feeblemindedness is an important factor as a cause of juvenile vice and delinquency, adult crime, sexual immorality, the spread of venereal disease, prostitution, illegitimacy, vagrancy, pauperism, and other forms of social evil and social disease" (Fernald, 1915, pp. 289–290). The dehumanization and brutalization of persons with retardation led to sterilization, segregation of the sexes and of retarded persons from other persons, and preventive marriage laws. This stance toward retardation can be summarized in the fact that the outstanding leaders in the field spoke in such terms as "stamping out idiocy and imbecility" (Johnson, 1898, p. 471). In 1901 Johnson, an extremely influential leader, also stated "I do not think that, to prevent the propagation of this class it is necessary to kill them off or to resort to the knife; but, if it is necessary, it should be done" (pp. 410–411).

In systems analysis terms, then, the function of the residential services system changed as the relationship between the retarded institutionalized individual and the end state of the social system altered. The immediate living environment as a temporary educational respite, whose purpose was to maintain strong ties between the individual and the larger community, shifted to loving and benevolent protection that resulted in increased severance from the rest of the social system. It then shifted again to a function of not simply isolating but forcefully turning all parts of the system inward and against that individual. The end state changed from an accepting, unified, and diverse community to self-sustenance of an increasingly homogeneous population, which became more and more willing to use force to maintain its boundaries.

The period of intense indictment peaked around 1910 and lessened due to the realizations that many retarded persons were not the menace originally thought, that complete segregation could not be achieved, and that courts and parents were often reluctant to commit individuals to a life of total confinement without any offense having been perpetrated. Still, institutions continue to exist as part of the entire mental retardation system. It is Wolfensberger's (1976) opinion that

> Many institutions still operate in the spirit of 1925 when inexpensive segregation of a scarcely human retarded individual was seen as the only feasible alternative to combat a social menace. I am not proposing that this view is still held; I am proposing that most institutions function as if the view were still held. (p. 69)

The structure of the system did not substantially change in the next 30 years and its function also remained the same: to isolate and congregate the deviant away from the undeviant. The status of the system was stable. In systems analysis terminology, synchrony was achieved: since the structure and function had not changed, they were operating as if all time were the same or simultaneous. Dynamic change within that structure was possible, such as a new institution opening or new individuals admitted; such temporal variations are possible within the bounds of the particular established synchrony (Cortés et al., 1974). However, no diachronic or structural change occurred; the system was intact.

2. FUNCTION OF MODERN RESIDENTIAL SERVICES

After two wars and in the prosperity of the 1950s, attention returned to social problems and concern over personal rights once again gained social and political attention. Civil rights laws, the Vietnam controversy, the definition of the rights of students, reformulation of the rights of accused persons, and revisions in the codes of ethics of many major professional societies all contributed to shifts in the structure, function, and response of the system encompassing those persons called retarded. Public outrage in response to well-publicized exposés of the conditions in several large institutions led to the emergence of the principles of the right to treatment and the least restrictive environment, as well as a professional commitment to "the community imperative" (Center on Human Policy, 1979). Better maternal health and neonatal care increased the population of those with disabilities and thus increased the input to the system. Those with retardation lived longer, increased in number, and increased in the number of those with more severe handicaps. As a result, different internal structures, functions, and outputs of the system emerged. Rather than maintaining the internal structural pressure to isolate the retarded individual from other parts of the social system, first the structure of residential services was enlarged to include alternative responses such as smaller types of publicly supported residences. Afterward, return to commitment to an integrated and pluralistic community resulted in such new proposals as supporting families in keeping their retarded children at home.

As increasing numbers of more severely handicapped children lived longer, the educational system also had to respond. First, there was an increase in the number of specialized schools, sheltered workshops, and teacher-training programs; this was a change accommodating larger numbers within a framework that remained segregated and based on restricted definitions of educability. Finally, however, the right of all children to a public education was recognized, and the application of principles such as the least restrictive environment led to more integrated school programs.

In systems analysis terms, a diachronic change has taken place in both the residential and educational systems. Since internal tension forced the very structure of the system to change, the system itself changed. It was not primarily from logical, rational, empirical research that the treatment system was or was not working that forced the system to modify, but rather, new models evolved from relatively irrational commitments to the liberty rights of all human beings and from a return to the earlier service principle of maintaining diverse and accepting communities.

C. Outputs

The function of a system can also be assessed by an examination of system outputs. One of the most typically examined is economic output. One analysis of the residential services system, for example, might suggest that although it appears that the retarded individuals at the center of the system are not making any economic contributions, the employment of thousands of institutional staff is one of the most concrete items of output. In the 1970s and 1980s, the measurement of economic outputs has been used to justify the input of public financial resources into many vocational training and employment programs for mentally retarded persons.

Although economic output is one outcome that can be gaged fairly easily, other outputs of the system of retardation services are unknown or barely addressed. For instance, the isolation of individuals in institutions has created such output as family stress and guilt, family relief, the alignment of significant amounts of public resources to buildings and employees, and perhaps the strengthening of public attitudes that persons with mental retardation are worthless, pitiful, and even dangerous. The effects of these outputs on the structure and self-maintenance of the system have largely remained unexamined.

Typically, resource input into the system and the existence of the entire mental retardation system itself has been justified through focus on the mentally retarded individual, the center of the system. Millions of dollars of resources (buildings, staff, programs, time) exist for the express purpose of helping individuals learn and grow. The function of the immediate environments in which persons with retardation find themselves are most often defined in terms of "maximizing development" or "enabling them to reach their full potential." Any change at that level of the system occurs only at that level, and has little, or only indirect, effect on any other level. The mental retardation system's relationship to the retarded person might appear to be one of caring for, training, and keeping retarded in order to maintain the existence of the system itself.

McKnight (1977) has proposed that the function of the helping profession is to encourage client dependency and deficiency in order to maintain the output of the employment of professionals. McKnight's arguments suggest that it is possible to recognize "human" services as systems in need of resources in order that economies may grow. Another result of this system, disguised under the mask that servicers are only doing their job in order to "help" people, is decrease in parental self-confidence in exchange for increased reliance on professional help. Thus, at Bronfenbrenner's (1979) level of exosystem, McKnight argues that an output of the mental retardation system is the employment of a significant number of nonretarded persons, as well as continued focus on personal and family dependency rather than independence. His theoretical arguments afford a framework in which to analyze the purpose and outcomes of the mental retardation system, and compel examination from the system perspective, rather than solely the perspective of the growth of the mentally retarded individual.

Research in the area of deinstitutionalization and community integration is beginning to make some attempts to address systems issues affecting persons with mental retardation and their movement from residence to residence. Deinstitutionalization research can be reviewed for its application to and grasp of the effects of each level of the residential services system, using the levels of the system outlined by Cantor (1979), Reiff (1971), Thompson and Wray (1985), and Bronfenbrenner (1977). Most of this research has centered on the individual within his/her immediate environment, with little attention paid to the exogenous forces affecting both the individual and the immediate environment: community and organizational influences; local, state, and federal governments; and the unconscious social forces of Bronfenbrenner's macrosystem. Trent (1983) has described how the content of most mental retardation research has been focused on the individual. His categorization of articles published in major mental retardation journals over 100 years revealed that the majority of research has been in such areas as medical-pathological classification, intelligence testing, the measurement of social adaptation, and behavior modification. Trent has described how this research has led to individualistic policies, such as education, institutionalization, and behavior change, with the system and societal context lacking. Almost no research attention has been paid to the verification and understanding of how the structure, function, response, and output of the mental retardation and community integration systems affect the movement and growth of persons with mental retardation, nor has the function and outputs of that system been clearly defined. Some theoretical analyses of the apparent function of the system such as Wolfensberger's (1976) have been attempted, but the effects of systems level decisions on the lives of persons subject to that system have not been widely documented using empirical methods.

A review of deinstitutionalization studies which have addressed environmental, ecological, and systems issues follows. The potential contributions of current research to comprehension of systems level issues and systems change is addressed in the last portion of this article.

III. DEINSTITUTIONALIZATION RESEARCH IN A SYSTEMS CONTEXT

Research about deinstitutionalization and the success in community living of persons with mental retardation appears to have taken place in at least two stages. Prior to approximately 1968, most research focused on the individual, the center of the mental retardation system. For instance, in McCarver and Craig's (1974) summary of research concerning the prognosis and outcome of community placement, almost all the variables utilized in the 175 studies reviewed were individual defined. These variables included such personal characteristics as delinquency, sexual behavior, age, and behavior problems. Even in more current research, this focus on individual characteristics is quite common in attempting to determine why some individuals succeed and why some fail at living in the community (e.g., Jacobson & Schwartz, 1983; Sutter, Mayeda, Call, Yanagi, & Yee, 1980). In systems analysis terms, this research is focused on change within only one component of a system, at Reiff's "individual level," or Thompson and Wray's "client level."

The legitimacy of this individual-based approach to understanding the reasons for successful community integration derives from the traditional approach to explaining service paradigms for any lower class, deviant, or devalued group: the cause of the problem, and hence the cure, lies in the individual. Ryan's (197) concept of "blaming the victim" applies to victims of racism and poverty as well as to persons with mental retardation: inequality is justified by finding defects in the victims of inequality. The narrowness of the focus on person fails to account for the fact that any individual behavior is a function of both person and environment (Sundberg, 1977). As Landesman-Dwyer and Sulzbacher (1981) have noted, failure of retarded persons to adapt to new environments requires consideration of the characteristics of both the environment and the individual. A systems analysis would have to begin with at least an analysis of an individual within an environment, such as the level of Bronfenbrenner's microsystem.

A few early studies on deinstitutionalization of persons with mental retardation (e.g., Hartzler, 1953) gave some consideration to factors in the individual's immediate environment, but the environmental analysis tended to focus almost exclusively on the division of postrelease environments into the categories of natural, foster, or group home. In such research, the category of the setting was the only environmental variable considered. Around 1967, several researchers began to attack the problem of how to describe and measure factors of the environment with as much specificity as had been applied to describing and measuring mentally retarded persons themselves.

A. The Individual within the Immediate Environment

Research attempts to describe individuals within the ecology of their immediate environments form the most substantial body of deinstitutionalization research addressing any systems issues. The level of the system addressed is the first, environmental microsystem, level (Bronfenbrenner, 1977; Reiff, 1971; Thompson & Wray, 1985). For instance, Edgerton's (1967) classic study of the everyday lives of persons living in the community examined such factors as the characteristics of the living environment, types of jobs held, and the role of benefactors in learning and "passing." Justice, Bradley, and O'Connor (1971) found that the primary reason for failure in foster placement was public misconception about mental retardation. Other problems in foster home failures in their study included lack of supportive services, problems with supervising institutions, and problems with the natural parents of the discharged individual.

Heal, Novak, Sigelman, and Switzky (1980), in their summary of research about characteristics of community living environments, found that there were four principal areas of environmental analysis which have been extensively explored. They include (1) taxonomies of environments and individual growth in different types of environments within those taxonomies, (2) the types of buildings used for community residences, (3) the degree of normalization of the environment, and (4) characteristics of caretakers.

Research more directly aimed at describing and characterizing the residential environments of persons with mental retardation has recently been initiated, specifically in three areas: (1) standardization of the measurement of specific qualities of an environment; (2) determination of the relationship between an individual's behavior and his/her environment in terms of what effects the environment has on the individual; and (3) determination of the effects the individual has on his or her environment. Research in each of these areas is summarized below, followed by a discussion of the issues of matching individuals with environments and larger system effects on both individuals and environments.

1. STANDARDIZED MEASUREMENT OF ENVIRONMENTS

As noted by Nihira, Mink, and Meyers (this volume), standardized scales which describe specific immediate environments are actually quite few in number. Although regulation and accreditation scales such as those of the Accreditation Council for Mentally Retarded and Other Developmentally Disabled Persons exist, only four scales have been commonly and frequently used in research. These include the Program Analysis of Service Systems (PASS) (Wolfensberger & Glenn, 1975), Moos's scales (1975), the Characteristics of the Treatment Environment Scale (Jackson, 1969), and the Residential Management Scale (King, Raynes, & Tizard, 1971).

Wolfensberger and Glenn's (1975) PASS is the standard instrument which has been used to measure the degree of normalization of an environment. Eyman, Demaine, and Lei (1979), Hull and Thompson (1980), and Lei, Nihira, Sheehy, and Meyers (1981) have all used PASS.

Moos (1975) has developed several scales to classify institutional and family environments, including the Correctional Institutions Environment

Scale, the Community-Oriented Programs Environment Scale, and the Family Environment Scale. Moos's categories for environmental climates measure such ecological concepts as cohesion, expressiveness, conflict, independence, achievement-orientation, moral–religious atmosphere, organization, and control. Willer and Intagliata (1980) have used Moos's Family Environment Scale extensively in their work on the classification of foster family care and natural home environments of deinstitutionalized individuals. They have found that, for instance, 85% of foster homes in their New York State study had a highly structured home environment (Intagliata, 1978), while only 50% of natural families accepting a retarded family member back into the home were structure oriented (Willer, 1978).

The Characteristics of the Treatment Environment Scale was developed by Jackson (1969) and used by Eyman, Silverstein, McLain, and Miller (1977). The Residential Management Scale is a revised version of the Child Management Scale (King et al., 1971) and indicates the use of resident-oriented compared to institution-oriented care practices in residential facilities in the domains of regimentation of routine, social distance between staff and residents, block or group treatment, and depersonalization of residents (Eyman et al., 1977; McCormick, Balla, & Zigler, 1975; Pratt, Luszcz, & Brown, 1980; Raynes, Pratt, & Roses, 1979). PASS 3, the Residential Management Scale, and the Characteristics of the Treatment Environment Scale are all standardized measurement scales used to describe the environments of community facilities in Pennsylvania into which Pennhurst residents are being deinstitutionalized (Conroy & Feinstein, 1982).

Raynes et al. (1979) measured four dimensions of quality of care in large institutions: management of daily events; staff–resident verbal interactions; community contact of residents; and the physical environment for residents. Pratt et al. (1980) adapted the Raynes et al. techniques to measure several environmental characteristics hypothesized as related to the quality of care in small community residences. First, they used King, Raynes, and Tizard's (1971) Management Practices Scale. Second, The Informative Speech Index measured the amount of staff speech to residents as well as the controllingness rather than informativeness of staff speech. Third, The Index of Community Involvement measured the degree to which residents participated in a range of community activities. The Index of the Physical Environment measured the amount of hominess and stimulation provided by the physical environment. Last, they used the Attendant Attitude Inventory (Butterfield, Barnett, & Bensberg, 1968), which had been shown to load on three factors of job dissatisfaction, strictness and rigidity of standards, and sociability and equality with residents. They found that scales measuring staff caretaking attitudes were only moderately related to actual care measures, and cautioned against the use of such attitude scales as proxy indices of actual behavior. Overall, they found these five dimensions of the caretaking climate varied independently of one another, providing strong evidence of the need for differentiated measurement techniques for environments.

Reynolds (1978) developed the Group Home Environment Scale specifically to measure the social climate of group homes, in an attempt to bridge the gap between the measurement of individual resident competencies and the measurement of physical characteristics of environments. Eight categories of the Group Home Environment Scale items measure residents' interaction with staff and other residents, staff interaction with other staff, and resident and staff interaction with the environment.

Lei *et al.* (1981) used three scales to assess the quality of small family care homes: PASS 3, the Home Inventory Form (an adaption of Caldwell's 1968 Home Observation for Measurement of Environment scale), and the Home Quality Rating Scale. The Home Quality Rating Scale had six interpretable factors: parenting quality and harmony in the home; additional support in providing care; quality and safety of dwelling and physical surroundings; size of home and sibling influence; residential; and preferences of the care providers using the Careprovider Preference Survey, which listed 50 behavior problems that residents might present. The survey assessed both the experience and the willingness of a care provider to handle certain behavior and other problems, and care provider perception of the degree of seriousness of each specific problem. Lei and Sheehy (1980) had found that the relationship between care providers' characteristics and the quality of the home environment is not of a simple linear nature; rather, complex curvilinear relationships were observed between care provider characteristics and the six factors of the Home Quality Rating Scale.

These attempts at standardizing several of the myriad, innumerable, and potentially infinite components of a living environment are steps in the direction of understanding the interaction between the behavior of one person and the daily situation in which he finds himself. Besides the definition and standardization of these components, however, is comprehension of their effects on retarded individuals.

2. EFFECTS OF THE ENVIRONMENT ON INDIVIDUALS

The effects of institutional settings on the behavior, social learning, and emotional growth of mentally retarded residents have been well documented (Pilewski & Heal, 1980). Researchers have begun to ask similar questions of the effects of community environments on residents, although these questions have arisen only after study of the variables related to characteristics of individuals who live in community settings (McCarver & Craig, 1974; Windle, 1962). The two-stage process of first inquiring about characteristics of retarded persons themselves for reasons of success in community living and afterward examining the environment for causes of success appears to follow a pattern easily recognizable in the research and policy phenomenon of retardation (i.e., first blame the individual, then look elsewhere). As opposed to either the individual or the environment being the singular cause, Landesman-Dwyer and Sulzbacher (1981) have pointed out that community failure is probably due to an interaction between the two factors of an inadequate facility (for instance, causing the client to act out) and the explanation that failing clients might have brought to the community residence more numerous problems or less general ability to adapt to a new setting than the individuals who were successful.

   a. Effects on Behavior and on Other Individual Characteristics. The effects of certain components of the environmental ecology upon residents have been studied. For instance, Rago, Parker, and Cleland (1978) found that maladaptive behavior of profoundly retarded male adults was significantly reduced in less crowded environments. However, the complexity of the issue of the effects of immediate environments on behavior has been evidenced in the controversy and conflicting findings regarding even a single factor, the relatively straightforward variable of size of a living unit. Landesman-Dwyer, Sackett, and Kleinman (1980) have summarized the provocativeness of the differing findings concerning the number of people in a living unit in relation to other variables such as social grouping, quality of care, location, and staff behavior.

   Several recent studies have explored the effects of residential environments on the behavior of persons with mental retardation. First, comparisons between effects of different categories of living environments have been conducted. Willer and Intagliata (1982), for instance, questioned the differential effects of group homes and foster (family care) homes on resident behavior and learning. They found that individuals in family care homes were significantly more likely to improve in their community living skills than individuals who lived in group homes. Individuals living in both settings were about equally likely to have friends, maintain their ongoing relationships with their families, and make use of community resources.

   Thiel (1981) examined the relationship between demands the environment made on an individual and that person's adaptive and maladaptive behavior. He found no significant results for environmental demand. However, the determination of environmental demand in this study was based on specialists' rankings of types of environments (own apartment, supervised apartment, natural family, group home, intermediate care facility), rather than on measures of specific demands made by specific environments. Seltzer (1981), in contrast, examined the environmental dimensions of different settings: institution, foster home, group home, family home, semiindependent, and independent apartments. The five dimensions measured included amount of autonomy afforded, extent of access to community and within-house resources, favorableness of expectations held by staff about residents, and the amount of training provided in unmastered skills.

Environments have also been examined for effects in other particular areas besides behavior improvement and skill learning. Landesman-Dwyer, Berkson, and Romer (1979) examined the effects of certain environmental characteristics on social affiliation and friendships. They found that the ratio of males to females in the group home, the average level of retardation of residents, the group home size, and the homogeneity of residents' backgrounds were more predictive of residents' affiliative behavior than were personal characteristics such as sex and intelligence.

b. The Importance of Staff Characteristics. One of the most important components of an environment is the staff or caretakers. The first steps taken to describe caretakers in community residential environments were evaluations of the effects of such demographic caretaker characteristics as age on resident success in community living (Intagliata, 1978). Another factor which has been examined is reported reason for engaging in work with mentally retarded persons. Scheerenberger and Felsenthal (1977) found that three fourths of the community caretakers in their study took the job because of "personal satisfaction" or "a specific interest in mental retardation." Intagliata (1978) found that 34% of foster family care providers had an altruistic motive in taking on this work.

Sanderson and Crawley (1982) analyzed the characteristics of successful foster (family care) parents using Holland's (1973) categories of vocational interests and preferences, which reflect the person's emotional life and personality structure. They found that successful male family care givers fell in the "realistic" category of personality structure, while successful female care givers more often fell in the "conventional" category. Penniman (1974) and Retherford (1975) found, respectively, "age" and "maturity" of caretakers to be predictive of more successful community placement.

Hull and Thompson (1980) examined four specific measures of staff attitudes: optimism, stereotyping, promotion of independence, and consciousness of normalization. Along with other environmental variables, they found these attitudes accounted for more variance in adaptive functioning of clients than did individual client characteristics such as IQ. Sutter (1980) found that caretaker experience and proximity of members of the caretaker's family to the home significantly influenced the success of community placement.

c. Measuring Success in Differential Ways. Most of the studies discussed above have measured "success" in terms of residents continuing to remain in the community without reinstitutionalization. A few studies have more closely attempted to categorize the success of community placements in terms of the provision of higher quality care, especially given the result of more resident learning and growth.

Intagliata, Willer, and Wicks (1981) have noted that using the categories of "foster home" or "group home" assumes that all foster homes or group homes are the same, whereas in actuality a single type of facility varies on innumerable dimensions. To measure the varying levels of the quality of care provided by foster family care providers in New York, they asked supervising social workers and nurses to rate the quality of care provided. They assessed nine areas of "quality," including provider participation in the development and implementation of resident treatment plans, the degree of encouragement of client growth, client independence, use of community resources, relating to clients in a warm and caring manner, the provider's level of emotional stability and organization, and the provider's ability to cope with routine and nonroutine client problems. When higher quality was defined as more normalized and more encouraging of client development and growth, several significant characteristics of the providers were related to the quality of homes. The significant provider characteristics included more education, having health-related training, motivation to take the job due to past experience in working with mentally retarded persons, living in urban areas, seeking out services and activities for the residents, actively involving themselves in resident treatment planning, establishing a stable and well-organized home, establishing warm, supportive, but not dependent relationships with residents, and encouraging residents to use community resources and develop new skills.

Intagliata and Willer (1982) found that the types and levels of behavior problems manifested by individuals after they were placed in the community may have depended on the amount, type, and degree of behavior problems that community care providers were willing to tolerate (George & Baumeister, 1981; Intagliata et al., 1981; Sutter et al., 1980). When individuals are experiencing difficulty in the community, Intagliata and Willer (1982) point out that attempts to modify only the clients' behavior see "reinstitutionalization as if it were entirely the client's fault rather than attempting to modify the characteristics of the residential setting that may have contributed to the client's difficulties" (p. 38).

d. The Influence of Several Different Environments and Outcomes. Another problem in assessing the environment's effect on individuals is that, in living in the community, several different environments impact on the same person. Different members of those environments can hold conflicting values, goals, and influences toward the same retarded person. Bartnik and Winkler (1981), for instance, found that parents, employers, and service agency staff members differed significantly on the issue of the personal responsibility of the client in adjusting to living in the community. They showed that adjustment of adults to independent community living involves adjustment to a number of different communities (work, home, parents, and social service agencies) and to social systems that have different norms for adjustment. Mercer (1973, 1978) has also emphasized the differences in expectations held by people having different roles in the different social systems with which retarded individuals interact.

In addition, there has not been consensus on desired outcomes for individuals. Although remaining in the community has easily been considered a preferred outcome, the measurement of success of community living and the influence of the environment on the individual has not yet taken into account the relative merits of an optimal balance between potentially differing outcomes in such areas as resident learning, greater use of community resources, quality of social relationships, resident satisfaction, and the expression of personal autonomy.

3. EFFECTS OF THE INDIVIDUAL
ON THE ENVIRONMENT

While some studies are beginning to address the issue of the effects of environmental characteristics on resident behavior, satisfaction, and learning, few take into account the individual's effect on the environment. At the first, environmental level of the microsystem is the retarded person's effect on staff or family members. While there has been extensive study on the effect of the birth of a retarded child on family members and family dynamics, and on family adjustment to a retarded child (e.g., Levinson, 1975), the work of describing family reaction to the reintegration of a deinstitutionalized family member has only just begun. Several authors (Atthowe & Vitello, 1982; Meyer, 1980) have researched family members' attitudes toward deinstitutionalization in general, such as into group homes. However, Willer, Intagliata, and Wicks (1981) have conducted one of the only studies so far that has addressed a deinstitutionalized person's effect on the family to which he or she returns. In their study of caretakers, Willer et al. gathered the typical demographic information, but also asked about the impact the residents had on the care provider's home life and psychological well being. Although many families frequently endured a crisis at the time of the child's release from the institution, they generally overcame their initial fears and later agreed that the return home was beneficial for the family as well as for the retarded member. Seventy-two percent of the families reported an enrichment of family life, 60% appreciated the retarded member's assistance in upkeep of the home, 72% reported an increased understanding of mental retardation, and 76% reported relief from feelings of loneliness.

This same study also reported the effects on the family in cases in which the retarded individual was returned to a community setting other than the natural home. Many of these families also experienced a crisis, but it was more likely to be extreme guilt. This guilt tended not to disappear as readily as did the anxiety experienced by natural families who accepted their retarded member back into the home.

The effect of retarded persons on the paid staff of community residential facilities has been addressed primarily through the single issue of staff turnover. Although Bruininks, Kudla, Wieck, and Hauber (1980) identified inadequate funding as the single most important concern contributing to staffing problems, they also found that other benefits and disadvantages of the job certainly came into play in staff turnover. Sarata (1975) found that the lack of resident progress was the greatest source of staff dissatisfaction. George and Baumeister (1981) also found that if staff lacked the training and support needed to deal with behavior problems presented by some residents, turnover was likely to be high. The more concrete effects of how resident behavior determines staff reaction and treatment of the resident, as well as staff performance, remains largely unexplored.

Another component of the immediate environment is the neighborhood. Although community attitudes toward mental retardation, deinstitutionalization, and specific group homes have been examined, these probes have tended to be limited to surveys. The effects of the interactions of neighbors and community members with their retarded neighbors on resident learning, and the effects of retarded citizens on their community, have not been rigorously documented. Although we know that community opposition to group homes decreases over a period of time (Moreau, Novak, & Sigelman, 1980), there are many unanswered questions. For instance, is mere community presence enough to contribute to that decline? What can group home staff or persons with mental retardation do to decrease opposition more quickly? What occurs in the cases in which opposition does not decrease? Is the decrease of opposition synonymous with acceptance?

One of the arguments that has been used to support community integration as a worthwhile goal has been that there are beneficial effects of integration for both retarded and nonretarded members of the community (Baumgart, Brown, Pumpian, Nisbet, Ford, Sweet, Messina, & Schroeder, 1982; Perske, 1981). However, the effects of integration of handicapped children into public schools, for instance, where the effects of such integration might be the most controllable and observable, are not well documented, nor are the effects of residential integration into neighborhoods.

Another component of the neighborhood, or town, is the adequacy of community support services. Gollay, Freedman, Wyngaarden, and Kurtz (1978) and Jacobsen and Schwartz (1983), among others, have shown that the lack of support services jeopardizes the success of community placements. Schalock, Harper, and Genung (1981) found that more persons were reinstitutionalized from community programs that were in smaller communities, perhaps because of the lack of, or inadequacy of, mental health services.

Intagliata, Kraus, and Willer (1980) described the effects that deinstitutionalized individuals had on a regional service system. As the types of clients changed, the types of services needed had to change. Service agencies had to hire new staff, develop special programs, and coordinate efforts with a wider variety of support agencies.

4. PERSON–ENVIRONMENT FIT

Given the current status of knowledge of how individuals succeed in community living, an oft repeated recommendation is that decisions on types of community settings should be based on matching relevant characteristics of retarded individuals with relevant characteristics of environments (cf. Sigelman, Novak, Heal, & Switzky, 1980; Willer & Intagliata, 1980). These recommendations imply large-scale planning and development of needed community environments with certain characteristics that would ideally match the identified characteristics of currently institutionalized persons.

From a systems theory approach, such recommendations fail to take into account the political, economic, and social influences of other elements of the system on residential decisions. The types of environments in which any mentally retarded person will live is subject to complex system interactions. For instance, Sitkei (1980) studied movement from group homes to less or more restrictive settings according to the licensure category of the home: publicly operated facilities, nonprofit homes, and private profit-making homes. He found that publicly operated facilities were much more likely to transfer residents to other settings, while profit-making homes transferred the least of the three groups. Bock and Joiner (1982) found that there were only very slight differences in the average performance of institution residents and residents of community facilities. Continued institutionalization of many people was attributable solely to the size limitations of community facilities.

Any research implication that calls for better matching of persons with environments ignores the small but important area of research focused on the method of selection of institution residents who do move to the community. The process by which certain individuals arrive at the point of leaving the institution and others do not has been examined in at least three studies. Willer and Intagliata (1980) found that the year in which a person was placed into the community was the most significant factor affecting whether he or she went to a group home or a foster home. The environment into which an individual was placed did not depend on any characteristics related to the individual, but rather on the primary option then in favor at the state planning and funding level. Calkins (1976) conducted an intensive case study of the community placement process for 14 New York State residents and found significant system effects for decisions in the process: illogical institutional procedures, a lack of a continuum of placement environments to match the range of individual needs, the influential persistence of advocates, and the existence of specific placement criteria which excluded various clients from certain sites where placements were available. Novak (1983) also found that system characteristics, rather than any individual characteristic or community "readiness" hypothesized in a particular retarded person, affected which institution residents moved to the community. Relevant system characteristics included the home county from which an individual came, the availability of a foster parent, funding availability, and local nursing home closings.

Windle (1962) has also underscored the almost total idiosyncrasy of the community placement process. Hence, it seems that individuals may end up in certain types of facilities, such as group homes, foster homes, natural homes, nursing homes, or institutions, not because of any logical analysis of individual need and environment characteristics but because of such factors as bed availability, year of placement, funding patterns, and county of residence. Given that persons may not end up residing in the types of community environments for which they were matched and recommended (Vitello, Atthowe, & Caldwell, 1983) and given such factors as limitations on community services funding and the permanence of large community residences already in existence, it is unlikely that any large-scale shifts in planning living spaces for people will occur in the near future. A possible exception might be through such substantially funded, mandated efforts as the deinstitutionalization of Pennhurst. Small amounts of individual-based attempts are likely to be the prevailing norm in most of the country.

These studies on the idiosyncratic ways that residents end up residing in the environments in which they live illustrate systemic effects on the lives of individuals. Identification of such systemic effects is necessary as a first step in the comprehension of the complexity and pervasiveness of the entire systemic context.

Given the idiosyncrasy of the process that places individuals in certain types of environments, it is unlikely that these effects can be eradicated or totally controlled. Research, however, could focus on understanding how environments themselves can be changed to better address the needs of individuals. Characteristics of programs or caretakers such as overprotection, promotion of independence, skill training of residents, and individualization of resident self-expression, could all be altered to more closely optimize individual growth and other desirable outcomes. The research on typologies and characteristics of residents and of environments has failed to account for the changing, dynamic flux possible in both.

There is almost no literature on the question of what characteristics an effective residential services worker has, much less on the staff qualities that would match different types of retarded residents. A small number of studies have attempted to determine what characteristics higher quality foster parents have. However, almost all the literature on group home staff seems to center on burnout and turnover. As previously noted, George and Baumeister's (1981) study indicated that homes with more resident behavior problems have higher turnover, and Sarata's (1975) study found that homes with less resident progress have more burnout. No intervention with the lack of resident progress and the number of behavior problems in either of these studies was indicated, reflecting the lack of consideration that certain components of the environment can be modified. Although many staff training programs exist, there is a marked lack of evaluation studies on the adequacy of that training and its impact on resident lives (Intagliata & Willer, 1981).

Thurman (1981) has recommended that the ecology of an individual with his/her environments should be "congruent," that is, exhibit mutual tolerance and acceptance between the individual and the environment. Thurman allows that congruence is obtained when the characteristics and behavior patterns of the individual are tolerated successfully by the social system and the individual enjoys enough support from the environment to maximize behavioral functioning. Methods to maximize congruence, such as pinpointing and improving the physical and attitudinal supports that maximize habilitation, would potentially be a useful direction for research.

B. Regional–State Level Analysis

At Reiff's (1971) and Thompson and Wray's (1985) higher organizational levels of the system, as well as at Bronfenbrenner's level of exosystem, some forces of influence, especially political and economic, have been identified. As it affects the mental retardation and residential services system, this type of study has tended to be limited to case study examinations or political analyses (e.g., Cohen, 1975).

Hogan and MacEachron (1980) have proposed one systematic structuring of the component variables in community-based regional service systems, possibly the controlling organizational variables at the regional level of the system. In their standardized tool, the Plan Evaluation Guide, three major areas are ideology, foundations of regional service systems (such as statutory bases for services, the empowerment of regional coordination, and comprehensiveness of the region), and operational features of regional service systems (such as use of resource control mechanisms, use of consumer coordination, administrative controls, resource and community development, individual service coordination, utilization of generic services, appropriateness of the regional governance structure, and quality safeguards). More documentation of the importance of these variables is needed.

At the level of regional adminstration, Zober (1980) compared two state systems of institutional services based on a "regional-decentralized model," and three different regional community-based service systems. He showed how each of these five systems evolved differently due, first, to environmental determinants such as the predominant and competing care and treatment paradigms, level of technology, existing social welfare arrangements, and economic and political constraints. The second major group of variables affecting the public intervention strategies adopted by each system were the roles played by key governmental decision makers, practitioners, and special interest groups.

Court orders have also played a significant role in many state's development of systematic deinstitutionalization plans (ARC/Michigan, 1979; Howse, 1979). In many states, the passage of Title XIX (Medicaid) of the Social Security Act in 1965 has significantly altered institutional populations (Zitske & Hallgren, 1980) as has the Title XIX amendments passed in 1971 funding intermediate care facilities for the mentally retarded (Taylor, Brown, McCord, Giambetti, Searl, Mlinarcik, Atkinson, & Wichter, 1981). Between 1965 and 1975 in Wisconsin, for example, the number of developmentally disabled persons living in nursing homes increased from approximately 300 to 4672, while the population of the three state institutions decreased from 3784 to 2618 (Griss, 1980).

Several researchers have addressed differences among the 50 states in operating services for persons with mental retardation. Bruininks, Hauber, and Kudla (1980) showed that the 50 states vary significantly in the degree to which they deinstitutionalize. Although approximately 20 of every 100,000 Americans live in community residences for retarded persons, the mean varies dramatically from state to state. For instance, in Minnesota, 70 of every 100,000 persons live in community facilities, while in West Virginia only 3 do. Janicki, Mayeda, and Epple (1983) have shown the wide variability in availability, size, and licensure of group homes throughout the 50 states.

Sigelman, Roeder, and Sigelman (1980) gave each of the 50 states a "deinstitutionalization score," based on the number of persons in community facilities compared to the number in institutions. They compared interstate differences in these scores to various political and socioeconomic measures to determine what types of factors relate to differences in community policies. Walker (1969), for instance, found that larger, wealthier, more industrialized states have throughout history adopted more "innovative" policies than smaller, poorer, more agrarian states. Sigelman *et al.* found, among socioeconomic indicators, that industrialization, education of the population, and more heterogeneous populations significantly though modestly correlated with deinstitutionalization scores. In terms of political measures, the use of community-based facilities was strongly determined by the extent to which states exhibited a liberal, pluralist, and reformist political system and culture. Overall, 38% of the interstate variance in deinstitutionalization was accounted for by three variables: political culture, legislative professionalism, and affluence.

Lippman (1976) established a set of criteria by which to assess the treatment accorded to mentally retarded persons falling under the responsibility of certain political categories such as the 50 states. He constituted a Set of Indicators of Societal Concern for Mentally Retarded Persons, a quantification of individual states' level of concern and nature and style of treatment afforded retarded persons by that entity. Based on the principle of normalization (Nirje, 1969; Wolfensberger, 1972) and the principle of "least restrictiveness," the 105 scale items were validated by parents, professionals, and public officials. They were intended to apply to a community as small as a county or as large as a nation, and included such items as numbers of retarded persons living in certain categories of facilities, the existence of a separate governmental unit addressing the needs of persons with mental retardation, and the prevalence of vocational programs. Application of this set of indicators is needed in order to determine the utility of such a method in the comprehension of system influences.

C. Federal Level Issues Affecting Deinstitutionalization Programs

The effect of federal funding on the lives of persons with retardation is well known to practitioners and administrators. For instance, services for persons dependent on public agencies for their care are, of course, bound by the strictures of federal regulations attached to allocations administered by a myriad of agencies. Boggs (1975) has enumerated how numerous legal, legislative, and bureaucratic factors affecting services for persons with mental retardation operate in such areas as the classification and definition of clientele.

Ross (1980) has summarized the federal dilemma of whether programs for persons with mental retardation should be funded and designated categorically or not. One argument is that federal and state categorical programs such as specific mental retardation programs promote waste, duplication, excessive paperwork, and high administration costs. Conventional public administration has instead promoted the idea of the umbrella agency. However, experience has demonstrated that low visibility groups such as various categories of disabled persons lose resources without the specific categorical designation (e.g., "mentally retarded" or "developmentally disabled") on funding and program initiatives.

The federal government's General Accounting Office report on deinstitutionalization (1977) documented the degree to which funding for these programs and persons is splintered: "at least 135 federal programs, operated by 11 major departments and agencies, have either a direct or indirect impact on the mentally disabled. An estimated 89 are operated by" the Department of Health, Education and Welfare (p. 5). Although deinstitutionalization of the mentally disabled has been a national goal since 1963, federal agencies that can influence this goal "have not yet developed a comprehensive and clearly defined national plan to achieve the goal" (p. 26). Specific illustrations of gaps and discontinuities in services due to the lack of interagency coordination at the federal level include (1) the lack of a joint Health and Human Services (HHS)–Housing and Urban Development (HUD) policy on the provision of support services to handicapped persons in community housing; (2) the failure to balance mass transit accessibility initiatives with paratransit specialized services for handicapped persons in the Department of Transportation and HHS programs; (3) the failure of Congress, HHS, and the Department of Labor to address the relationship between income maintenance programs such as SSI and wage supplement proposals for persons employed in sheltered work environments; and (4) the seeming failure of HHS and Congress to develop a rational, agency-wide policy on services to mentally handicapped persons in nonmedical, community residential settings (Ross, 1980).

One example of the apparent inability of the federal government to provide coherency and consistency in service delivery is the regulations governing federal intermediate care facilities for the mentally retarded. These regulations allow for all programs and services to be provided within the facility itself, inviting the development of large, centralized, segregating, and isolating facilities. Professional and special programs, training and rehabilitation, recreation, and social services can all be provided internally with internal staff, and even vocational training programs and sheltered employment can be conducted within the facility itself. Thus, it is allowable within the "rules and regulations," for a resident of such a facility to never leave the building (Zitske & Hallgren, 1980).

On the one hand, both the executive and legislative branches of the federal government have proclaimed deinstitutionalization as a national goal. On the other hand, institutional services are funded at a rate nearly five times that of community-based services. In 1980, for instance, the federal budget for Medicaid was $11.25 billion, while $2.7 billion was alloted for Title XX community services.

It is this national level, with its myriad regulations and funding patterns, which is the largest exosystem encompassing and defining the context of the entire system of deinstitutionalization. It is no wonder that, to many, the mental retardation and residential services system fails to look like a "system" at all. Some writers, like Singer (1980), have evocatively described the insanity of our "crazy systems."

In relation to mental retardation services, Elias (1976) has examined the network of Canadian services for persons called mentally retarded and noted that service agencies obviously do not function as a single system. In his case study examination of the Canadian network, no component in the mental retardation system existed through which coordinated action could be demanded. No body existed which could demand and ensure that various direct service components acted together as a synergistic system. The network lacked an effective "decider" which would determine the purposes, set primary goals, and control component elements or subsystems of the whole (Miller, 1972), as demanded by a truly functional system. The functions and outputs of the apparently noneffective system were implicit, unconscious, and became clear only upon examination of the whole. Canadian agencies apparently functioned in isolation as closed systems, admitting people, providing services they deemed appropriate, and discharging them back, with little vision of a desired end product and with little regard for the capabilities of other community agencies. Often an individual component of an agency ceased to function, or changed its input or output to other component agencies, and precipitated crisis reactions in the other elements. Further, these closed components did little to build capacity, enhance life quality, or offer hope to the persons they served.

In his application of systems theory to the Canadian services system Elias summarized the ineffectiveness with which this apparent nonsystem reacted to the pervasive problem of scarcity of resources. There was a wastage of resources as capital expenditures were tied up in the renovation of old institutions and construction of new ones. Manpower practices involved a massive misallocation of resources, since they relied on degree and diploma requirements with loyalties divided between professions and clients. Specialized rather than generic services were used. Services were denied, postponed, or diluted without taking into account the immediate or long-term consequences of those decisions. Only a fraction of the information available on prevention of mental retardation was utilized. With a wide range of needs and narrow range of options, there was a tendency for existing services to be used even when they were only marginally appropriate. Residential, developmental, and vocational services were not typically structured to promote movement from dependence to relative independence. Staff subverted policy by "hoarding," i.e., continuing to serve clients even when service was no longer needed, and when others would have benefited.

These maladaptations and others contributed to the inertia which made it highly difficult if not impossible for this system or nonsystem to adapt to new demands from members and from the community. The system had experienced extensive growth and institutionalization. The exosystem of the community had to a large extent failed to forcefully demand change. The system continued to justify some of its activities on the basis of earlier rationales and practices. Last, it seemed to have displaced its goal of habilitating mentally retarded persons in favor of system maintenance and survival (Elias, 1976).

IV. THE POSSIBILITY OF SYSTEM CHANGE

Durkheim (1951) has delineated that what holds a society together is, first, the presence of a commonly held, commonly shared structure of goals and values. Second, the institutions of the society must be held by the people they serve to be legitimate, and to have a moral authority which is willingly accepted by the people. Third, the individuals who make up the society must have a clear sense of self. One can then examine the cohesiveness of any society from the point of (1) its structure of goals and instrumental values, (2) the state of the institutional legitimacy of the institutions in the society, and (3) the extensiveness of the sense of self and degree of identification or alienation of the people within that society (Yankelovich, 1979). Since the ways in which a society treats its more needy members reflect the values of that people, an analysis of the basic values expressed in that treatment raises several questions. If that treatment is problematic, if it is not in accordance with the basic values, or if the values themselves appear questionable as reflected in the treatment, the most important questions raised center on whether shifts in the basic values, the treatment, and in the system itself are possible. If so, the next question is how those shifts can be realized.

On the one hand, the forces that resist change provide the equilibrium and duration of the societal institutions that are at the basis of the sense of civilization and culture of a society. "All of the forces which contribute to stability in personality or in social systems can be perceived as resisting change" (Watson, 1969, p. 488). Watson's analysis of the common sources of resistance to change in social systems indicates that all those sources focus on what is required to maintain the equilibrium and stability of the system. Vested interests resist change, but the causes of greatest resistance are matters which are connected with what is held to be sacred. Conformity to prevailing norms is another source of resistance to change, and is reflected in the systemic and cultural coherence which recognizes that one part of a system cannot be changed without affecting other parts. Any changes in mental retardation services, for instance, are inextricably linked to changes in other service systems, larger systems, and cultural values. From this point of view, change in mental retardation services can occur only as corresponding changes occur in the other levels of the system. The analysis of changes in the history of residential services discussed above reflected this principle. In considering current attempts on the part of some to effect major systemic changes toward deinstitutionalization and community integration, the necessity for and interaction of change at different levels must be taken into account. Even arguments for a continuum of care including the institution must take into account the forces resistant to change and forces contributing to internal systemic tension.

While there are established techniques to change the behavior of the individual, there exists no thorough and systematic understanding of how to activate, move, and alter the larger levels constructing the system which surrounds the individual. Thompson and Wray (1985), in addressing a desired systems change toward community integration, have proposed methods for changing the current system in behavior analysis terms. In their view, if all levels of the systems were clearly defined, then changing the behavior at any one level could be addressed. Although the technology for altering the behavior of individuals is understood, as is the manipulation of variables in the immediate environment, the behavior analysis approach has not yet been extended to entire service systems and to complex human service issues. The rearrangement of major social and economic networks of people and groups of people who provide services to handicapped individuals can only be accomplished once the behavior of these networks is analyzed. Once the goals of change are defined, in Thompson and Wray's view, the failure to achieve the desired outcomes at one level would dictate moving one step upward in the organizational hierarchy to identify the controlling variable at the next level. Thompson and Wray postulate that at some point the manipulation of the appropriate controlling variable should enable the variables at each of the lower levels to operate properly in order to produce the desired outcome for the individual. They propose the application of Skinner's (1938, 1953) three-term contingency analysis to the changes in organizational behavior required to successfully implement community integration; this analysis would determine the presenting situation, agency responses, and consequences of agency actions in a wide variety of classes of variables. "A thorough contingency analysis of current controlling variables inconsistent with community integration policy will lead logically to suggestions for manipulating variables to produce necessary organizational changes consistent with community integration" (Thompson & Wray, 1985, p. 4). However, at this time Thompson and Wray admit that the controlling organizational variables are poorly defined.

What is required for system level change has been alternately explained by Watzlawick, Weakland, and Fisch (1974) in their description of the differences between first-order and second-order change. At the level of first-order change, logical levels of analysis are kept strictly within the system in order to prevent paradox and confusion. First-order change is limited to one level of the system, as opposed to diachronic (or structural) change. An example is the maintenance of institutions as part of the residential services system. When dehumanizing living conditions were publicly exposed, a response in some institutions was to place children on chairs rather than on the floor, to ensure that all residents were clothed, and to install private showers. That was first-order change, making a difference at one level without any higher order shift. In order to effect change from one level to another, a jump, discontinuity, or transformation in the very system itself is necessary. Watzlawick *et al.* summarize these two distinct types of change as "one that occurs within a given system which itself remains unchanged, and one whose occurrence changes the system itself" (p. 10). Analogous to this relationship is the fact that a person having a nightmare can do various things inside the dream—run, hide, fight, scream, jump off a cliff, etc.—but none of those behaviors can terminate the nightmare. The only way out of the dream is to wake up, an altogether different state. Changes within the nightmare are first-order changes, and waking up is a second-order change. In mental retardation services, one possible avenue to second-order change might be through such decrees as all children having the right to an education or all people having the right to live in the community.

Rapaport (1977) has delineated how the strategies and tactics for system change differ depending on the definition of the problem or the source of difficulties. His levels of the definition of the problems are similar to Bronfenbrenner's (1977) ecological environments. For instance, at the first level, if social problems are defined as the result of the inability of some people (such as those who are labeled retarded) to fit into the structure of society, the focus is on the individual level of analysis and on the deficits of particular persons. The problem is then summarized in such terms as "John is noncompliant" or "Mary has to learn to control her tantrums before she can move out to the community." Change strategies at this level focus on changing people, and interventions will be person-centered strategies such as training programs.

At the next level of group, social problems can be conceptualized as created by interpersonal difficulties within primary groups such as the family, peer, and work groups (Bronfenbrenner's microsystem). The problem is seen in terms of "If only the family cooperated in this toilet training program, everything would be fine." Resulting strategies focus on such techniques as training for families and competitive employers on interpersonal communications and behavior modification techniques.

At the third level of analysis, social problems are defined as caused by the organizations of society which fail to implement the desired values and goals of our social institutions (Bronfenbrenner's mesosystem). The aim remains to enhance the ability of organizations themselves rather than the persons served. The problem can be defined in such terms as "We want to move these people to apartments, but that would take too many staff" or "We want to teach them how to talk, but we don't have the money for a speech therapist." On this level, change strategies center on organizational development and resource development techniques, such as systems-centered consultation and development of new structures and communication styles within organizations.

At the last level of analysis, that of institution and community, social problems are conceived of as created by the institutions of society rather than by persons, groups, or organizations (Bronfenbrenner's exosystem and macrosystem). The problem might be defined in such terms as "We don't like this institution, either, but the community isn't ready for our people." The key to social change is the attitudes, values, goals, and political–economic ideology and social policies of which the institutions themselves are composed and on which the organizations are based. An important variable is the distribution of power and change principles of social action, social policy, and community organization.

Changes in mental retardation services have tended to follow prescribed steps, or "recipe-like" guidelines of *process-dominated* change (White, 1977, p. 164). In contrast to the prescribed steps of process change, *goal-dominated* procedures effect change by first setting a goal or specifying some end product, then designing suitable processes for attaining the goal. Goal systems are future oriented, with an image of the future energizing and directing movement into the future. For instance, O'Brien (1982) has proposed the goal of building communities competent to care for all their members, which would result in an end product of pluralistic, diverse communities. Some hope to change the structure of the mental retardation system to be one that values every individual, with respect for his or her uniqueness, individuality, and contribution to a multidimensional society.

The most clearly articulated vision of a mental retardation system different from the current one has been put forth by the proponents of the principle of normalization (e.g., Bank-Mikkelson, 1976; Flynn & Nitsch, 1980; Wolfensberger, 1972). Since normalization requires the physical and social integration of persons as the cornerstone of service delivery, as well as "community presence" and community participation (O'Brien, 1982), the implementation of this principle would require a significant change at all levels of the system. Flynn and Nitsch (1980) have pointed out that, to date, adoption of the underlying principles of normalization has been limited to "adoption-in-theory" and has yet to become "adoption-in-practice" (p. 374). They have argued that limited resources have hindered the adoption of normalization in practice, while Pieper and Cappuccilli (1980) have argued that agencies have failed to translate normalization theory into daily service provision due to erroneous interpretations of the principle. In contrast, McCord (1982) has argued that, as opposed to fiscal and political constraints or a misunderstanding of the principle, the theoretical rather than practical adoption of normalization is more functionally due to the overriding historical function and identity of human services; in his view, the prior purposes ("functions") continue to dominate a self-maintaining system. He reiterates that the major historical role of our human services rests inextricably within the context of society's reaction to deviant persons, and that the function of those services has been and continues to be social control. He maintains that mental retardation programs have operated historically as social control mechanisms to remove, contain, and isolate deviant persons.

From this viewpoint, members of a society attempt to distance themselves from people whose appearance or behavior is negatively judged. As a result, they have empowered formal mechanisms of control to accomplish the task of isolating people (Blatt, Bogdan, Biklen, & Taylor, 1977; Pomerantz & Marholin, 1977; Schur, 1980). "Agencies operate within a social, political, and economic framework that rewards practices which increase the dependence of deviant people on the human service sector" (McCord, 1982, p. 248). In McCord's analysis, human services have four overriding tasks (i.e., the system has four functions): (1) to point out deviancy through labeling procedures and thus assure society that containment is warranted (Murphy, 1980; Scott, 1969); (2) to keep deviant people isolated so that society experiences neither embarrassment nor the burden of caring (Dexter, 1972; Perrucci, 1974); (3) to control deviant people so that new societal members can be socialized to the accepted boundaries of traditional values and norms (Erickson, 1966); and (4) to perpetuate deviance by "teaching people to conform to their deviant status and to willingly accept their containment" (Berger & Luckmann, 1967; Vinter, 1963). Although not every researcher would agree, it is possible to view the principle of normalization as challenging the maintenance of these functions. From this orientation, attempts to restructure the system would be subject to the challenges opposing the adoption of a new paradigm of knowledge as described by Kuhn (1963). According to Kuhn, challenges to any new paradigm include tenacious defense of the previously held construction of reality, insecurity and crisis in response to the new "anomaly of knowledge," and resistance to a substantive change in beliefs and actions. Other tools used to defend the old paradigm include assertions of competence of the old paradigm and symbolic acceptance of the new concept in order to create the illusion of change. It is possible to view the acceptance of the new paradigm of the principle of normalization as subject to all of these defensive tools.

Several factors indicate that the prospects for system change are somewhat positive (Elias, 1976). First, there is the very fact of the emergence of a new set of values, attitudes, and beliefs underlying mental retardation services. New service methods have increased, and there is a new surge of public interest and activism concerning people with handicaps, including mental retardation. The fact that the argument continues as to whether community living is possible for all persons with retardation, or whether the institution will continue to be required for some individuals, is also a healthy sign reflecting the questioning of the basic values underlying the system.

The view is shifting from focus on how to change the retarded person to make him/her "ready" to move to the community, to how to build the competence of our communities to care for all our members, including the most handicapped. As Best-Sigford, Bruininks, Lakin, Hill, and Heal (1982) have noted, "The future of deinstitutionalization will be determined more by the ability and willingness of perspective-shapers and policy-makers to adapt the community based service system to today's needs than it will be by the extent of the needs of today's institutionalized population" (p. 139).

Our lack of understanding of the effects of different levels of the system, and by what methods they can be transformed, contributes to the apparent hesitancy of research to grapple with the systemic context. More complicated and more important than the description of certain factors that exist, as is the content of much current community integration research, would be acceptance of the challenge to research to describe the structure, function, and output of the system and to describe how it works and fails to work, how it influences the lives of retarded individuals, how decisions that are made by each individual involved in human services is affected by the systems context, and how that system responds to and can be influenced by forces of change.

REFERENCES

Association for Retarded Citizens/Michigan. *The Plymouth case and decree.* Lansing, Michigan: ARC/Michigan, 1979.

Atthowe, J. M., Jr., & Vitello, S. J. *Deinstitutionalization and the family.* Paper presented at the annual meeting of the American Association of Mental Deficiency, Boston, June 1982.

Bank-Mikkelson, N. Denmark. In R. B. Kugel & A. Shearer (Eds.), *Changing patterns in residential services for the mentally retarded* (rev. ed.). Washington, D.C.: U.S. Govt. Printing Office, 1976.

Bartnik, E., & Winkler, R. C. Discrepant judgments of community adjustment of mentally retarded adults: The contribution of personal responsibility. *American Journal of Mental Deficiency,* 1981, **86**(3), 260–266.

Baumgart, D., Brown, L., Pumpian, I., Nisbet, J., Ford, A., Sweet, M., Messina, R., & Schroeder, J. Principle of partial participation and individualized adaptations in educational programs for severely handicapped students. *The Journal of the Association for the Severely Handicapped,* 1982, **7**(2).

Berger, P. L., & Luckmann, T. *The social construction of reality: A treatise in the sociology of knowledge.* Garden City, New York: Doubleday, 1967.

Bertalanffy, L., von. *General system theory: Foundations, development, applications.* New York: Braziller, 1968.

Bertalanffy, L., von. *A systems view of man.* Boulder, Colorado: Westview Press, 1981.

Best-Sigford, B., Bruininks, R. H., Lakin, K. C., Hill, B. K., & Heal, L. W. Resident release patterns in a national sample of public residential facilities. *American Journal of Mental Deficiency,* 1982, **87**(2), 130–140.

Blatt, B., Bogdan, R., Biklen, D., & Taylor, S. From institution to community: A conversion model. In E. Sontag, J. Smith & N. Certo (Eds.), *Educational programming for the severely profoundly handicapped.* Reston, Virginia: Council for Exceptional Children, 1977.

Bock, W., & Joiner, L. From institution to community residence: Behavioral competencies for admission and discharge. *Mental Retardation,* 1982, **20**(4), 153–158.

Boggs, E. M. Legal, legislative and bureaucratic factors affecting planned and unplanned change in the delivery of services to the mentally retarded. In M. J. Begab & S. A. Richardson (Eds.), *The mentally retarded and society: A social science perspective.* Baltimore, Maryland: Univ. Park Press, 1975. Pp. 441–468.

Brim, O. G. Macro-structural influences on child development and the need for childhood social indicators. *American Journal of Orthopsychiatry,* 1975, **45**, 516–524.

Bronfenbrenner, U. Toward an experimental ecology of human development. *American Psychologist,* 1977, **July,** 513–531.

Bronfenbrenner, U. *The ecology of human development: Experiments by nature and design.* Cambridge, Massachusetts: Harvard Univ. Press, 1979.

Bruininks, R. H., Hauber, F. H., & Kudla, M. J. National survey of community residential facilities: A profile of facilities and residents in 1977. *American Journal of Mental Deficiency,* 1980, **84**(5), 470–478.

Bruininks, R. H., Kudla, M. J., Wieck, C. A., & Hauber, F. A. Management problems in community residential facilities. *Mental Retardation,* 1980, **18**(3), 125–130.

Butterfield, E., Barnett, C., & Bensberg, G. A measure of attitudes which differentiate attendants from separate institutions. *American Journal of Mental Deficiency,* 1968, **72**, 890–899.

Caldwell, B. *Instruction manual: Home observation for measurement of the environment.* Unpublished manuscript, 1968.

Calkins, C. F. *The emergence of mentally retarded adults from a private culture to a public culture: A case of the community placement process.* Doctoral dissertation, George Peabody, College for Teachers, 1975. *Dissertation Abstracts International,* 1976, **36**, 5988-A. (University Microfiles #76-3714, 185).

Cantor, M. Neighbors and friends: An overlooked resource in the informal support system. *Research on Aging,* 1979, **1**, 4.

Center on Human Policy. *The community imperative: A refutation of all arguments in support of institutionalizing anybody because of mental retardation.* Syracuse, New York: Syracuse Univ. Press, 1979.

Cohen, H. J. Obstacles to developing community services for the mentally retarded. In M. J.

Begab & S. A. Richardson (Eds.), *The mentally retarded and society: A social science perspective.* Baltimore, Maryland: Univ. Park Press, 1975. Pp. 401–422.

Conroy, J., & Feinstein, C. *The longitudinal study of the court-ordered deinstitutionalization at Pennhurst.* Paper presented at the annual meeting of the Association for the Severely Handicapped, Denver, November, 1982.

Cortés, F., Przeworski, A., & Sprague, J. *Systems analysis for social scientists.* New York: Wiley, 1974.

Dexter, L. A. On the politics and sociology of stupidity in our society. *Social Problems,* 1972, **9,** 221–228.

Dunphy, M. D. Modern ideals of education applied to the training of mental defectives. *Proceedings of the National Conference on Charities & Corrections,* 1908, p. 331.

Durkheim, E. *Suicide, a study in sociology.* Glencoe, Illinois: Free Press, 1951.

Edgerton, R. B. *The cloak of competence: Stigma in the lives of the mentally retarded.* Berkeley, California: Univ. of California Press, 1967.

Elias, J. W. *Computer simulation of a comprehensive community service system for the mentally retarded.* Doctoral dissertation, Department of Psychology, York University, Toronto, Ontario, September, 1976.

Eyman, R. K., Demaine, G. C., & Lei, T. Relationship between community environments and resident changes in adaptive behavior: A path model. *American Journal of Mental Deficiency,* 1979, **83,** 330–338.

Eyman, R. K., Silverstein, A. B., McLain, R., & Miller, C. Effects of residential settings on development. In P. Mittler & J. M. deJong (Eds.), *Research to practice in mental retardation: Vol. 1, Care and prevention.* Baltimore, Maryland: Univ. Park Press, 1977.

Fernald, W. E. The history of the treatment of the feeble-minded. *Proceedings of the National Conference on Charities & Corrections,* 1893, pp. 206, 209.

Fernald, W. E. What is practical in the way of prevention of mental defect? *Proceedings of the National Conference on Charities & Corrections,* 1915, p. 96.

Flynn, R. J., & Nitsch, K. E. *Normalization, social integration, and community services.* Baltimore, Maryland: Univ. Park Press, 1980.

George, M. J., & Baumeister, A. A. Employee withdrawal and job satisfaction in community residential facilities for mentally retarded persons. *American Journal of Mental Deficiency,* 1981, **85**(6), 639–647.

Goffman, E. *Asylums.* New York: Anchor Books, 1961.

Gollay, E., Freedman, R., Wyngaarden, M., & Kurtz, N. R. *Coming back.* Cambridge, Massachusetts: Abt, 1978.

Griss, R. *Funding for alternative residential services for persons with developmental disabilities.* Division of Policy and Budget, Wisconsin Department of Health and Social Services, September, 1980.

Hartzler, E. A ten-year survey of girls discharged from the Laurelton State Village. *American Journal of Mental Deficiency,* 1953, **57,** 512–518.

Heal, L. W., Novak, A. R., Sigelman, C. K., & Switzky, N. N. Characteristics of community residential facilities. In A. R. Novak & L. W. Heal (Eds.), *Integration of developmentally disabled individuals into the community.* Baltimore, Maryland: Brookes, 1980.

Hogan, M. F., & MacEachron, A. E. *Plan evaluation guide.* Downsview, Ontario: National Institute on Mental Retardation, 1980.

Holland, J. L. *Making vocational choices: A theory of careers.* New York: Prentice-Hall, 1973.

Howe, S. G. *Third and final report on the experimental school for teaching and training idiotic children: The first report of the trustees of the Massachusetts schools for idiotic and feeble-minded youth.* Cambridge, Massachusetts: Metcalf, 1852.

Howse, J. Maintaining a standard of quality. *Third annual report of the New York City/Long*

Island County Service Group, April 1, 1978 to March 31, 1979. State of New York, Office of Mental Retardation and Development Disabilities, Office of Planning and Evaluation, 1979.

Hull, J. T., & Thompson, J. C. Predicting adaptive functioning of mentally retarded persons in community settings. *American Journal of Mental Deficiency,* 1980, **85**(3), 253–261.

Intagliata, J. *Use of family care homes as a community placement for mentally retarded persons in New York State.* Paper presented at the annual convention of the American Association on Mental Deficiency, Denver, May 1978.

Intagliata, J., Kraus, S., & Willer, B. The impact of deinstitutionalization on a community-based service system. *Mental Retardation,* 1980, **18**(6), 305–307.

Intagliata, J. & Willer, B. A review of training programs for providers of foster family care to mentally retarded persons. In R. H. Bruininks, C. E. Meyers, B. B. Sigford, & C. Lakin (Eds.), *Deinstitutionalization and community adjustment of mentally retarded people.* Washington, D.C.: American Association on Mental Deficiency, Monograph No. 4, 1981. Pp. 282–315.

Intagliata, J., & Willer, B. Reinstitutionalization of mentally retarded persons successfully placed into family-care and group homes. *American Journal of Mental Deficiency,* 1982, **87**(1), 34–39.

Intagliata, J., Willer, B., & Wicks, N. Factors related to the quality of community adjustment in family care homes. In R. H. Bruininks, C. E. Meyers, B. B. Sigford, & K. C. Lakin (Eds.), *Deinstitutionalization and community adjustment of mentally retarded people.* Washington, D.C.: American Association on Mental Deficiency, Monograph No. 4, 1981.

Jackson, J. Factors of the treatment environment. *Archives of General Psychiatry,* 1969, **21**, 39–45.

Jacobson, J. W., & Schwartz, A. A. Personal and service characteristics affecting group home placement success: A prospective analysis. *Mental Retardation,* 1983, **21**(2), 1–7.

Janicki, M. P., Mayeda, T., & Epple, W. Availability of group homes for persons with mental retardation in the United States. *Mental Retardation,* 1983, **21**(2), 45–51.

Johnson, A. Concerning a form of degeneracy. *American Journal of Sociology,* 1898, **4**, 465.

Johnson, A. Report of committee on colonies for segregation of defectives. *Proceedings of the National Conference on Charities and Corrections,* 1903.

Justice, R., Bradley, J., & O'Connor, G. Foster family care for the retarded: Management concerns for the caretaker. *Mental Retardation,* 1971, **9**(4), 12–15.

Kerlin, I. N. Report of standing committee. *Proceedings of the National Conference on Charities and Corrections,* 1885, p. 159.

Kernberg, O. *Leadership and organizational functioning: Part II: Regression in leadership.* A paper presented at the Sterling Forest Conference, New York, October, 1974.

King, R. D., Raynes, N. V., & Tizard, J. *Patterns of residential care: Sociological studies in institutions for handicapped citizens.* London: Routledge & Kegan Paul, 1971.

Kuhn, T. S. *The structure of scientific revolutions.* Chicago, Illinois: Univ. of Chicago Press, 1963.

Landesman-Dwyer, S., Berkson, G., & Romer, D. Affiliation and friendship of mentally retarded in group homes. *American Journal of Mental Deficiency,* 1979, **83**, 571–580.

Landesman-Dwyer, S., Sackett, G. P., & Kleinman, J. S. Relationship of size to resident and staff behavior in small community residences. *American Journal of Mental Deficiency,* 1980, **85**(1), 6–17.

Landesman-Dwyer, S., & Sulzbacher, F. M. Residential placement and adaptation of severely and profoundly retarded individuals. In R. H. Bruininks, C. E. Meyers, B. B. Sigford, & K. C. Lakin (Eds.), *Deinstitutionalization and community adjustment of mentally re-*

tarded people. Washington, D.C.: American Association on Mental Deficiency Monograph No. 4, 1981, Pp. 182–194.

Lei, T., Nihira, L., Sheehy, N., & Meyers, C. E. A study of small family care for mentally retarded people. In R. H. Bruininks, C. E. Meyers, B. B. Sigford, & K. C. Lakin (Eds.), *Deinstitutionalization and community adjustment of mentally retarded people.* Washington, D.C.: American Association on Mental Deficiency, Monograph No. 4, 1981. Pp. 265–281.

Lei, T., & Sheehy, N. *Physical and parenting characteristics of foster homes for retarded children.* Paper presented at the annual meeting of the American Academy on Mental Retardation, San Francisco, May 1980.

Levinson, R. *Family crisis and adaptation: Coping with a mentally retarded child.* Unpublished doctoral dissertation, University of Wisconsin at Madison, 1975.

Lippman, L. Indicators of societal concern for mentally retarded persons. *Social Indicators Research,* 1976, **3**, 181–215.

McCarver, R. B., & Craig, E. M. Placement of the retarded in the community: Prognosis and outcome. In N. R. Ellis & N. Bray (Eds.), *International review of research in mental retardation* (Vol. 7). New York: Academic Press, 1974.

McCord, W. T. From theory to reality: Obstacles to the implementation of the normalization principle in human services. *Mental Retardation,* 1982, **20**(6), 247–253.

McCormick, M., Balla, D., & Zigler, E. Resident care practices in institutions for retarded persons: A cross-institutional, cross-cultural study. *American Journal of Mental Deficiency,* 1975, **80**, 1–17.

McKnight, J. The professional service business. *Social Policy,* 1977, **8**(3), 110–116.

Mercer, J. *Labelling the mentally retarded.* Berkeley, California: Univ. of California Press, 1973.

Mercer, J. Theoretical constructs of adaptive behavior: Movement from a medical to a social-ecological perspective. In W. A. Coulter & H. W. Morrow (Eds.), *Adaptive behavior: Concepts and measurement.* New York: Grune & Stratton, 1978.

Meyer, R. J. Attitudes of parents of institutionalized mentally retarded individuals toward deinstitutionalization. *American Journal of Mental Deficiency,* 1980, **85**(2), 184–187.

Miller, J. G. Living systems: The organization. *Behavioral Science, 1972,* **17**(1), 1–182.

Moos, R. H. *Evaluating correctional and community settings.* New York: Wiley, 1975.

Moreau, F. A., Novak, A. R., & Sigelman, C. K. Physical and social integration of developmentally disabled individuals into the community. In A. R. Novak & L. W. Heal (Eds.), *Integration of developmentally disabled individuals into the community.* Baltimore, Maryland: Brookes, 1980.

Murphy, S. T. Vocational rebabilitation counseling and advocacy: An analysis of dissonant concepts. *Rehabilitation Literature,* 1980, **41**, 2–10.

Nirje, B. The normalization principle and its human management implications. In R. Kugel & W. Wolfensberger (Eds.), *Changing patterns in residential services for the mentally retarded.* Washington, D.C.: President's Committee on Mental Retardation, 1969.

Novak, A. *Facilitators and barriers in the community placement process for developmentally disabled individuals facing deinstitutionalization.* Doctoral dissertation, University of Illinois at Urbana-Champaign, 1983.

O'Brien, J. Personal communication, March 28, 1982.

Penniman, T. L. Initial screening and identification of predictors for possible use in selecting foster mothers for the mentally retarded. *Dissertation Abstracts International,* 1974, **35**(6–A), 3879.

Perrucci, R. *Circle of madness: On being insane and institutionalized in America.* Glencoe, Illinois: Free Press, 1974.

Perske, R. *New Life in the neighborhood: How persons with retardation or other disabilities can help make a good community better.* Nashville, Tennessee: Abingdon Press, 1981.

Pieper, B., & Cappuccilli, J. Beyond the family and the institution: The sanctity of liberty. In T. Apolloni, J. Cappuccilli, & T. P. Cooke (Eds.), *Achievements in residential services for persons with disabilities: Toward excellence.* Baltimore, Maryland: Univ. Park Press, 1980.

Pilewski, M. E., & Heal, L. W. Empirical support for deinstitutionalization. In A. R. Novak & L. W. Heal (Eds.), *Integration of developmentally disabled individuals into the community.* Baltimore, Maryland: Brookes, 1980.

Pomerantz, D. J., & Marholin, D. Vocational habilitation: A time for change. In E. Sontag, J. Smith, & N. Certo (Eds.), *Educational programming for the severely profoundly handicapped.* Reston, Virginia: Council for Exceptional Children, 1977.

Pratt, M. W., Luszcz, M. A., & Brown, M. E. Measuring dimensions of the quality of care in small community residences. *American Journal of Mental Deficiency,* 1980, **85**(2), 188–194.

Rago, W. V., Parker, R. M., & Cleland, C. C. Effect of increased space on the social behavior of institutionalized profoundly retarded male adults. *American Journal of Mental Deficiency,* 1978, **82**(6), 554–558.

Rapaport, J. *Community psychology: Values, research and action.* New York: Holt, 1977.

Raynes, N., Pratt, M., & Roses, S. *Organizational structure and the care of the mentally retarded.* London: Croom-Helm, 1979.

Reiff, R. R. Community psychology and public policy. In J. C. Glidewell & G. Rosenblum (Eds.), *Issues in community psychology and preventive mental health.* New York: Behavioral Publications, 1971.

Retherford, R. Selected characteristics of foster parents and acceptance of the retardate into the family structure. *Dissertation Abstracts International,* 1975, **35**(7-A), 4289.

Reynolds, W. M. *Assessing the social climate of group homes for developmentally disabled persons.* Paper presented at the annual convention of the American Association on Mental Deficiency, Denver, May 1978.

Ross, E. C. Developing public policy for persons with disabilities: The case for a categorical approach. *Mental Retardation,* 1980, **18**(4), 159–163.

Ryan, W. *Blaming the victim.* New York: Random House, 1971.

Sanderson, H. W., & Crawley, M. Characteristics of successful family-care parents. *American Journal of Mental Deficiency,* 1982, **86**(5), 519–525.

Sarata, B. Employee satisfaction in agencies serving retarded persons. *American Journal of Mental Deficiency,* 1975, **79**, 434–442.

Schalock, R. L., Harper, R. S., & Genung, T. Community integration of mentally retarded adults: Community placement and program success. *American Journal of Mental Deficiency,* 1981, **81**(5), 478–488.

Scheerenberger, R. C., & Felsenthal, D. Community settings for mentally retarded persons: Satisfaction and activities. *Mental Retardation,* 1977, **15**(4), 3–7.

Schur, E. M. *The politics of deviance: Stigma contests and the uses of power.* New York: Prentice-Hall, 1980.

Scott, R. A. *The making of blind men: A study of socialization.* New York: Russell Sage Foundation, 1969.

Seltzer, G. B. Community residential adjustment: The relationship among environment, performance, and satisfaction. *American Journal of Mental Deficiency,* 1981, **85**(6), 624–630.

Sigelman, C. K., Novak, A. R., Heal, L. W., & Switzky, H. N. Factors that affect the success of community placement. In A. R. Novak & L. W. Heal (Eds.), *Integration of developmentally disabled individuals into the community.* Baltimore, Maryland: Brookes, 1980.

Sigelman, L., Roeder, P. W., & Sigelman, C. K. *Social service innovation in the American states: Deinstitutionalization of the mentally retarded.* University of Kentucky, 1980.

Singer, B. D. Crazy systems. *Social Policy,* 1980, Sept./Oct., 46–54.

Sitkei, E. G. After group home living—what alternatives? Results of a two year mobility follow-up study. *Mental Retardation,* 1980, **18**(1), 9–13.

Skinner, B. F. *The behavior of organizations; An experimental analysis.* New York: Appleton, 1938.

Skinner, B. F. *Science and human behavior.* New York: Macmillan, 1953.

Stein, I. *Systems theory, science, and social work.* Metuchen, New Jersey: Scarecrow Press, 1974.

Sundberg, N. *Assessment of persons.* New York: Prentice-Hall, 1977.

Sutter, P. Environmental variables related to community placement failure in mentally retarded adults. *Menta Retardation,* 1980. **18**(4), 189–191.

Sutter, P., Mayeda, T., Call, T., Yanagi, G., & Yee, S. Comparison of successful and unsuccessful community-placed mentally retarded persons. *American Journal of Mental Deficiency,* 1980, **85**(3), 262–267.

Taylor, S. J., Brown, K., McCord, W., Giambetti, A., Searl, S., Mlinarcik, S., Atkinson, T., & Lichter, S. *Title XIX and deinstitutionalization: The issue for the 80's.* Syracuse, New York: Center on Human Policy, 1981.

Thiel, G. Relationship of adaptive behavior, age, and environmental demand to community-placement success of mentally retarded adults. *American Journal of Mental Deficiency,* 1981, **86**(2), 208–211.

Thompson, T. & Wray, L. A behavior analytic approach to community integration of persons with developmental disabilities. In K. C. Lakin & R. H. Bruininks (Eds.), *Strategies for achieving community integration of developmentally disabled citizens.* Baltimore, Maryland: Brookes, 1985.

Thurman, K. Least restrictive environments: Another side of the coin. *Education and Training of the Mentally Retarded,* 1981, **16**(1), 68–70.

Trent, J. W. Technology without logos: The idea of mental retardation in the journals of the American Association on Mental Deficiency. *AAMD Special Interest Group on Humanism Newsletter,* 1983, **2**(1), 3–16.

U.S. General Accounting Office. *Returning the mentally disabled to the community: Government needs to do more.* Washington, D.C.: U.S. Govt. Printing Office, 1977.

Vinter, R. D. Analysis of treatment organizations. *Social Work,* 1963, **8**(3), 23–25.

Vitello, S. J., Atthowe, J. M., & Caldwell, J. Determinants of community placement of institutionalized mentally retarded persons. *American Journal of Mental Deficiency,* 1983, **87**(5), 539–545.

Walker, J. L. The diffusion of innovation among the American states. *American Politics Science Review,* 1969, **63**, 880–899.

Watson, G. Resistance of change. In W. Bennis, K. Benne, & R. Chin (Eds.), *The planning of change* (2nd ed.). New York: Holt, 1969. Pp. 488–498.

Watzlawick, P., Weakland, J., & Fisch, R. *Change: Principles of problem formation and problem resolution.* New York: Norton, 1974.

White, J. D. Process directed change vs. goal directed change in normative and natural systems. In J. White (Ed.), *The general systems paradigm: Science of change and change of science. Proceedings of the annual North American meeting, Denver, Colorado, February 21–25, 1977.* Washington, D.C.: Society for General Systems Research, 1977. P. 164.

Wilbur, *Journal of Insanity,* 1852.

Willer, B. *Post-institutional adjustment of the retarded returned to the natural families.* Paper presented at the annual convention of the American Association on Mental Deficiency, Denver, May, 1978.

Willer, B., & Intagliata, J. *Deinstitutionalization of mentally retarded persons in New York state: Final report*. New York: State University of New York at Buffalo, 1980.

Willer, B., & Intagliata, J. Comparison of family and group homes as alternatives to institutions. *American Journal of Mental Deficiency*, 1982, **86**, 588–595.

Willer, B., Intagliata, J., & Wicks, N. Return of retarded adults to natural families: Issues and results. In R. H. Bruininks, C. E. Meyers, B. B. Sigford, & K. C. Lakin (Eds.), *Deinstitutionalization and community adjustment of mentally retarded people*. American Association on Mental Deficiency, Monograph No. 4, 1981.

Wilmarth, A. W. Report of the committee on feeble-minded and epileptic. *Proceedings of the National Conference on Charities & Corrections*, 1902. P. 160.

Windle, C. Prognosis of mental subnormals. *American Journal of Mental Deficiency*, 1962, **66** (Monogr. Suppl.), 1–80.

Wolfensberger, W. *The principle of normalization in human services*. Toronto: National Institute on Mental Retardation, 1972.

Wolfensberger, W. The origin and nature of our institutional models. In R. B. Kugel & W. A. Shearer (Eds.), *Changing patterns in residential services for the mentally retarded* (rev. ed.). Washington, D.C.: U.S. Govt. Printing Office, 1976.

Wolfensberger, W. (Ed.), *Training Institute Publication Series*, 1982, **2**(2), 14.

Wolfensberger, W., & Glenn, L. *PASS 3: Program analysis of service systems: Field manual*. Toronto: National Institute on Mental Retardation, 1975.

Yankelovich, D. Two truths: The view from the social sciences. In D. M. Borchert & D. Stewart (Eds.), *Being human in a technological age*. Athens, Ohio: Univ. Press, 1979. Pp. 89–105.

Zitske, J., & Hallgren, B. *Life in limbo: A report on people with disabilities in nursing homes*. Madison, Wisconsin: Wisconsin Coalition for Advocacy, 1980.

Zober, M. A. *Alternative public intervention strategies affecting mentally retarded persons in the United States*. Paper presented at the annual meeting of the American Association on Mental Deficiency, San Francisco, May 1980.

Autonomy and Adaptability in Work Behavior of Retarded Clients

JOHN L. GIFFORD,* FRANK R. RUSCH,*
JAMES E. MARTIN,[†] AND DAVID M. WHITE[‡]

*DEPARTMENT OF SPECIAL EDUCATION AND [†]DEPARTMENT OF PSYCHOLOGY
UNIVERSITY OF ILLINOIS AT URBANA–CHAMPAIGN
CHAMPAIGN, ILLINOIS
AND
[†]DEPARTMENT OF SPECIAL EDUCATION
SCHOOL OF EDUCATION
UNIVERSITY OF COLORADO AT COLORADO SPRINGS
COLORADO SPRINGS, COLORADO

I. INTRODUCTION

That significant advances have been made to expand the concept of employability to include persons with obvious disabilities cannot be disputed.

INTERNATIONAL REVIEW OF RESEARCH IN
MENTAL RETARDATION, Vol. 12

This expanded concept has resulted from advances in training technology, litigation and legislation, and substantial documentation of the variables positively affecting community adjustment. Although residential-related variables have been the focus of the vast majority of research in the area of the deinstitutionalizaion process, employment-related variables have been regarded as important to long-term community adjustment.

Employment-related variables that have been the focus of recent research include reasons why mentally retarded individuals lose their jobs (Greenspan & Shoultz, 1981; Greenspan, Shoultz, & Weir, 1981), what behaviors are considered critical for competitive employment (Rusch, Schutz, & Agran, 1982), and what setting should be utilized to best instruct mentally retarded adults to acquired entry level work behavior (Rusch, 1983). A growing area of concern has been the investigation of procedures that promote response maintenance. This latter area of concern has risen in importance as we recognize that the sheltered workshop is an ineffectual model for promoting one's transition from sheltered to nonsheltered, competitive environments (Rusch & Mithaug, 1980).

In this article, a framework is proposed upon which a systematic technology for the vocational training of mentally retarded individuals[1] may be based. Current deficiencies in sheltered workshop training programs can be attributed to a lack of identified procedures to promote employability (Pomerantz & Marholin, 1977; Whitehead, 1979) and to existing practices that encourage workers' dependence upon training personnel (Gold, 1973, 1975; Martin, 1980). This article focuses upon the work behavior literature as it pertains to the maintenance of behavior in transitional employment efforts, i.e., investigations of best practices for advancing people from sheltered workshops to competitive employment in nonsheltered contexts. Following a review of recent developments in the work behavior literature, a theoretical framework is proposed that identifies two categories of behavior required in competitive employment: autonomy and adaptability. This framework is offered to suggest ways to generate, combine, and implement training strategies systematically, and to provide direction for future research on maintenance programming.

II. DEFICIENCIES IN CURRENT VOCATIONAL TRAINING APPROACHES

Many adults can become productive, contributing members of our society rather than nonproductive, costly wards of the government (Martin, Schneider, Rusch, & Geske, 1982). Ideally, these individuals should progress

[1]Throughout this article, individuals, persons, etc., should be considered to be diagnosed as mentally retarded unless otherwise specified (e.g., physically handicapped, nonhandicapped).

toward employment objectives that prepare them to participate to their fullest potential. Unfortunately, the majority of these adults are currently unemployed or underemployed in day-care, work activity, and sheltered workshop settings (Whitehead, 1979). Examination of the procedures used by the sheltered workshop, the predominant setting for vocational training of mentally retarded persons, can help to explain why few workers attain their vocational promises.

Upon referral to a sheltered workshop, an individual is typically evaluated for 90 to 120 days to determine his/her work potential (Menchetti, Rusch, & Owens, 1983). Based upon this evaluation, the individual is either placed into work activity, extended sheltered employment, or transitional employment programs. Individuals whose production rate is 25% that of the normal workforce qualify for work activity programs. Extended sheltered employment is available for individuals whose production rate exceeds that of those in work activity programs but who are believed incapable of attaining the skill levels or independence required in the community. *Transitional employment,* the process of training skills needed for competitive employment, is available only to those individuals with the highest vocational potential. Ideally, upon completion of transitional employment training, an individual leaves the sheltered environment for employment in the competitive labor market.

Unfortunately, transition to competitive employment is atypical, due to deficiencies in existing vocational training programs. Typical sheltered workshop staff lack knowledge of what skills should be trained, how best to train these skills, and how best to structure their programs to facilitate movement toward nonsheltered, competitive employment (Gold, 1975; Pomerantz & Marholin, 1977; Rusch, 1983). Sheltered workshops traditionally rely upon staff who have little knowledge about the instructional technology or industrial design necessary in developing an individual's potential for employment (Pomerantz & Marholin, 1977; Whitehead, 1979). Thus, the primary method of training, supervision with vague instructions and occasional prompts to stay on task, further encourages dependence upon sheltered placement and emphasizes working on overly simplified tasks, rather than developing marketable work skills (Gold, 1973, 1975; Martin, 1980).

Rusch and Mithaug (1980), in their interpretation of Department of Labor (Whitehead, 1979) data, indicated that persons placed from sheltered workshops into competitive employment are generally "work ready" upon entering the sheltered workshop. Rusch and Mithaug suggest that individuals who lack survival skills do not acquire them in the typical sheltered workshop program. They assert that unless the existing vocational training system is modified to include community-based, transitional programs for the development of social and vocational survival skills, most individuals in sheltered workshops will remain relatively nonproductive and dependent upon state and federal welfare.

III. A NEW APPROACH TO TRANSITIONAL EMPLOYMENT

Recently, a number of attempts have been made to mitigate the difficulties inherent in transitional employment. Bates and Pancsofar (1983), Mithaug (1981), Schutz and Rusch (1982), Rusch and Mithaug (1980), Rusch (1983), Rusch and Schutz (1981), and Wehman (1981) have provided transitional employment models making it possible for hundreds of adults, previously regarded as unemployable by existing rehabilitation standards, to become employed in the community as productive members of the work force (cf. Martin, 1980). In this model the community is first *surveyed* to identify possible job placements and their associated social and vocational survival skills (Rusch, 1979a). Next, *community-based, (nonsheltered) training sites* are established within actual community work settings. Third, the individual is trained in the community work setting (i.e., the nonsheltered training site) and then *placed into a targeted job* within a 6-month period. Finally, *training and long-term follow-up of decreasing intensity* is provided to facilitate the maintenance of acquired skills, in addition to training skills unique to the new employment site. By addressing the transition from sheltered to competitive employment, this model offers the advocacy and coordination necessary to provide the opportunity for vocational training and, ultimately, community placement and adjustment. However, this model is relatively new, and the best practices to use to facilitate individuals' participation in society must still be delineated. A review of recent advances in vocational training procedures is followed by our proposed theoretical framework designed to unify established research findings, as well as to guide future research needed to advance a transitional employment approach to competitive employment.

IV. EFFECTIVE STRATEGIES FOR MAINTAINING VALUED WORK BEHAVIOR

A very recent trend in the work behavior literature has been the investigation of strategies for use in training adults in competitive employment settings (Connis, 1979; Connis & Rusch, 1980; Cuvo, Leaf, & Burakove, 1978; Rusch, 1979b; Rusch, Connis, & Sowers, 1979; Schutz, Rusch, & Lamson, 1979; Sowers, Rusch, Connis, & Cummings, 1980). These studies are distinct from previous work behavior studies in that the problems of maintenance (durability) and generalization (transfer) have been addressed. These issues are defined as the degree to which behaviors are maintained once formal training (intervention) is terminated, and the extent to which newly acquired behavior generalizes to extratraining settings, people, and behaviors (Stokes & Baer, 1977), respectively. Historically, the issues of maintenance and generalization have been largely neglected because it has been presumed that behaviors changed via intervention programs adapt to the natural contingencies of reinforcement and, thus, are maintained and/or transferred to novel environments (see, for example, Allyon & Azrin, 1968). Today it is widely recognized that maintenance and generalization do not occur automatically, but that procedures ensuring their operation must be built directly into the behavior change program (Baer, Wolf, & Risley, 1968; Kazdin & Bootzin, 1972; Kazdin & Craighead, 1973; Kazdin & Polster, 1973; Marholin, Siegel, & Phillips, 1976; O'Leary & Drabman, 1971; Rusch & Schutz, 1981; Stokes & Baer, 1977; Walker & Buckley, 1972).

Despite the obvious importance of maintenance and generalization, these topics have until recently received very little attention in the field of vocational rehabilitation (Rusch & Schutz, 1981). Research appearing to date in the work behavior literature has focused primarily upon demonstrating that adults are capable of acquiring specific task-related skills and on improving their production performance (Bellamy, 1976; Bellamy, Horner, & Inman, 1979; Rusch, Schutz, & Heal, 1983). Yet, in order to facilitate the movement of individuals from sheltered to competitive employment, both maintenance and generalization must be systematically explored. This section reviews all representative studies reported in the work behavior literature that reflect efforts to identify parameters facilitating the maintenance of vocational and social survival skills (Rusch, 1979a). Undeniably, transfer of training is centrally important when considering extratraining placement; however, the scope of this chapter is limited largely to maintenance—one form of generalization. The literature review of strategies for achieving improved maintenance of vocational skills includes (1) traditional training methods, (2) sequential-withdrawal and partial-withdrawal designs, (3) self-control procedures, and (4) self-verbalization and mediation techniques. Following this review, a theoretical framework is presented to unify current findings and suggest additional maintenance strategies.

A. Traditional Behavior Change Procedures

The majority of maintenance studies have incorporated externally produced cues, where cues are generated and managed by a change agent (e.g., trainer, co-worker, supervisor). A few of these studies, while not addressing the issue of maintenance directly, have incorporated short periods of observation following training to assess whether behavioral changes have endured. For example, Schutz, Jostes, Rusch, and Lamson (1980) used contingent preinstruction with two moderately mentally retarded workers to acquire sweeping and mopping skills. Contingent preinstruction, which consisted of verbal directions to correct an error, was administered by trainers whenever a completed task component was unacceptable. Training procedures resulted in acceptable performance on seven out of seven tasks. Follow-up probes over a 3-month period indicated that sweeping and mopping performance was maintained at the same level demonstrated during acquisition criterion (i.e., seven out of seven tasks performed acceptably).

Matson and Martin (1979) examined a social learning approach to improve production rates and various social skills of severely mentally retarded adults. Prior to starting work, seven workshop clients were required to engage in a discussion regarding work behavior. Staff contingently praised various aspects of the previous day's performance across each target behavior. Additionally, information concerning how to improve the behaviors was provided verbally and through role playing. The social skill training improved all 12 target behaviors. Representative treatment effects included 25–50% improvement in work skills and 100–400% decrease in occurrence of behaviors incompatible with work skills, such as "eyes off task." Four weeks after training was terminated the target behaviors were assessed across 3 consecutive days. The follow-up probes indicated that the behaviors had maintained in the absence of the social skills training package.

Compliant work behavior of a moderately mentally retarded kitchen laborer employed in a nonsheltered vocational setting was increased and maintained in a study reported by Rusch and Menchetti (1981). Prior to externally imposed intervention, the worker responded inconsistently to co-workers' requests for assistance. Following two practice sessions on how to respond appropriately to co-worker requests, and being suspended and sent home in one instance, the worker complied appropriately to all subsequent co-worker requests. Following day-by-day data collection, his performance level remained high during the follow-up checks conducted over a 10-week period.

Six adolescents in a class for mildly and moderately mentally retarded students were trained in janitorial skills in a study by Cuvo *et al.* (1978). External change agents utilized a training package comprised of various levels of instructional assistance in conjunction with the administration of primary reinforcers. Immediately upon introduction of the training package, all cleaning tasks improved across both the men's and women's bathroom. Four postchecks over a 2-week period, conducted after training, indicated that the acquired skills were maintained.

Although technically not a maintenance study, Bellamy, Inman, and Yeates' (1978) investigation of cable harness production rates by three severely mentally retarded adults is important because performance was measured over an 18-month period. Generally, the short duration of most work behavior studies has precluded the demonstration of sustained improvement in work performance. In this study, the experimenters sought to utilize a supervision method that could be adopted by employers. Specifically, a timer contingency was used to differentially reward production rates. This intervention enabled two of the three workers to produce at or very near industrial standards, some 12–18 months after acquisition was initiated. One omission by the study was failure to assess performance in the absence of the timer. If performance would not maintain in the absence of the timer contingency, workers whose employers felt timers were inappropriate might regress to baseline.

Gold (1972) examined the retention of vocational skills trained in sheltered environments via intensive, externally generated cue procedures. One year after acquisition, significant retention of bicycle brake assembly skills was noted in workers previously trained with redundant relevant cues to a rigorous performance criterion. High retention levels were observed despite lack of practice and the absence of the redundant cues employed initially during acquisition. However, careful documentation of work experiences between acquisition criterion and the retention test was not kept. Thus, it is quite possible that subsequent training, practice, and the interaction of other historical factors may have accounted in part for these high retention rates.

Several investigators have also addressed the issue of fading extrinsic reinforcement, instructional cues, and bringing work behavior under the control schedules of reinforcement existing in targeted, posttraining environments (Crosson, 1969; Rusch et al., 1979). For example, Rusch et al. (1979) trained a mildly mentally retarded woman to work continuously throughout a 6-hour day in a restaurant setting. The results of this investigation suggested that a combination of praise and feedback (token points) for continuous work and response cost (loss of points) for discontinuous work resulted in maximum work performance as compared to praise or praise and feedback without response cost. Data collected following the gradual withdrawal of the major training components indicated that these response gains were maintained. Further, the results indicated that work performance maintained following an extension of the daily token–point exchange ratio to weekly exchanges and, finally, to a weekly paycheck. The difficulties of traditional behavior change procedures are exemplified by the Bellamy et al. (1978) investigation which did not explicitly bring work behavior under the control of stimuli and reinforcers common to the workplace. Without explicitly planning the transition to naturally occurring cues and reinforcers, maintenance of these behaviors is jeopardized. In contrast, the Rusch *et al.* (1979) gradual transition from a daily token-point exchange to weekly exchanges, and finally, to a weekly paycheck, is an example of a carefully planned transition from trainer produced to naturally occurring reinforcers.

B. Systematic Withdrawal of Treatment Components

Certainly, all of the studies discussed thus far are noteworthy in that the methodologies utilized are pertinent to maintenance. However, few of these studies were specifically designed to program for long-term maintenance. Because most of these studies utilized treatment "packages," the need also exists to isolate which components contribute most to maintenance. Unfortunately, such analyses have decreased in the applied literature (Hayes, Rincover, & Solnick, 1981). Exceptions include research reported by Rusch and his colleagues. For example, as indicated above, Rusch *et al.* (1979) employed a sequential-withdrawal design in a study that utilized the combined effects of praise, tokens, and response cost to increase a single subject's time spent working in a restaurant setting. Once experimental control was established relative to the three combined treatment components, a sequential-withdrawal of single components was initiated, i.e., individual components comprising the larger token reinforcement program were withdrawn one at a time with the effect of the withdrawal on performance assessed. Vogelsberg and Rusch (1979) utilized a partial-withdrawal design within a multiple-baseline framework while training three severely mentally retarded adolescents to cross intersections. The experimenters withdrew one component (feedback) from one of the subjects, which resulted in a loss of appropriate looking responses. These data strongly suggested that a complete loss of acquired looking response in all subjects would result if the feedback component was similarly withdrawn from each. Therefore, after the withdrawn component was reinstated and the performance level reestablished with the original subject, all subjects in this study were required to model the performance of a second trainer in order to promote maintenance. Vogelsberg and Rusch's (1979) study demonstrates the value of the partial-withdrawal design in predicting potential maintenance failures before they occur.

C. Self-Control Procedures

Behaviorists have contributed to an understanding of self-control that suggests much human behavior appearing to be internally directed is actually controlled by environmental events (Kanfer & Karoly, 1972). Though internal processes are often suggested to explain their occurrence, self-control behaviors remain under the control of reinforcement, even though these stimuli may sometimes be covert and relatively independent of externally occurring consequences (Bandura, 1969). Self-control can facilitate the generalization of behavior in natural settings where systematically imposed external controls are not feasible (Atthowe, 1973; Bandura, 1969; Gardner, 1977; Marholin *et al.*, 1976; O'Leary & O'Leary, 1976) or desirable (Kanfer & Phillips, 1970). Mentally retarded persons, however, appear deficient in mediational self-control processes in that their behaviors often fail to meet environmental demands unless they are under external control (Gardner, 1977). Consequently, these individuals need to be explicitly trained to use self-control procedures (Gardner, 1977; Rusch & Schutz, 1981), thereby attaining internal control via external control procedures (O'Leary & O'Leary, 1976).

Self-control has been defined as a process in which an individual's response alters the probability of the occurrence of a subsequent response (Skinner, 1974). Kazdin's (1980) definition of self-control includes the additional concept of intention: "those behaviors a person deliberately undertakes to achieve self-selected outcomes" (p. 248). Though minor differences exist with respect to the definition of self-control, numerous authors agree that such procedures can be used profitably with mentally retarded individuals. Rimm and Masters (1979), for example, suggest that self-control procedures are likely to be effective with individuals of almost any intellectual level. Shapiro (1981) and Mahoney and Mahoney (1976) point out the efficacy of self-control procedures in promoting an individual's independence. Self-control procedures are also recommended for enhancing the acquisition and maintenance of behaviors required in an increasingly complex society (Kurtz & Neisworth, 1976).

After an examination of the self-control research literature, Kurtz and Neisworth (1976) determined that self-monitoring, self-reinforcement, and antecedent cue regulation strategies were especially useful. *Self-monitoring* refers to initial awareness of the occurrence or nonoccurrence of a behavior, followed by the recording or reporting of that behavior (Nelson, 1977; Shapiro, 1981). *Self-reinforcement* involves the self-determination and self-administration of reinforcement (Jones, Nelson, & Kazdin, 1977). Finally, *antecedent cue regulation* limits the range of discriminative stimuli controlling the desired behavior, and might incorporate procedures such as the use of picture cues (Connis, 1979; Martin, Rusch, James, Decker, & Trtol, 1982; Wacker & Berg, 1983) Use of these strategies is most promising to promote the maintenance of independent behavior, since mentally retarded individuals would be able to evaluate and report their own behavior, manage self-rewards, and attend to antecedent cues.

Recently, a small body of research has emerged concerning the use of self-control strategies for facilitating the acquisition and maintenance of work behavior. The ability to determine and administer one's own reinforcers was examined by Wehman, Schutz, Bates, Renzaglia, and Karan (1978) in three case studies. Two of the studies compared the effects of external, self-administered, and self-determined reinforcement upon the work production rates of three adults in a sheltered workshop setting. In the first study a severely mentally retarded adult was introduced to external, self-administered, and, finally, self-determined reinforcement in a sequential manner. The results indicated an increase in work production rates with the introduction of each new reinforcement strategy. Interestingly, self-determined reinforcement produced the highest level of production.

In the second study, a mildly mentally retarded adult was exposed to similar reinforcement conditions. As in the first study, self-administered and self-determined reinforcement were more effective than external reinforcement, with self-determined reinforcement being the most effective in increasing production rates. The third study compared the effects of noncontingent, externally administered, and self-administered reinforcement upon a profoundly mentally retarded individual's production of floor pulleys. Unlike the other two studies, external reinforcement was the most effective strategy, followed by self-administered, then noncontingent reinforcement. However, this last study may not have been directly comparable to the earlier two studies. It differed in that a liberal definition of self-administered reinforcement was used, and the individual's level of mental retardation was more severe. Since some minimal level of cognitive ability is required for self-administered and self-determined reinforcement, this subject's cognitive deficit may explain failure to replicate.

Helland, Paluck, and Klein (1976) compared the effect of self-reinforcement and external reinforcement on workshop task production. Twelve mildly and moderately mentally retarded young adults were divided into two groups. Individuals in the self-reinforcement group were trained to compliment themselves and to select a reinforcer upon completion of collating 10 sets of paper. The individuals in the external reinforcement group were given a reinforcer and praised following every set completed. Analysis of the results indicated that both reinforcement conditions significantly improved performance, and that self-reinforcement was as effective as external reinforcement. This finding is especially noteworthy since the self-reinforcement group members were free of external supervision.

In a more sophisticated study involving complex vocational tasks in a competitive employment site, Connis (1979) examined the effects of sequential pictorial cues, self-recording, and praise on the sequencing of job tasks. Utilizing antecedent cue regulation, four mildly to moderately mentally retarded adults were sequentially introduced to the use of picture schedules and self-recording. Each subject's picture schedule depicted his or her assigned tasks. The results indicated that use of picture schedules combined with self-recording enabled subjects to successfully sequence their job tasks. Further, withdrawal of picture cue training resulted in continued high levels of independent task change. The self-directed use of sequenced photographs in conjunction with other treatment approaches appeared to enable the subjects to successfully maintain the behavior independent of external supervision.

Finally, Sowers *et al.* (1980) trained time management in a vocational setting by also employing self-control strategies. Three adults, ranging from mildly to moderately mentally retarded, were trained in a competitive employment site to go to and return from lunch and breaks on time. After an initial baseline period, preinstruction in time management, instructional feedback, and the use of a pictorial time card (an antecedent cue regulation procedure) were introduced. This self-control training package enabled the individuals to quickly learn to manage their time. When preinstruction and instructional feedback were sequentially withdrawn, acquired time management skills maintained, under the self-directed use of the pictorial time cards.

The success of the last two efforts in producing and maintaining vocational skill speaks to the need for the sophisticated use of combined strategies in facilitating maintenance. The use of self-control within the context of a withdrawal procedure must be noted as particularly suited to promote the maintenance of learned skills. After control over behavior has been established, movement to increased levels of self-control and gradual withdrawal of treatment components can successfully facilitate maintenance of behavior in the targeted natural setting.

D. Self-Verbalization and Mediation Techniques

Blackwood (1972) has suggested that speech is a verbal chaining process that produces both discriminative stimuli and conditioned reinforcers. Consequently, self-verbalizations should modify motor responses through "mediating between stimulus situation and target behavior" (Bornstein & Quevillon, 1976, p. 179). Since the pioneering work of Meichenbaum and Goodman (1969a,b, 1971) in establishing verbally mediated self-control through cognitive self-instructions with impulsive children, a number of articles have appeared in this area (see Goetz & Etzel, 1978; Israel, 1978; O'Leary & Dubey, 1979; Rosenbaum & Drabman, 1979, for excellent reviews).

According to Karlan (1980), research on self-instruction as a means to modify behavior focused initially only upon changing verbal behavior. Subsequently, individuals were trained directly to self-instruct as a means to modify target behavior. These first two approaches assumed a direct relationship between what was said and what was done. More recently, research has examined the relationship between, and the procedures used to develop, correspondence between what a person says and actually does (cf. Karlan & Rusch, 1982). However, the research literature has to date primarily examined self-regulation of internal verbal stimuli with children and adults of normal intelligence (Burgio, Whitman, & Johnson, 1980). Fortunately, a small but growing body of similar research has addressed mentally retarded individuals in work settings. The remainder of the present section will examine these investigations.

Recently, Rusch, Morgan, Riva, and Martin (1984) examined the effects of self-instruction with mildly and moderately mentally retarded adults who were competitively employed. Two components of this study were unique. First, massed trial self-instruction periods (Bornstein & Quevillon, 1976), rather than the customary spaced practice trials (Meichenbaum & Goodman, 1971) were used. Second, performance of nonhandicapped co-workers was utilized to validate treatment goals and procedures. During baseline the percentage of 10-second intervals spent working was assessed for both groups of workers. Massed trial self-instruction then took place, followed by maintenance assessments of the acquired skills. Each individual was separately trained on different days, during two 30-minute sessions before lunch and dinner service periods. "Traditional" self-instructional training procedures were repeated during these training periods. The results indicated that prior to massed self-instruction training the two handicapped individuals were working an average of 48 and 60% of the intervals, respectively. Their co-workers were working well above this level. After the massed self-instruction training, the handicapped individuals either equaled or surpassed co-worker performance levels.

In another study conducted at a competitive employment site, Crouch, Rusch, and Karlan (1983) investigated whether reinforcement of verbal statements would produce changes in speed of task completion. Three employees had been taking more time in completing certain tasks than allowed by their kitchen managers. Additionally, comparative validation data (Rusch & Mithaug, 1980) indicated that nonhandicapped co-workers were completing the tasks faster. Following a baseline condition, each worker received co-worker prompts regarding how to use a wrist watch to complete tasks on time. Prompting was found to increase one worker's speed in setting up the lunch line above the manager-identified standard and near that of his nonhandicapped co-workers; it had no effect on the remaining subject's speed. Next, the three employees were individually prompted to say when they would start and complete their task by describing how their watch or clock would look when they began. Also, at the halfway point of their task, each was instructed to say when they would finish. Following each time related statement (*say*), the person was verbally praised. This second procedure resulted in two employees increasing their time to that above the standard and slightly above that of co-workers. However, with this intervention, the third employee still failed to meet the time standard established by the management, although he did work as fast as his co-workers. Even the addition of a phase that would have enabled him to be reinforced for completing the task with 5 additional minutes did not produce the desired result. It is noteworthy that, during this phase, the third employee never finished within 25 minutes to be reinforced. Eventually the kitchen manager raised the time standard by 5 minutes, which resulted in this employee finishing on time. The results of Crouch *et al.*'s study suggest that the reinforce–say procedure was generally effective in increasing task speed. Also, this study highlights two important points. First, in order to reinforce correspondence between saying and doing the person must initially be able to perform the task to criterion. In this study, the third worker simply did not finish in time to be reinforced. Second, the use of co-worker data resulted in a standard being changed that would otherwise have arbitrarily constrained the reinforcement schedule of one employee.

E. Summary

The present section has summarized strategies utilizing externally and internally generated cues to promote work maintenance. Although both strategies are of value, external cue strategies contain certain limitations. One problem associated with the external control approach is that it may paradoxically preclude development of self-directed behaviors (Kazdin, 1973; Zisfein & Rosen, 1973). Indeed, this deficit has been cited as a primary obstacle to the community integration process (Wehman, 1975). In addition, external control may fail to promote generalization of the newly acquired response over settings and time. Typically, adults are trained to acquire setting-specific skills (e.g., bus riding) under direct supervision and are expected to continue to perform the skill correctly without supervision and in different settings. That the majority fail to maintain such skills is commonplace and contributes to our definition of mental retardation (i.e., the failure to maintain use of externally generated cues in the everyday performance of adaptive behavior).

This limitation may be overcome by utilizing external strategies in conjunction with internal strategies to develop the necessary self-control to achieve maintenance. Karlan and Rusch (1982), for example, suggest the use of verbal statements as a "mediational" strategy. Karlan and Rusch suggest that a relation exists between what one says and what one does; this relation is strengthened if correspondence is reinforced. At this time, correspondence research has centered upon reinforcing the accurate reporting of doing (do–say sequence). No studies, apart from Crouch *et al.* (1982), have reported the value of the say-then-do sequence. It is possible that direct instruction on task-specific components (e.g., completing each step of one's work assignment in sequence) would lead to the production of valued work behavior. For instance, Leon and Pepe (1978) used a self-instruction strategy, termed response guidance, to teach mathematical computational skills in a resource teaching classroom. They observed that students improved their computational abilities on training tasks and generalized the use of the response guidance strategy to new, untreated arithmetic operations. Clearly, future research combining such external response guidance procedures (e.g., preinstruction and corrective feedback) and various existing self-control strategies is warranted.

To summarize, a growing body of work behavior research has begun to examine maintenance issues. Most of these studies have employed external change agents who have arranged antecedents or delivered consequences in order to change behavior. A few of these investigations have also assessed short-term maintenance through follow-up checks to suggest that target behaviors maintain once treatment is withdrawn. Recently, self-control strategies have been advanced as a means to facilitate maintenance. These procedures could enable individuals to manage those cues that, historically, have been externally controlled. Self-monitoring, self-reinforcement, and antecedent cue regulation are three self-control strategies that appear promising.

The implications of these self-control strategies for long-term, competitive employment are obvious. After external change agents introduce the self-control procedures to the workers, and train the workers in how to use these procedures, they could withdraw from the environment, and fade the treatment to allow independent use of self-control strategies. External control used to train self-control appears to be an excellent means to facilitate long-term maintenance of the wide variety of complex survival skills adults require to become independent.

V. A PROPOSED THEORETICAL FRAMEWORK

Applied research is most vulnerable to criticism in its ability to demonstrate maintenance and generalization of behavior once treatment is withdrawn. A powerful technology for behavior change has been built, and yet a technology to ensure that acquired skills endure beyond termination of training remains to be developed (Rusch & Schutz, 1981; Walker, 1979; Warren, Rogers-Warren, Baer, & Guess, 1980). Procedures for ensuring maintenance and generalization of behavioral changes are not necessarily equivalent to those procedures leading simply to acquisition. Consequently, a technology of maintenance and generalization must be built upon a new framework, incorporating traditional behavior change methods where they are appropriate, but in the main superseding these approaches.

Traditionally, generalization has been regarded as "absence of discrimination" (Bijou & Baer, 1961; Marholin et al., 1976). In contrast, Baer et al. (1968) avoided traditional laboratory conceptualizations when they stated, "A behavioral change may be said to have generality if it proves durable over time, if it appears in a wide variety of possible environments, or if it spreads to a wide variety of related behaviors" (p. 96). Baer and Wolf (1970) suggested that generality of behavior change occurs when behavior exhibited in one environment transfers to another environment.

The most comprehensive conceptual scheme for generalization, to date, has been developed by Drabman, Hammer, and Rosenbaum (1979). Drabman et al. (1979) considered Kazdin's (1975), O'Leary and O'Leary's (1976), and others' definitions of generalization simplistic and as excluding many important exemplars encountered in applied settings. They presented a classification scheme that possesses conceptual precision and explanatory power, but which has not yet been utilized in applied research. A conceptual framework was developed to identify 16 classes of generalization. The descriptive categories of generalization included generalization across time, nonredundant settings, behaviors, and subjects. The generalization classes produced were viewed as distinct, i.e., each generalization class represents a different treatment strategy. Table I clarifies each of these strategies by depicting whether treatment is present or absent (time), and whether the setting, behavior, and subject is the same for each of 16 generalization classes.

Each of the categories provides a concise means to identify a specific form of generalization. For instance, if none of the four categories differ from those in effect during treatment (including any experimenter controlled contingencies still intact beyond the formal treatment program) this class is termed *maintenance*. When behavioral changes endure in the treatment setting after program contingencies are withdrawn, this class is termed *time generalization*. When behavioral changes are demonstrated in a setting other than that in which training occurred, this class is termed *setting–time generalization*. The focus of the present chapter is upon the last two classes, time generalization and setting–time generalization, which in this article will be referred to as maintenance in keeping with the traditional definition (Rusch & Kazdin, 1981).

TABLE I
CLASSES OF GENERALIZATION

Generalization class	Time treatment Present	Time treatment Absent	Setting Same	Setting Different	Behavior Same	Behavior Different	Subject Same	Subject Different
Maintenance	X		X		X		X	
Subject generalization	X		X		X			X
Behavior generalization	X		X			X	X	
Subject–behavior generalization	X		X			X		X
Setting generalization	X			X	X		X	
Subject–setting generalization	X			X	X			X
Behavior–setting generalization	X			X		X	X	
Subject–behavior–setting generalization	X			X		X		X
Time generalization (no treatment)[a]		X	X		X		X	
Subject–time generalization		X	X		X			X
Behavior–time generalization		X	X			X	X	
Subject–behavior–time generalization		X	X			X		X
Setting–time generalization (no change agent)[a]		X		X	X		X	
Subject–setting–time generalization		X		X	X			X
Behavior–setting–time generalization		X		X		X	X	
Subject–behavior–setting–time generalizaion		X		X		X		X

[a]The classes of generalization examined in this article.

A. Vocational Training Goals

The goals of transitional employment programs can be considered along two dimensions, autonomy and adaptability of performance. *Autonomy* refers to the ability of a worker to perform vocational skills correctly with minimal supervision. *Adaptability* refers to the ability of a worker to perform vocational skills correctly across a range of environment contexts and task requirements. Table II displays hypothetical worker profiles along these two dimensions. Worker D represents a profile that is the objective of vocational training: maximal autonomy and adaptability. That is, Worker D remains on task without supervision and exhibits high skill transfer. Worker C displays a deficit in adaptability, Worker B a deficit in autonomy, and Worker A deficits in both autonomy and adaptability. Because this chapter emphasizes maintenance, autonomy will receive primary consideration, though adaptability will be discussed when pertinent. Autonomy is discussed in relation to the self-control literature, withdrawal strategies (Rusch & Kazdin, 1981), and to selected traditional behavioral change strategies. Adaptability is considered in relation to general case programming (Horner, Sprague, & Wilcox, 1982).

B. Autonomy

An employee's autonomy is a critical factor in job retention. As suggested in the literature review, self-control training techniques and systematic withdrawal procedures can promote autonomous work skills. As noted, self-con-

TABLE II
HYPOTHETICAL WORKER PROFILES ALONG THE DIMENSIONS OF AUTONOMY AND ADAPTABILITY

	Adaptability	
Autonomy	Minimal	Maximal

Minimal	Worker A
	Remains on task
	  only with supervision
	Transfers to new
	  tasks with difficulty
		Worker B
		Remains on task
		  only with supervision
		Transfers to new
		  tasks easily

Maximal	Worker C
	Remains on task
	  without supervision
	Transfers to new
	  tasks with difficulty
		Worker D
		Remains on task
		  without supervision
		Transfers to new
		  tasks easily

trol is "an individual's class of responses applied to the modifications of one's own specific behavior that is deemed 'maladaptive' or needing change" (Goetz & Etzel, 1978). In the following section, this definition of self-control is adopted and a more detailed examination of this concept is undertaken. In the subsequent section, systematic procedures for the withdrawal and reinstatement of treatment components are described. Finally, traditional behavior change strategies promoting autonomy are discussed.

1. SELF-CONTROL

Goetz and Etzel's (1978) definition of self-control centers upon a process in which a subject's own set of responses influences his/her behavior. In the context of employment, performance can be modified in three progressively higher levels of self-control—he/she can manage his/her own training procedures, select his/her own training procedures, or select his/her own training goals. In general, familiarity with procedures involved in a lower level of self-control is necessary for progression to a higher level. For example, an employee must have experience managing several different antecedent cues before being able to select among optional cue presentation procedures. To date, only the self-management of training procedures has been investigated among mentally retarded persons.

In self-management of training procedures, the subject regulates antecedent cues (Connis, 1979; Martin *et al.,* 1982), monitors his/her own performance (Nelson, 1977; Shapiro, 1981), and/or administers his/her own reinforcement (Jones *et al.,* 1977). That is, the employee can manage his/her own antecedents, responses, consequences, or any combination of these three facets of the training procedure. As the employee becomes proficient at managing his/her own training procedures, s/he can proceed toward self-selection of training procedures. As noted before, the self-management of training procedures is most powerful when combined with a withdrawal procedure.

2. WITHDRAWAL OF TREATMENT COMPONENTS

Rusch and Kazdin (1981) proposed three designs for selectively withdrawing training components after behavior control is achieved so as to facilitate and assess maintenance: (1) sequential-withdrawal, (2) partial-withdrawal, and (c) partial–sequential-withdrawal. A sequential-withdrawal design consists of the gradual withdrawal of selected components of the training package in consecutive experimental phases to determine if behavior is maintained. If, during any phase, performance decreases below acceptable levels, a treatment component (or all of the components) is replaced; when the behavior is built back to an acceptable level, a different order of withdrawal is instigated.

As cited previously, the Rusch *et al.* (1979) study exemplifies the sequential-withdrawal design. In their study, prompts and praise, tokens, and response cost comprised the treatment package used to increase the subject's time spent working in a restaurant setting within an ABABCBC design (see Fig. 1). Once experimental control was established relative to the three combined treatment components, a sequential-withdrawal of single components was initiated. First, response cost contingencies were no longer in effect each day; rather, they were in effect only on predetermined, randomly selected days. Second, a four-step withdrawal of the token economy was initiated. In a final phase, praise was withdrawn. Within each withdrawal phase no loss in acquired behavior was noted.

The partial-withdrawal design "consists of withdrawing a component of the intervention package or the total package from one of several different baselines (behaviors, persons, or settings) in a multiple-baseline design" (Kazdin, 1982, p. 215). In this design, the intervention is gradually withdrawn across different baselines. If withdrawing the intervention does not result in loss of the desired behavior, then the intervention can be withdrawn from other baselines as well. If the withdrawal results in a loss of behavior, the component(s) are replaced; following reinstatement to the original performance levels, different withdrawal procedures are attempted to obtain maintenance of performance.

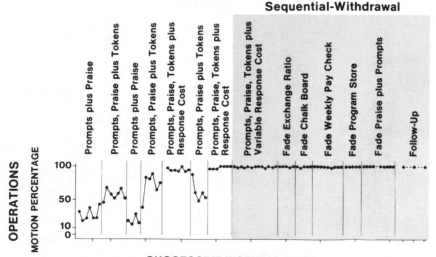

FIG. 1. Sequential-withdrawal assessment of maintenance of attending to task (from Rusch *et al.,* 1979).

Vogelsberg and Rusch's (1979) study demonstrates the value of the partial-withdrawal design in predicting potential maintenance failures before they occur. In their investigation, three severely mentally retarded individuals were trained to cross intersections. When one training component, feedback, was withdrawn from one of the subjects, approaching, stepping, and walking behaviors were maintained (see Fig. 2). However, a critical feature of crossing—looking—decreased in frequency. These data suggested that a loss in looking might have resulted for all subjects if a similar withdrawal were introduced for each. Therefore, the investigators undertook a different training strategy with the two remaining subjects. Behavioral rehearsal and a trainer model resulted in maintenance of each of the criterion behaviors in these two subjects. In addition, this revised strategy was applied to the first subject after successfully rebuilding the diminished looking skills, resulting in successful maintenance. With the partial-withdrawal design, either a single component, several, or all components of a training package are withdrawn from one of the baselines of a multiple-baseline design. This withdrawal strategy is an excellent means of determining what can happen if similar withdrawals are replicated across the remaining baselines. Once again, if the withdrawal results in loss of behavior, the components can be replaced; following reinstatement of the original performance levels, a different withdrawal order may be tried across the same or another baseline (subjects); or the same withdrawal could be replicated across another baseline.

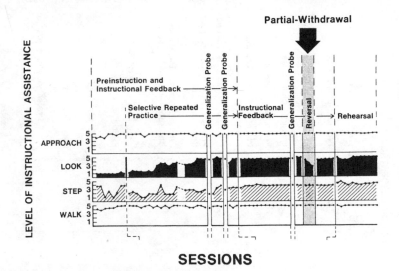

FIG. 2. Partial-withdrawal assessment of maintenance of intersection crossing skills (from Vogelsberg and Rusch, 1979).

Last, in a partial–sequential-withdrawal design, the two previous strategies are combined. First, all or part of a treatment package is withdrawn from one of the baselines (behaviors, persons, or settings) of a multiple-baseline design. If the behavior maintains, the withdrawal is advanced to include other components, or replicated across other baselines. If the behaviors do not maintain, however, the withdrawn components may be reintroduced simultaneously with the withdrawal of the same or different components across one or more of the other baselines.

Combining the partial and sequential-withdrawal designs allows for the orderly withdrawal of the various components of the treatment package in an effort to decrease the probability that subjects will discriminate the absence or presence of the contingencies. By combining the partial and sequential-withdrawal design strategies investigators can predict, with increasing probability, the extent to which they are controlling the treatment environment as the progression of withdrawals is extended to other behaviors, subjects, or settings. (Rusch & Kazdin, 1981, p. 136)

Martin's (1982) assessment of facilitation of meal preparation through the use of pictorial cues incorporated a partial–sequential-withdrawal design (see Fig. 3). Instructional feedback and preinstruction were included in the treatment package for the three subjects in the study. Following acquisition by the first subject, instructional feedback was withdrawn, followed by withdrawal of preinstruction. Each withdrawal was so successful that a more rapid withdrawal strategy was undertaken with the second subject. Simultaneous withdrawal of both instructional feedback and preinstruction resulted in a minimal loss in performance. A similarly rapid withdrawal strategy was utilized with the third subject. Not only was performance maintained, in some instances it improved, due in part to the reduction in behavioral outbursts triggered by trainer feedback.

Clearly, withdrawal methodology provides a flexible sequence of procedures for assessing maintenance. The successful implementation of withdrawal methodology is indicated by the presence or absence of change in the dependent measure. Although an a priori plan is needed, withdrawal methodology is "open ended" in the sense that change or lack of change in the dependent measure influences decisions with regard to the sequence of withdrawals. This methodology uses orderly withdrawal of training components to decrease the detection of the absence of those training components by the subject. In total, these designs can aid work behavior researchers to explore alternative means of terminating interventions without prolonged loss of desired behavior (Kazdin, 1982). In the next section, traditional behavior change methods are characterized. They, like withdrawal strategies, often exploit a gradual transition from training interventions to natural settings.

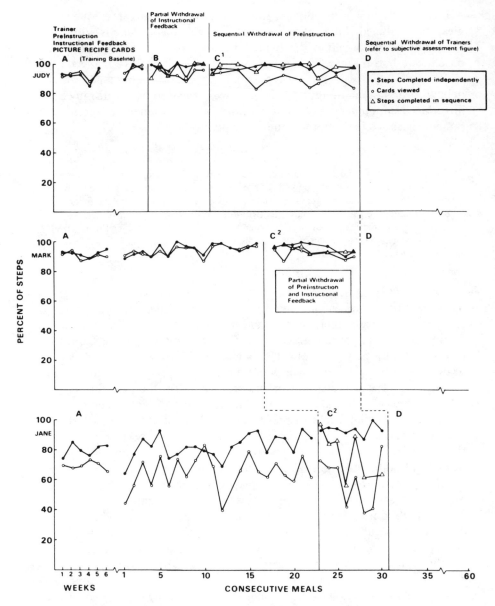

FIG. 3. Partial–sequential-withdrawal assessment of maintenance of meal preparation skills (from Martin, 1982).

3. TRADITIONAL BEHAVIOR CHANGE STRATEGIES

In addition to the self-control and component withdrawal procedures just discussed, several traditional behavior change strategies are effective in promoting maintenance. Essentially, these strategies have as their common aim the minimization of the difference between the training setting and the natural environment in which the behavior is ultimately to be maintained. A basic strategy is simply to design the training setting as similar as possible to the natural environment in which the behavior is to endure (O'Leary & O'Leary, 1976). A slight variant involves making gradual transitions in the training task until it is equivalent to the target task in the natural environment. The transitions can take place with respect to reinforcement schedules (Rusch *et al.*, 1979), discriminative stimuli, e.g., errorless learning (Terrace, 1963), or other aspects of the task.

Another method of achieving congruence between the training and maintenance settings is engineering the natural environment. For example, reinforcers delivered by the change agent in the training setting can be applied by significant others in the natural environment (Stokes & Baer, 1977), preserving the basic training procedure. Still another tactic that prepares the worker's transition from the training setting to the natural environment is rehearsal in the natural environment prior to termination of the training program (Marholin & Touchette, 1979). A final strategy, overlearning, can be used in conjunction with the minimization technique. To the extent that responses and response rules in the natural environment approximate those in the training setting, subjects' maintenance performance will profit from overlearning procedures (Atthowe, 1973; Gifford, Rusch, Martin, & Karlan, 1983; Sundel & Sundel, 1975).

Taken together, self-control techniques, selective withdrawal procedures, and traditional behavior change strategies comprise training approaches promoting autonomy of behavior. The following section will address the concern for adaptability of behavior. General case programming is discussed as a strategy particularly suited to promoting adaptability.

C. Adaptability

Employees must not only perform vocational skills correctly with minimal supervision in a setting similar to the training site, but they must also be able to function relatively independently across a wide range of environmental contexts and response requirements. General case programming (Horner *et al.*, 1982) suggests a technology to that end. As characterized by Horner *et al.* general case programming represents "behaviors performed by a teacher or trainer to increase the probability that skills learned in one training setting will be successfully performed with different target stimuli, and/or in different settings, from those used in training." The greatest impediment to success for many individuals in community educational and rehabilitational programs is insufficient generalization of newly acquired skills across tasks, settings, persons, and time (Barrett, 1977). As Baumeister (1969) suggested "It is one thing to show that well-defined response sequences can be shaped in a highly structured, controlled, and atypical environment and quite another matter to demonstrate that conditioning can produce permanent adaptive changes in complex areas of adjustment over a wide variety of environmental circumstances" (p. 50).

General case programming addresses these concerns in its systematic process of defining the instructional universe, selecting appropriate examples from that universe, and properly sequencing the examples to promote generalization of performance across varied target environments. Concepts central to general case programming are stimulus class and response class. A *stimulus class* refers to any group of stimuli that share a common set of stimulus characteristics. For example, when selecting an apple in a grocery store, an individual is to obtain an instance of the stimulus class "apple." All stimuli that do not fit within the "apple" stimulus class (e.g., oranges, tangerines) are outside the stimulus class. A *response class* is defined using similar criteria. "The primary factors determining a class of responses are that all instances of the class produce the same functional effect (i.e., produce the same outcome) and that all members of the class share common topographical characteristics" (Horner *et al.,* 1982, p. 67). For example, the response class "using a screwdriver to tighten a screw" is defined by a previously loose screw being tight and by the response topography required to achieve this outcome using a screwdriver. General case learning is achieved when a given stimulus class exhibits stimulus control over a given response class, i.e., any member of the stimulus class controls the appropriate member in the response class. Several considerations guide the definition of the instructional universe, selection of examples from that universe, and sequencing of the examples. These include providing sufficient variation within stimuli and response requirements so as not to train too narrowly. Control by irrelevant stimuli is reduced, and control by relevant stimuli is accentuated so that stimulus control is maximal.

Recently, Horner and McDonald (1982) compared single-instance and general case instruction in teaching four severely mentally retarded high school students the vocational skill of crimping and cutting electronic capacitors. A multiple-baseline mirror design was utilized in which each subject received baseline assessment, single-instance training, and finally, general case instruction (see Fig. 4). In this design, Student A entered single-instance instruction first, followed by Students B, C, and D, respectively. During general case instruction, the order was reversed, with Student D be-

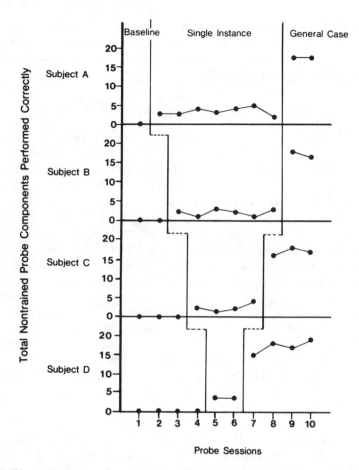

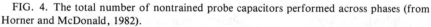

FIG. 4. The total number of nontrained probe capacitors performed across phases (from Horner and McDonald, 1982).

ing the first to receive the treatment. During each of the three phases, probe sessions were conducted on 20 types of capacitors on which students had received no instruction. The results indicated that general case instruction can be utilized successfully to train crimping and cutting of electronic capacitors as a functional vocational skill and that general case instruction is superior to single-instance training for promoting performance across nontrained examples. Further, errors following single-instance training are functionally related to the restricted range of training stimuli found within the single-instance training format. These results suggest the value of proper selection and sequencing of training examples to develop behavior change that is enduring and functional across varying environments. By promoting generalization across tasks, settings, supervisors, and other environmental factors, the general case approach is a powerful technique that can provide for greater adaptability by employees since each situational variation does not require additional training.

D. Overview of the Proposed Framework

In its broadest sense, our theoretical framework suggests a means for selecting strategies to facilitate autonomy or adaptability of work behavior. Thus far, strategies have been proposed to facilitate either autonomy or adaptability of performance, but not both. A study conducted by Wacker and Berg (1983) suggests a broader strategy. In this study, several strategies to promote autonomy of performance were combined with a generalization strategy. In a multiple-baseline design (across subjects and tasks), five moderately and severely retarded adolescents were first trained to use picture cues to guide their performance on complex assembly and packaging tasks. This was followed by training on two of the tasks themselves, using picture cue guidance. During training, modeling, verbal correction, and contingent praise were delivered. Following training, both maintenance and generalization were assessed (see Fig. 5). In the first phase (Posttest 1), subjects were tested on training tasks using picture prompts, but with modeling, verbal correction, and contingent praise withdrawn. Posttest 2 assessed subjects with the picture cues withdrawn as well. A third posttest phase, designated maintenance by Wacker and Berg, assessed subjects under the same conditions as Posttest 2, but 2 to 4 weeks later. Generalization testing was conducted by presenting novel tasks under the same conditions as subjects received in Posttest 1 and Posttest 2. Results indicated that picture prompts can be used successfully to promote acquisition, maintenance, and generalization of complex vocational tasks.

Although Wacker and Berg's (1983) study is interesting in its own right, it is presented primarily to demonstrate the manner in which strategies for facilitation of autonomy and adaptability can be combined. Wacker and Berg utilized three strategies that promote primarily autonomy of performance: external mediation, antecedent cue regulation, and sequential-withdrawal of the treatment package. The use of picture cues can be considered external mediation; the fact that the subjects learned to manage the picture cues themselves constitutes antecedent cue regulation; and the withdrawal of modeling, verbal correction, contingent praise, and the picture cues at different assessment points comprises a form of the sequential-withdrawal technique.

Additionally, Wacker and Berg attempted to facilitate adaptability of behavior by presenting training procedures that could be considered a

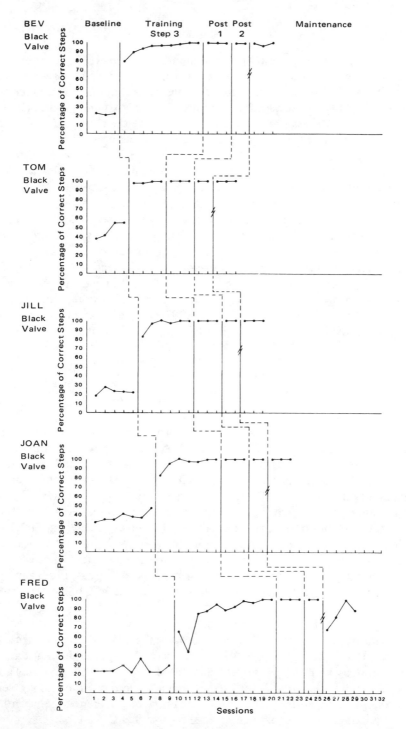

FIG. 5. Percentage of steps completed correctly on the black valve taks across phases (from Wacker and Berg, 1983).

rudimentary form of general case programming. In their training procedure, two different vocational tasks (e.g., valve assembly and circuit board assembly) were presented and their subsequent effect upon maintenance and generalization was assessed. By presenting multiple training examples, the authors promoted adaptability of performance by their subjects.

The complexity of the training and testing procedures found in Wacker and Berg's study suggests the value of a theoretical framework to guide and evaluate research on the maintenance and generalization of behavior. The present framework considers procedures utilizing self-control, withdrawal of treatment components, and traditional behavior change techniques attempting to reduce the difference between training settings and targeted natural environments, as strategies primarily promoting autonomy of performance. General case programming is the major strategy to promote adaptability of performance. To develop a truly effective technology for promoting autonomy and adaptability, each of the strategies suggested must be assessed alone and, more importantly, in optimal combination, as suggested by Wacker and Berg's (1983) study. The following section reexamines the work behavior literature previously presented in light of the proposed theoretical framework.

VI. GENERAL DISCUSSION

The current article has stressed the importance of the development of a technology for maintaining work behavior. A summary of the existing work behavior literature as it pertains to maintenance was presented, highlighting effective strategies. Further, a theoretical framework addressing maintenance and generalization of behavior was presented. In this framework, two overarching goals of transitional employment programs were identified, promotion of autonomy and adaptability. Under each category, relevant training strategies were discussed. Self-control procedures, withdrawal strategies, and certain traditional behavior change strategies were discussed under the category of autonomy of performance. General case programming was considered as a strategy promoting primarily adaptability of performance.

The proposed theoretical framework highlights certain characteristics of the literature on the maintenance of vocational skills. Of the maintenance studies cited earlier, only one (Wacker & Berg, 1983) combined a maintenance strategy with one promoting adaptability of performance (see Table III). The remaining studies utilized strategies selected from among self-control, withdrawal designs, and minimization of differences between the training setting and the targeted natural environment.

When the existing work behavior literature was examined in light of our

TABLE III
Strategies Utilized within Vocational Training Studies That Promote Worker Independence (Autonomy) and Performance (Adaptability)

Investigators	Autonomy			Adaptability
	Self-control	Withdrawal design	Traditional strategies	General case programming
Wehman et al. (1979)	X			
Helland et al. (1976)	X			
Connis (1979)	X	X		
Sowers et al. (1980)	X	X		
Rusch et al. (1979)		X	X	
Vogelsberg and Rusch (1979)		X		
Schutz et al. (1980)		X		
Matson and Martin (1979)			X	
Rusch and Menchetti (1981)			X	
Cuvo et al. (1978)			X	
Gold (1972)			X	
Crosson (1969)			X	
Gifford et al. (1983)			X	
Rusch et al (1983)	X			
Crouch et al. (1982)	X			
Horner and McDonald (1982)				X
Wacker and Berg (1983)	X	X		X

proposed theoretical framework, one fact became apparent. Work behavior research has made little use of multiple strategies to promote autonomy or adaptability of performance. Only Wacker and Berg (1983) combined strategies across the two categories (autonomy and adaptability). Aside from Wacker and Berg, only Connis (1979) and Sowers et al. (1980) have employed multiple strategies in their efforts. It cannot be taken as given, of course, that multiple strategies are superior to single strategies or fewer strategies in combination. However, since sophisticated strategy combinations have not yet been assessed systematically, their potential power remains unknown.

Only a few of the many possible strategy combinations have been attempted, indicating the potential for several productive lines of research. First, optimal combinations of strategies must be found. In addition, general combining rules must be determined to enable the selection of strategies appropriate to a given training setting and targeted natural environment. Only as these goals are approached will a systematic technology exist for maintaining valued work behaviors.

ACKNOWLEDGMENTS

This article was prepared with partial support by grants to the second author from the Graduate College, University of Illinois at Urbana—Champaign and from the Illinois Department of Public Aid.

REFERENCES

Atthowe, J. M. Behavior innovation and persistence. *American Psychologist,* 1973, **28,** 34–41.

Ayllon, T., & Azrin, N. H. *The token economy: A motivational system for therapy and rehabilitation.* New York: Appleton, 1968.

Baer, D. M., & Wolf, M. M. The entry into natural communities of reinforcement. In R. Ulrich, T. Stachnick, & J. Mabry (Eds.), *Control of human behavior* (Vol. 2). Glenview, Illinois: Scott, Foresman, 1970.

Baer, D. M., Wolf, M. M., & Risley, T. R. Some current dimensions of applied behavior analysis. *Journal of Applied Behavior Analysis,* 1968, **1,** 91–97.

Bandura, A. *Principles of behavior modification.* New York: Holt, 1969.

Barrett, B. H. Behavior analysis. In J. Wortis (Eds.), *Mental retardation and developmental disabilities: An annual review* (Vol. 9). New York: Brunner/Mazel, 1977.

Bates, P., & Pancsofar, E. Project EARN (Employment and Rehabilitation = Normalization): A competitive employment training program for severely disabled youth in the public schools. *Education and Treatment of Children,* 1983, in press.

Baumeister, A. A. More ado about operant conditioning—or nothing? *Mental Retardation,* 1969, **7,** 49–51.

Bellamy, G. T. Habilitation of the severely and profoundly retarded: A review of research on work productivity. In G. T. Bellamy (Ed.), *Habilitation of severely and profoundly retarded adults.* Eugene, Oregon: Research & Training Center in Mental Retardation, University of Oregon, 1976.

Bellamy, G. T., Horner, R. H., & Inman, D. P. *Vocational habilitation of severely retarded adults: A direct service technology.* Baltimore, Maryland: Univ. Park Press, 1979.

Bellamy, G. T., Inman, D. P., & Yeates, J. Workshop supervision: Evaluation of a procedure for production management with the severely retarded. *Mental Retardation,* 1978, **16,** 317–319.

Bijou, S. W., & Baer, D. M. *Child development, a systematic and empirical theory* (Vol. 1). New York: Appleton, 1961.

Blackwood, R. O. *Mediated self-control: An operant model of rational behavior.* Akron, Ohio: Exordium Press, 1972.

Bornstein, P., & Quevillon, R. The effects of a self-instructional package on overactive preschool boys. *Journal of Applied Behavior Analysis,* 1976, **9,** 179–188.

Brown, A. L. Knowing when, where, and how to remember: A problem in metacognition. In R. Glaser (Ed.), *Advances in instructional psychology* (Vol. 1). Hillsdale, New Jersey: Erlbaum, 1978.

Burgio, L. D., Whitman, T. L., & Johnson, M. R. A self-instructional package for increasing attending behavior in educable mentally retarded children. *Journal of Applied Behavior Analysis,* 1980, **13**, 443–459.

Connis, R. T. The effects of sequential cues, self-recording, and praise on the job task sequencing of retarded adults. *Journal of Applied Behavior Analysis,* 1979, **12**, 355–361.

Connis, R. T., & Rusch, F. R. Programming maintenance through sequential withdrawal of social contingencies. *Behavior Research of Severe Developmental Disabilities,* 1980, **1**, 249–260.

Crosson, J. E. A technique for programming sheltered workshop environments for training severely retarded workers. *American Journal of Mental Deficiency,* 1969, **73**, 814–818.

Crouch, K. P., Rusch, F. R., & Karlan, G. *Utilizing the correspondence training paradigm to decrease time spent completing vocational tasks.* (Submitted for publication, 1983).

Cuvo, A. J., Leaf, R. B., & Burakove, L. S. Teaching janitorial skills to the mentally retarded: Acquisition generalization and maintenance. *Journal of Applied Behavior Analysis,* 1978, **11**, 345–355.

Drabman, R. S., Hammer, D., & Rosenbaum, M. S. Assessing generalization in behavior modification with children: The generalization map. *Behavioral Assessement,* 1979, **1**, 203–219.

Gardner, W. I. *Learning and behavior characteristics of exceptional children and youth.* Boston, Massachusetts: Allyn & Bacon, 1977.

Gifford, J. L., Rusch, F. R., Martin, J. E., & Karlan, G. R. *Promoting vocational skills through attentional strategies.* The Fifteenth Annual AAMD Conference, Illinois Chapter, Homewood, Illinois, 1983.

Goetz, E. M., & Etzel, B. C. A brief review of self-control procedures: Problems and solutions. *Behavior Therapist,* 1978, **1**, 5–8.

Gold, M. Stimulus factors in skill training of the retarded on a complex assembly task: Acquisition, transfer, and retention. *American Journal of Mental Deficiency,* 1972, **76**, 517–526.

Gold, M. Research on the vocational rehabilitation of the retarded: The present, the future. In N. Ellis (Eds.), *International review of research in mental retardation* (Vol. VI). New York: Academic Press, 1973.

Gold, M. W. Vocational training. In J. Wortis (Ed.), *Mental retardation and developmental disabilities: An annual review* (Vol. 7), New York: Brunner/Mazel, 1975.

Greenspan, S., & Shoultz, B. Why mentally retarded adults lose their jobs: Social competence as a factor in work adjustment. *Applied Research in Mental Retardation,* 1981, **2**, 23–28.

Greenspan, S., Shoultz, B., & Weir, M. M. Social judgment and vocational adjustment of mentally retarded adults. *Applied Research in Mental Retardation,* 1981, **2**, 335–346.

Hayes, S. C., Rincover, A., & Solnick, J. V. The technical drift of applied behavior analysis. *Journal of Applied Behavior Analysis,* 1981, **13**, 275–285.

Helland, C. D., Paluck, R. J., & Klein, M. A comparison of self- and external reinforcement with the trainable mentally retarded. *Mental Retardation,* 1976, **14**, 22–23.

Horner, R. H., & McDonald, R. S. Comparison of single instance and general case instruction in teaching a generalized vocational skill. *Journal of the Association for the Severely Handicapped,* 1982, **7**, 7–20.

Horner, R. H., Sprague, J., & Wilcox, B. General case programming for community activities. In B. Wilcox & G. Bellamy (Eds.), *Design of high school programs for severely handicapped students.* Baltimore, Maryland: Brookes, 1982.

Israel, A. C. Some thoughts on correspondence between saying and doing. *Journal of Applied Behavior Analysis,* 1978, **11**, 271–276.

Jones, R. T., Nelson, R. E., & Kazdin, A. E. The role of external variables in self-reinforcement. *Behavior Modification,* 1977, **1**, 147–178.

Kanfer, F. H., & Karoly, P. Self-control: A behavioristic excursion into the lion's den. *Behavior Therapy,* 1972, **3,** 398–416.

Kanfer, F. H., & Phillips, J. S. *Learning foundations of behavior therapy.* New York: Wiley, 1970.

Karlan, G. Issues in communication research related to integration of the developmentally disabled adult. In A. Novak & L. Heal (Eds.), *Community integration of developmentally disabled individuals.* Baltimore, Maryland: Brookes, 1980.

Karlan, G. R., & Rusch, F. R. Correspondence between saying and doing: Some thoughts on defining correspondence and future directions for application. *Journal of Applied Behavior Analysis,* 1982, **15,** 156–162.

Kazdin, A. E. Role of instructions and reinforcement in behavior change in token reinforcement programs. *Journal of Educational Psychology,* 1973, **64,** 63–71.

Kazdin, A. E. *Behavior modification in applied settings.* Homewood, Illinois: Dorsey Press, 1975.

Kazdin, A. E. *Behavior modification in applied settings.* Homewood, Illinois: Dorsey Press, 1980 (revised).

Kazdin, A. E. *Single-case research designs: Methods for clinical and applied settings.* London and New York: Oxford Univ. Press, 1982.

Kazdin, A. E., & Bootzin, R. R. The token economy: An evaluation review. *Journal of Applied Behavior Analysis,* 1972, **5,** 343–372.

Kazdin, A. E., & Craighead, W. E. Behavior modification in special education. In L. Mann & D. A. Sabatino (Eds.), *The first review of special education* (Vol. 2). Philadelphia, Pennsylvania: Buttonwood Farms, 1973.

Kazdin, A. E., & Polster, R. Intermittent token reinforcement and response maintenance in extinction. *Behavior Therapy,* 1973, **4,** 386–391.

Kurtz, P. D., & Neisworth, J. T. Self-control possibilities for exceptional children. *Exceptional Children,* 1976, **42,** 212–217.

Leon, T. A., & Pepe, H. *Self-instructional training: Cognitive behavior modification as a resource room strategy.* (Final Report, DHEW, BEH Grant G007701991) Washington, D.C.: Government Printing Office, 1978.

Mahoney, M. J., & Mahoney, K. Self-control techniques with the mentally retarded. *Exceptional Children,* 1976, **42,** 338–339.

Marholin, D., Siegel, L. J., & Phillips, D. Transfer and treatment: A search for empirical procedures. In M. Hersen, R. M. Eisler, & P. M. Miller (Eds.), *Progress in behavior modification* (Vol. 3). New York: Academic Press, 1976. Pp. 293–343.

Marholin, D., & Touchette, P. E. The role of stimulus control and response consequences. In A. P. Goldstein & F. H. Kanfer (Eds.), *Maximizing treatment gains: Transfer enhancement psychotherapy.* New York: Academic Press, 1979.

Martin, J. E. Work productivity and the developmentally disabled. In J. A. Leach (Ed.), *Productivity in the workforce: A search for perspectives.* Office of Vocational Education Research, Department of Vocational and Technical Education, College of Education, University of Illinois, Champaign, 1980.

Martin, J. E. *Time-setting generalization assessment of mentally retarded adults acquired self-control in the preparation of complex meals after withdrawal of training components and trainers.* Unpublished doctoral dissertation. Department of Special Education, University of Illinois at Urbana-Champaign, 1982.

Martin, J. E., Rusch, F. R., James, V. L., Decker, P. J., & Trtol, K. A. The use of picture cues to establish self control in the preparation of complex meals by mentally retarded adults. *Applied Research in Mental Retardation,* 1982, **3,** 105–119.

Martin, J. E., Schneider, K. E., Rusch, F. R., & Geske, T. R. Training mentally retarded individuals for competitive employment: Benefits of transitional employment. *Exceptional Education Quarterly,* 1982, **3,** 58–66.

Matson, J., & Martin, J. A social learning approach to vocational training of the severely retarded. *Journal of Mental Deficiency Research,* 1979, **23**, 9-17.

Meichenbaum, D., & Goodman, J. The developmental control of operant motor responding by verbal operants. *Journal of Experimental Child Psychology,* 1969, **7**, 553-565. (a)

Meichenbaum, D., & Goodman, J. Reflection-impulsivity and verbal control of motor behavior. *Child Development,* 1969, **40**, 785-797. (b)

Meichenbaum, D. H., & Goodman, J. Training impulsive children to talk to themselves: A means of developing self-control, *Journal of Abnormal Psychology,* 1971, **77**, 115-126.

Menchott, B. M., Rusch, F. R., & Owen, S. D. Assessing the vocational needs of mentally retarded adolescents and adults. In J. L. Matson & S. E. Breuning (Eds.), *Assessing the mentally retarded.* New York: Grune & Stratton, 1983.

Mithaug, D. E. *Prevocational training for retarded students.* Springfield, Illinois: Thomas, 1981.

Nelson, R. E. Assessment and therapeutic functions of self-monitoring. In M. Hersen, R. M. Eisler, & P. M. Miller (Eds.), *Progress in behavior modification* (Vol. 5). New York: Academic Press, 1977. Pp. 263-308.

O'Leary, K. D., & Drabman, R. Token reinforcement programs in the classroom: A review. *Psychological Bulletin,* 1971, **75**, 379-398.

O'Leary, S. G., & Dubey, D. R. Applications of self-control procedures by children: A review. *Journal of Applied Behavior Analysis,* 1979, **12**, 449-465.

O'Leary, S. G., & O'Leary, K. D. Behavior modification in the school. In H. Leitenberg (Ed.), *Handbook of behavior modification and behavior therapy.* New York: Prentice-Hall, 1976.

Pomerantz, D., & Marholin, D. Vocational habilitation: A time for a change. In E. Sontag (Ed.), *Educational programming for the severely and profoundly handicapped.* Reston, Virginia: Council for Exceptional Children, Division on Mental Retardation, 1977.

Rimm, D. C., & Masters, J. C. *Behavior therapy: Techniques and empirical findings* (2nd ed.). New York: Academic Press, 1979.

Rosenbaum, M. S., & Drabman, R. S. Self-control training in the classroom: A review and critique. *Journal of Applied Behavior Analysis,* 1979, **12**, 467-485.

Rusch, F. R. Toward the validation of social/vocational survival skills. *Mental Retardation,* 1979, **17**, 143-145. (a)

Rusch, F. R. A functional analysis of the relationship between attending to task and producing in an applied restaurant setting. *The Journal of Special Education,* 1979, **13**, 399-411. (b)

Rusch, F. R. Competitive vocational training. In M. Snell (Ed.), *Systematic instruction for the moderately and severely handicapped.* Columbus, Ohio: Merrill, 1983.

Rusch, F. R., Connis, R. T., & Sowers, J. The modification and maintenance of time spent attending to task using social reinforcement, token reinforcement and response cost in an applied restaurant setting. *Journal of Special Education Technology,* 1979, **2**, 18-26.

Rusch, F. R., & Kazdin, A. E. Toward a methodology of withdrawal designs for the assessment of response maintenance. *Journal of Applied Behavior Analysis,* 1981, **14**, 131-140.

Rusch, F. R., & Menchetti, B. M. Increasing compliant work behaviors in a non-sheltered setting. *Mental Retardation,* 1981, **19**, 107-112.

Rusch, F. R., & Mithaug, D. E. *Vocational training for mentally retarded adults: A behavior analytic approach.* Champaign, Illinois: Research Press, 1980.

Rusch, F. R., Morgan, T. K., Riva, M., & Martin, J. E. *The effects of a self-instructional training package on the attending and producing behaviors of competitively employed handicapped adults.* Submitted for publication, 1984.

Rusch, F. R., & Schutz, R. P. Vocational and social work behavior: An evaluative review. In J. L. Matson & J. R. McCartney (Eds.), *Handbook of behavior modification with the mentally retarded,* New York: Plenum, 1981.

Rusch, F. R., Schutz, R. P., & Agran, M. Validating entry level survival skills for service occupations: Implications for curriculum development. *Journal of the Association for the Severely Handicapped,* 1982, **7**, 32–41.

Rusch, F. R., Schutz, R. P., & Heal, L. W. Vocational training and placement. In J. L. Matson & J. A. Mulick (Eds.), *Handbook of mental retardation.* New York: Pergamon Press, 1983.

Schutz, R. P., Jostes, K. F., Rusch, F. R., & Lamson, D. S. The use of contingent pre-instruction and social validation in the acquisition, generalization, and maintenance of sweeping and mopping responses. *Education and Training of the Mentally Retarded,* 1980, **15**, 306–311.

Schutz, R. P., & Rusch, F. R. Competitive employment: Toward employment integration for mentally retarded persons. In K. L. Lynch, W. E. Kiernan, & J. A. Stark (Eds.), *Prevocational and vocational education for special needs youth.* Baltimore, Maryland: Brookes, 1982.

Schutz, R. P., Rusch, F. R., & Lamson, D. S. Evaluation of an employer's procedure to eliminate unacceptable behavior on the job. *Community Services Forum,* 1979, **1**, 4–5.

Shapiro, E. S. Self-control procedures with the mentally retarded. In M. Hersen, R. M. Eisler, & P. M. Miller (Eds.), *Progress in behavior modification* (Vol. 12). New York: Academic Press, 1981. Pp. 265–297.

Skinner, B. F. *About behaviorism.* New York: Knopf, 1974.

Sowers, J., Rusch, F. R., Connis, R. T., & Cummings, L. E. Teaching mentally retarded adults to time manage in a vocational setting. *Journal of Applied Behavior Analysis,* 1980, **13**, 119–128.

Stokes, T. F., & Baer, D. M. An implicit technology of generalization. *Journal of Applied Behavior Analysis,* 1977, **10**, 349–367.

Sundel, M., & Sundel, S. S. *Behavior modification in the human services.* New York: Wiley, 1975.

Terrace, H. S. Discrimination learning with and without "errors." *Journal of the Experimental Analysis of Behavior,* 1963, **6**, 1–27.

Vogelsberg, R. T., & Rusch, F. R. Training severely handicapped students to cross partially controlled intersections. *AAESPH Review,* 1979, **4**, 264–273.

Wacker, D. P., & Berg, W. K. Effects of picture prompts on the acquisition of complex vocational tasks by mentally retarded adolescents. *Journal of Applied Behavioral Analysis,* 1983, **16**, 417–433.

Walker, H. M. *The acting-out child: Coping with classroom disruption.* Boston, Massachusetts: Allyn & Bacon, 1979.

Walker, H. M., & Buckley, N. K. Programming generalization and maintenance of treatment effects across time and across settings. *Journal of Applied Behavior Analysis,* 1972, **5**, 209–224.

Warren, S. F., Rogers-Warren, A., Baer, D. M., & Guess, D. Assessment and facilitation of language generalization. In W. Sailor, B. Wilcox, & L. Brown (Eds.), *Methods of instruction for severely handicapped students.* Baltimore, Maryland: Brookes, 1980.

Wehman, P. Behavioral self-control with the mentally retarded. *Journal of Applied Rehabilitation Counseling,* 1975, **6**, 27–34.

Wehman, P. *Competitive employment: New horizons for severely disabled individuals.* Baltimore, Maryland: Brooks, 1981.

Wehman, P., Schutz, R., Bates, P., Renzaglia, A., & Karan, O. Selfmanagement programs with mentally retarded workers: Implications for developing independent vocational behaviour. *British Journal of Social and Clinical Psychology,* 1978, **17**, 57–64.

Whitehead, C. Sheltered workshops in the decade ahead: Work and wages, or welfare. In G. T. Bellamy, G. O'Connor, & O. C. Karan (Eds.), *Vocational rehabilitation of severely handicapped persons.* Baltimore, Maryland: Univ. Park Press, 1979.

Zisfein, L., & Rosen, M. Personal adjustment training: A group program for institutionalized mentally retarded persons. *Mental Retardation,* 1973, **1**, 16–20.

Index

Contents of Previous Volumes